Bowhunting Tactics of the Pros

Other Books by Lamar Underwood

Man Eaters

The Greatest Hunting Stories Ever Told

The Greatest Fishing Stories Ever Told

The Greatest War Stories Ever Told

The Greatest Survival Stories Ever Told

The Quotable Soldier

The Bass Almanac

On Dangerous Ground

Bowhunting Tactics of the Pros
Strategies for Deer and Big Game

EDITED BY
LAMAR UNDERWOOD

THE LYONS PRESS

Guilford, Connecticut
An imprint of The Globe Pequot Press

The Lyons Press is an imprint of The Globe Pequot Press.

Printed in the United States of America

10 9 8 7 6 5 4 3 2

Library of Congress Cataloging-in-Publication Data is available on file.

Acknowledgments

Articles in this book by the following authors originally appeared in books and magazines and are reprinted here by permission of the authors.

Charles J. Alsheimer, *Hunting Whitetails by the Moon*, Krause Publications, 700 E. State St., Iola, WI 54990-0001

"The Real Dirt on Scrapes and Rubs" by Peter Fiduccia originally appeared in the book, *Whitetail Strategies*, and is reprinted by permission of the author.

Jerome B. Robinson, *In the Deer Woods*, The Lyons Press, 123 West 18 St, New York, NY 10011

The article "The Art of Seeing" by Jay Cassell originally appeared in *Sports Afield* and is reprinted by permission of the author.

All other articles originally appeared in the following maagazines published by Harris Publications, Inc., 1115 Broadway, New York, NY 10010, and are reprinted by permission of the authors and Harris Publications.

Whitetail Hunting Strategies, Deer & Big Game Bowhunting, Guns & Hunting, Tactical Bowhunting, Bowhunting Yearbook, Sportsman's Bowhunting Annual, Full Draw Bowhunting, Deer, Deer 2001.

Editor's Note

My deepest gratitude and appreciation go out to the following people who helped make this book possible:

To Jay Cassell, the Lyons Press Editor who shepherded the book through every stage of production, from original conception to press time. To all the contributors, not only for their illuminating articles but for their thoughtfulness in allowing us to reprint them here. To Harris Publications for their unstinting support of bowhunting in the many magazines they publish, from which most of these selections were taken. To Gerry Bethge, the Harris Publications Editor who worked with many of the authors during the original publication of the articles. And to Brad and Carol Herndon for the jacket photograph.

Contents

Introduction

It is probably safe to say that in its fledgling years, bowhunting was distinguished as being the "sport of challenge." Or, as the hyperbole swelled among its faithful, "the ultimate challenge." Back then, such colorful language wasn't meant for going out to bag a whitetail deer with a bow. These were the years when legendary figures like Fred Bear and Howard Hill transformed bowhunting into high adventure as they stalked dangerous game with their longbows. Cameras whirred with film, and articles and books made sure their feats were not private and secret. The very title of Hill's first book, *Hunting the Hard Way*—still in print, by the way—states exactly the point the man was trying to make. And did make with his extraordinary hunting achievements. Fred Bear too.

Today, bowhunting still earns the stripes that make it "hunting the hard way," but the "sport of challenge" has become the sport of challenge *and* opportunity. From equipment options that would have boggled Howard Hill's mind, to special bow-only seasons that begin amid autumn's greatest splendor, bowhunters have a great deal to be thankful for. The thrill of locating game and closing to a position where a shot is sensible and likely to succeed is as powerful as ever. But the advantage of the extended seasons and the fact that access to good uncrowded hunting ground is easier for the bowhunter than the gun hunter give bowhunting additional tremendous appeal. No doubt, this combination of challenge and opportunity is the reason the ranks of serious bowhunters have swelled in recent decades.

For the man or woman who truly likes nature—and not just the Disney-like idea of nature—who truly would rather be outdoors than indoors, a day spent bowhunting can be filled with rewards and pleasures that are not tainted by the failure to bag game. The woods and fields are bountiful with sounds and images that stir the soul and imagination. Did that sound of a stick breaking up ahead mean a buck on the move? What are the blue jays scolding in the stand of pines off to the right? Is the mast crop failing this year? Why are so many geese moving today? Do they know a storm is coming? Did a big buck make this rub? Is this a hot scrape or cold and old?

As the old saying goes, "The journey is the glory." As in fishing and other forms of hunting, the failure of the bowhunting mission does not mean a wasted day. The old memory bank picked up lots of good stuff to reflect on. Every experienced angler or hunter has uttered the expression dozens of times, "Nah, I didn't get a thing. But it was a great day to be out there."

There comes a time after repeated failures when that old suck-it-up attitude starts to go lame. Other bowhunters are being successful. What's wrong with me? What do I have to do to put some points on the board?

The answer to this common malady lies, in my opinion, not with forming a new relationship with Lady Luck, but in putting, figuratively and even literally, some new arrows in your quiver. I presume that's the reason you picked up this book.

I can promise you that help is on the way in the pages ahead. Help in the form of learning from the experiences of others.

Forgive the "stretch" that stems from my personal interest in aviation, but there is an old flying bromide, applicable to hunting, that pins the cause of failure—a crash!—on any one of four possibilities:

1. You did nothing, just when you should have been doing something,
2. You did something, just when you should have been doing nothing at all.
3. You did something, but it was too little.
4. You did something, but it was too much.

Somewhere in those four broad categories lurk the reasons for a hunt ending in failure. The most common culprit is Number One. For it is with that category in mind that you must ask yourself—please forgive the aviation again—"Have I been running my hunt on automatic pilot?" If you have been, watching and waiting for things to happen, then it's time you took over the controls and started *making* things happen!

The expert hunters who share their experiences and observations here are some of the most respected authorities in bowhunting history. As an editor, it has been my great fortune to publish their articles and photographs in hundreds of magazine issues over the years. Their no-nonsense tips and advice have helped thousands of bowhunters at all levels of skill increase their enjoyment of bowhunting. From the beginner eager to learn, to the veteran looking for new ideas and challenges, those readers have become better bowhunters because of experts like Charlie Alsheimer, Peter Fiduccia, Dwight Schuh, Jeff Murray, John Weiss, Greg Miller, and Gary Clancy to name but a few of the contributors here.

Bowhunting will never be easy. And there never will be any sure things, despite what the covers of many magazines try to tell you. Skill and preparation are absolute necessities, and attaining them totally on your own will require a long stay in the famous School of Hard Knocks. There's a better path to building your skills: By spending some time with the bowhunters whose specific strategies are detailed here, you will find your confidence on the upswing as you put their game plans into practice. Once you are hunting confidently, you will start hunting well. Your share of great days will follow, whether your goal is to bag a buck—*any* buck!—or a bull elk out in the high country.

—Lamar Underwood
March 2001

Part One
Seize Bowhunting's First-Strike Advantage

For whitetail bowhunters, opening day occurs in September or October, a time when gun hunters are still many, many weeks away from their first day in the field. Your chances of bagging a buck will never be better than this time when pressure on the deer is at its lowest. In the woods, signposts pointing to the places deer can be found are everywhere—*if* you know how to read them.

1 The Whitetail's Autumn Behavior

BY CHARLES J. ALSHEIMER

Here's the perfect place to start forming your whitetail bowhunting game plan. The fact that the whitetail deer is a creature of strong habits is the biggest chink in his armor.

From the book *Hunting Whitetails by the Moon*, copyright 1999 by Charles J. Alsheimer, Krause Publications

Have you ever sat on a stand and tried analyzing the whitetail's autumn behavior? Have you ever wondered when the pre-rut, rut, and post-rut begin and end, or which aspect of the rut is most fascinating?

When I began deer hunting, I didn't know much about the whitetail's rutting behavior. During my youth, I viewed the rut as one frenzied two-week period in the whitetail's life. After 30 years of extensively hunting and photographing whitetails, I now realize the rut's chemistry is more complex than I originally thought.

Understanding whitetails during autumn, especially as it relates to the rut, requires knowledge of deer behavior and what triggers the rut's various phases. Everything that precedes breeding—velvet peeling, rubbing, scraping, chasing and fighting—has a purpose. No aspect of the rut is an isolated occurrence. All the activities blend to create one of nature's most incredible spectacles.

The Preparation

Photoperiodism—the behavioral and physiological responses to changing amounts of daylight—drives nature's timetable, from leaves growing on trees to antlers growing on deer. Though summer's growing season is leisurely for whitetails, subtle changes within the buck population shape a herd's pecking order for fall. Dominant bucks engage in stare-downs, shadowing and, in some cases, flailing with their hoofs. These behaviors help determine which buck could become the bull of the woods when the breeding game begins.

Nature does not load bucks with their full arsenal before the precise time each weapon is needed. Can you imagine what the woods would be like if a buck's testosterone level peaked in early September rather than early November?

By late August, bucks' velvet dries, cracks and peels. About the same time, just enough testosterone surges through their system to inspire rubbing. Then, near the end of September, the testosterone "valve" opens wider, stimulating scraping.

By mid-October, with the days cooler and testosterone levels higher, bucks move more during daylight. Does' estrogen levels climb, and they begin smelling differently. By early November, bucks' testosterone levels and does' estrogen levels have peaked, setting the stage for what deer hunters call "the rut."

The Rut's Confusing Terms

When someone mentions pre-rut, rut or post-rut to me, I always ask them to define what those terms mean to them so I can best answer their question. Those terms have been used so many ways the past 50 years that it's difficult to define them universally.

For biologists and researchers, pre-rut usually defines all behaviors that occur before full-blown breeding. In contrast, most hunters think of the pre-rut as the early autumn period when days are warm and little rubbing, scraping or fighting occurs.

To researchers, the word "rut" usually means the actual breeding period. But most hunters think it means that much and more, namely the time bucks are going bonkers while rubbing, scraping, chasing and fighting.

Hunters and biologists agree the post-rut is the period and behavior associated with the time after breeding ends. So, the mere study and use of these words can be confusing. Though I believe pre-rut, rut and post-rut are good ways to describe a whitetail's autumn behavior, I break it down more precisely.

The Dominance Phase

Dominance among white-tailed deer is progressive and ever-changing. Once a buck's velvet peels, it begins the physical training for its greatest game—breeding. In many ways, this period reminds me of an athlete's preseason training regimen. A buck is fat-laden as summer ends, far different from what it will be by Oct. 1. Once its antlers are hard, a buck begins to rub more frequently as daylight continually shortens. A buck rubs frequently for two obvious reasons. First, like a boxer working a speed bag, a buck rubbing a tree is strengthening its neck and shoulder muscles. Second, rubbing allows a buck to leave its scent and visual markers so other deer know it has been there and will return when breeding begins.

With ever-increasing testosterone in its system, a buck adds another dimension to its identity by making scrapes. Scraping, like rubbing, allows a buck to make its presence known by dispensing scent throughout its area.

Hunters debate whether scraping is primarily a "buck thing" or if it's done to attract does. In more than 30 years of photographing and hunting deer from Texas to Canada, I've seen less than 20 does interact at scrapes. During this time I've seen and photographed hundreds of bucks making scrapes. So, based on this, it's my view that scraping is a buck behavior; in this case a way to show its dominance.

I believe scraping is also a satisfying, conditioned response for bucks. When working an overhanging licking branch, a buck is greatly satisfied by the branch massaging its forehead, preorbital and nasal glands. I don't believe a buck consciously knows it is spreading its scent to other deer.

Judging by the hundreds of photos I've taken of scraping bucks, it appears the satisfying and stimulating aspects of scraping might largely explain why a buck performs the behaviors frequently. I'm not saying scent-depositing isn't a big part of scraping, because it is. But I'm convinced the dynamics of scraping are incredibly complex and serve several functions, probably more than we'll ever realize.

Physical Competition

With rubbing and scraping comes physical competition. Once free of velvet, most bucks begin sparring. This is a way to exercise while testing the herd's competitive waters. For the most part, sparring matches are playful skirmishes between two bucks of equal size and stature. However, on occasion, sparring can get out of hand and become ugly. The best analogy I can offer is two teen-age brothers playfully wrestling on the living-room floor. Before they realize it, one gets his nose bloodied and tempers flare. While photographing in fall, I've often seen sparring contests between bucks follow a similar sequence.

As breeding time nears, bucks become adventurous, and trouble often befalls a traveling buck. A buck's range often expands from about 600 acres in summer to 4,000 or more acres by early November. A whitetail's summer and early-fall pecking order falls apart, because strange bucks continually trespass on each other's turf. Chaos invades the whitetail's world!

The Seeking Phase

Bucks are more vocal in autumn than at any other time of the year. By November, bucks communicate with other deer by emitting grunts, bleats, snorts and snort-wheezes.

With maximum levels of testosterone now flowing, bucks look feverishly for an estrous doe. Their noses dictate when and where bucks go. No doe group is safe as bucks weave across their expanded territory. At this time, all the dynamics of buck behavior unite. Bucks are now finely tuned physical specimens that spend every waking hour rubbing, scraping and looking for does. Judging by research I've conducted for several years, an active buck might make six to 12 scrapes per hour during this rut phase. The frequency depends on how sexually active a given buck is.

At this time, bucks also lip-curl—a behavior scientists call "Flehmening"—far more than in previous months. They exhibit this behavior when they find a place where a doe has urinated.

Lip-curling allows a buck to learn if a doe is entering estrus. The buck traps scent from a doe's urine in its nose and mouth, and then lip-curls. This helps the buck's scent-analyzing device—the vomero-nasal organ in the roof of its mouth—pinpoint the doe's status.

When a mature buck or an aggressive yearling buck encounters a stranger or a recognized contender, one or two things usually occur. Stare-downs or shadowing usually occur first. It's generally a buck's antlers and body size that cause one antagonist to cut short the encounter by shying away. Most bucks are aware of the size of their antlers and body, and can quickly size up the situation. However, if two bucks of similar size—with testosterone-injected attitudes to match—find each other, the results can get ugly.

If a fight to the death begins, the scene can be spectacular. Antlers become ice picks, and there are no rules of fair fighting. A buck's objective is to knock his opponent to the ground, and then stick his antlers into his opponent's abdomen or hindquarters. Such fights can be gruesome, and when it's over, victor and loser alike often need time to recover before resuming their pursuit of does. Combatants even die from their wounds.

Of all the times to hunt, the seeking phase is one of the best, especially for a tree-stand hunter. The peak of this period is usually three to four days before and two to three days after the rutting moon. During this time, bucks are on the move but not yet chasing every doe they encounter. Their movement patterns through funnels and along scrape and rub lines are more predictable. Unfortunately, the seeking phase only lasts a short time before blending into the chase phase.

The Chase Phase

The chase phase often gets confused with the seeking phase. The two behavior periods overlap, but they're different. This phase usually begins a couple days after the rutting moon and lasts three to four days into the full blown breeding phase. During the chase phase, does are almost entering estrus, and bucks are frantically trying to be the first to find them. Now a buck will chase every doe it encounters. Such meetings often resemble a cutting horse trying to cut a calf out of a herd of cows. A buck can be persistent, knowing it will eventually find a doe that won't run. During the chase phase, scraping and rubbing continue, and in many cases can be intense, especially in a well-tuned herd. The chase phase often brings more intense fights, especially if two bucks pursue the same doe.

The chase phase can be a great time to hunt, but it often gets frustrating because the action can take bucks out of range as they chase does.

Tending and Breeding Phase

This is the stage that gives the rut its name. When a doe finally enters estrus, it will accept a buck's company wherever it goes. In many parts of North America, the doe-to-buck ratios are so weighted toward females that all available bucks can easily find a hot doe. When breeding begins, scraping nearly ceases and bucks curtail much of the activity that took place throughout the rut's dominance, seeking and chasing phases.

This phase usually begins five to seven days after the rutting moon and lasts about 14 days. During this time, 70 percent to 80 percent of mature does will be bred.

Rather than traveling, a buck will stay with a hot doe for up to 72 hours. For the first 24 hours, a doe will smell right, but won't be ready to breed. During the second 24 hours, the doe will be in full estrus and allow the buck to breed her several times. Then, because she continues to smell right for the last 24 hours, a buck will continue to stay with her.

During those three days, a buck will move only when the doe moves. Because most does cover little ground, deer activity can seemingly halt during this time. Only when the doe cycles out of estrus will the buck move on to look for another estrous doe.

The first does to come into estrus will often cause a commotion by attracting several bucks. When that happens, a dominant breeder buck never rests as he tries to run off all intruder bucks in order to stay in position to breed the doe. Because they have no time to rest or eat, breeder bucks can lose up to 25 percent of their weight during the rut's seeking, chasing and breeding phases.

Of all the rut's phases, the breeding time can be the most difficult to hunt because movement is limited. At this time, about the only way tree-stand hunters will see action is to place their stands in the hot doe's core area or sites frequented by doe groups.

Post-Rut: The Recovery Time

By the time a whitetail's prime breeding period ends, a buck's testosterone level is plummeting. A breeder buck is also so rut-worn that its body is in a near meltdown. Researchers have found that some bucks are so worn down by the time breeding is over that they'll have trouble surviving a hard winter. With less testosterone to drive them, bucks go into a resting and feeding mode as soon as the November breeding ceases. In regions with high doe-to-buck ratios, the stress of an extended breeding season decreases the survival chances of many breeder bucks.

Even with does entering estrus at nontraditional times, such as December and January, the rutting behavior of bucks will not be as intense as it was earlier. Limited, subdued chasing will occur, but scraping and serious fighting is mostly over. Most post-rut behavior is done by subordinate bucks in the form of sparring, but minor scraping and rubbing will likely occur.

Survival again becomes more important than breeding. The post-rut is a time for bucks to restore fat and energy reserves. The bucks seem to know their only chance of surviving a Northern winter is to rest and feed heavily.

Conclusion

The whitetail's rut is an amazing and complex phenomenon. It's made up of an array of behavioral traits, each distinctly different but interwoven. Each rut phase works in concert with the others to ensure the species' survival.

2   Reading Rubs:
The Whitetail Sign That Says, "Hunt Here!"

BY GREG MILLER

The author has been an avid student of learning to "read" rub sign for over 15 years. The knowledge that has helped him put bucks in the Pope & Young and Boone and Crockett books can help you locate and bag a buck next season!

Twelve years have passed since I wrote my first article on the benefits of using antler rubs and rub lines as hunting aids when pursuing trophy whitetails. Interestingly, prior to my writing that piece, I thought I'd learned nearly everything there was to know about rubs and rub lines. To say I had made a slight error in judgment would be a gross understatement.

The past 12 years could be viewed as an age of enlightenment for me. Not only have I learned a great deal more about rubs and rub lines, I've also discovered some interesting facts regarding the way big bucks relate to these highly visual bits of sign. Has this additional information proved valuable? Without a doubt! In the last eight years I've harvested two bucks that gross-scored better than the Boone and Crockett minimum. And I've arrowed four others that exceeded Pope & Young's minimum entry score. My increased knowledge of antler rubs played a role in each and every one of those kills.

I believe that most whitetail deer hunters have a basic understanding of antler rubs and rub lines. But that's only a start. For as I've discovered, achieving a consistent level of success on mature bucks is possible only after your "rub knowledge" has increased beyond the basic stages. The good news is that this increase in knowledge really isn't all that difficult to acquire.

For instance, a lot of hunters I talk with express concern about not being able to figure out rub lines entirely from one end to the other. At one time I was under the impression that this was an absolute must. However, countless experiences I've had in recent years would indicate that gaining an intimate familiarity with entire rub lines, while certainly okay, isn't necessarily a prerequisite for success. The key is being able to tell exactly which parts of a buck's rub lines he's most likely to utilize during daylight hours at specific times during the season.

While this might sound like a nearly impossible task to accomplish, it isn't. All it takes is some close study of topo maps and aerial photos and a willingness to do a bit of legwork. The final ingredients required are some basic woodsman's skills and a dose of good ol' common sense. (Sadly, it's this last ingredient that seems to be missing from the repertoires of so many modern day whitetail deer hunters.)

Along with helping you gain familiarity with the lay of the land in a specific area, topo maps and aerial photos can drastically shorten your searches for bedding areas. And what exactly should you be looking for? Well, some places I've found to be favored big buck bedding spots include thick regrowth areas, briar thickets, south-facing hillsides, blowdown-rich areas, river and creek bottoms and just about any swamp (whitetails relate strongly to drainages in general). All these places usually are relatively easy to pick out on topo maps and/or aerial photos. Just make sure you have the most recent maps and photos available for the targeted area(s).

Topo maps and aerial photos also can prove helpful for pinpointing the location of primary feeding areas. Trust me, once you've determined exactly where the deer in your hunting areas are feeding and bedding, the task of locating the most potentially productive rub line stand sites then becomes much easier. This is simply because the vast majority of rub line activity occurs in these two places.

It's a well-known fact that whitetail bucks do a good deal of rubbing around the outside perimeter of feeding areas. Indeed, this is one of the best places to start your searches for active rub lines. But for most of the season this really isn't the best place to wait in ambush for a big buck. With the exception of the latter stages of the pre-rut, daylight activity along rub lines, especially by mature bucks, is going to be relatively restricted. You'll notice I said restricted, not nonexistent. What this means is that, provided they set up in the right spots, hunters can fully expect to see big bucks traveling along their rub lines during this part of the season.

Anyone who has spent even a little time chasing mature bucks knows that, for most of the season anyway, animals in this age class seldom wander close to feeding areas during legal shooting hours. Obviously then, the restricted daylight activity I spoke of occurs some place other than near food sources. In truth, this activity normally occurs on the very opposite end of preferred buck travel routes, in relatively close proximity to their established bedding areas.

Just like with their preferred food sources, whitetail bucks do a lot of rubbing around the outside perimeters of their favored bedding areas. Of even more interest to hunters, though, nearly all of the big bucks I've chased over the years had several well-defined rub lines leading into and out of his bedding area. These rub lines denoted the buck's most preferred morning and afternoon travel routes.

Although each whitetail buck seems to possess his own very unique personality, almost all of the mature bucks I've hunted have displayed one similar behavioral trait. They did at least some moving around during daylight hours. Further, this activity occurred along an active rub line, but very close to the buck's preferred bedding area. In fact, during the early to mid pre-rut period, I've seldom seen this activity extend further than 75 yards beyond a bedding area; big bucks often display this same behavior trait again during the post-rut period.

Ideally then, hunters should strive to establish stand sites somewhere within the 75 yard radius mentioned. Of course, the closer you set up to a big buck's bedding area, the greater your chances for catching him up and moving around during legal shooting time. Just remember that closing the distance also increases the chances that the buck could somehow detect your presence.

For the very reason cited above, I personally like to start out by placing my stands a minimum of 75 yards away from the bedding area. I'll consider moving closer only if I don't see any buck activity after two or three sits. I might also take a chance and relocate closer if I repeatedly see a big buck wandering around just outside of his bedding area. Regardless of where I set up, however, I'll hunt my bedding area rub line stands a maximum of only two times per week.

My choice of stand site locations changes dramatically during the final week of the pre-rut. This is that one time of year when it's okay to sit near preferred food sources. Personally, I prefer to set up approximately 100 yards back away from the edge of the actual feeding area, but still along an active rub line. I'm not, however, just picking a rub line at random. In most cases, I already know which rub lines are playing host to the greatest amount of buck travel. I'm able to figure this out by periodically checking for fresh rubs throughout the early part of the season.

At the beginning of this article I stated that a lot of hunters still have trouble figuring out the middle sections of rub lines. I'd like to reiterate that being able to accomplish this task really isn't all that important. This is because there really isn't a gradual relaxation of the restrictive travel patterns big bucks adhere to during the early part of the season. From what I've seen, big bucks dramatically increase their daylight activities literally overnight. A big buck that wouldn't think of venturing away from his bedding area before dark one day could very well show up at a feeding area in broad daylight the very next day. Buck temperaments really do change this quickly during the final days of the pre-rut!

I'm sure there's a question lingering in the minds of some readers at this point. Why not spend the entire season hunting from the stand sites you've established along rub lines near buck bedding areas? Two reasons. As already mentioned, the more time you spend hanging around a big buck's bedroom, the greater the chance that the buck will eventually detect your presence. Also, continual intrusions deep into a mature buck's home turf will eventually cause all the deer in that area to become suspicious and flighty.

A.M. or P.M.?

It's my opinion that quite a few hunters are still committing what I consider to be some basic blunders regarding their rub line setups. One of the most obvious and costly of these blunders sees hunters spending the morning hours sitting along travel routes that, in reality, are being used by bucks only in the afternoon—and vice-versa. Although I've seen instances where big bucks have used the same travel routes both in the morning and afternoon, it's far from a common occurrence. In most cases, mature deer will use distinctly different travel corridors for their morning and afternoon wanderings.

Differentiating between morning and afternoon travel routes entails applying a bit of that common sense I mentioned earlier. If the rubs are facing toward a known feeding area, then it's a fairly safe bet that you've discovered a morning travel route. Conversely, rubs that face away from a food source and toward a suspected bedding area almost always indicate a preferred afternoon travel route. Here's a simple rule of thumb to keep in mind when trying to determine direction of travel: The rubs found along a whitetail buck's rub lines will face away from the direction the buck is traveling. It really is that simple!

Over the years, I've discovered another interesting aspect of rub line behavior. Initially I believed that this particular aspect of rub behavior was exclusive to big woods whitetails. However, a bit more study on the subject showed me that this just isn't the case. In reality, the behavior surfaces in those situations where whitetail bucks are routinely visiting an in-woods food source. As is their normal tendency, bucks will establish rub lines along the routes they use to travel back and forth between their bedding areas and the food source. But instead of ceasing their rubbing activities upon reaching the food source, they continue to make rubs all the way along their feeding routes.

A big buck I arrowed some years ago was relating strongly to this exact type of rub line. The rub line actually had its beginnings near the buck's bedding area, which was located in a thick spruce swamp a half-mile from the food source. After leaving his bedroom, the buck would make his way through several hundred yards of mature poplar forest. He would then cross an old logging road and head into an expanse of mixed birch, poplar and oak. His rub line coursed through this part of the woods and continued on through the grove of acorn laden oaks where my stand site was located.

It's important to note that I shot the above mentioned eight-point, 220-pound bruiser along his rub line during the early stages of the rut. Now normally, whitetail bucks abandon their rub lines once breeding begins. Or at least they abandon the travel route rub lines that they established during the pre-rut. However, mature bucks continue to relate to feeding area rubs right on through the rut. Why? Because, in their searches for hot does, prolific breeding bucks will continually cruise through feeding areas. These "cruises" often take them along the feeding route rub lines they used earlier in the fall.

I've recently incorporated a new wrinkle into my rub hunting philosophies. Simply put, I now pay a lot more attention to those rub lines and rub areas where bucks have also laid down a good number of scrapes. My decision to concentrate more of my hunting efforts on such spots has been tremendously reinforced during the past several archery seasons especially. Almost without exception, the mature bucks my hunting partners and I have chased during that time have related more strongly to those areas where both rubs and scrapes were found in good numbers.

I've unearthed a lot of important hunter-useful facts regarding big buck rub behavior during the past 12 years. And I know for certain there's still more to be learned about this very interesting and informative aspect of whitetail buck behavior. For that reason, I seriously doubt if I'll ever again make the mistaken assumption that I know all there is to know about antler rubs and rub lines.

Rub Size = Buck Size?

I'm sure that most deer hunters have heard the old saying, "Big rubs mean big bucks!" However, I'm not so sure that everyone who has heard the saying really believes that big antler rubs are a true indicator of big buck presence. Trust me, they are. Actually, it takes only a bit of common sense to realize the truth in this belief. Spikes, forkhorns or even basket-racked bucks simply don't have the strength or the aggressive nature required to strip the bark from thigh-sized trees.

That's not to say, however, that smaller bucks won't rub on large trees. They most definitely will. But in almost every instance, smaller bucks will rub on larger trees only after those trees have first been "opened up" by a real stud buck. In fact, all the bucks living within the same core area will work many of the same rubs— just as they will work many of the same scrapes.

A word of warning about using rub size alone as a guideline when deciding on hunting spots: Don't have unrealistic goals. For instance, I'd like nothing better than to be able to limit my hunting efforts strictly to bucks that rub on nothing but leg and telephone-pole-sized trees. However, I learned long ago that rubs of this size can't be found in any great abundance anywhere. For this reason, I've adopted a "wrist-sized and larger" rub hunting policy. In a nutshell, if I find a buck that's consistently rubbing on wrist-sized and larger trees, I'll hunt him. So far, this policy has proved to be quite reliable.

Identifying Buck Travel Routes

Hunters obviously will see more action by setting up along those travel routes bucks use most often. But how do you go about identifying exactly which of his many travel routes a particular buck prefers to use? Again, it's merely a matter of applying some common sense and paying attention to the on-going rub activity in your hunting areas.

Personally, I continually check suspected buck runways throughout the early and middle part of the archery season. I keep a mental note of the amount of rubbing activity that's occurring along those runways. By the time the late pre-rut period rolls around, I'll know exactly which runways are hosting the most buck travel. Almost without fail, these runways will show a lot more rub action than all others. By the way, a good deal of rub activity along one particular runway could denote a couple things. It could be that one buck is using that trail nearly every day. Or it could mean that several bucks are using the trail with regularity.

There's one exception to the rub-frequency rule that hunters should know about. Studies have shown that some whitetail bucks actually rub less as they grow older. I should add that I'm referring here to bucks 5½ years old and older. These deer just seem to become more concerned with survival than breeding. And as far as establishing their dominancy, these huge deer seldom have to prove their prowess. Their appearance alone is usually enough to intimidate any potential rivals.

So if you happen to be hunting a buck that fits into the above-mentioned age class, don't become concerned if you find a low number of rubs scattered about his suspected home range. More than likely the buck is still spending all his time right in the immediate vicinity. He's just not quite so eager to advertise his existence. Nor is he likely to leave an obvious line of rubs along his most preferred travel routes. But this is exactly what makes mature bucks such tough customers.

Tactics at a Glance

- Although bucks do a great deal of rubbing around the perimeter of feeding areas, it's not a great place to set up.
- Most mature whitetail bucks will do at least a little moving around during daylight—usually on a rub line.
- If rubs are facing toward a feeding area, it's a morning route.
- If rubs are facing away from a food source, it's an afternoon route.
- Mature bucks will abandon travel-route rub lines once breeding begins, switching to feeding route rub lines to intercept does.

3 Scrape Savvy: How to Read Autumn's Critical Clues to Buck Movements

BY CHARLES J. ALSHEIMER

Renowned photographer and author of several books and hundreds of articles on whitetail deer, Charlie Alsheimer is also one of the leading figures in promoting whitetail deer research, particularly in the area of rut timing. Assisting in studies of the moon and other influences on whitetail behavior, Charlie has been involved in breakthrough studies of the rut with leading researchers such as Wayne LaRoche. Charlie's book Hunting Whitetails by the Moon *is a landmark work on the subject. In addition, he is the author of* Whitetail: The Ultimate Challenge *and* Whitetail: Behavior Through the Seasons. *He is also Northern Field Editor of* Deer & Deer Hunting Magazine. *Alsheimer's contributions that have greatly rewarded readers in magazines that I personally have been associated with include this piece from* Sportsman's Hunting Yearbook 2000.

Ribbons of clouds began turning amber as the sun inched closer and closer to the horizon. In the east, a full moon was making its ascent into the November sky. What an incredible sight! For the better part of two hours, I had been perched in my treestand overlooking a hot scrape hoping a whitetail buck would come my way. Unfortunately only gray squirrels entertained me throughout the sit.

With half an hour of hunting light left, I stood to stretch and wait for the hunt to wind down. Before I could take my bow off its hanger, brush started snapping to my left in the direction of the scrape I was hunting over. I strained hard to see a deer. In the midst of breaking limbs, the unmistakable sound of grunts pierced the air. The sound grew louder and a doe bounded past the scrape and straight toward my stand, with a trophy 10-point on her heels. Before I could get ready to shoot they ran under the stand and stopped 50 yards away.

For the next 10 minutes, the two stood yards apart staring at each other. Occasionally the big buck would grunt at the doe. The more I looked at the buck's rack the more excited I became. After what seemed an eternity the doe began retracing her steps. When she got under my stand I lost sight of her, as I didn't want to take my eyes from the buck. It sounded like she walked another 30 yards before stopping. Now I was caught in a crossfire with the buck and doe on opposite sides of my treestand. I was sure one of them would spot me.

Luck began dealing me a winning hand when the doe bounded off. The buck started slowly in her direction and I figured if he kept on course he would pass within 15 yards of my stand. The last rays of sunlight reflected off his body as he approached. With nose to the ground, the grunting buck stepped into a shooting lane. I came to full draw just as he looked up at me. I released and the arrow buried itself behind his front shoulder. In a flash the buck bounded off, stopped 50 yards from me, looked back in my direction and collapsed. Although this experience happened over 20 years ago, it illustrates the type of behavior that takes place around a hot scrape during the rut.

Anatomy of Scraping Behavior

It wasn't until I began seriously photographing whitetails in 1970 that I started to understand the entire whitetail scraping process. It's a fascinating aspect of whitetail behavior and one I love to witness. Since 1970 I've been able to observe over 1,000 scrapes being made. Though some of these observations have been in enclosures, over half of them have been in areas where deer could come and go as they please. I also discovered early on that whitetail bucks performed a part of their scraping ritual year round.

When I first saw a buck working a scrape during the velvet-growing season, I couldn't believe my eyes. That was over 25 years ago and at the time I had never heard of such a thing, so I thought it was extremely rare. As I began spending more time afield with my camera, I came to realize that scraping activity during winter, spring, and summer wasn't rare at all, just not as frequent as in the fall months. Since the first sighting I've witnessed and photographed many bucks working licking branches during non-rutting months.

When a scrape is worked during the autumn months, a buck is trying to leave as much of his scent (pheromones) as possible. In the process of making a scrape he rubs his preorbital, nasal, and forehead gland, as well as salivating on the scrape's overhanging licking branch. He also paws away debris beneath the branch so he can urinate into the scrape's exposed earth. In the North, a buck will usually splay his legs during the urination process, if the scrape is made prior to about October 25. After this time, he'll place his hind legs together and urinate through his tarsal glands into the scrape, while rubbing these glands together. This is commonly known as rub-urination. By urinating through his tarsal glands a buck is able to leave even more of his scent.

It should be pointed out that more than one buck will use the same scrape. A few years ago while bowhunting over an active scrape on our farm, I had seven yearling bucks work the same scrape between dawn and 9 a.m. Though I've never seen this repeated I have photographed bucks working the same scrape within five minutes of each other on numerous occasions.

In a well-tuned deer herd (where the buck to doe ratio is 2-3 adult does for every antlered buck) with a good representation of mature bucks it's not uncommon for mature bucks to make between 6 and 12 scrapes per hour. This is primarily because bucks are moving a lot during this period of the rut and in some cases they'll be active for up to six hours between bedding periods.

For the most part scrapes are "buck things." Research has documented that does work a scrape's overhanging licking branch. I've seen this take place many times in the woods and have photographed it often. However, a doe's frequency at scrapes is at best minimal compared to a buck's level of scraping activity.

Factors That Influence Scraping

As summer fades into autumn, the frequency of scraping intensifies. The level of intensity depends on a number of factors. The two most important are the adult doe to buck ratio and number of mature bucks in the population.

Volumes have been written on how high adult doe to buck ratios shut down the rut. If you hunt an area where there are more than four or five adult does for every antlered buck the rut will be light, with little chasing, rubbing and scraping. If you hunt an area where the ratio is three adult does to every antlered buck, the rut should have a fair amount of visible rutting activity. If the ratio is one to one or two adult does for every buck rutting activity in the form of chasing, fighting, rubbing and scraping can be outstanding. And yes there are a few places in North America where there are more antlered bucks than adult does. In these areas, the rut tends to be unbelievable, beyond imagination.

Another thing that's required for a high level of scraping to be present is the presence of mature bucks. In areas where a deer population has adequate numbers of mature bucks, scraping intensity is much greater.

Timing

Researchers are in some disagreement as to the level of scraping activity that can be expected during daylight hours. Some biologists have found that 70 percent of all scraping behaviors takes place under the cover of darkness while others say it is over 95 percent. It's been my experience that the 70 percent figure is more accurate. Regardless, most of it occurs in the dark, which doesn't bode well for hunters. However, by timing the rut the chances of catching a buck working a scrape in broad daylight increase dramatically.

The arrival of mid-October sets the stage for aggressive scraping to begin. With ever-increasing amounts of testosterone being released into a buck's system, the switch is thrown for them to begin increasing the size of their territory. When this happens they begin leaving their scent wherever they can.

Several research projects have shown that the peak of scraping activity occurs just prior to the full-blown breeding beginning. The trick is knowing when the prime-breeding window takes place. For the past four years, Vermont researcher Wayne Laroche and myself have been involved in an in-depth research project dealing with the timing of the doe's estrus cycle. Specifically, we have been looking at the moon's influence on this cycle. In over 70% of the cases our research does (which number over 50) are cueing off the second full moon that follows the autumn equinox in the North. Approximately seven days after this moon (which I call the Hunter's Moon), the does begin breeding, with the breeding window lasting roughly 14 days. Armed with this information, it's possible for hunters to know that during the 10-day period before the breeding window, commonly known as the seeking or chase phase, scraping will be intense.

Scrape Classification

Prior to and when the seeking and chase phase of the rut arrives and intensifies, three types of scrapes will show up: boundary, secondary and primary. I pay little attention to boundary scrapes, except for checking the size of the track in them. If the track in the scrape is over 2½ inches wide (with no more than ½-inch split in the toes), the buck probably weighs over 175 pounds and is a mature buck.

Boundary scrapes are random scrapes bucks make as they travel through their territory. They often show up along the edge of fields, fencerows, old roadways and along creeks. So, as the name implies, they are along boundaries. Yearling bucks make many (but not all) boundary scrapes as they try to figure out their first rut.

Secondary scrapes can offer excellent chances to kill bucks because they are generally found along well-used trails between the bedding and feeding area. In many instances, bucks make a line of these scrapes (20 to 50 yards apart) along trails between the bedding and feeding areas. Because they are on trails or in funnels, bucks will frequently rework and freshen them. In all my years of hunting I've probably killed more bucks along secondary scrapes than any other place.

The "mother lode" of scrapes is the primary scrape. Unfortunately, they are often few and far between as it normally requires a mature buck population for them to exist. The primary scrape can be a true "bus station" for whitetail bucks and the one all hunters yearn to find. Unlike secondary scrapes that are usually found along trails and in funnels, primary scrapes are usually found in strategic locations during the course of the rut. You'll usually find well-worn trails to them and more often than not they are in very thick cover where mature bucks feel secure.

The Setup

I've found that huntable scrapes need to be on flat or fairly flat ground. From a scouting standpoint, always remember that favorite scraping areas are traditional. In other words they show up in the same place or area year after year, providing man or nature doesn't destroy the habitat. Therefore you can scout for many of these areas in the off season.

Setting up the ambush over a primary or secondary scrape can be tricky. Because it takes little to cause whitetails to become nocturnal, it's important to not overhunt a scrape location. I plan my scrape hunting near three different scraping locations, rotating among them to avoid overhunting a particular scrape. Because I'll be rattling and calling from these ambush points, I look for hot scrapes where there is medium to heavy cover. I also know that my chances of bagging a buck rise if these locations are in funnels or prime travel corridors.

Hanging the stand as close to the bedding area as possible increases the potential for buck sightings. This allows you to intercept a buck when he leaves his bedroom at the end of the day. If you set up too far from a bedding area, the buck won't reach you before quitting time. The same holds true in the morning though it is not as important because during the rut bucks will be on the prowl through midday. But by being close to the bedding area, you can catch a buck returning to his bedroom.

Stand placement in relation to the scrape or scrape line is critical when bowhunting. Often terrain will dictate where this will be. If possible I hang the stand 15-20 feet high, 20 to 40 yards downwind of the scrape rather than right on top of it. Years ago I used to set up right on top of the scrape, but consistently found mature bucks going downwind of me as they passed through the area scent checking the scrape. In a few situations these lessons were learned the hard way. By moving farther from the scrapes my opportunities to kill mature bucks increased.

Tease 'Em in Range

Hanging bow stands over 30 yards from a scrape means that other techniques are required to get a buck close enough for a shot. Two methods I use successfully are calling with a grunt tube and rattling.

When I began using communication methods with deer, I did so with only antlers. Though there were successes, it wasn't until I began using a grunt tube, alone and in conjunction with the antlers, that my successes increased significantly. During the last 14 years, I've discovered that using a call will cause deer to be more responsive than anything else will. Whether a novice or seasoned veteran, it's important to realize that you don't need to know how to make every vocalization a whitetail makes. The key is to be able to master two or three and know how and when to use them.

My favorite calls are the bleat, trailing grunt and tending grunt. I find the bleat to be a good locator call, much like a turkey yelp. I often use the bleat a couple times just before and after I do a rattling sequence. I'll also use it when the action is slow and I haven't seen deer in a while. Basically it sounds like *neeeeaah*.

The trailing grunt is a short grunt that bucks make when they are traveling through the woods or when they are around other deer. It's not uncommon for a rut-crazed buck to make a short grunt every one to 10 steps he takes when he's in the right mood. If I see a buck walking through the woods, I'll use this grunt to stop him and to coax him in my direction. This is also a call that I'll use when no deer are in sight. If a buck is sexually active and not with a doe, there is a good chance he'll respond to the grunt if he can hear it.

The tending grunt can be a lethal weapon if used properly. When a buck is with a hot doe and is either frustrated by her rejections or another buck tries to intrude on his party he'll make a grunt that has a ticking cadence. The tending grunt can last from five to 30 or more seconds at a time. Often if I'm hunting in thick cover and a buck walks through I'll use a tending grunt to bring the buck to my stand. This is a great call to use when bucks are on the move and the rut is hot-to-trot.

During the full-blown chase phase of the rut, bucks are very aggressive and often all it takes for a fight to occur is for one buck to look at another buck the wrong way. Over the years I've found that the best time to use antlers to bring a buck close to my stand is the 14-day period prior to the prime-breeding window.

When I rattle around scrape sites, I do so aggressively with a sequence that seldom lasts longer than five minutes. Few fights I've witnessed have ever lasted longer so I keep it short and loud and make it as aggressive sounding as possible. Generally I rattle for a minute and a half, pause for 30 seconds, rattle for a minute and a half, pause for 30 seconds and end the sequence by rattling for a minute and a half. I also find that the two hours either side of daylight work best. But don't rule out midday during this period because I've rattled in some nice bucks during this time.

Also, when rattling do it in the thickest cover possible, especially if you're bowhunting. When a buck responds to antlers, he almost always comes in cautious, looking for the combatants. If he can't see them he'll usually hang up. So, thick cover forces him to come closer. Though you can't make as many natural sounds, like breaking branches and raking the ground, rattling from a treestand gives greater concealment, allows you to see the buck coming, and keeps the incoming buck from spotting you.

As October's days fade into November, the woods become a chaotic place for bucks and does, and both use scrapes to preserve the species. Because of this hunting prime scraping locations is one of the most challenging and rewarding ways to hunt whitetails.

4 The Real Dirt on Scrapes and Rubs

BY PETER FIDUCCIA

"What's this?" you might be thinking right now. "We just had chapters on scrapes and rubs. Do we need another?" The answer is a hearty "Yes!" I guess I'm sort of like an airline pilot I heard about. Someone asked him, "Why do you prefer four-engine planes?" He answered, "Because they don't make one with five!" You see, like that pilot, I'm always looking for an edge. And when it comes to bagging a whitetail buck, you should be doing the same. I'm sure you know that already, or you wouldn't be bothering to read this book. You see, the subject of scrapes and rubs is vastly important in how you go about getting a decent shot at a buck. And as helpful as Greg Miller and Charles Alsheimer have been on the subject in previous chapters, I'm not willing to close the book on the subject. We need a clincher—someone to wring scrapes and rubs out one more time until the ultimate morsels of wisdom and experience have been extracted from all his past hunts and days afield. I have just the man for the job, and in sharing what he has learned on this subject he may just possibly be giving your bowhunting strategies the biggest boost toward success you'll likely ever receive.

Peter Fiduccia's book Whitetail Strategies, *from which this excerpt is taken, is a no-holds-barred, no-nonsense titan of a book. It "cuts to the chase" quite literally in details and meaningful observations and conclusions about deer hunting that are irresistibly fascinating and helpful. A whitetail hunting authority of many talents and interests, Peter is host and head man at the* Woods N' Water *tv series, and author of scores of magazine articles.* Whitetail Strategies *is available from the Outdoorsman's Edge Book Club (www.outdoorsmansedge.com); or from* Whitetail Strategies, *1-800/652-7527.*

Without a doubt—more bucks—especially big bucks have been shot by hunters watching over scrape sites than any other hunting strategy used. However, since I have been hunting deer, I can say that the subject of scrape hunting has generated more controversy, disappointment, apprehension and misinformation among buck hunters than any other of the hunting methods combined.

Right up front, the information I'm sharing with you about scrape hunting is functional, common sense based information I have learned the hard way— through trial and error. Over the years, I have been just as confused about scrapes as you. By making a lot of mistakes while hunting over scrapes and having more than my fair share of success, I have formulated certain ideas and theories about this subject. I can state unequivocally, that scrape hunting is more successful when you apply a healthy dose of common sense to this tactic.

Let me also say, I have learned the success you encounter when hunting over scrapes is positively related to the balance of the deer herd in the area you hunt (buck to doe ratio). In areas where there is a one-sided ratio of bucks to does, the purpose of the scrape is no longer as consequential to the buck. Bucks living within any given area where the doe population is greater than the buck population, may simply, out of instinct, paw out several scrape sights and briefly attend them. But, when most of the does begin to enter their primary estrus cycle, these bucks no longer have an interest or the time to make new scrapes or tend established ones. There are simply too many estrus does roaming the woods willing to give the buck all the amorous attention he is seeking. Therefore, he has no need to hang out at one of his scrape locations waiting to meet a doe and accomplish his lifelong goal—to mate with as many does as possible.

This is why those who hunt in wilderness areas that don't have a high population of deer, but have a buck and doe population equitably balanced, have better success when hunting over scrapes. Areas like the remote regions of northern Maine, the Adirondack Mountains. of New York and a province like New Brunswick in Canada are classic examples. In these remote areas the scrape site plays a critically important role as a convenient meeting site for deer. It is the most practical place for a horny buck to meet a hot doe.

Want a comparison? When you were in your teens did you go to the library to meet a girl? Or, did you go to a dance club, bar, or the beach. I'll bet the latter. You knew where the odds were best for you to meet someone from the opposite sex who was looking to enjoy a night out. The same holds true for a buck. Instinctively, he knows the best and quickest place to meet a hot doe is over a scrape. Therefore, it's important to keep in mind these factors as we discuss scrapes. Not only do they work best in areas where the ratio balance and age structure of both sexes of the deer herd is ideal, but also in remote places where there are so few deer (again equally balanced) that the quickest and easiest way to locate each other is at a scrape site. These factors will determine how often scrapes are used by resident bucks. It's also important to understand that although one buck may make a scrape (does also make scrapes), other bucks and does may use this scrape. Most of the time this is related to the pecking order established in July and August.

According to some biologists and experts, the optimum sex ratio of one buck to every three deer creates terrific scrape hunting conditions, providing all the other factors related to scrape hunting are favorable. The best sex ratio for any deer herd is ideally a herd managed with a ratio of 1:1. At this point, I know you're asking what are the other factors. In talking with several biologists while writing this book, they analyze the following components when figuring out if an area will have optimum scrape making and activity levels.

- Buck-to-doe ratio
- Numbers of mature bucks within the herd
- Number of mature does within the herd
- Age structure of both sexes
- General health of the herd

In addition, there are hunting factors to also consider when determining how successful scrape hunting will be.

- Time of year
- Wind patterns in the area hunted
- Weather conditions
- How far the deer move between bedding, social, and feeding areas

(And, my favorite, because I think it's the most important factor when it comes to everything related to deer hunting, whether you are hunting disturbed or undisturbed deer:)

- Hunting pressure—Are you hunting deer that are relaxed or spooky?

Getting back to optimum sex ratios, as the sex ratio increases, which means the balance becomes less than one buck for every three does, scrape making and activity and the results from hunting over them, decreases appropriately. For most of you reading this book, the real hard truth is that you probably don't live in an area with an ideal sex ratio. You probably hunt in an area that is heavily hunted. Therefore, you are probably hunting deer that are disturbed. So, can scrape hunting be an effective hunting strategy for you—you bet! It will just take a common sense approach and plan for hunting scrapes to make you a successful scrape hunter.

First, try to locate areas that don't receive much hunting pressure. Some of my best success with scrape hunting has been in populated suburban areas while chasing bucks I call Backyard Bucks. By just simply doing a little research—by yourself and without making any fanfare to your hunting companions about what you're doing, you can find ideal out-of-the way places to hunt scrapes. Remember whenever you locate a good scrape or discover a big buck, keep it to yourself. It doesn't take but the slightest bit of pressure—and that could mean just one other hunter entering this buck's bailiwick—to alert him to the fact that he is being hunted. The result will be the buck will become more cagey and hunting him will become much more difficult. Hunting pressure is a hunter's second worse enemy (with wind being the first).

Ideal places to search out secluded scrape areas include small islands in rivers, small patches of brush or wood lots, private estates (the smaller the better), lands owned by corporations, military bases, manufacturing plants, church properties, land surrounding suburban reservoirs, golf courses, country hospitals, small outlying strip malls, rural airports, and one of my favorites, prisons. All these areas usually get overlooked by hunters who are afraid to ask for permission to hunt from these property owners. Or, simply because hunters don't believe these small pieces of land can offer great deer hunting. I could tell you here and now it is worth your effort to carefully check these places out. If you can't hunt within the areas I mentioned, hunt as close to the property borders as possible.

If none of these types of places are available to you and you hunt on public lands that are heavily hunted, here is the key to successful scrape hunting on public land. Get off the beaten track. I normally don't recommend a hunter must go "way back in" to score on a good buck. However, when it comes to using a scrape hunting strategy on public land, it's better to hunt further in. Besides getting yourself away from the crowd, you are likely to discover some remote swamp or cedar patch that will be alive with fresh primary scrapes. The bucks in these areas are usually bigger and there are usually more of them. When you find an area with undisturbed bucks, especially mature bucks, you have found a scrape hunting hot spot. The competition between mature bucks not undergoing heavy hunting pressure is intense and this is the single most desirable factor when scrape hunting.

For years, I have listened to disappointed hunters explain to me how they have had little success when hunting scrapes. Their reasons are wide and varied, "The primary scrape I was watching was abandoned by the buck" or "The buck is only checking the scrape nocturnally" or "I don't know how to tell the difference between a primary scrape and any other scrape" and the one I used relate to, "I watched a primary scrape for days without ever seeing a buck."

Not only have I heard them all, but I've lived them all, as well. That is until 15 years ago when I decided to figure out how to successfully identify and hunt active scrapes. Scrape hunting isn't easy despite what anyone including the experts may tell you. If scrape hunting was so foolproof, hunters wouldn't need any other tactic and all of us would be killing big bucks every year.

Some hunters and most experts say it's important to classify scrapes. Hunters must know whether the scrape they are hunting over is a primary or secondary scrape and so on. To this, I simply reply, "Bull dinky!" Not necessary. In fact, it can lead to more confusion about the subject. Through experience, I've learned that in some areas, there might not even be a single primary scrape to be found. Instead of wasting a lot of time looking for PRIMARY or SECONDARY scrapes, remember, just find a fairly large scrape (3 feet x 3 feet or larger) and you'll have found as good a scrape to hunt over as any other. The scrape you're hunting should be:

- moist, or at least damp
- fresh and dark-looking
- pawed cleanly to the bare earth
- almost free of debris (no branches, leaves, etc.)
- and has an overhanging branch, (especially if bitten in two)

If the additional following conditions exist, the scrape is even better than the one described above:

- is surrounded by rubs
- has a strong musky or urine odor
- has visible droplets of blood (from the estrus doe, most visible in scrapes made in the snow)
- tracks in and around the scrape (the bigger the better)
- lots of droppings (look for clumped dung from bucks)

If you find a scrape showing most or all of the above, worrying about whether it's a primary or secondary scrape is ridiculous. Stop and please read that sentence again. Instead, stop worrying about trying to find primary or secondary scrapes. Look for a scrape like I described above. Then go downwind and set up. Just hunt the darn thing—confidently.

With that said, for the sake of providing you with the information to be a more informed deer hunter, here is how you can simply and quickly identify primary and secondary scrapes. Primary scrapes are usually 4 feet x 4 feet and are often larger. They are usually churned up, muddy from buck urine and are free of debris. They will ALWAYS be accompanied by an overhanging branch. This branch, more often than not, will show signs of having been chewed and frayed by the buck as he deposits scents from his mouth, eyes and forehead while he refreshes his scrapes by urinating down his legs, over his tarsals and into the scrape. Most times, the buck leaves a hoof print somewhere near the center of the scrape. Primary scrapes are made in areas off the beaten trail. They are still placed where the buck has learned he will receive the most attention by passing does. A buck does not make many primary scrapes.

Secondary scrapes are made with much more frequency than primary scrapes and receive much less attention by a buck. They are usually much smaller (3 feet x 3 feet and less) and are not given the meticulous construction attention a buck pays to creating his primary scrape. Secondary scrapes are often erratic in shape and contain a small amount of debris (leaves, twigs, etc.). They are generally made close together and often form a line of direction. This collection of scrapes is often called a "scrape line" and, although they attract both bucks and does, they are not as productive as primary scrapes.

Remember that scrapes can be abandoned by bucks for a variety of reasons. In the pre-rut, scrapes are abandoned almost as soon as they are made because the bucks are too busy chasing mature does who came into a brief estrus cycle. During the primary rut, scrapes are abandoned for many reasons. Most often, however, it is when many does (in a herd with an unbalanced sex ratio) all come into estrus simultaneously. Remember what I said above, in this situation, a buck doesn't need scrapes.

Some hunters sit over abandoned scrapes not realizing another hunter may have already killed the buck that made the scrape. Or, estrus doe activity levels may be altered and the bucks moved to another area with a higher concentration of estrus does. One of the most common reasons for abandonment, at least daytime abandonment, is hunting pressure . . . and so on.

Bucks use these single scrapes as meeting places for does. They create scrape lines to "lure" does in. These scrapes are often left in areas where does frequent, such as fence lines, edges of fields, and brush lines. A scrape line is designed to encourage does to follow these smaller scrapes. Resembling the trail of bread left by Gretel (in the fairy tale Hansel & Gretel), this scrape line is used not as a rescue effort, but rather to lead the hot doe to a secure place where the horny buck is waiting.

Many hunters ask me how long should they hunt over an active scrape before giving up. This is probably one of the most difficult questions to answer. A realistic answer depends on a myriad of factors. To be quite candid, I'd have to see the hunting area, figure out the pressure from other hunters and look at the actual scrape to give an educated answer. However, generally, if the area you are hunting has a buck to doe ratio of about one buck to every four does, you'll see enough buck activity at active scrape sites that should last right through the peak of the primary rut. If the ratio is higher than 1:6 when the peak begins to fall off, I recommend abandoning the scrape and, instead, concentrating your efforts on locating does.

As many of you have often heard me say, "I am not a buck hunter, I am a doe hunter." What I mean by that is I always concentrate my efforts during the frenzy and rut phases on locating does. If you locate the does during this time of year, you'll locate the bucks. I only abandon this theory in the early part of October during the archery season when hunting the more secluded areas I think the bucks are using this time of year.

I have found most scrapes left by bucks are left in areas most frequented by does in late October. Look for scrapes where you find heavy doe activity during that time of the year. When you find a scrape opened up in November, you can rest assured it will be more active than any of the October scrapes described above.

So, now let's get down to it. Now that you understand scrapes, how can you hunt them successfully? There are several methods to increase your scrape hunting success. Some require some imagination; and others just require standard hunting tactics—both work. I have had much more success by getting creative. I'll touch on them here.

First, let's look at the more traditional strategies you can use. The overall goal in hunting over scrapes should be to attract the buck to you, rather than waiting for the buck to come in to check the scrape on his own. Many of my hunting strategies are directed to this end. I believe big bucks are like spiders in a web. They can hang out all day without ever moving, unless they are INSTINCTIVELY MOTIVATED to do otherwise. By using these motivating tactics, you eliminate having to wait on a buck who may or may not make his way past your stand.

By using these active strategies, you are no longer a passive hunter. You are a hunter who has now taken much more control of his deer hunting destiny—and success.

The most common error made when hunting over scrapes occurs when hunters investigate the scrape too closely. Don't walk right up to it, walk around it, poke at it, or handle the overhead branch. Obviously, all you accomplish is forewarning the buck via his most effective sense—his nose—that trouble has arrived! If the buck isn't immediately alerted to your presence after such a close investigation, he's certain to pick it up when he checks it out after you have left. If the human odor left behind is too strong when he arrives at the scrape, the buck may even abandon the scrape for a few days.

So, Scrape Hunting Rule #1 is to investigate all scrapes from a distance of several yards. If you want to investigate a scrape more closely, make sure the soles of your boots, whether they are rubber or leather, are washed clean with a nonscented cleanser. I wash the bottom of my hunting boots at least every other day. Also, carry surgeons' gloves and use them if you think you have to poke around (or plan to create a mock scrape) and touch anything in and around the scrape. Next, even if you take all the precautions above, don't stay at the scrape longer than necessary.

Scrape Hunting Rule #2—The next thing to avoid is setting up too close to the scrape. For bowhunters, I recommend setting up no closer than 15 yards no farther than 30 yards. Getting within 15 to 20 yards is a "roll of the dice" as any buck approaching a scrape usually checks out his surroundings before he comes in. When I get this close, I make sure I am thoroughly concealed. For firearm hunters, I recommend never getting closer than 30 yards and, most times, I suggest setting up 50 to 75 yards away, depending upon how thick the cover is. Always set up downwind of the scrape.

If you've ever been at one of my seminars, you've heard me say this again, the problem with hunting scrapes is that most bucks have learned to check their scrapes downwind and from the safety of cover. They only venture forth when the wind currents tell him that a hot doe has come into the scrape or when he smells the urine or tarsal gland of a competitive buck. In either case, he'll come in to investigate. It is this type of behavior response that has enabled me to create several unusual tactics that can provide you with some amazing results.

Spider Syndrome

I discovered this when a hunter at one of my seminars related the following story to me. At the end of my seminar he said, "Peter, I was hunting a big primary scrape when I was in Maine. Every morning when I went back to the stand, I saw that the buck used the scrape the night before. After spending several days watching the scrape all day long without ever seeing a buck, I decided on the last day to leave early and slowly stalk along a logging road on my way back to the lodge. I thought I would get lucky and jump a buck and not go back home empty-handed."

Without taking a breath, the discouraged hunter went on to say, "When I decided to get up, I grabbed my wool day pack. When I swung it around my shoulder to put it on my back, the strap got caught in the brush behind me and it made noise when I pulled it free. Then, I grabbed my bow and, as sure as heck, it got hung up in the brush and made more noise when I pulled it free. At this point I was thoroughly pissed off. So, when I took a few steps, I snapped a branch. Now, I was really mad. So, I kicked the branch as hard as I could I was so angry. Once the branch stopped skidding along the leaves, I heard branches breaking and leaves crunching. Almost instantly there was a big racked buck standing less than 10 yards from me! Before I could come to full draw, he made me, whirled and was gone."

Before I could say a word, the hunter turned and melted off into the crowd. That night in the hotel, I thought about what he said. It was so obvious that I couldn't believe I never thought of it before then. This hunter motivated the buck into responding. He was probably sitting within 100 yards of this buck the entire week he was hunting the scrape. For whatever reason, perhaps the wind was carrying his human odor toward the buck, the buck never approached his scrape while the hunter was there. Perhaps the buck had been hunted hard by other hunters before this hunter arrived and decided the best time to check the scrape was nocturnally.

In any event, the buck acted like a spider in a web. If you look at a spider, she'll stay in the same spot all day long until something shakes the web. It could be an insect, or an eraser from a pencil. Whether it's a food source or a foreign object, the spider is motivated by the vibrations to run down the web to investigate. This is exactly what happened with this hunter.

The sounds he made unintentionally imitated the natural sounds another buck or doe might have made as it approached his scrape. Both bucks and does can be very possessive about a scrape even if they didn't make it themselves. These natural sounds sparked the buck's interest enough to have him abandon his caution and run in and check out whether a hot doe had moved in or to see if it was a competitive buck scent-marking his scrape. Had the hunter been ready, his hunt would have ended successfully. Noise is not nearly as bad as we have been lead to believe, especially if the noise you make is made with a healthy dose of good ol' common sense.

Proof that some foreign noises attract deer is brought home each year by hunters I talk to. Often, I've been told about how a buck ran in as a hunter was climbing a tree with his portable tree stand. Obviously, the buck responded to the sounds of the stand scraping against the bark of the tree. Others have told me about bucks running in after snapping off branches to clear shooting lanes. Still others, have related stories how bucks have come in while they sawed or chopped saplings. Many times, as I am raking a trail free of leaves and debris to my stand, I have had bucks and does trot in to investigate the noise. All these types of natural noises can trigger an instinctive reaction by bucks to investigate what they may perceive to be a competitive buck or hot doe.

Other than seeing a big buck frequenting your hunting area, the first big scrapes will confirm that a mature buck is present. Big mature bucks start making *nonactive* scrapes as early as September. These scrapes are made, I believe, through instinct rather than being initiated by any onset of the rut. I firmly believe immature bucks don't start scraping until mid to late-October.

The best time to hunt scrapes is not during the actual peak of the primary rut, but, rather a week earlier during the frenzy period. By being informed and knowing how to take advantage of hunting scrapes, you will capitalize on this interesting and challenging facet of deer hunting.

Other than finding a fresh scrape, discovering a rub irrefutably gets the adrenaline flowing in deer hunters. Without actually seeing the buck, we know he passed this way. It gives us momentum. We become confident that we are hunting in an area with bucks.

Like scrapes, however, rubs have also been a source of controversy and misinformation, creating a quagmire of confusion about the subject. Determining why a buck makes a rub and when and where he makes it has been the preoccupation of many biologists and deer hunters alike. Unfortunately, the information gathered about rubs for the most part has only created more questions than answers.

The trick with rubs is to separate fact from misinformation. Rubs have important implications for deer hunters. To begin with, bucks do not make rubs solely for the purpose of removing velvet from their antlers. Bucks remove their velvet on bushes, saplings, and with their rear hooves. In fact, many bucks even tear off loose velvet with their teeth and eat it. On occasion, they remove small pieces of stubborn velvet by rubbing their antlers on a tree.

However, the primary reason bucks make rubs is to first establish a visual and olfactory (scent) sign post to other bucks and even does. **Rubs are part of their complex system of communication.** Understanding this single fact can help you sort out all the other important implications of rub making by bucks.

Bucks don't rub a tree just to rub it or solely to strengthen their neck muscles. They rub trees to establish their position in the herd, to warn off inferior bucks, to attract does, and to release frustration. But, the behavior of rubbing goes much farther. As a buck rubs a tree he releases scent from his forehead gland. This pheromone, or scent, also acts as a sexual stimulant to does. Some biologists believe the scent left after a buck has rubbed a tree can actually stimulate does into their estrous cycle. It is something similar to how horse breeders use a stallion as a teaser to get mares primed to breed. Does interpret rubs as sexual sign posts. The more they see and smell, the more primed they become.

I once read that some biologists believe that these pheromones act as biological stimulants which can induce early ovulation in does. Instinctively, bucks realize this and, even before the rut begins in earnest for the does, bucks begin to make rubs. Made lethargically at first, these are the rubs you see in September and early October. Then as the buck's own testosterone levels increase, his instinct to make and deposit scent on more and more rubs becomes a preoccupation with him accounting for the dramatic increase in rub sightings by hunters in late October and early November.

Some biologists go as far as saying that the more bucks rub in a given area, the more likely an early estrus will take place among does! The bottom line here is that if you are hunting in an area with an exceptional amount of buck rubs you may experience rutting behavior earlier than normal—a fact that would be overlooked if you weren't aware of the consequences of excess rubbing activity.

Rubs indicate a lot more, too. Many of us have heard that small rubs are made by bucks with small racks and big rubs are made by bucks with large racks. While this is generally true, it is not written in stone. In order to better determine if a rub was made by a yearling or by a mature buck, examine each rub very carefully—even if it was made on a small sapling tree. Big bucks leave a couple of telltale signs on their rubs. Inevitably, a mature buck will leave small gouges (from the points on his antlers) in the tree. In addition, a lot of times rubs made by mature bucks will be longer than a normal rub, starting almost at the base of the tree and going up higher than a normal rub. Also, the tree will usually have some broken branches or may even have its trunk bent or broken.

Rubs can also indicate a travel pattern. During my early days of deer hunting, I found a single rub entering the woods from a cornfield. As I examined it, I discovered several more rubs in somewhat of a line heading deeper into the woods. Obviously, a buck came from the field where he was eating or attending does and on his way back to his bedding area made or added to the rubs I had discovered.

As I continued into the woods looking over the rubs I glanced back toward the field. To my surprise I saw another line of rubs—about fifty yards away from the rubs I was looking at. Interestingly they were made on the opposite side of the trees I was looking over. Clearly, the buck made this line of rubs as he exited the woods and made his way to the field. Most bucks will take a morning route that is different then their evening route. At any rate, after finding several small gouges in the rubbed trees I determined the buck had some points on his antlers. I decided to hunt the area that evening.

I posted along the line of rubs that made their way into the field. At 4:30 PM an 8-point buck made his way through the woods heading to the field. As he stopped to rub a small sapling tree directly in line with the other rubs I had examined earlier in the day—I shot him. I have used rubs to determine the general direction or travel patterns of bucks ever since—and so can you!

I've also used rubs to help me determine the core area of bucks. When you discover an area of rubs that are clumped in close proximity of one another and are in a semicircle, you've more than likely discovered the very heart of a larger buck's core area. Often, but not always, these spots are off the beaten trail. They are frequently very close to a buck's preferred bedding spot. A spot a big buck will go to when he seeks solitude from hunting pressure.

I use this tactic on a mountain I hunt in my hometown. Early in the season, I search out a spot that has the kind of rubs I described above. From that point on, I leave the area alone until hunting pressure sends the bigger bucks sulking for cover. When the pressure is on, I hunt the area. Over the years, I have taken several trophy size bucks using this tactic. The most recent being a 12-point buck that I shot after posting in a spot with an excess of rubs in a semicircle. The buck scored 149⅝ Boone and Crockett points. Bucks this size often revert to using these types of areas after the firearms season gets underway.

I also like to look for rubs that are concentrated next to beds, droppings, and in and along thick cover. When I find rubs with this type of additional sign and terrain, I have found a hot spot. If, however, after a diligent search, I have not discovered a normal amount of rubs in my area, it's time for me to think about hunting elsewhere. A lack of rubs in a given area could be a good clue to a low buck population. A lack of substantial size rubs could indicate a lack of mature bucks. In either event, I look for another spot to hunt. The only exception to this rule according to some biologists, is that there will be less buck rubbing activity when the acorn crop is low. I have never been able to prove or disprove that theory.

Another interesting point about rubs takes place during the frenzy period of the rut. That's when buck rubs take on a completely different look. They begin to make much larger rubs during this time. These "frenzy period rut-rubs" can be seen for quite a distance by other deer. The bucks even change the types of trees they rub on during this period using sumac, cedars, pines, and other aromatic type trees. The more mature bucks will make lots of rubs now and hunters will begin seeing a lot more scarred trees in their hunting area.

Finally, I strongly believe that aggressive mature bucks within a herd will make different types of rubs than the lesser or subordinate bucks do. These rubs tend to be VERY LARGE and are made on big cedar trees. These individual trees are often revisited by the same buck year after year. These types of rubs also attract other large bucks. However, they are not left all over the woods. They are few in number in heavily hunted areas—but they are there. In fact, I have noticed this behavior more in areas that are specifically managed for trophy bucks.

I once found such a rub a few years back. It was on a cedar tree that measured 10 inches around! In fact, I have never found one on any other type tree other than a cedar. I think that's because cedar trees are the only trees that can withstand the onslaught of this type of rub. After a long three day vigil of hunting the area, I shot a 12-point buck as he was walking toward the exact tree. Until this day I am not sure if he was the buck who made the original rub, or, if he was just another dominant-type buck who was coming in to check the large rub out and refreshen it with his own scent.

The simple fact is, big rubs attract BIG bucks. A few big bucks may even use the same tree to rub! It's also why I strongly recommend that hunters make big false rubs to attract big bucks. These visual sign posts are hardly ever ignored by big bucks. They instinctively HAVE to check the rub out. They want to identify through scent deposited on the tree by the last buck if that buck was more dominant (aggressive) than them or not.

Rubs are too often ignored for nothing more than an indication of a buck being in an area. They shouldn't be. Look them over carefully to determine what they mean. They can and will provide you with several important clues. When you become proficient at reading rubs, you will be able to identify the size of the buck that made the rub, a direction he was traveling, whether or not it was his core area, and even the time of day it was made (i.e., morning or afternoon route).

Keeping in mind everything I've said above, here's a hunting strategy that I named several years ago, "Shake and Break." Simply put, bucks sometimes react to sounds that they think are being made by other bucks. A buck that hears branches being snapped, leaves shuffling, or the grating sound of a tree trunk being rubbed, can be fooled or, more precisely, instinctively motivated into believing these noises are being made by a competitive buck or bucks.

Many times, especially during what I call the "Big Chase" (the 48 to 72 hour period when bucks are frantically chasing after estrous does), bucks respond to these fraudulent natural sounds by throwing caution to the wind and enthusiastically running in to check out what they believe to be a racket being made by another buck. Bucks have even responded when I took small saplings and brush and shook them violently for several minutes. Other times, bucks have reacted to the sounds when I took a single antler and rubbed it up and down a small tree. I intentionally look for trees with loose bark and rub high enough so that the bark can fall to the leaves below. The added noise of the bark landing on the leaves acts as an additional motivational stimulus. As you will discover when using this tactic, however, you must be ready to shoot quickly. Most bucks that respond to these noises often race in, look around briefly, and then leave in as big a hurry as when they arrived. Be creative when deer hunting; don't be afraid to make noises that imitate natural sounds made by rutting bucks.

5   Deer Diet in Bow Season

BY BOB MCNALLY

Respected author and bowhunting authority Bob McNally builds his whitetail hunting game plan around food sources. Sure the rut is important. But deer have to eat somewhere—and that's the place Bob wants to be!

The surest way to a buck's heart is knowing what he eats, and where to find it.

It was a still, steamy, hot and buggy October morning when Ed Jones climbed to his treestand in southern Arkansas, not far from the Mississippi River. It wasn't the best weather for bowhunting deer, but it was opening day, and that made it traditional, almost mandatory, for Jones to be in the woods. He had grown up hunting whitetails in his home state of Wisconsin, and every year over the last decade he and his father, Tom, had bowhunted opening weekend on family land.

Though their best bucks usually fall later in autumn, the Joneses have a remarkable record of taking plenty of venison with bows and arrows during the hottest part of the Arkansas early archery deer season. They've even downed a number of heavy bucks, including a few eight- and 10-pointers, some pushing the Pope & Young record book.

So while Ed Jones knew the best of the deer season was still a month or more away, he settled into his oak-top perch thinking of all the opening-day deer he'd taken from the same spot over the years.

As gray light slowly filled the forest floor below him, Ed began to hear the soft sounds of morning. An owl hooted from a not-too-distant swamp. Gray squirrels chattered, and woodpeckers rat-tat-tat-tatted on hardwood bark. Every now and then there was slight understory rustling from unseen animals as they moved in fallen leaves and twigs.

As the growing day's light gave more definition to the woods, Ed could plainly see long, sickle-shaped seed pods hanging on a trio of honey locust trees he hunted 20 yards from. The dried, foot-long, quarter-moon-shaped seed pods didn't look like the kind of food deer relished. But none of the dozens of pods Jones had knocked onto the ground with a long limb just the previous afternoon could be seen still there.

"They've all been devoured by deer," he thought, which was why this particular treestand had always been one of the best early bow bets he'd discovered in 25 years of deer hunting.

3 3

When the new-day light was good enough to shoot, Jones stood in his tree-stand, nocked an arrow and waited quietly, alertly. A few moments later he heard the steady shuffle of deer hooves moving closer from a creek bottom, and soon a doe and two yearlings stood beneath the honey locust trees. The deer nosed leaves around, sniffing and searching for seed pods. They looked and looked, and ate a few pod morsels that had been overlooked by other deer. Then the animals moved off, disappearing in the distance.

A short time later, another doe approached the honey locust grove. It was a heavy 120-pound doe, with big floppy ears having nicks and cuts from old age. The doe's gray muzzle was rooting in leaves for seed pods when Jones loosed his PSE bow's string and the Satellite 125-grain Titan found its mark low behind the animal's shoulder.

The doe exploded into a blur of motion, turning back the way she'd come to the seed pods, but traveled only 50 yards before Jones watched her stumble and fall.

Only a few minutes passed, and Jones again heard the soft shuffle of leaves from approaching deer—this time from the opposite direction where the does and yearlings had appeared.

The light was still too poor to see well through the woods, especially looking at the ground for tan-camouflaged deer. But Jones finally pinpointed the source of the leaf sounds after seeing a buck's head turn, its ivory-white rack standing out starkly in the gray of the early-morning woods. It was a basket-rack six-pointer, the type buck Jones had long since stopped shooting with his bow so it could live longer growing a heavier bigger rack.

Ed knew such a little buck early in the season was likely to be the companion of a bigger buck or two. He looked beyond the six-pointer as it moved into the grove of honey locusts, and two larger-body deer stood in the low-light shadows. He could just barely make out their rack sizes, and both were "keepers," especially one, which had a non-typical rack and a big, single drop tine on one side. The bucks were not spooky, as they generally are during the opening weeks of bow season. So they stood their ground for a time, browsing on shrubs, while moving closer and closer to the honey locust trees—and well within shooting range.

Finally, the smaller of the two "keeper" bucks stepped boldly into the honey locust understory, probing for seed pods. Ed hesitated for just a second as he surveyed the buck's rack. He wanted the larger of the two bucks, but the bigger one showed no interest in coming closer. Experience told Ed to take the lesser deer while he had the chance. So he drew his bow, anchored and sent a broadhead through the chest of the 197-pound, 10-pointer that later measured 121⅝ Pope & Young points.

"I really wanted the bigger buck, which I know now was a sure P&Y size animal," says Jones. "But I learned a long time ago that to be consistently successful bowhunting you must take the *first good opportunity* to shoot when it becomes available. That's especially true during the early bow season because everything is still so green and lush you may only get a small open shot for just a moment or two at even close animals. Deer also can feed on just about everything early in the year, so you can have a hot spot like a honey locust grove where you expect every deer within miles to show up. But whitetails—especially good bucks—rarely do what you expect them to do. Many times I've seen a deer coming my way, been ready for a shot, and for no apparent reason it drifted off in another direction. That can happen anytime, anywhere, but especially in the early season because of the abundance of deer browse.

"There is so much choice deer food during bow season, you can't be sure where animals travel and roam. That's why I shot that 10-pointer when I had the first good opportunity. I might have sat in that treestand for another month before another nice buck came within range. Deer don't travel a great deal during the early bow season because the weather is still very warm. In Arkansas it can be downright hot—sometimes in the 90s. When it's that hot, deer don't travel much. They stick pretty much to river bottoms, creek draws and drainage ditches. And they seldom travel far from shady, cool thickets with plenty of leaf canopy. I try to hunt those places, setting up stands near primary food sources that are very close to cool bedding areas."

Deer hunters used to walking and scouting for "hot" oak trees dropping acorns to concentrate whitetails often are disappointed in the early archery season. Even cultivated crops like soybeans and corn may not be much to the liking of deer in hot weather. Yet deer still must feed, but often their choice foods are over-looked by even experienced hunters.

It's important to remember that deer are browsing animals, not grazing ones. So a multitude of shrubs are to a whitetail's liking, especially in the bow season when much of the woods is green with mature growth. Greenbrier (smilax) is an important deer food wherever it's found, especially in the South where it can grow year-round. Deer relish the glossy-green broad leafs of the woody, thorny vine, which can be found in lowlands and uplands. Look for telltale signs of deer "nip-ping" the vines, shown by brown blunt ends on the plants, found along trails near creeks and side ridges. Other choice deer browse that bowhunters should be able to identify afield include: jasmine, honeysuckle and, yes, even poison ivy. Other deer foods that can concentrate whitetails for bowhunters early in the year are wild grapes, watermelons and persimmons. Such foods mature earlier in the year than many plants whitetails dine on during late autumn and winter.

One oak variety, however, that can be an important food source early in the season is the water oak, which is abundant throughout the Southeast. Not only does this tree drop acorns much earlier than many other oaks, but it's a consistent mast producer and thrives in wet, thick areas deer prefer to inhabit early in the bow season.

Experts say water oaks don't produce the most preferred acorns for deer. Other trees like white oaks and red oaks have more succulent acorns that white-tails desire. But water oaks are consistent producers, usually offering lots of acorns early in the year during seasons when other oak mast may fail to develop.

The trouble with water oaks, however, is that often a "bottom" or creek drainage with such trees has hundreds of oaks "raining" acorns at the same time.

Thus deer can be scattered throughout the low area, which makes it a difficult bowhunting proposition. Some savvy hunters, however, have learned they can "sweeten" select deer forage plants, like water oaks, by fertilizing them with simple, inexpensive fertilizers like 6-6-6 or 10-10-10. By spreading fertilizer around a specific tree or two, many hunters say the acorns such trees produce are favored by deer. Fertilizing not only works to concentrate whitetails feeding around specific water oak trees, but it's effective in "sweetening" other early season foods like grapes, honeysuckle and greenbrier. Fertilizing also aids grapes, persimmon and apple trees to bear fruit when other similar plants in a given region have none.

Apples, pears, persimmons and grapes are some of the best and earliest foods deer key on during bow season. All of these fruits respond well to fertilizing, and anywhere they're found bowhunters should take careful note of them. An old apple or pear grove on an abandoned homestead can be especially attractive to deer. I've seen in-velvet bucks, good ones, stand on their hind legs to reach still-hanging apples when ones on the ground had been devoured. In wild apple groves you can "hold" feeding deer in the area by knocking down fruit, but do it with a stick or rake not your hands, because you don't want lingering human scent.

When I was a teenager in Illinois a friend and I lucked into one of the best bowhunting deals I ever experienced. It was late summer and we stopped at a roadside fruit stand to buy some apples and pears and the fruit seller was grumbling to another customer about how deer had been eating his young sapling apple trees and killing them. We prodded the guy with questions, and by being tactful and friendly we "volunteered" to bowhunt the pesky deer that were costing him big bucks in the apples and trees they were consuming.

We had a 70-acre, manicured and very private apple orchard to hunt, and the deer were huge and abundant. Only trouble was the guy wouldn't let us put stands in his apple trees, and the best spots only could be hunted from the ground. Still, we arrowed plenty of deer, including some good bucks. But if only we could have used treestands I'm sure some of the record-book animals we habitually saw would have been ours.

There are surprising numbers of wild apple, plum and pear trees throughout America, particularly around old homesteads. Some of the very best spots for hunting are a bit off the beaten track and not always easy to locate. One of the best ways of finding fruit trees is to scout areas in spring and look for bright blossoms which by bow season turn to fruit. Blossoms are easy to spot with binoculars from even long distances, especially in hilly terrain. Mark their locations on a topo map, and check them in fall for fruit and deer sign.

As plants ripen, mature, die and rot, deer stay on the move to other foods, sometimes on a week-to-week basis. So a consistently successful bowhunter has got to have a mind-set for locating the best deer foods like he's in nature's grocery store. Whitetails move around, feeding on agricultural crops like soybeans and corn, then to native browse, acorns, then perhaps clover or rye grass.

Another important element to choosing hunting spots according to the preferred foods of deer is that rarely do whitetails linger long feeding on even the most succulent forage. Their diets are widely varied, and they stay mobile munching mushrooms over there, to nipping greenbrier over here, while on their way to a clover or bean field on the next ridge.

It sounds obvious, but deer can change food preferences overnight, so you've got to keep on your toes and move bow stand locations, too. When you pinpoint a hot apple or honey locust tree, or a lush honeysuckle jungle, don't automatically assume deer are waiting in line to dine there. Read the sign around the food source to determine if whitetails *currently* are feeding there. Fresh tracks and *very fresh* droppings are best evidence. When in doubt, hang a stand and hunt the spot a time or two. But don't get married to the place, because deer aren't.

6 Beds: The Secret Spots Where Bucks Spend 90 Percent of the Daylight Hours

BY JOHN WEISS

Yes, you heard John right. New research has proven that bucks spend 90 percent of their daylight hours in and around their bedding zones. Here's how this respected authority and dedicated whitetail hunter finds and cracks into these sanctuaries. Author of hundreds of magazine articles on whitetail deer and several books, John's latest work is The Whitetail Deer Hunter's Almanac, *published by* The Lyons Press.

Several years ago Arkansas hunter Todd Henderson relayed one of the most incredible big-buck hunting stories I've ever heard. He'd located a small pocket of cover so thick it would choke a mouse and, from a distance, using binoculars, spotted a bedded buck right in the middle.

There was no way Henderson could approach the cover without alerting the buck so he decided to back off and come back another time to find a stand site. Trouble was, over several days, he returned at random times and the buck was always there.

Then one night, coming home late from work, he spotted the buck in an open field and had a brainstorm. Since the deer clearly was a nocturnal animal, as most trophy bucks are, Henderson decided he'd have to enter the buck's bedding area and hang his stand in darkness, well before the deer returned early the next morning.

Knowing he'd probably have only one chance at getting this particular buck, Henderson hiked to the bedding area at midnight, carrying with him his bow and two stands.

Working in the dim glow of a flashlight, Henderson found the trail leading to the spot where the buck habitually bedded. Then, about 30 yards away, he located two trees spaced about six feet apart. Next, he hung one stand in each tree so they faced each other with the front edges of their base platforms nearly touching. Finally, he hung his bow on a hook, and then laid down on the two facing stands and went to sleep!

Five hours later, Henderson's wristwatch alarm gave several soft "beeps" to waken him. And 45 minutes after that, when it was just barely light enough to see, the enterprising hunter arrowed the buck from 30 yards as it returned to its day-time seclusion.

"In being a long-time fisherman and hunter, I've come to notice many parallels between big bass and big bucks," Henderson explained. "Fish biologists tell us that 90 percent of a lake's bass population resides in only 10 percent of the total amount of water present. And similarly, deer biologists conducting radio-tracking studies have learned that a mature buck, on average, spends 90 percent of his daylight hours in only 10 percent of his familiar home range."

Consequently, it sounds logical that if a hunter likewise devotes 90 percent of his time to stand hunting in the immediate area where a buck is spending nearly all of his time, eventually taking that buck should be a no-brainer.

But it's not quite that easy. First comes the matter of finding one of these high-security bedding areas. Then it's necessary to recognize that these fortresses are such safe havens it's virtually impossible to enter them undetected when the buck is there. You have to enter when he's gone and be waiting for his return.

When they're subjected to moderate hunting pressure, whitetails tend to feed early and late and then evaporate into heavy cover to bed during the midday hours. And if the hunting pressure is intense, the animals, especially mature bucks, become fully nocturnal and remain sequestered in their beds throughout the entire daylight hours.

I've heard some hunters claim they've sneaked right up on bedded deer and caught them completely asleep, but there's too much evidence that this rarely happens.

Biologists say that, anatomically, deer lack what is called a super-chiasmatic nuclei, or "sleep clock," in their brains. This is a ganglion of nerve endings which humans do indeed possess because our far more complex brains require a much deeper level of rest if we are to awaken completely refreshed.

Consequently, when the alarm clock goes off in the morning, we are not capable of instantly reacting with a state of full alertness. Our sleep clocks simply prohibit this, causing us to gradually stairstep up from the depths of deep slumber into eventual full consciousness.

As I said, deer (and other animal species commonly preyed upon) do not possess so-called sleep clocks in their brains. This is nature's way of giving them the ability to be at complete rest, and to derive the mental and physiological benefits of that rest, without actually "falling asleep."

Because of this, resting deer are able to react instantly without having to first return from a state of unconsciousness. Clearly, this is a valuable attribute to possess because, otherwise, the world's predators would quickly and easily bring all prey species to the brink of extinction and we'd have a shattering imbalance among our wildlife populations.

It's also interesting to note that, according to studies conducted by the South Carolina Department of Wildlife and Marine Resources, although mature bucks spend most of their time within that 10 percent of their home range where they feel the most secure, they generally spend less than two hours at a time actually bedded. It's rather common for them, in fact, to periodically stand, stretch, walk around a bit, nibble upon something, urinate, and then lay down again in the same immediate area.

The above studies also revealed that when a deer is indeed lying down, it frequently lays its head right on the ground and even briefly closes its eyes. Nevertheless, these apparent interludes of "sleep" rarely last more than two minutes, and even then the animal's sensory apparatus can bring it to a state of instant arousal and total alertness.

Never lose sight of the fact that whitetails select certain places to bed for the most important reason of achieving safety. As a result, if they are unexpectedly surprised at close range and spooked from that region, chances are they will not return for a long time and will attempt to find some other place that affords an equal or higher level of security.

Therefore, during the course of scouting for bedding sites, it is extremely important that you move slowly and yet present a highly visible appearance and make plenty of noise. I even whistle to myself and smoke my pipe!

The illusion you want to present is that of a person who is engaged in some type of routine outdoor work. Throughout the year, whitetails become accustomed to numerous encounters with utility line workers, foresters, surveyors, and farmers. The deer see them in the distance, hear them talking and working with tools, and simply move out of their way for the time being.

By simulating this normal human activity afield and by giving the deer plenty of advance warning and opportunity to hide or sneak away undetected, they'll usually retain full confidence in the security of their chosen bedding sites and will undoubtedly return shortly after you've left.

Conversely, if you prowl around very quietly and periodically alarm the deer at close range, forcing them into a frantic escape mode as they snort and bound away with their tails waving, you'll destroy their feeling of security and cause them to seek seclusion elsewhere.

Due to the infinite number of terrain and cover variations around the country, it is impossible to describe specific places where bucks will bed. We can only give generalizations and then it is up to the hunter himself to apply this insight to his own chosen hunting grounds.

All regions of the country fall into one of three categories: mountainous, rolling, or flat. In mountainous regions, bucks commonly bed about mid-elevation, or halfway up the mountain, while does bed in the bottomlands. In terrain characterized by rolling topography, bucks commonly bed on the highest ground available, while does bed midway up the slopes. And in predominantly flat country, bucks usually bed within the innermost sanctuaries of thick cover while does locate themselves more toward the outer periphery.

In mountainous terrain, pay special attention to hillside benches or terraces. In rolling terrain, scout well-defined ridges, promontories, heads of hollows, and similar cover-saturated areas that give a good view from above. In flat country, search for the thickest cover you can find, such as dry hummocks in swamps, dense pine plantations or cedar bogs, regenerative thickets where a forest fire or logging operation previously took place, or wherever the terrain is choked with jack-strawed logs, blowdowns, or undergrowth such as honeysuckle or rhododendron.

It stands to reason that most hunters will want to home-in upon those particular bedding sites used by bucks, so naturally it's important to know how to identify buck beds versus doe beds.

The very best time of year to locate deer beds is after the season closes and there is snow-cover on the ground. Not only are the beds now quite visible, but due to the recent hunting pressure they will be the very types of bedding sites the deer will probably use again next year shortly after hunters begin infiltrating their habitat.

In the absence of snow-cover, spend time scouting immediately after several days of very rainy weather. This will cause deer to "lie up" for several consecutive days, and in so doing their beds will be more pronounced due to the continual compacting of the grass and weeds beneath their body weight.

In examining the beds first-hand, recall what we said earlier about bucks generally bedding in different locations than does, in accordance with the topography of the landscape. Also, the largest bucks are most often loners while does tend to be highly gregarious; therefore, a single bed in a typical "buck bedding location" is very likely to indeed be a mature male. New Jersey biologist C.J. Winand has another way of confirming whether a bed was occupied by a buck.

"Bucks and does alike commonly defecate upon rising from their beds," C.J. explains. "But does usually drop less than 50 pellets at each defecation, while bucks usually drop more than 75 pellets. So simply count 'em."

The final confirmation I rely upon is whether a cluster of beds reveals matted impressions of different sizes. Bucks have a strong tendency to avoid bedding too close to yearlings, yet such younger deer have a very high inclination for bedding with their mothers. As a result, if you find, say, seven beds clustered in rather close proximity to each other, and three of the beds are large and four of them relatively small, it's a safe assumption you've found a social group consisting of several does, with two of them being accompanied by their most recent offspring.

Certain types of weather conditions are highly conducive to hunting bedded deer. Likewise, there are certain times you absolutely do not want to hunt bedding sites.

Keep in mind that when whitetails are bedded they have several distinct advantages in their favor.

First, they are spending the greater part of their resting period laying down, which makes them far less visible.

Second, they'll have selected their bedding sites in such a manner that all of their senses can be used with peak efficiency to monitor their immediate surroundings for the approach of possible danger.

In other words, they'll be able to see very well in that direction which affords the best long-range view, and yet they'll simultaneously be able to smell and hear in that direction which does not lend itself well to visibility.

So it's imperative to have your stand in place long before the season opens, and it's equally important to hike in to occupy that stand under cover of darkness well before the animal returns. And the worst possible conditions for hiking to a stand situated in a bedding area is quiet weather accompanied by ground cover, which is dry and noisy when trod upon. Even though you'll be entering the bedding area long before dawn's first light, when the deer most likely is feeding elsewhere, you never can be entirely sure he's not there during many of the darkness hours as well.

The very best time to hunt a bedding site is immediately after it has rained and when there is a gentle, prevailing wind. The precipitation will dampen the ground cover, muting any human error as you hike in. And if there is a deer in the immediate vicinity, the moderately gusting breezes will tend to confuse its senses of hearing and smell.

Although hunting a buck's bedding area carries a higher success percentage when done from a treestand, still-hunting bedding areas with a partner is worth considering if you have a special rapport with someone whose hunting style meshes well with your own. It becomes almost like a marriage or other relationship in which you intuitively know what each other is thinking and then are able to second-guess what each other will do in varying circumstances. You become so intimately familiar with each other's pace and method of negotiating certain types of terrain configurations it's almost as though the two of you are one.

I have one such partner like this. And as amazing as it sounds, we can space ourselves 300 yards apart, enter a mile-long stretch of mixed cover, never have visual contact with each other as we hunt, and yet nevertheless eventually emerge somewhere along the opposite side within just a couple of minutes of each other. That's how in-tune we are with each other's hunting style and movement patterns.

There is one particular set of circumstances we like to team-hunt more than any other. It's a situation in which a rather steep ridge clearly travels a lengthy distance. He'll take one side of the ridge, and I the other, and we'll still-hunt our own respective terraced benches. Even though we may be only 75 yards apart, we can't see each other because of the intervening crest of the ridge between us.

As we each sneak along, we visually pick the cover apart just ahead of our line of travel, hoping to spot a bedded buck. We also periodically look over the edge of the bench, where it pitches off steeply downhill, in hopes of seeing bedded deer on the next lower terrace.

The thing that makes this technique so lethal is that if my partner inadvertently jumps an unseen buck from its bed, and no shot is possible, the buck's behavior is fairly predictable.

It will usually bolt in a fairly straight line for a 100 yards or so, then turn sharply and go up and over the crest of the ridge to the opposite side and begin doubling back, apparently intending to travel along that bench a given distance and eventually climb back over the crest of the ridge still again to return to its original bedding site. And, in so doing, the deer often runs headlong into the hunter on that opposite side.

So whenever either of us bumps a deer from its bed we instantly give a crow call. This signal tells the other hunter on the opposite side of the ridge to immediately get behind the nearest tree or other screening cover and freeze, because in moments a buck will likely be coming straight in his direction.

It has been said that a trophy buck is where you find it. But now, we also know something else. No matter how large a buck's adopted home range may be, he'll be spending nearly all of his time in only 10 percent of that available area. Find it, move in during one of his brief forays elsewhere, and chances are you'll get lucky.

7   Setting the Stage

BY GARY CLANCY

No big buck in his right mind ever waltzes out into the middle of a crop field in broad daylight, right? Yeah, but they aren't very far away.

Field edges are tempting places to hunt, especially when you have seen a good buck using the field. In this case I had watched not one, but three dandy bucks, still hanging together in their summer bachelor group, feed in the secluded alfalfa field for a week before the bow season opened. Things looked promising for opening day. The bucks showed on the first evening of the season, but used a trail about 80 yards away from the one I was perched over to enter the field. I tried some soft grunting and sparring, hoping to arouse enough curiosity in one of them to cause him to wander over in my direction, but all I got was a long, hard stare and after that they ignored the soft grunts and tickling tines.

They were still in the field, along with several does and fawns when my wife drove into the field and up to my tree to pick me up when shooting hours ended. The next evening I sat in a stand overlooking the trail the bucks had used to enter the field the previous evening. You guessed it. All three of them walked out on the trail I had been sitting on the first night. The third evening was a bust. Only the does and fawns entered the field. I knew better but I gave it one more try the next evening. Same deal. The does and fawns and one spindly 7-point showed, but the big boys stayed hidden. Even though I had taken every precaution to prevent the bucks from knowing I was hunting them, I now knew the gig was up. A mature buck catches on in a hurry. I would not be seeing those bucks in the field during shooting light again. I was convinced of that. So the next morning I went snooping. I was certain that the bucks had not abandoned the field, but they were now wary enough not to step foot in the field until after dark. I was betting that somewhere between the buck's bedding area and the feeding field was a staging area. If I could find it, there was still a good chance I could connect on one of the bucks.

A staging area is nothing more than a place where a buck or sometimes multiple bucks will spend some time on a regular basis. Usually they are related to feeding sites, although, as we will see in a minute, they can also relate to bedding areas. What happens to create a staging area is this. I'll use the three bucks I was hunting as an example. Once the bucks had an inclination that they were being hunted they became reluctant to enter the field until after dark. But odds are good that the bucks were still rising from their beds at the same time every afternoon to begin the trip from bedding area to the alfalfa field. Deer do not vacate their primary food source easily and it is natural for a deer to rise from his day bed in late afternoon to begin the journey to his favorite food source. Along the way, the buck will establish a location where he will spend anywhere from 15 minutes to an hour rubbing saplings, sparring with other bucks, doing a little browsing and, as the season progresses, pawing out a scrape or two just for the heck of it. A staging area is a place for a buck to kill some time while he waits for darkness so that he will feel comfortable venturing into the open feeding area.

How to Locate Staging Areas

Staging areas are fairly easy to locate in agricultural areas, more difficult to find when hunting extensive timber. In agricultural areas, the best way to locate a staging area is to backtrack from the field along the trail the deer are using to enter the field. Very often there will be a number of trails the deer are using and you may need to backtrack on more than one before finding the staging area. Because bucks will use the same staging area from year-to-year, my favorite time to locate these buck magnets is during early spring scouting trips. However, I realize that is not always possible. Many times, as in the case of the bucks in the alfalfa field I end up being forced to do my detective work during the season. Either way, spring or during the season, rubs are the key to identifying a staging area.

I've spent a lot of hours sitting in a treestand observing bucks on staging areas and from my observations, it appears that rubbing is the primary activity they engage in while waiting for darkness. Backtrack along a trail and when you find an area with multiple rubs, both along the trail and off to the sides of the trail, you can feel confident that you have found a staging area. Many times the staging area will include the intersection of two or more trails. And all of the staging areas I have found have been in fairly thick cover as opposed to open woods. Another key location for staging areas in hill country seems to be on a flat shelf or bench or along the route the bucks travel between bedding and feeding sites. On occasion I have found staging areas on the fringe of the feeding field. In all instances, when this has occurred, the fringe provided the bucks with the thickest cover along the route from the bedding area to the feeding field. Although I never overlook the field fringes, it is more common for the staging area to be found 100 to 300 yards back from the field.

Although rubs are the sign which most often alerts me to the presence of a staging area, I also keep my eyes open for trails, tracks, droppings of various age and, as the rut approaches, scrapes. Because bucks will spend some time browsing while killing time at the staging area, signs of browsing are often abundant as well. Sign at staging areas is often subtle and easily missed. This is especially true if the area you are hunting has a poor population of mature bucks. Since mature bucks do the bulk of the early rubbing, a lack of mature animals in the population means fewer rubs, which makes it more difficult to locate staging areas. Also, if only a single buck has been using a staging area, even though he is using it on a daily basis, there will not be an abundance of sign, which again makes the staging area difficult to spot. Take your time, look close, and don't expect to find a lot of sign when searching for a staging area.

Acorns and Staging Areas

Although the most common staging areas are related to agricultural fields, there have been a half dozen times when I have encountered staging areas where deer have been feeding heavily on acorns. One farm I hunt in southern Minnesota provides the classic example. On this farm, there is a small riverbottom and a connecting block of timber. This parcel was logged for the oak many years ago and is now comprised mainly of ash, basswood, and maple. The larger parcel of timber provides good bedding cover for the deer but oaks and thus acorns are scarce. However, only 100 yards to the west of the larger chunk of timber is a smaller stand of timber which has never been logged. The oaks here, mostly white oak with a smattering of red, are ancient and huge. The broad canopy of these giant trees ensures that little sunlight reaches the forest floor, so here the understory is bare, like a pasture. There is a grassy slough separating the two woods. Does, fawns, and small bucks amble across this slough in broad daylight, drawn by the acorns, but the big boys just can't bring themselves to be so bold. Instead, the mature bucks make their way up from the riverbottom in late afternoon and stage in an especially thick section of the bigger woodlot. Here they wait for the sun to set so that they too can cross the slough and feast on the fallen mast. In this example, the slough provides an obvious transition from the thicker and larger woodlot to the smaller, oak-laden woodlot. But the transition is not always so obvious. I've found the same situation when hunting big timber. The bucks, reluctant to join the does and smaller bucks on the more open oak ridges, hung back in a staging area until dark. No question, these staging areas can be difficult to find, but if you are hunting oaks and seeing lots of deer feeding on acorns, but not seeing any good bucks, don't just assume that it is because there are no big bucks in the area. It is very possible that the bucks are spending that last hour of shooting light at a nearby staging area. Find it and you are in business.

Evening Only

When a staging area is related to a food source, whether agricultural or a big timber situation, evening is the best time to hunt the staging area. It is in the evening that bucks spend the most time at the staging area. In fact, I've found that most staging areas are not worth hunting in the morning. Bucks have little reason to spend time at a staging area relating to a food source in the morning. Plus, getting into a staging area stand near a food source without spooking deer on the way to the stand is difficult. No sense in messing up a good evening stand by trying to hunt the stand in the morning too. However, staging areas near bedding sites are sometimes worth a shot in the morning.

Bedding Area Staging Sites

The jury is still out on whether bucks spend more time at staging areas near their beds in the evening or in the morning. My personal theory, backed up by a lot of treestand time, is that bucks tend to use bedding area staging sites most frequently upon their return to the bedding area in the morning. It appears to me that before bedding down for the day, a buck will use this staging area to do a little rubbing, maybe paw out a scrape and generally just nose around for a little while before re-tiring. I'm sure that bucks probably use these bedding area staging sites frequently in the evening as well. However, because most of the bedding area staging sites I have found have been very close to the actual bedding area, it is very difficult to sneak into a stand at the staging site without alerting the buck in the bedding area. I'm sure that the reason I have not seen more bucks in the evening when hunting staging sites near bedding areas is because the buck has been aware of my presence. In fact, I no longer attempt to hunt staging sites near bedding areas in the evening, but I consider them to be an excellent location for a morning stand. I should also mention that bedding area staging sites generally do not have the amount of sign that staging sites near feeding areas have, which makes them difficult to locate. Spring is definitely the best time to search for staging areas near places bucks are likely to bed.

The Rut and Staging Areas

The rut is one of those good news/bad news deals when it comes to hunting stag-ing areas. The good news is that as the pre-rut winds down you will find an ever increasing amount of sign at staging areas, mainly in the form of rubs and scrapes. This makes a staging area much easier to locate. The bad news is that about a week before the first wave of does comes into estrous, bucks will become too antsy to spend much time lingering at staging areas. And when the first does enter their es-trous cycle you can forget about hunting staging areas entirely. What you are left with is a short window of opportunity, a time span of about 10 days, when the bucks are really into rubbing, but have not yet developed a bad case of rut-induced wanderlust.

Alfalfa Field Bucks

It took some serious detective work, but I found what I was looking for on a brush-choked bench about 200 yards back off of the alfalfa field. Rubs were not plentiful, but there were enough to convince me that more than one buck was spending some time at the location. Droppings were plentiful, some still shiny, oth-ers dry and dull, indicating that the deer had been using the area on a regular basis. I hung my stand high in a towering hickory within easy range of the intersection of two trails and the greatest concentration of rubs. It was a warm day and I knew the bucks would not move until late in the day, so I vacated the area and then snuck back into the stand about two hours before sunset. It was nearly two hours later, the sun already out of sight behind the bluff, the welcome coolness of evening descending on the valley when the trio of bucks made their appearance. Even though I had been watching the two trails closely, it was a calm evening and the movement easily caught my eye. One of the bucks was rubbing his antlers on the thumb-thick sapling. The buck was to my left about 30 yards, too far for a shot in the thick, early season underbrush. I waited and prayed that one of the three would work his way closer before shooting hours ended. Minutes dragged by, sometimes I could see patches of hide or a glimpse of antler as one of the deer moved, but I never did get a good look at all three of the bucks together. When one of them, a 10-pointer with distinctive, dagger-like brow tines stepped into a narrow shooting lane 20 yards away, I drew, aimed, and released. I'm not sure if my arrow deflected or if the buck ducked it, but I watched the white and yellow fletching slide just over the back of the buck.

Hey, staging areas are good places to hunt for deer, but you still have to hit them!

8 The Biggest Secret in Bowhunting

BY THOMAS L. TORGET

Tom Torget puts in a strong word urging bowhunters to tread lightly in their early-season operations. A whitetail, Torget believes, behaves according to the book only when he's left alone. Sounds simple, but a lot of bowhunters just don't get it!

Picture this: Bowhunters Bob and Beau are like a pair of puppies desperate to break out of the yard so they can run and chase. Nine months they've waited for opening day. Nine months! Another 96 hours of agony separates them from the October 1 archery opener.

"Let's check our stands after work tonight," says Bob during a coffee break at the plant. "See if there are any fresh tracks since yesterday."

"Good idea," agrees Beau. "I hope that 9-pointer sticks to his pattern. I've got a surprise waiting for him when he comes by my stand on Saturday!"

An hour before dark, Bob's pickup bounces noisily along the seldom-used rutted farm road that winds through the middle of the woodlot. He stops just north of the creek and shuts off the engine. The two hunters pile out in a flash, slam doors and step quickly through the timber toward the treestand that Beau set up on Labor Day. Seconds later two bucks erupt from their beds and race down the hill toward the creek.

"Bucks! Bucks!" shouts Bob, pointing at the pair of white flags a moment before they disappear from view.

"I see 'em!" screams Beau. "Eight pointers! Both of 'em! And they're headed right to my stand!"

"Awesome!" hollers Bob. "Totally awesome! Hey, Beau. Is this gonna be a great season or what?"

Three weeks later Bob and Beau sit in the plant cafeteria staring glumly into their lunch buckets. Their perky puppy personae are no longer in evidence. "I just don't get it," grumbles Bob. "We scouted that area every single day for a month in preseason and we've hunted our stands at least five times a week since opening day. All we've seen is one forkhorn, two spikes and seven does and yearlings. It just doesn't make sense."

"And we haven't spotted a buck since Sunday of opening weekend," notes Beau. "I think we need to start looking for another place to hunt."

Think a new hunting venue will make any difference? Me neither. Bob and Beau aren't about to tag a whitetail until they learn to back off. They need to appreciate that when it comes to bowhunting whitetails, less is always more. But like so many others, Bob and Beau believe that if their stand sites are chosen carefully and are well-camouflaged, they can go to them day after day without alerting deer to their presence. They convince themselves that whitetails will simply ignore evidence of human intrusion—such as noise and human odor—and hold fast to their pre-disturbance patterns.

Whitetails are creatures of habit, particularly in early season. A buck will more or less hold to his travel pattern and daily schedule as long as he's not disturbed. But because survival is every whitetail's number-one priority, once he's alerted to human presence in his area, he'll adjust his activity to avoid encountering that presence again. That's particularly true for any buck that has seen his third birthday. No whitetail grows to maturity by ignoring or tolerating hunting pressure. He grows old only by paying acute attention to even scant evidence of human pressure and by adjusting his activity to avoid it. He may move to another area where there's no sign of human activity or he may alter his schedule to avoid all travel during daylight. Either way, the bowhunter who disturbed him has almost no chance of tagging him. Were this not true, whitetails would long ago have disappeared from our forests and farmlots.

"We go out of our way to avoid putting any pressure whatsoever on the whitetails we hunt," says Jim Hole, operator of Edmonton-based Classic Outfitters. "Up here in Alberta we don't have the heavy concentrations of deer like you have in some of the states. So our whitetails aren't as used to seeing hunters as deer might be in Ohio or Michigan. A big buck up here is hypersensitive to hunting pressure. If we get too aggressive in our stand placement or stand use, we'll just push him deeper into the timber and make him more nocturnal. That's why we're so careful about little things. For example, we make sure we don't leave scent along the trail and we carry our treestands out with us when we leave. We don't want a buck to have any hint that we're in the area, much less that we're hunting him. I'm convinced that minimizing the pressure we put on the deer is the real key to the success we've enjoyed."

One tactic that Hole uses to avoid pressuring bucks relates to stand placement. He strongly prefers hanging stands at the edge or just inside the perimeter of a woodlot rather than deep inside the timber. "I just believe it's almost impossible to get in and out of a grove of timber without making enough noise and leaving enough scent to alert deer," he says. "We find it's better to position our hunters so they only have to move a short way into the woodlot before reaching their stands. There's less noise, less scent and therefore the deer don't know they're being hunted. That may mean a hunter doesn't see the buck until right at dark, but that's okay. I'd rather be in a stand for 30 minutes and not have the deer know I'm around than be there for three hours and have him aware of my presence."

As our friends Bob and Beau learned, scouting "hard" isn't always the best way to set up an archery ambush. Roaming noisily through woodlots and jumping whitetails out of their beds immediately before you hunt them is never a good idea.

As much as possible, it's best to conduct preliminary scouting from afar. By studying aerial photos and topographic maps, a hunter often can identify likely bedding areas and terrain features that influence where deer travel. On-the-ground scouting is best performed soon after the end of the previous season. Trees are still bare of foliage, rubs are still easily seen and there's no downside to disturbing the deer. When circumstances require in-field scouting immediately prior to a hunt—a common occurrence—it's best to tread lightly. When possible, such as when scouting a crop field just prior to opening day, use binoculars to observe the deer from afar. They'll hold to their pattern as long as it's not disturbed and that's precisely what you need to stage an ambush.

"A lot of hunters get bogged down searching for every rub line and scrape in the area," says Minnesota bowhunter Myles Keller, who's tagged more Pope & Young-class whitetails than any other archer. "When I'm scouting a big buck, I do everything possible to avoid moving right in on him as I try to figure out his routine and what his point of origin is. If I can learn the general vicinity of his bedding area, I can then look over my opportunities to intercept him as he travels to or from that area. Obviously, I'd like to know the exact location of his security area, but it's often hard to pin that down without alerting him to the fact that he's being hunted. So I keep my distance."

Even when Keller locates an abundance of fresh sign indicating a mature buck is using an area, experience has taught him to avoid the temptation to set up right next to the sign. "For years I used to hang stands right on top of the best sign I could find," he says. "Then I realized what a mistake I was making. I was hurting—rather than helping—my chances to kill the deer that left that sign. It's a natural tendency to want to hunt right there because everything looks so great. But I've learned that with a mature whitetail, it's critical that you back off and give him room. Now I usually hang my stands some distance away from that sign. I've learned that it's easier to kill a deer as he approaches that area than it is to wait until he gets there."

The best-placed stand won't provide shooting opportunities if area whitetails are alerted each time you go there. Which is why it's so important to choose approach and departure routes that allow you to get to and from your stands undetected. Most bowhunters pay scant attention to such details. Perhaps they assume that any deer disturbed during stand approach will "calm down" soon afterwards and then forget the episode even happened. Dream on!

Ask yourself this: If you knew for certain that a big buck was bedded 50 yards from your stand, how would you travel there? Obviously, you'd move with excruciating care and caution, stepping as lightly as possible and taking whatever time was needed to avoid alerting the deer. Given that you can never be certain a buck is not bedded near your stand, that go-slow approach is precisely the way you should proceed every time. You should, in effect, stalk your stand. Since adopting this approach myself, I've frequently had whitetails pass within a few yards of my stands only minutes after my arrival.

Stand departure requires an equal degree of caution. It's tempting to scramble down from a treestand after dark and hustle quickly back to camp, particularly if the weather's cold or wet. But such hustle will cost you dearly if you disturb a nearby deer. He needn't see or smell you to know that you're something he wants no part of. If he hears a commotion near your stand, you've given him a reason to stay away from that area. Minimizing this risk is not difficult. Simply take an extra 15 minutes to travel out of the woodlot. Move slowly and silently until you're completely away from your stand area.

"Some guys believe that if they hang a stand in a good spot and keep going there over and over again, that sooner or later they'll eventually get together with a mature buck," says Myles Keller. "But it rarely works that way. More likely, they end up not seeing any good bucks at all."

Keller concedes that it's very difficult to stay away from a stand that's located adjacent to abundant buck sign. "You know the buck has been there and you believe—correctly—that he's probably going to come back," says Keller. "So that's where you want to be. I've done it myself plenty of times. But it's never worked for me and I finally learned not to do it. But I understand the temptation and how hard it is to resist."

Experienced bowhunters know that the best chance to kill a mature whitetail from any given stand site occurs the first time you hunt there. Your second-best chance occurs the next time, and so on. Simply put, no stand site ever got better the more it was used. And while you may think you're approaching and leaving without creating noise or leaving scent, the truth is that your presence will be noted. And deer that encounter your presence will make adjustments to avoid encountering it again.

That's why rotating your hunting among multiple stand sites is one of the most effective tactics for minimizing pressure on whitetails. A good rule of thumb is to avoid using any single stand site more often than once each week. Relocating a stand just 75 to 100 yards can keep it fresh while allowing you to continue hunting the same general area. There is no single tactic that will do more to minimize pressure on whitetails than to avoid repeated use of one or two stands.

If your preference is for the fixed-position style of treestand, you needn't purchase six of them in order to rotate your hunting among six stand sites. Several treestand manufacturers (including Aero Adventure Products, Basic Innovations, Iron Creek Outfitters, Screaming Eagle, Trailhawk and Trax America) offer fixed-position models that attach to a separate mount that's hung on the tree independently of the platform and seat. With multiple mounting units, one or two platforms can be rotated easily among several locations, keeping each of them fresh.

Perhaps the surest way to pressure whitetails is to hunt from a permanent treestand. You can be certain that every deer older than six months knows the location of every such stand in the area and have learned to skirt around them in their travels. Permanent stands are almost always more visible than a fixed-position or climbing stand because they're usually "over built" and set up at fairly low elevations. A bowhunter who makes repeated use of a permanent stand commits two pressure-related sins. So don't expect to see him posing for pictures near the camp game pole any time soon.

Tactics at a Glance

- Don't set up in the middle of fresh buck sign.
- Spooking a big buck may kill any chance of taking him in that location.
- Scout more with maps and binoculars than on foot.
- Stalk your stand.
- In evenings, leave your stand silently.

9   The Fine-Tuned Bowhunt:
An Early-Season Review

BY CHARLES J. ALSHEIMER

As a review for early-season planning, a master bowhunter and whitetail authority walks you through his personal game plan for success. As you might imagine, Charlie believes that chance favors the prepared, and that goes double for bowhunters!

How many times have you had a whitetail buck approach your stand only to have it spook as you attempted to bring an aluminum arrow to full draw across a metal rest? Ever had a whitetail spook as you attempted to move on the frosty metal platform of your treestand? Worse yet, how many times have you shot over a deer's back from a lofty treestand perch? Does this all sound painfully familiar? If you're a serious or novice bowhunter, the chances are better than 50/50 that these scenarios have left you with a sour taste in your mouth.

I learned early in my bowhunting career that the art of arrowing a whitetail, any whitetail, was far more difficult than taking one with a gun. Certainly, much of this handicap is due to the fact one must be within 25 yards of a whitetail to score with a bow. However, when I reflect on some of my whitetail bowhunting blunders and why they occurred, one thing stands head and shoulders above everything else: I failed to pay attention to details. The bottom line is that bowhunting for whitetails is a details game. Nothing more, nothing less. If you can master the details you can be a success in the woods. Unfortunately, human nature, being what it is, causes us to attempt shortcuts. And whether you're flying an airplane or shooting a bow and arrow, shortcuts will always get you into trouble.

There's a famous quote that says, "Chance favors the prepared man." This quote can apply to many things, but I can't help but think that a bowhunter authored these five words. So, with details in mind I'll attempt to share with you the pitfalls I've tried to overcome during nearly 30 years of bowhunting whitetails. When I think of fine tuning a bowhunt I think of five things that always need improvement. They are; 1) your bow 2) your shooting ability 3) your stand and its placement 4) the clothing you wear 5) how you scout. If you can fine-tune and master these five you can't help but be better.

The Bow

When thinking of a hunting bow remember that speed is not king in a deer woods; never has been—never will be. There will never be a bow capable of beating the speed of sound and even the fastest bows on the market pale in comparison. For this reason bowhunting whitetails is a 20-yard game, 25 at tops. Seminar speakers often talk of whitetails jumping the string. I can assure you that after taking nearly a half million whitetail photos over a 28-year period, that the behavior referred to as "string jumping" is nothing more than a deer reacting to an oncoming arrow. In its attempt to flee, it lowers its body for leverage before pushing off and running. Usually at ranges under 20 yards, a whitetail cannot react in time to dodge the arrow. At ranges over 20 yards, it has the physical makeup to succeed in dodging an arrow. The key thing to remember is that the bow should be set up to function under hunting conditions and hunting situations are far different than 3-D conditions.

A key in successful whitetail hunting is how quiet a bow is when the moment of truth arrives. Whenever I get my hands on a hunting bow I go over it to see where the noises are. After pulling it back a few times and then shooting it, I'm able to determine if there are any noises in the bow's eccentrics. Often, when pulled to full draw, a wheel will squeak. To eliminate the sound, I apply unscented Pledge or vegetable oil to the wheel axle or string channel. Some people suggest using a light lubricant such as WD-40. However, I shy away from any petroleum-based lubricant because of its odor.

After silencing the bow's eccentrics I go to work on the arrow rest. Having a silent arrow rest is critical when it comes time to draw on a buck. I cut a piece of rawhide and glue it below and above the arrow rest so that if the arrow falls off the rest it does not hit any metal surface. If you prefer to be aesthetically pleasing there are a number of commercial pads that will do the same thing.

When it comes to the actual arrow rest there are a number of ways to go. Though metal spring rests are popular with 3-D shooters, I stay away from any metal rest as nothing is louder than the sound of metal to metal coming together. I keep it simple and use a rest compatible with aluminum and carbon arrows. In other words the rest must be dead silent when the arrow is pulled back.

Once the arrow rest is taken care of it's important to make sure the cable guard slide performs in both wet and dry conditions. Most bow manufacturers skimp when it comes to cable guard slides, so it's important to find one that is quiet in all weather conditions and a number of aftermarket slides can fill the bill.

The last step in a bow's noise creation comes when the arrow is released. Upon release all the stored energy in a bow is released in a millisecond. Because of this, vibration is at its peak. To eliminate as much noise as possible, I tighten most screws on the bow and quiver with Loc-Tite to make sure they stay tight no matter how much I shoot. I use two rubber cat whisker silencers to quiet the string. Avoid using fabric puff silencers because they take on moisture when it rains and the added weight slows arrow flight up to five feet per second. Should noise in the bow persist, I opt for a bow stabilizer.

One other bow silencing tip is to make sure that the arrow's feathers or vanes in the bow's quiver are not touching. If they do touch, they will rub together during the release, causing unwanted noise. I used to leave my quiver attached to the bow when hunting from a treestand. I no longer do this. Instead, I take the quiver off, affix it to the tree, and shoot my bow without the quiver on. This makes for a smoother release and less physical movement.

Bow sights have improved greatly in the last few years. And with the aging of the American bowhunter these sight improvements couldn't have come at a more opportune time. With the most productive bowhunting hours occurring at the fringe of daylight the old bead type sight pins simply don't cut it anymore, especially for the older bowhunter. I've lost count of the number of bowhunters who said to me, "I had a great chance to take a buck but I couldn't see my sight pins." Well, this problem has been solved. Fiber-optic pins are now the answer. With a sight equipped with these pins you'll be able to shoot under any condition.

Shooting Ability

Once the bow is set up for silence, the task of sighting-in the bow is at hand. But before sighting-in it's important to paper test for arrow flight to make sure the arrows are exiting the bow properly. You can do this by shooting the arrows through a large sheet of white paper tacked to a square wood frame positioned in front of bales of hay to stop the arrows. By shooting through the paper you can examine the tear-hole made by the broadhead and determine if your arrow is fish-tailing or porpoising in flight, which is remedied by very slightly moving the plunger-button in or out or adjusting the arrow rest.

Once the arrows are flying from the bow correctly it's important to work on accuracy. When all is said and done, accuracy with a bow and arrow boils down to a smooth release and pin control. Over the years, I've struggled with both of these aspects of archery hunting. When target practicing, work hard at perfecting a smooth release. If you shoot fingers (glove or tab) make sure there is no dirt buildup or creases in the glove or tab. If there is, there's a high probability that no matter how hard you try your release will not be smooth, resulting in decreased accuracy. Because residue builds up on both a tab and leather glove it's wise to use a new one each year, even if they don't show wear. If you're a release shooter keep the release clean and lubricated. Though perfecting a smooth release is key, I find that proper pin control is the lynchpin of good shooting ability. A tip is to force yourself to keep the pin on the target for a second or two after the arrow is released and never take your eye off the target.

When I began hunting with a bow and arrow in the late '60s my practice sessions consisted of shooting off the ground into bales of hay. Though I thought this honed my shooting skills the reality was that it didn't prepare me for the moment of truth. You see, I've always been a treestand hunter and practicing from ground level at hay bales left a lot to be desired when it came to shooting out of stands 15 feet in the air. It's only been during the last 15 years that I've taken my practice sessions to the next level and started shooting from elevated positions. As a result, my success has soared.

As with everything there seems to be a "next level" we all must strive for to become better at what we do. And with target practice this means using a 3-D deer target from an elevated position. Shooting at a life-size deer target from above will not only make you keenly aware of arrow flight from above but also enable you to perfect shot placement. An added bonus is that the more you shoot at a 3-D target, the better you're able to overcome buck fever.

It's no secret that practicing with field points can be a big mistake because they fly differently than broadheads. For this reason it's essential to practice with broadheads, the more the better. I do this by shooting into a sandtrap broadhead target I've made in my backyard. It works slick and the sand that clings to the arrow and broadhead can be removed quickly for the next round of shooting by merely dipping them in a bucket of water.

If you're not into making broadhead targets there is another option for broadhead tuning. In the past year Satellite Archery Company has introduced their innovative MatchPoint. The MatchPoint looks like a long field point, is the same length and weight as a broadhead, and flies like a broadhead. By using this point, the need to shoot broadheads a great deal for hunting is over.

Probably the greatest number of bucks missed each year can be attributed to bowhunters misjudging the shooting distance. You might be good at judging distances on level ground but attempting to do it from a treestand is another matter. This is another reason that practicing from an elevated position is important. If, after elevated practice, you are still having trouble judging distances, buy or make your own color-coded markers and stick them into the ground around your treestand. Deer will never notice them, and you'll know how far they are from you. Of course, the foolproof way to know the distances around your stand is by using one of the many range finders on the market.

Stands/Stand Placement

Next to bow noise nothing blows a bowhunter's cover faster than a squeaky stand. It's probably safe to say that few bowhunters recondition their treestands from year to year. If you don't you're only kidding yourself and setting the stage for a big miscue. Every August I get all my stands together and go over each in my backyard. Not only do I give them a quick coat of flat black and gray paint, but I also check the fasteners and retighten the bolts and connectors. In addition, I attach each stand to a tree and simulate different bowhunting positions to make sure there are no creaks and squeaks. This might seem like overkill, but I've been on enough hunting trips to know that nothing sets a whitetail buck in motion faster than the noise of metal scraping together.

Stand placement is another area that can make or break a fall's bowhunt. Too many bowhunters hang a stand and exit the woods without giving thought to whether there is clearance to pull their bow to full draw. Unfortunately, upon returning to the stand to hunt they find out there is a clearance problem when their elbow or bow limb comes in contact with a branch. Unfortunately, most realize this problem when deer show up. On more than one occasion, I've learned this lesson the hard way. I now test the clearances as soon as I hang a stand.

Treestand safety belt clearance is a minor detail that can quickly become a major problem when trying get in position for a shot. A belt that often looks like a great device in a catalog or on a showroom floor easily becomes an entanglement problem if you don't practice with it on your body a few times before actually hunting with it. Many safety harnesses provide the utmost in safety but severely limit mobility within a treestand. The trick is to know how you can—and can't— move before mister big shows up.

Camo

I'm amazed at how little thought goes into one's choice of camouflage. In sales they say, "form follows function." In the majority of situations this is not the case when it comes to buying camo. Instead of letting function be the key ingredient in the purchase the buyer lets form dictate. So, rather than buying a camo pattern that meets a particular need buyers select a pattern based on what their favorite hunting hero or their peers wear. One of the true acid tests for a camo pattern is what it looks like from 50 yards away. If it looks like a black blob you might as well save your money and buy work coveralls. The key is that the hunter must blend in with the surroundings he hunts. This may mean that two different patterns are required to meet one's hunting needs. Once the leaves fall from the trees most ground patterns will not work well for treestand hunting. A dark camo pattern on a hunter perched 15 feet in the air is a dead giveaway and the least little movement will spook a deer when the moment of truth arrives. Many of the larger camo companies have great patterns but don't overlook the little guys for some of them have designs equal to the big boys. A tip to pass on is for the hunter to wear light-colored camo patterns when hunting from a tree (without leaves) and darker blends for ground hunting.

While discussing clothing there is one small detail regarding forearm bulk that often causes problems for bowhunters. The fabric on the arm with which you hold your bow (left forearm on right-hand shooters) cannot be loose in the forearm area when you shoot. If it is the bow string will strike the fabric upon release and one or two things will happen. First, the string hitting the fabric makes a loud snap. Secondly, when the string makes contact with the fabric, the obstruction will cause improper arrow flight. This often occurs and is a classic case of a small detail becoming a huge one in a millisecond. As distracting and uncomfortable as it may seem the key is to wear an arm guard to keep this from happening.

Fine-Tuned Scouting

Scouting during the summer for this fall's hunt cannot be as thorough as in the winter months. This is because too much human activity in the woods just before the bow opener will cause deer to change their patterns or become nocturnal. But even with less time spent walking around a sound plan can be arrived at with a minimal amount of time spent. First, if you're going to be hunting a new area try to get your hands on an aerial photo of your hunting land. Every county seat in America has an aerial photo file of their county, and there's a good chance you can pick one up in time to plan for your hunt. In looking at an aerial photo, remember a few things. Whitetails are creatures of habit and they seek out the path of least resistance, just like you and I do. So, check the photo for the presence of hedgerows, diversion ditches or thin necks of woods which connect a feeding area and big piece of woods. Nine times out of 10, bucks will use these corridors traveling to and from their bedding and feeding areas. Next look closely at the inside corners, where a woodlot wraps around a field. Again, bucks will opt to go around a field rather than going across it during daylight. So, inside corners are excellent places to intercept deer.

If your area has a good apple crop this year, check these locations as soon as you can. If the apples are in abundance and not far from thick cover look for a good treestand setup at the edge of the orchard along well-used trails. The tendency is to want to put a treestand right in the orchard. Don't do it unless you have to. This is because you never know which tree a buck will gravitate to when the apples begin falling, so my advice is to set up just out of the orchard rather than in it. Also, make sure the wind is in your favor and try to get 15 yards off the trail for concealment purposes. Never think you can beat a whitetail's nose. They have more than 10 times the amount of nasal surface as we do and it's believed that their ability to smell is far greater than 10 times more than humans.

In late summer begin checking the acorn mast as inconspicuously as possible. The first acorns will begin falling around September 1, and though having a green appearance, deer and other animals will be gravitating to them quickly. Knowing where the mast is will help you plan your strategy. The key is to know what's going on long before the season begins.

Of course, early bow season means that alfalfa and clover fields are prime locations to ambush a buck coming to feed. In most cases, the plants have not been frosted and are still lush. If this is the case these fields will be worked heavily. However, don't make the mistake of setting up at a field's edge. Hang your stand 75 to 100 yards inside the woods along well-used trails so that the animal will move past you during legal light. During the early part of bow season these setups will usually be better in the afternoon than the morning. This is because whitetails will usually be feeding in such locations all night and exit them at the first hint of light, long before you have a chance to get into your stand. After they have bedded all day they get hungry and are anxious to get back to the field before nightfall.

Miscellaneous, But Important

Just because your bow, shooting, stands, clothing and scouting have been fine tuned don't be lulled into thinking everything is going to be easy. Veteran bowhunters know that there are a few other things that can make or break you while passing the hours on stand. Experienced hunters know very well that holding your bow in the stand can be a tedious task, especially if you sit for hours on end in cold weather. Therefore, it's important to have the bow hanging in just the right place for easy access when a buck shows up. "Just the right place" means within inches of your grip hand so that you don't have to move a great deal to grab on to it. For hunters who like to sit on stand this means a bow holder attached to the stand. For hunters who like to stand this means attaching a screw-in hook to the side of the tree or to an overhanging branch.

Also, it's important that the arrow nocks are tight in order to prevent the arrow from falling off the string. Personally, I like the Bjorn or similar style nocks that grip the string. Also, some type of arrow snubber is a critical piece of equipment to have on the bow. These attach to the riser handle to securely hold the front portion of the arrow on its rest. As soon as the arrow begins to be drawn the snubber releases and moves clear of the arrow's flight path. Without one, the least little breeze or wrong movement will knock the arrow off the rest.

One last piece of equipment that helps to fine-tune your hunt is a lower hip or knee pocket. This is a small fabric cup that hangs from your belt and supports the lower end of the bow when a deer is approaching. If you have never used one you know how heavy a bow can feel as you're waiting for a buck to get into shooting position. This little holder takes the weight off the bow and allows you to relax (as if that's possible!) until a shot presents itself.

Fine-tuning the bowhunt is not difficult but it does take planning and a great deal of attention to detail. In many ways the sport of deer hunting is a game of chance. But one thing is certain: "Chance favors the prepared man."

Tactics at a Glance

- Your bow's silence is far more critical than speed.
- Be certain that your arrows are flying straight before sighting in your pins.
- Most bucks are missed because the hunter has misjudged distance to the target.
- Winter may be the most ideal time to scout.

Part Two
All About the Rut

Like kids waiting for Christmas, bowhunters anticipate the coming of the rut with the kind of intensity that can be downright excruciating. Supposedly, the rut will bring the advent of the season when bucks literally go bonkers, when they will be following and chasing does hither and yon with caution thrown to the winds. At least, that's what the legends say. The truth is a little more focused. Yes, bucks can be taken during the rut, but defining the exact period when their interest in does will be at its peak is difficult. Thanks to studies by whitetail experts like Wayne LaRoche, Jeff Murray, and Charlie Alsheimer, we know a lot more about how the rut kicks in than we did years ago, and more-precise timing is possible. Also in recent years, more attention has been paid to the various phases of the rut, all of which require tactics to fit the rut situation as it exists at that time. So, as it turns out to be true with so many things, that rut has no "one-size-fits-all" strategy, but instead requires a well-tuned, flexible game plan. You can start building yours right here.

10   The New Rut Strategy

BY JOHN WEISS

Because the rut is so important—after all, it's the season when supposedly sly and smart bucks go completely bonkers in their pursuit of does—a universal question pops up wherever bowhunters gather: "When's the rut going to happen?" Not content with mere "guessing," some researchers and hunters have come up with new systems they believe give them the edge on predicting peak rutting activity. Here's John Weiss' report on some of the theories that are earning new believers every season.

Hunters living north of the Mason-Dixon Line have become so conditioned to believe the peak of the rut is November 15th that quite often they actually miss the best rut-hunting action in their region.

Undoubtedly this goes back to an early, widely published study conducted by New York deer biologists Lawrence Jackson and William Hesselton who spent seven years studying the embryos of 864 road-killed does. By determining the ages of the embryos and then back-dating, it was possible to determine the date each doe was bred. The findings of the biologists subsequently concluded that a majority of the does were bred during a 20-day "window" spanning the dates of November 10 to November 20; or, on the average, November 15, which is the date that has long since been stenciled on the foreheads of deer hunters.

It all sounds logical and scientific but we've since become aware of flaws in the interpretation of Jackson and Hesselton's study; keep in mind, their work was conducted from 1961 to 1968. In the 30-plus years since this landmark research, other scientists have made other investigations and learned there is at least a full week's time, plus or minus, of variability in which the onset of the rut may be triggered each year.

Now, after three decades of pursuing deer, I finally realize why some years I experienced little or no rut-hunting action at all while other years the intensity of the rut could only be described as incendiary.

During those particular years when it seemed like there was no rut, hunters could expect to see a plethora of magazine hunting articles offering various explanations. I always found humor in those specific articles which claimed that not much breeding took place, probably because of unusual weather that turned the deer off; proof that this assertion was false always came the following spring when a new crop of fawns could be seen following their mothers. Other deer hunting writers, including myself, speculated that perhaps weather had indeed influenced the rut and it was the excessive heat or other adverse conditions that had simply caused the majority of the breeding activity to take place after dark.

Now, however, still new research information has come to light that strongly suggests that, due to cosmic influences, hunters simply missed the rut because it occurred much earlier or later than they expected.

According to Vermont biologist Wayne LaRoche, there are five factors that can cause variations in the dates that deer breeding activity takes place from one year to the next.

The age structure of the local population has a critical influence upon the timing. Since young does breed later than mature does, areas that have high populations of young deer often have an almost unnoticeable first rut followed weeks later by a second rut that is quite intense. Conversely, if the local deer population has a high percentage of mature does, intense breeding will take place earlier than the norm.

The sex ratio of the local population is a determining factor because areas that have low buck populations have lengthy rutting periods of low intensity, simply because there are not enough males to quickly get the job done of impregnating all the available females. Conversely, areas with high buck populations have shorter, more intense mating seasons in which the majority of the females may be bred in just a few days; in this latter case, if you've miscalculated and missed getting afield at precisely the right time, you're out of luck.

The health of the local deer herd is vital to successful breeding. Bucks and does alike, which live on prime range and are in excellent body condition, breed earlier and with more intensity than deer living on poor range.

The genetics of the subspecies inhabiting a given region are important because widespread transplanting of deer took place 50 to 75 years ago. This is why Georgia whitetails, for example, which were transplanted from Wisconsin, breed almost two months earlier than native whitetails living in neighboring Alabama.

Variations in latitude, as one travels farther north, cause the breeding season to be compacted and intense, yet as one travels farther south the rut is protracted and less intense. At the equator there is no specific breeding period and in fact mating is so subtle it's barely noticeable and takes place throughout the entire 12 months of the year.

"Trying to sort through all of this and get your ducks in a row is a real headache for the hunter," Wayne LaRoche grins, "but it's a real turn-on for research biologists.

"The earth wobbles in a cycle on its axis as it orbits the sun," LaRoche continues, "and it's this solar cycle that sets the breeding season for whitetails in non-equatorial regions."

Interestingly, since fall in the southern hemisphere occurs at the same time as spring in the northern hemisphere, some peculiar experiments have been performed. In one study, northern U.S. whitetails which always rutted in November were transplanted to New Zealand where they immediately shifted to an April rutting period.

The importance of this experiment is that it conclusively proved that whitetail mating behavior is not triggered and synchronized by calendar dates (a human invention created solely for our living convenience) but by annual changes in solar and lunar influences.

Whitetails have a pineal gland, which is sometimes called "the third eye," that is present in the brain of all animals having a cranium, including humans. The sole function of this gland is the secretion of the hormone melatonin and how much of this substance is secreted is controlled by light intensity; low light levels stimulate the production of melatonin and high light levels inhibit it.

So how does an organ inside the brain know how much light intensity is taking place outside the skull? Researchers contend this information is received through nerve pathways from the pineal gland to the eye. Moreover, when light levels are low over prolonged periods of time, high levels of melatonin trigger the release of sex hormones from the pituitary gland to steadily bring the animal to a height of sexual readiness.

In northern bucks and does, this date is approximately November 1. Look upon the scenario as a gun that first has been loaded and then cocked. It's ready to go off at the slightest impetus and in the case of bucks it's the full moon that serves as the trigger. This is the pre-rut chase phase when bucks do goofy things and act like reckless teenagers with their testosterone faucets wide open.

With does, however, the surge in their mating receptiveness occurs shortly thereafter when the full moon ends and the so-called peak of the rut begins.

Why all of this is important to the hunter was the question that caused Wayne LaRoche to develop a computer program demonstrating how deer rutting behavior changes in relation to diminishing light levels from day to day and week to week; equally significant, Wayne learned how rutting activity within the time frame decreed by nature is slightly different from one year to the next.

What resulted was the Whitetail Rut-Predictor in the form of a series of annual fall/winter calendars. At a glance, any hunter can scan the calendar of the current month and he'll see each day of the week has a representative symbol. These symbols tell him exactly what deer are doing on each particular day as solar and lunar influences steadily change and cause a subsequent reactive change in deer behavior.

The five calendar symbols are represented by silhouettes of bucks engaging in feeding, seeking, chasing, tending, and resting body postures, each of which tell the hunter which hunting strategies are likely to be the most successful on each given day.

"If there is a seven-day stretch on the calendar depicting feeding deer, naturally you'll want to hunt each day at a prime food source," LaRoche explains. "Little rutting action is evident as yet."

If several days on the calendar reveal bucks in a seeking mode, the pre-rut is underway and scrape hunting is now the hot hunting tactic, along with using a grunt call and rattling antlers.

If there is a string of daily chasing symbols, the pre-rut is intensifying. Now, hunting doe-bedding areas and doe-feeding areas is undoubtedly the best bet, with a doe bleat call coming in handy. For the time being, the effectiveness of scrape hunting is beginning to taper off.

If tending symbols predominate, the peak of the rut is taking place. Now, calling bucks is futile. Hunting scrapes is getting even worse. Hunt doe travel corridors and use a doe bleat call or fawn-bleater.

If there are long strings of resting symbols, the peak of the rut is over and exhausted bucks are trying to recoup body strength. Since bucks may now lay up in their beds for days at a time without moving, stand hunting is a waste. The tactic of the day should now focus upon gathering partners and staging drives through heavy-cover bedding areas.

A similar method of predicting deer activity levels is the popular Moon Guide developed by Minnesota hunter (and *Whitetail Hunting Strategies* columnist) Jeff Murray. Yet it's different from the standpoint that it doesn't focus upon the rut alone and therefore can be used throughout the hunting season.

"I've pegged three universal strategies in accordance with the moon's position, not its phase," Murray explains. "Confirmed by radio-telemetry studies, we now know the best hunting success near open food sources is only when the moon is overhead near sunset because during the rest of the lunar month deer won't show up until after dark. When the moon times occur during early morning and late afternoon, hunt bottlenecks or travel corridors connecting evening bedding and feeding areas with daytime feeding and bedding areas. And for the rest of the lunar month, hunt strictly near bedding areas.

"Regarding the rut, a three-year lunar cycle is comprised of early, middle, and late phases," Murray continues. "This is why hunters frequently claim to experience hot rutting action one year but little or no rutting the next year. Actually, what happened was that they entirely missed the rut because the deer's sexual cues were triggered earlier or later than usual."

I've found both Wayne LaRoche's Whitetail Rut-Predictor and Jeff Murray's Moon Guide to be highly accurate in assessing deer activities across the entire northern half of their range. But since LaRoche's research is based upon a computer model of solar and lunar changes in light levels, and since Murray's is based upon moon position cues, localized weather conditions may slightly affect those light levels and thus slightly accelerate or retard certain phases of the rut.

"For example," Wayne LaRoche explains, "dense cloud cover shortens day length by 15 to 20 minutes per day and diminishes the intensity of moonlight at the ground surface. Similarly, heavy rain or snow falling through the atmosphere blocks sun and moonlight by defracting and diffusing light and prevents nearly all moonlight from reaching the earth. Storm conditions may shorten day length by more than 30 to 40 minutes each day. Conversely, a long stretch of bright, sunny weather tends to suppress deer movement and may delay the onset of rutting activities in other regions. As a result, weather-induced changes in day length may explain slight differences in breeding times at different locations each year at the same latitude."

This is why it's important for any hunter to stay in tune with what's going on in his own bailiwick. Continuously dark, overcast weather in his region may accelerate all aspects of the rut by a day or more. Yet at the same time, his friend living at the same exact latitude but 100 miles away where the weather has been continuously sunny, may not expect to see the onset of rutting activity for several more days or until dark clouds associated with a storm front move into his area.

Every year we continue to learn more about whitetail rutting behavior but biologists admit that many mysteries still remain to be unraveled.

Strategies at a Glance

- Although most hunters believe that the rut peaks on November 15, it usually peaks anywhere from November 1 to 10.
- Numerous factors influence rut intensity including population dynamics, weather, and moon phase.
- Most researchers now agree that it's the moon that triggers the rut.

Deer Activity Indicators on Order

To obtain Wayne LaRoche's Whitetail Rut Predictor, write to Stonefish Environmental, Dept. HP, P.O. Box 216, Enosburg Falls, VT 05450. The price is $9.95 plus $1.75 s/h. Or call (800) 858-3213 to order.

To obtain Jeff Murray's Moon Guide, write to Fool Moon Press, Dept. BT, P.O. Box 15013, Duluth, MN 55815. The price is $9.95 plus $2 s/h. Or call (800) 449-6645 to order.

11   Just a Matter of Time

BY KENN YOUNG

The rut is known as the best time to harvest a really big whitetail buck, but hunting the rut can be an intricate puzzle unless you understand its specific phases and why they happen when they do.

Ed Schwartz had seen a lot of unusual deer behavior over the years, but on this cold November day even Ed was having trouble believing the scene taking place in the overgrown field in front of him.

"My stand was in a large oak overlooking a good trail intersection," Schwartz explained. "There was a large sage field beyond that. But after I climbed into my stand that particular morning there were sounds like I had never heard coming from the direction of that old field. Wheezes, bawls, snorts, even shrill whistles, all combined with sounds I knew had to be deer running."

It probably should be mentioned here that Ed is a hunter who makes even the term "fanatic" seem less than appropriate. His largest whitetail, a 19-point, non-typical taken in 1988, was for a long time the largest bow kill listed in the Arkansas Big Bucks Association record book.

"I go in early, two hours or more before even first light," Schwartz stated. "That lets the disturbed nightlife have time to calm down after my passing. I'm as careful as I can be, but no one can be completely quiet in the dark, so that extra time helps things get back to normal. I can tell you this: Sitting there that morning in the total blackness that happens just before dawn, listening to those sounds, well . . . it was eerie!

"Finally it was light enough to make out what was going on in that field, and it sure was something to see! First a doe burst from the thick brush along the edge, running like the devil was chasing her . . . maybe he was from her viewpoint. Because right behind her, his outstretched nose nearly touching her tail, came a huge, 10-point buck! A second later, another buck, a large eight-point, charged into the opening and raced after them! Then, not more than a second or two later, still another eight-point broke from the opposite edge and joined the chase!"

Schwartz paused for breath, his eyes alight at the memory, his voice actually quavering as he continued.

"For a good five minutes, those three bucks chased that old doe around that field, it looked for all the world like same sort of furry train. Her tongue was hanging out and the bucks slung saliva with every step, their grunts and wheezes were even more pronounced now that they were closer. After about five minutes, the whole group crashed back into the thick cover, and disappeared out of hearing.

They never came into range, and it was probably a good thing. I was shaking and sweating at the same time, my heart about to give out. I guarantee you, it was an experience I'll never forget!"

It is a well-documented fact that the period we call the rut can have a drastic effect on the hunter's chances of taking a good buck. Without the sexual urge, which causes even the older bucks to occasionally let their guard down, prospects for success would definitely be far less. Where those oldest, most dominant bucks are concerned, not only is the rut the best time to hunt them, in many cases it is the only time!

But even today, many hunters still believe the rut to be only that short period when the bucks are actually with the does. However, experts such as Drs. R. Larry Marchinton and Karl Miller of the University of Georgia School of Forestry Resources, logically argue that the rut is actually composed of the entire period from velvet shedding until antler casting. This would encompass a total time frame of more than five months in most regions! During that entire period the buck undergoes gradual but continual changes, all brought about by the effects of his breeding urge. Knowledge of what is happening, but more importantly when it is happening, will certainly improve your hunting chances.

From the hunter's viewpoint, there are four distinctive periods within the overall rut time frame. These are: (1) The early fall period, (2) the pre-breeding frenzy, (3) the breeding period itself, and (4) the post-breeding. Each of these periods offers hunting opportunity, but only to the hunter who is adaptable.

As a youngster, I was taught by the old-timers that the rut was triggered by the first cold snap of the fall. Other tales have it being the first frost, or the first full moon, or even the rise and fall of the sap in the trees. While each of these may somewhat coincide to the rut taking place, none have any real physical or internal effect on breeding.

The breeding urge is brought about by photoperiodicity, the amount of light reaching the eye (or amount of darkness, whichever you prefer). Daylight naturally decreases in the fall and increases in the spring, due to the earth's rotation on its axis. Because this is an annual cycle, once you have determined the dates for your area, they will remain the same year after year. External factors, such as hot weather, intense hunting pressure, and out-of-balance buck:doe ratios, may affect breeding intensity and visibility, but the actual times remain the same.

One single day, the peak breeding date, is the fulcrum of our whole rut diagram. That is the day when the most does are bred annually in any given area. It is important that you know the date for the exact locale in which you hunt, since it can vary slightly from one location to another. If you can't determine this date through actual in-the-woods observation, your state game department keeps extensive records on breeding activity, and can pinpoint the date for you.

Once you know that date, it is simple to make a time frame calendar of the various rut stages. Let's say the peak occurs around November 15, a somewhat common date throughout much of North America. One breeding normally lasts 10 to 14 days, making the time frame approximately November 7 to 22. The pre-breeding frenzy (that brief period that provides the very best rut hunting of the entire year) takes place three to five days before that first doe reaches estrus, November 1-7. The long early fall period stretches backward from that point to the time of velvet shedding (which normally occurs during the first two weeks of September), or September 15 to November 1.

On the other end of the spectrum, there is the post-breeding period, which lasts for about seven to 10 days immediately after the breeding period ends: November 22 to December 1.

When completed, your calendar should provide an accurate visual guide to rut activity for your individual hunting area. While each period is a part of the overall rut, buck attitudes and activity during each will be far different.

The Early Fall Period

In early September, a burr forms around the antler base, cutting off the blood supply to the velvet. This formation is caused by a rise in testosterone, a form of steroid within the buck's blood, and is triggered by photoperiodicity.

The most visible effect of the testosterone increase is enlargement of the neck muscle. While many hunters still believe that a rutting buck's neck swells, this is not actually the case. The muscles enlarge primarily as a result of the buck "fighting" saplings, with the steroid aspect of the testosterone enabling that buildup to occur at a rapid rate.

The rutting urge and subsequent activity during the entire fall are progressive. Early, the bucks are somewhat nocturnal and invisible, but their increasing desire and frustration gradually force them to move more and more. I compare the males during the entire rut cycle to a clock being slowly wound, tighter and tighter, and then suddenly allowed to unwind. The tightest point occurs during the pre-breeding frenzy, and is when the most visible activity will occur.

Scrapes may be made as early as mid-September, but these are only boundary markings and seldom revisited. Rubs occur at almost any time, and will often be evident even when scrapes are not. Scrapes are seldom found in some areas for the most basic of reasons; these pawed spots are advertisements, spots where bucks meet does. If there are high numbers of does in any area, the buck can pick and choose; he doesn't have to advertise!

I concentrate on travel routes during the early fall period, usually from an elevated platform. I start out hunting access trails to food and bedding areas, then switch to areas of scrape and rub concentration as November nears. I also search out doe areas during midday nonmovement periods, knowing these locations will become vital as actual breeding nears. Why? When the does are ready, the bucks will be with them.

The Pre-Breeding Frenzy

This brief period is without a doubt the most productive few days of the entire season for the knowledgeable rut hunter.

For roughly a week prior to that first doe reaching estrus, the bucks move far more often—their inner sex drives even causing them to occasionally prowl during daylight hours. Their attitude is now openly belligerent, and real fights can occur (not to be confused with the early fall shoving matches that hunters more normally see). They occasionally take "jaunts," long circular trips, during which they search for receptive does and in general just "go on the prowl." They move closer to the doe areas, finding bedding spots in thick cover near the concentration zones. Rubs and scrapes are made and worked with increasing vigor. In short, particularly during the last few days before that first doe reaches estrus, even older bucks come close to being totally out of control!

Virtually any hunting method that is based on a buck's desire to breed may work at this time. Scrape-watching is certainly at its most productive, as the bucks continually check for does. Remember that occasionally a doe, or even a subordinate buck, will stay in the immediate vicinity of a working scrape. Be careful on your approach to your nearby stand; nothing can ruin a day of hunting more than spooking deer on your way in. When watching scrapes, doctor them with estrous doe urine, and never forget wind direction or get careless with your human scent.

Rattling will be effective, particularly in areas of high buck concentration. Inject violence into your technique; bang and grind the antlers together for periods of 20 to 30 seconds, stomp the ground, thrash underbrush, and rustle leaves. All these are natural fighting sounds that bucks expect to hear. After you complete a sequence, give a few tending grunts and then wait, keeping your eyes trained downwind. In most instances, rattling is a two-man operation; the rattler and a shooter located 75 to 100 yards downwind overlooking dense cover. It is simply a buck's nature to check with his nose before he sees with his eyes. But never forget that the really dominant buck in that area may not care which two governments are fighting. If his urge is high, he may simply walk in from any direction at any time.

One frosty December morning, I was set up rattling along the edge of a small pear flat on a well-known south Texas ranch. My companion was a dentist and friend from New York who had never hunted with horns before, and was more than a little skeptical of the whole idea.

He had just voiced that opinion for about the 10th time, low-voiced to be sure, when suddenly a buck neither of us had seen crashed through the surrounding brush within yards of our position! The large nine-pointer took one look at the two "does," and immediately reversed his direction, actually kicking sand on us for good measure! The New Yorker, who tumbled backward into a patch of prickly pear as the buck nearly jumped over him, still considers rattling to be dangerous!

Scent canisters, 35mm film containers filled with unscented cotton saturated with estrous doe urine, will attract a buck when placed upwind of scrapes or bedding areas. Scents can work, if timed right and handled correctly. There can be nothing more exciting than listening to a large buck, grunting with every step, heading your way through the predawn dimness. It can make even a veteran's neck hairs stand on end!

The frenzy is the one period when even old bucks are most likely to do un-usual things at unusual times. This often makes sheer amount of time spent in the woods the deciding factor in success. It's an old truism: "You can't kill him if you're not there." Take a lunch, water, and hunt from "can see" to "can't see." You have no better chance of killing a good buck!

The Breeding Period

This period begins the moment that first doe reaches estrus. While it may not be the best time for the expert hunter, it is undeniably the period during which most really large bucks are taken.

Why is that true? Because bucks are doing something they do at no other time of the year; they are seeking out and breeding does. Even the real oldsters sometimes lose just an edge of their caution, due to that overriding desire to breed. That explains why a few real monsters are taken each year standing in open fields, crossing busy roads, or in bare clearcuts, definitely not your normal big buck spots.

Two things normally occur when a buck encounters a receptive doe: (1) If he is the dominant buck of the area, and if no other bucks are following her, he will merely stay with her. In essence, he will briefly adopt her travel patterns, a change which can prove to be his undoing. Does seldom live in areas as thick and inaccessible as bucks, and are not as cautious in their movements. This puts the buck in a precarious position when hunters are in the woods. (2) If competition is heavy, he will try to herd her to a more secluded spot. This trait is naturally more common late in the breeding period when fewer does are available.

Normally he will remain with the doe until she passes out of estrus, 24 to 36 hours. When she loses her appeal he will immediately leave her and head for the nearest doe area, checking any working scrapes in the vicinity.

Scrape watching, rattling, and calling become something of a hit-or-miss proposition during the actual breeding period, at least for the bigger deer. The most dominant bucks will be with the does, leaving the scrapes and fights to the younger stuff.

Smart hunters become what amounts to doe hunters at this time, either still hunting around doe areas or setting up stands along travel routes within them. Once again, the sheer amount of time spent in the woods becomes a primary in-gredient in success. Even the most mature buck will occasionally do stupid things while under the rut influence, but you have to be there to take advantage of those momentary mistakes.

Three years ago, I nearly ran over a good 10-point standing within yards of a busy highway, at 11 o'clock in the morning, with cars passing almost under his nose! For a long minute, with brakes squealing all around him, he stood gazing into a field on the other side of the road. Finally he turned and walked uncon-cernedly back into the woods, but not before giving several passing hunters severe heart checks!

Why was he there? Although I never saw them (or even thought to look), I imagine there were does in that field across the road. But whatever the reason, for the briefest of moments he was preoccupied and therefore vulnerable.

Slip-hunting, still-hunting, whichever term you prefer, can be very effective when hunting the breeding period, especially during windy or damp weather. Many authors today fail to recommend this hunting form because few hunters do it well enough to be effective. But for those with the patience, easing through a doe area, maybe throwing in an occasional tending grunt, can definitely pay some big dividends. While the breeding period may not be the best time for the more experienced hunter, it is without question the average hunter's best chance of harvesting a lot of horns. Once again, total time spent in the woods is often the deciding factor.

The Post-Breeding Period

Many hunters regard the post-breeding phase as the hardest of the various rut periods to hunt. This is at least partially true because many bucks have been taken, and the survivors are doubly wary and reclusive. But as always, the successful hunter will be the one who understands and adapts his methods to what is actually taking place.

During the first two to three days after that last doe passes out of estrus, hunting may be similar to that of the pre-breeding frenzy, in a word, outstanding! The bucks are once again searching for nonexistent ready does. Try all the effective hunting methods of the frenzy: rattling, scraping, and scents. They will work, but for a far briefer time. The bucks have now been in perpetual motion for many long weeks, and are just plain tired. As no available does are found, their interest quickly wans.

Mother Nature has thrown her subjects a serious curve at this time. The combined pressures of the rut and hunting season have left the bucks in their poorest physical condition of the entire year. This at a time when they are looking the dead of winter, the time of lowest food availability, squarely in the face. Older males again become extremely reclusive, resting as much as possible, moving only to feed and becoming completely nocturnal if there is even a hint of hunting pressure.

With the bucks in that reclusive state, the hunter must go to them to be effective. The actual places they retire to will almost invariably be remote and hard to hunt. Forced movement, drives, pushes, even dogs (where legal, of course), may become the alternative to flush a good buck from such heavy cover. Group hunting does not appeal to some, myself included, but late in the season it may well be the only way. Slow, silent drives by a small group of veteran hunters, who know the terrain like the back of their hands, can be deadly. Drivers and standers have about equal opportunity in most cases, because big bucks will lie close. You literally have to step on them to make them move. Even then there will be no wild, headlong flight through the woods; it's out of sight and back into cover, the quicker the better. A trick of old bucks who have played this game before is to slip back through the drivers at some point within dense cover. Shots are generally close and safety should always be the primary concern.

In summation, understanding rut chronology will certainly have a direct effect on your rut hunting success. Knowledge, and practical application of that knowledge, is the key. Once you know the peak breeding date for a particular location, you can use or modify the various time frames to make your own guide. From that point it actually gets simple. You know what the deer are most likely to be doing, and you know when they will be doing it, often even before they do! Employ the correct hunting method(s) at the correct time, and you just may have that "edge" that will let you harvest your buck of a lifetime! Good hunting.

12 Two Ruts Are Better Than One

BY JEFF MURRAY

In John Weiss' earlier chapter, "The New Rut Strategy," we were introduced to the research being done by Jeff Murray and others on the effect of the moon on the rut and deer activity in general. Although he is rightly famous as the innovator and publisher of the Deer Hunters' Rut Guide, Jeff is also one of today's most respected and trusted bowhunting authorities. From his home base in Minnesota, he is constantly on the prowl for new tactics to make bowhunting more successful, and when he discovers something interesting, you can bet he'll be anxious to share it with others.

No matter how hard you rub the crystal ball, you'll have a hard time predicting whitetails. You'll never know, for instance, why that buck did an about-face at the last instant, even though you were motionless as a bronze statue and the wind was in your face. And Lord knows why big bucks freshen some scrapes but not others. And the rut: Why are some days—and some years—hotter than others?

I'm as helpless as the next guy on the first two counts, but some recent revelations on what triggers the rut have revolutionized by rut-hunting success. All that jazz about being in the right place at the right time will become, for the most part, a reality and not a cliche once you learn how to tap the "twin peaks" of the rutting season.

The Right Time

The whitetail rut is a dynamic event undergoing several distinct stages, or phases. We'll look at the Big 3: Pre-rut, peak breeding and post-breeding "trolling."

According to conventional wisdom, the so-called pre-rut stage of the fall breeding season is the best time to see big bucks on the move. These monarchs are allegedly "on edge" as they eagerly anticipate the first does of the year entering estrus. Now, aggressive tactics like rattling, calling, mock scrapes and deer lures can help tip the odds on dominant bucks that are "up and looking." Apart from this period, the theory goes, bucks won't respond to these tactics.

I no longer subscribe to this concept. The key to understanding the rut is the principle of "rut economics." Simply stated, when the demand for does exceeds the supply, hunting is best. During the pre-rut, as an example, daytime buck activity is at a near-seasonal high, but only because bucks must work to find receptive does. But which bucks? The monarchs we all dream about or adolescent bucks jockeying for position on the right-to-breed ladder?

Here's a classic example of what I'm talking about. A few years ago while scouting during midday in his home state of Oklahoma, Eddie Claypool sneaked up on a pair of 2½-year-old bucks hounding a doe.

"I got to within 50 yards and decided to just watch," Claypool recalled. "I carefully took one more step for a better view when all of a sudden I noticed a huge 12-pointer staring at me from his bed. Of course he bolted the instant our eyes met, but I'll never forget how indifferent he was to those young punk bucks pestering his does. He knew they weren't quite ready to breed, and he wasn't about to expose himself. It just wasn't time. This is typical pre-rut stuff. Big bucks are occasionally on the prowl, but they're pretty discreet about it." Smaller bucks, Claypool contends, are more like hormone-charged, teenage boys—off the wall over the ladies, regardless of the social cues.

This all changes during the succeeding stage—peak breeding, or tending—when the majority of does enter estrous. Now an ample supply of does more than meets the demand. As bucks pair off with receptive partners, deer activity declines—so drastically it seems as if the adult whitetail population has migrated out of the county.

But if this was all there was to the rutting season, hunters wouldn't harvest a fraction of the super bucks that end up in the record books. Fortunately, a second peak period occurs, one that most hunters don't even know exists. Shortly after peak breeding, buck activity springs to life almost overnight. While it only lasts a few days, it's the trophy whitetail hunter's finest hour. We call it the "trolling stage," because that's exactly what top-end bucks of the pecking order do. When you see a decent-racked buck with a trance-like dog-trot, glassy eyes and tongue hanging out like a bloodhound, you're looking at a troller.

"The pre-rut is good, but the trolling [stage] is best," Claypool claims. "Now a buck not only has a hard time finding willing does, but he's used to breeding. Put the two together and he's going to be a little desperate. He should go into hiding and recuperate the instant his nose tells him there are no more hot females in his domain. But he isn't ready to give up breeding, so he trolls—from doe family group to doe family group." This explains the memorable stories of lucky hunters who kill monster bucks they never knew existed in their area. We contend these bucks were caught out of position in unfamiliar territory during the trolling stage.

So much for theory. Here's a real world testimonial to the power of the trolling stage. During a recent fall, five bowhunters within a 75-mile radius in central Illinois arrowed bucks grossing from 140 to 160 Pope & Young points. We're talking bully bucks, likely the biggest on their block. And each was taken during a narrow three-day window: November 12—Wellington Outdoors' Terry Rohm (155 P & Y); November 13—Eddie Claypool and his brother-in-law, Mark Perkins, (140 and 160 P & Y, respectively); November 14—Primos Game Calls' Will Primos (160) and me (150 P & Y).

Coincidence? Just a great place to go deer hunting? Perhaps. But consider, too, our combined 500 hunting-hours prior to these three days. If you still need more proof, consider Todd Amenrud's experience in southern Manitoba. As usual, he hunted hard the first two weeks of November but the pre-rut action was spotty and the rut seemed over. "I was packed up ready to head for home but I got snowed in," he recalled. "Good thing: The next two days, big bucks were everywhere." The dates? You guessed it: November 13 and 14.

Intercepting a troller won't be easy.

"You've got to be extra-patient during the pre-rut," Claypool says, "because it's the best time [of year] to see lots of bucks. Can you really let a good animal walk in hopes of a better one showing up later? If your hunting area produces trophy racks but you only see mediocre bucks, I'd say you've got something to think about."

Another obstacle separating you from a troller is the law. We now know the whitetail rut does not fall on the same dates each fall (more below), meaning some years bowhunters will get a good crack at trollers and some years it's the gun-hunters' turn. For example, when the rut falls late, gun-hunters in many states get a crack at the best hunting in years. Conversely, when the rut falls early, bowhunters who hunt hard through the final stage of the rut will be rewarded.

Which leads to yet another problem associated with the trolling stage: To get to this stage, you've got to endure the "passive peak" breeding stage.

"Most hunters see very few deer [when bucks and does are paired up]," Claypool says. "The temptation is to give up on the rut; you're convinced it's over and you've missed out. But just when you're about to throw in the towel, the action picks up. Location is extremely important, of course, because it only takes a day or two for the bucks to realize there are no more [willing] does." In practical terms this means you've got, at most, four days to capitalize, since not all does are on the same estrous cycle. No wonder timing the rut over the years has been a fickle affair!

Timing the Rut

Biologists define the rut as the time when deer breed. And they've long said it's governed mainly by photoperiodism (defined as the diminishing ratio of daylight to dark). Meanwhile, when we hunters think "rut," visions of hyper buck activity dominate our thoughts. We need to be careful not to confuse breeding activity with rutting activity. For instance, anyone intentionally targeting the peak of the breeding season is going to miss out on the rut's hottest action. When bucks are paired off with does, they evacuate traditional core activity areas to avoid competition. Further, a breeding buck doesn't travel far during this period because he's got the real deal. The twin peaks preceding and succeeding breeding are where it's at. Nevertheless, the ability to predict peak breeding is an excellent start, because it allows you to intercalate these twin peaks.

The secret to forecasting peak breeding lies, I believe, with the moon. Briefly, a whitetail doe's pineal gland tells her when the breeding season rolls around by measuring sunlight levels. This is why she always cycles in the fall (when daylight diminishes rapidly) and why North American deer transplanted to the Southern Hemisphere breed during our spring (which is their fall). It now appears this pineal gland is equally sensitive to waxing and waning moonlight that interacts with photoperiodism to help synchronize the rut each fall.

An interesting relationship between the New Moon phase and peak breeding can be seen across the board among the ungulate family, of which deer are members. For example, first-hand observations of Indian buffaloes involving 2,457 mating bulls and cows coincided with the New Moon (Ramanathon, 1932). This jibes with Eddie Claypool's notes and data compiled by Michigan bowhunter Bob Scriver, which I published in my latest book, "Moonstruck!" Plug in estrous dates of captivity deer and harvest statistics from the Midwest and Canada, and an odd, three-year cycle emerges. Coincidentally, this cycle was confirmed by independent research conducted by Vermont biologist Wayne LaRoche and also observed by top outdoor photographer Charles Alsheimer.

No-Fail Rut Strategy

Before we can translate the twin peaks of rut activity into practical hunting strategies, we must have a working understanding of the relationship between bucks and does. Apart from the rut, adult males and females live segregated lives. Bucks bed together during nonhunting months, separating themselves from does and their preferred bedding areas. Meanwhile, doe groups center around an alpha female and her offspring (plus a niece or two and perhaps their direct descendants). Furthermore, does usually dominate bucks when it comes to preferred food sources. But as the rut approaches, these patterns morph into new ones. In fact, buck behavior of the three main rut stages is pretty cut-and-dried, and this largely determines where they'll spend most of their time. Here's the scoop.

Pre-rut—Orthodox whitetail philosophy calls for hunting buck sign during the pre-rut. There is some merit to this. Bucks gradually shift their primary bedding areas closer to that of the does' and they end up marking them with rubs and scrapes. The bucks are in a "monitoring mode" during the pre-rut. They don't want to miss out on the first few does entering estrus.

But during the pre-rut stage, Claypool rarely hunts over classic rut sign. Instead, he plugs it into the overall pattern of where bucks and does are bedding, where they're feeding, and how he might best slip in between undetected.

"If you hunt over buck sign you're going to blow the bucks out," he says. "I mean, you're literally invading their turf. I'd much rather hunt fringe areas catching the bucks coming and going. They're less wary in these areas, and these spots are easier to get into without making a ruckus."

The pre-rut is also the best time of year to put deer lures to work. Communication between the sexes centers on olfactory messages, allowing a buck's nose to help him differentiate infertile does from those in their critical 24- to 48-hour heat cycle. Why not give him what he's looking for?

Peak Breeding—When bucks and does pair off, deer activity dies in traditional high traffic spots. Now's the time to go looking, because bucks aren't; they've got their does. But where? Like a cattle dog, a dominant buck will herd his companion where he wants her to go, in this case away from potential rivals. Unusual out-of-the-way pockets are prime, including: offbeat drainage ditches, "swamp islands" (patches of high ground surrounded by the mire), isolated knolls and similar fringe habitat. But after you relocate, don't expect to see many deer at this time. If you're in the wrong place, you can tell by the "lost" yearlings and fawns left behind. Incidentally, neither rattling nor scents work now. This is strictly a waiting game.

Within about a week, all available does will have been bred. Soon the brief-but-sublime trolling period hits, and some bucks fall into a predictable routine. Because they must now cover as much ground as possible to find the next doe, they follow familiar travel corridors connecting doe groups. Bucks are prone to cut corners whenever possible, so take terrain features into account, and you might intercept a frantic buck crisscrossing to and from doe bedding areas. Just don't get sidetracked with buck sign. Bucks are searching, not monitoring. Which makes for the best rattling of the year, as evidenced by the following incident.

"I saw a nice 10-pointer hot on the tail of a doe about 300 yards away, so I rattled to him," Claypool recalls. "It was at the tag end of the breeding cycle, and he stopped briefly before resuming the chase. Well, apparently the doe didn't want any part of him, because he returned about two hours later. I'll never forget it. I heard leaves rustling behind me and here comes the same buck trotting toward me on a steady gait. I couldn't even get my bow drawn by the time he made it under my tree. He knew exactly where the rattling came from, and he wasn't going to miss out. The crazy part was that this was midday." Claypool coolly waited the buck out and slipped a 100-grain Rocky Mountain Premiere behind the shoulder of the 150-class buck.

The rut opens a window of opportunity unequaled the rest of the year. But why single out a part of the rut when twin peaks are there for the taking?

Editor's note: Jeff Murray has pioneered research on how the moon affects hunting strategies. His latest innovation, Jeff Murray's Moon, predicts the three main stages of the rut. For more information call: 1-800-449-6645.

Rut Terminology

We cannot use familiar terms loosely when it comes to the rut. Here are some working definitions to keep everyone on the same page:

RUT: The breeding season of whitetail deer comprised of several distinct stages, each exhibiting measurable changes in behavior.

PRE-RUT: The unique stage of the rut when does are entering their estrous cycle and initial breeding activity is imminent. This stage lasts, more or less, about 10 days. When represented on a graph, this is the up-slope of courtship just prior to peak breeding.

PEAK BREEDING: The period of the rut when all available adult female deer are in heat and accompanied by sexually mature bucks. This is the peak of the graph lasting approximately five to seven days.

POST-BREEDING TROLLING: The period of the rut when bucks have exhausted the supply of estrous does and aggressively pursue courtship, often outside their core area. It takes between one and four days for bucks to scent-check a rutting territory. On a graph, this is the downslope of the rut immediately following peak breeding.

SECONDARY RUT(S): Subsequent rut stage(s) following the primary rut.

RUT ECONOMICS: The law of supply and demand in the whitetail woods. When the demand for does exceeds the supply of bucks, hunting is best thanks to increased competition for the limited supply. Conversely, when the supply of does exceeds the demand of bucks, hunting is poor; bucks have little difficulty finding receptive does.

ESTRUS: The heat cycle (ovulation) of adult female deer lasting from 24 to 48 hours. The reproductive cycle repeats itself 21 to 32 days later, depending on the geographic area, if the doe does not conceive during her first estrus.

NEW MOON: The dark moon phase when little or no sunlight can be seen reflecting off the moon's surface.

FULL MOON: The brightest moon phase when the entire surface of the moon facing Earth reflects sunlight.

QUARTER-MOON: The phase when half of the moon's observable surface reflects sunlight back to Earth (there are two such Quarters, First and Third).

LUNATION: The 29.5-day period (lunar month) it takes for the moon to go from New Moon to New Moon.

13   How Bucks Find Does

Most hunters have seen whitetail bucks hot on the heels of a doe in heat but just how does he locate her in all those woods?

From my treestand, a good 30 feet above the ground, I could tell what was going to happen before it happened. I'd seen it a zillion times: a buck trailing an apparent estrous doe. Still, I was so mesmerized by the buck's mannerisms that I just had to sit back and drink it all in. This animal, it was clearly evident, was a buck on a mission.

For example, first he made a predictable semicircle when he hit the corner of the freshly picked cornfield bordering a meandering creek bottom. Next, the muscular eight-pointer looped along the lower edge of the field with his nose held high. Then, after pausing momentarily, he backtracked for about 20 yards and picked up the trail precisely where he'd left it at the end of the semicircle.

Semicircles. Loops Backtracking—the name of the tracking game. No question, the process by which bucks find does during the rutting season is both intriguing and enlightening. It's intriguing, of course, because it represents one of Nature's most captivating wonders, the courtship ritual. But the process is also enlightening for enterprising hunters who take the time to translate the phenomenon into practical hunting strategies. I promise you this, once you fully comprehend the significance of this subject, you'll never hunt the rut the same. Here, then, are the keys to the courtship kingdom.

The Eyes Have It

Yogi Berra had it right when he said you can observe a lot just by watching. That whitetail bucks and does use body language to communicate with one another is an established biological fact. But too many hunters fail to capitalize on potential opportunities by simply not paying attention; bucks certainly keep their eyes peeled, and so should you.

Over the years I've watched a lot of bucks watch a lot of does. The record time-period for a buck monitoring a particular doe is when I glassed a distant Dakota 10-pointer stand in one place, practically motionless, for nearly three hours before making his next move. So if bucks can find does simply by watching, why can't hunters find bucks by watching does?

Indeed, I do a great deal of doe-watching. First and foremost, I don't automatically rule out any individuals; I carefully and patiently glass virtually every bald-headed whitetail in the whitetail woods. I know this doesn't jibe with mainstream thinking—we're after bucks, not does, so why bother with the distractions?—but monitoring does really is a terrific tactic during the rut. Look at does as bait—like a worm or fly for trout—and sooner or later a doe in your immediate vicinity is going to cycle. Then all you have to do is lay back and wait for the bucks.

On the other hand, you could be hunting the wrong does at the right time. After all, not all does go into heat on the same day or even the same week in the fall, meaning you must read each does' body language to tell where they are in their reproductive cycle. One helpful visible clue is dark-stained hock glands of does. Research shows that does rub-urinate on a daily basis just like bucks in order to refresh their hock, or tarsal glands. During the fall, these glands on bucks and does appear to grow successively darker as the rut approaches, ostensibly from increased rub-urination.

Incidentally, a doe entering estrus is also more vocal than her midcycle counterparts. I've watched does blowing their shrill, piecing whistle every 10 or 20 minutes as they highball through the woods for no apparent reason. (Often an aggressive buck appears shortly thereafter, but just as often one does not.) Translation? The next time you hear a deer whistling repeatedly, don't assume it's a spooked animal. By all means grunt back—estrous does actually respond better to buck grunts than bucks—and you might call in the best possible bait for luring a dream buck within range.

All of these clues can help, but the general appearance of a doe is probably the best indication of her willingness (or refusal) to breed. Believe me, bucks "study" does, looking for these classic estrous characteristics: erect, horizontal tail, often cocked sideways (rather than a vertical "warning" tail or a fully relaxed dangling tail); accentuated side-to-side head bobbing (rather than vertical head bobbing); agitated demeanor telegraphing tension (rather than contentment); and repeated urination (while most deer urinate about 10 times a day, does in heat will urinate several times in one area before moving on).

Parallel Trails & Buck Routes

The doe-finding behavior patterns of a dominant alpha buck are easy to spot, and once you lock onto them you can better predict where to set up (and when and where to move). First, keep in mind that this particular buck begins the courtship stage of the rut by monitoring a familiar social group of does within his home range. He does this so he can breed them one-by-one as they become receptive to his advances. Most of the buck's undercover surveillance is quite secretive, but some fairly predictable tactics are used.

For example, a favorite buck trick is scent-checking field edges where does feed in the open after dark. Note that if a buck attempted to scent-check individual trails back in the woods, before they converged, the buck would waste a lot of time. (This tactic is used by desperate bucks, typically adolescent 2½ year olds.)

Older, experienced animals, on the other hand, have learned to reduce their exposure while checking trails just inside dense cover. And knowing how cruising bucks vacuum these trails can help pinpoint rut-time stand placement.

Ears to Hear

During the rut, bucks listen for does and does listen for bucks. Research on the whitetail's brainstem response to pitch (sound frequency) yields an unimpressive range of 500-12,000 Hz, compared to man's range of 20-20,000 Hz. But to make up for their "less acute" auditory system, deer adopt several survival tactics that end up giving them the edge in hearing perception. Keep in mind that listening isn't necessarily hearing. My teenage daughter can hear what I say but she doesn't know what I'm talking about until she listens.

The ability to listen is greatly enhanced by a deer's radar dish-like ears. By constantly swiveling its ears—up to 270 degrees—a deer can measure the difference in time it takes for an approaching sound to reach each ear lobe. This, in turn, allows the deer to home in on your exact location with surprising accuracy—almost as keen as a spring gobbler pinpointing a hen's yelp.

What exactly are bucks listening for? Experience teaches that another buck's "tending grunt" can be effective, but so can the softer grunts and mews of does. It pays to carry an assortment of commercial deer calls since deer are individuals and what works on one may not work on another. Also, be patient: Somewhere out there deer are actually listening.

"I can't tell you how many times I've set up over 'hot' deer trails and watched bucks ignore them as they zipped by just out of range," recalled Rob Evans, a trophy bowhunter from southern Minnesota with a dozen monster racks to his credit. "I'm talking about bucks that intentionally cut across trails, rather than running with them. That's why I hardly ever prepare a stand site along a specific trail when the rut's hot 'n heavy. Instead, I prefer general areas where bucks tend to funnel through."

An alternative is hunting spots that resemble, for all practical purposes, a tic-tac-toe grid. If you look hard enough, you'll discover main trails adorned with so-called parallel trails. They're not there because the deer traffic is so thick that the bucks and does need passing lanes. They're a function of terrain. Take a fairly steep sidehill, for instance. Typically, you'll find tic-tac-toe grids at key points and saddles and along the slope. Edges of swamps are also prime candidates for parallel trails as are smaller woodlots.

Which brings us to the other main method bucks use to find does during the breeding season—buck routes. As the local supply of does dwindles and becomes exhausted—or the does simply do not go into estrus when olfactory clues indicate they should—bucks follow rather prescribed routes to take them from doe group to doe group. This is my favorite method for bowhunting the brief but helter-skelter post-breeding "trolling" stage of the rut. Rather than camping out near a preferred food source or even a red-hot rub or scrape line, I like to set up shop along the most direct route connecting two or more doe bedding areas.

Again, it's not all that difficult to figure out buck routes, especially if you think like a rutting buck who has places to go and does to visit. With topographic map in hand, simply ask yourself what would be the easiest and quickest way to get from Doe Group A to Doe Group B. It's no secret that bucks, especially mature, large-bodied animals, are basically lazy creatures preferring the easy route to the more taxing one when they're not spooked. (No wonder key fence and river crossings are good places to hang a treestand or erect a ground blind.) And this goes double for the rut when bucks literally wear themselves thin, losing up to 25 percent of their body weight, as they pursue estrous does.

Simply stated, rutting bucks cut corners. The best buck routes sometimes leap off the map—such as the heads of hollows, ridge saddles, and intersections like a fenceline and a creek bottom. But most such routes are largely void of buck sign. Why? Because bucks simply do not spend much time along these corridors. To a buck, they're merely a means to an end and not a destination. A lack of buck sign is irrelevant if the timing is right.

Sniffing Out Does

So much for buck locomotion. Just how do they go about singling out prospective mating partners? With their noses, of course. You already know that. But did you know that bucks use airborne scent as much, if not more, than ground scent during courtship? In fact, contrary to popular belief, bucks do not rely heavily on urine deposits for distinguishing receptive females from unreceptive females.

A pair of landmark studies on the fascinating subject of "chemical signals" of whitetails during the breeding season bear this out and help point hunters in the right direction. A relatively obscure report, published in 1995 in the Journal of Chemical Ecology by Indiana and Georgia researchers, discovered 44 volatiles (extremely fragile compounds) in the vaginal mucus of female whitetails and 63 volatiles in their urine. Another study, conducted at the University of Georgia, showed that "control" bucks definitely responded more aggressively to does "anointed" with vaginal secretions from estrous females over those receiving "voided" urine (lacking the secretions) from females that were in heat. In fact, the estrous urine void of vaginal mucus proved to be no more attractive than urine from midcycle females.

Drawing hard-and-fast conclusions on this subject will always be controversial, but three key insights can be gleaned. First, it appears that compounds in vaginal mucus play a major role in pairing up bucks with fertile does. Because the pheromones discharged by a doe are extremely volatile and frail, they must literally be tasted by a buck to be verified. This is why bucks are often observed licking the rumps of does during courtship (ultimately the doe decides if and when copulation will take place).

Second, these volatile compounds likely last hours in the real world, not days or weeks. So be realistic about doe-in-heat scent usage. Even the best scent products under ideal conditions are likely a short-range game.

And third, the popular notion that a rutting buck is a nose-to-the-ground machine is grossly misleading; if they were, successful hunters would routinely notice lacerations on their bucks' noses, which just isn't the case. To the contrary, bucks follow their noses in tracking down mainly airborne scents. This is a good reason to elevate commercial deer scents to maximize their potency rather than placing the scents at ground level. In addition, scents should never be left in the woods overnight and should always be reapplied each day.

Analyzing how bucks find does can translate into better hunting strategies. Perhaps this is the true meaning of "think like a buck."

Bed and Breakfast Bucks

Many hunters do not realize that older bucks are largely solitary animals, whereas mature does are the opposite—socialites preferring the company of other deer, usually their offspring and, in some cases, sisters and cousins. As a result, bucks never bed in close proximity to does—until the pre-rut stage of the breeding season hits.

Indeed, when the first few does begin emitting olfactory clues that suggest they're nearing estrus, nearby bucks relocate their bedding areas. The bucks move from reclusive, dense cover, (typically at higher elevations) to security cover immediately downwind of a social group of does. In my opinion, most rubs and scrapes in the deer woods are the result of bedded bucks monitoring and marking doe bedding areas. Granted, hunters occasionally encounter rub lines along strategic topographic barriers, such as rivers and bluff lines, but the majority of hard-core buck sign is the result of "bed and breakfast bucks." This moniker fits because most preferred doe bedding areas are within commuting distance of primary food sources high in protein and rich in calories.

The so-called sign-post markers of bucks are thought to involve the process of biostimulation. In other words, the exchange of hormones and other selective compounds from the bucks' urine, forehead and saliva, deposited while rubbing and scraping, help "prime" the does to go into estrus. As one biologist friend put it, "If a buck can't find an estrus doe, he'll do his part to create one."

The bottom line for the pre-rut, then, is concentrating on cover directly downwind of doe bedding areas, because that's where the bucks will be.

14   Roaming for Romance

BY JOHN WEISS

Despite the widely accepted idea that bucks are supposed to be a cinch to take during the rut, veteran whitetail addict John Weiss likes to fine-tune his tactics. His ideas about where the bucks will be just might be the edge you need to draw on a trophy this season.

The mood is one of tense excitement and apprehension. And it messes with the minds of bowhunters by bombarding their senses with stimuli fitting of the arrival of a new season in which change is the only constant.

The long, muggy dog-days of summer are slowly drawing the curtain down, and suddenly one's eyes are dazzled with a collage of brilliant colors straight from the Great Artist's palette. There is an unmistakable and refreshing crispness in the air, accompanied by the heady fragrance of woodsmoke. The feel of soft wool, and the heft of archery equipment in one's hands, completes the picture, but you knew what was in store because you've been waiting for it since this time last year.

Now, bucks are becoming increasingly more visible, and the reason for this is simple: The courtship rituals of deer are a lot like those of humans. With both species, more time, energy, and emotion are invested in the pursuit than in the actual consummation of the relationship.

Consequently, it's commonplace for a hunter to pattern one or more bucks, diligently put in his time on stand, and eventually take a buck, but quite often the buck he takes is one he never saw before or even suspected was around. Rather, it was a buck that was roaming for romance.

Yet, just as often, exactly the opposite occurs. In our annual camp we've frequently doped out a nice buck's routine prior to opening day, seen him on such a regular basis and eventually named him, when suddenly, "poof," he'd disappear never to be seen again.

It was entirely by coincidence that one day I was talking with Larry Marchinton, the noted Georgia biologist who specializes in radio-tracking deer, that the answers to some of these questions began to come into clear focus. Moreover, I like to think that what we've learned has since enabled us to double our chances of taking nice bucks.

"When we first began using radio telemetry to evaluate deer movement patterns, we'd occasionally lose track of one of our radio-collared bucks," Larry explained. "When this happened, we figured the deer in question was either killed on a highway or the transmitting device on the collar had simply malfunctioned.

But then maybe as much as a full month later, we'd suddenly begin detecting the collar's beeping signal again in the very area where the deer previously disappeared. This told us the deer had in fact not been killed, nor had the transmitter failed. Clearly, the deer had merely traveled far away, well out of range of our radio receiver, and then at a later time returned."

Then Marchinton emphasized that these occasional, unpredictable travel tendencies of whitetails almost always involve bucks and not does. Does are essentially homebodies that grow to maturity, breed, and raise their offspring within a two-square mile area of where they were born.

As fawns, young bucks and does alike remain close to their mothers. However, when an adult doe is about to give birth again the following spring, she drives the yearlings away. Her former daughters remain in the general area and can be expected to eventually reunite with their mother, but the young bucks leave their home range altogether to take up residence elsewhere. This "dispersal," as biologists refer to the phenomenon, is nature's way of preventing inbreeding among blood-related family members. Consequently, from the time he becomes a yearling, a buck's natural instinct inclines him to engage in widespread travels whenever he is faced with a lack of food, feels the urge to breed, or fears for his safety, whereas does pretty much stay put and tough-out the existing conditions.

This isn't meant to imply that whitetail bucks become eternal nomads. In fact, they are actually more paranoid than does and therefore cling tightly to certain areas they perceive to afford the utmost in safety. As a result, if a buck locates a particular piece of real estate that offers several prime food sources, thick security cover not disturbed by repeated human intrusion, and an abundance of does that will become receptive at the onset of the rut, he'll remain within that ideal habitat for much of the entire year. Moreover, if a human, or other infrequent source of danger such as a free-roaming dog, causes him to hastily retreat, he'll eventually return to his home turf.

This is exactly the type of situation that hunters capitalize upon when they diligently scout a given region, peg a buck's daily behavior pattern, hang a portable stand, and hours or days later eventually succeed in taking that very animal.

Yet there are several circumstances in which a mature buck will entirely abandon his bailiwick, move into an adjacent territory, and become known as an "alien" or "immigrant."

The first situation involves repeated human intrusion. This may involve intense hunting pressure, but it may also result from the continued daily activities of foresters, loggers, utility-line workers, surveyors, or others. In any case, the buck in question quickly begins feeling his security cover has been so repeatedly violated that it's time to seek quietude and safety elsewhere.

The second element which is sure to cause a buck to begin traveling afar is the onset of the rut with few available does to breed on his familiar home grounds. As a result of this sex-ratio imbalance in any given region, bucks begin making excursions beyond their customary home ranges in search of pockets of doe family units. This can be dangerous business for a traveling buck because his journey is sure to take him into territory he is not intimately familiar with. Plus, he stands the risk of running headlong into the adjacent region's dominant buck and perchance being subjected to a whipping. Nevertheless, it is nature's decree that he go forth and breed and that is a cosmic force he must obey.

The exciting thing about all of this is that radio-tracking studies conducted by biologists have revealed very well-defined ways in which bucks leave an existing range they've been inhabiting and travel into new territory. It doesn't make any difference whether an immigrant buck was literally spooked out of his former region by human intrusion, or whether he's searching for receptive does, because in both cases his travel behavior is rather predictable.

Knowing this in advance, an astute hunter can actually stack the odds in his favor. While engaging in pre-scouting of his favorite hunting grounds, he'll obviously want to concentrate upon locating whatever sign he can find that, likely as not, was left by resident animals and then place his stand accordingly. But if he's also aware of the fact that immigrant bucks may periodically filter through his region, and how they're likely to be moving about, he can substantially increase his chances of encountering more deer than otherwise.

Probably the most important thing to keep in mind is that when a buck ventures far from his home turf into an unfamiliar region he doesn't move in random or haphazard fashion. Radio-telemetry studies have revealed most such bucks travel along well-defined, natural terrain features.

For example, in one South Carolina study, a seven-point buck wearing a radio transmitter was carefully monitored and determined to be holing-up in a black oak thicket along the banks of the Edisto River. The deer remained within that several hundred square yard piece of cover for the entire months of September and October and an enterprising bowhunter who carefully scouted the area would have undoubtedly found it quite easy to ascertain the buck's daily movements between his bedding and feeding areas and eventually take him.

But then the pre-rut began and the buck, feeling the restless urge to mate, began searching for does. Yet he didn't wander cross-country in aimless fashion. Instead, he followed the east bank of the Edisto River downstream for a distance of seven miles, eventually crossed the river at a shallow riffle, began working back upstream along the opposite bank in a westerly direction, eventually crossed the river again, and ultimately found himself right back in the core area of his original home turf. Biologists plotting his movements say the journey took four weeks.

This classic illustration provides answers to the types of questions that often perplex hunters. A bowhunter who previously scouted the black oak thicket and patterned the deer's behavior, only to have the deer suddenly disappear, might have asked, where did he go? Was he taken by a poacher at night, or did he perhaps come out second-best in a highway skirmish with a truck? The answer is neither. The deer just temporarily left his home area.

By the same token, a second hunter sitting in a treestand several miles downstream could have conceivably taken this buck and likewise been faced with the puzzling question, "where did this buck come from because I've never seen him around here before?"

Consequently, whenever I'm on a preseason scouting mission, searching for trails, scrapes, and other sign indicating the regular presence of deer, one type of location I always investigate is the presence of a riverbottom.

Typically, most riverbottoms are like magnets to deer because they provide lush vegetation and thick security cover for hiding. Therefore, finding sign indicating how the animals are moving around in a bottomland is not overly difficult. Yet after you've pegged the routines of local, resident deer, there's a potential bonus to look forward to, and that is the possibility of also encountering immigrant bucks traveling through the region as they make their way either upstream or downstream.

In other words, if there is intense hunting pressure upstream or downstream, or a distinct lack of does in those regions, you stand a good chance of seeing not only the resident deer in the particular area where you've set up but also other bucks that may periodically filter through your locale from elsewhere.

There's one other important thing to keep in mind about riverbottoms and it is that they are often quite wide. Therefore, unlike a gun hunter, a bowhunter must refine his search for a bottleneck. This is simply a narrow constriction in the cover or steepness of adjacent sidehills that deer must squeeze through in order to continue along in their travels. After you've marked several such bottlenecks on your topo map, scout only these locations for trails and other sign, then place your stand in the particular bottleneck revealing the most travel activity.

Yet riverbottoms certainly are not the only type of terrain feature bucks use when traveling away from areas of existing hunting pressure or in search of does. Virtually any well-defined landform that clearly runs uninterrupted for a long distance may serve as a type of "highway" used by migrating deer.

Throughout the eastern states, for example, where the Appalachian Mountains stretch from Maine to Georgia, ridgelines extending uninterrupted for many miles can be hot spots worth investigating. The same is true of the Ozarks in the Midwest. In either of these cases, or wherever else mountain ranges exist, simply examine a topo map and look for unbroken sections of ridgeline terrain at least five miles in length. Along those ridges are likely to be mast-bearing hardwoods, evidence of scrapes and rubs, and trails that have been religiously adhered to by deer for hundreds of years. Not only are these excellent sites for ambushing nice bucks, particularly in specific regions where sign is concentrated, but there's also the likelihood of bushwhacking a wide-roaming deer looking for female companionship.

Similar to a riverbottom is any canyon-like gorge where sheer rock facings literally contain deer travel activities and channel their movements in certain directions.

But landforms need not be this dramatic for deer to use them as travel byways. In Iowa, Nebraska, Illinois, and other farmbelt states where agriculture is intensively pursued, it is common to be faced with vast plowed fields as far as the eye can see. Sometimes it almost seems as if those croplands extend all the way to the horizon.

Yet if you examine an aerial photo, you'll see that somewhere in the distance the cropland is actually bordered on at least two sides by terrain which is too rugged to be plowed and planted. That rugged terrain might be in the form of a forest, wet swale or terrain pockmarked with sinkholes. Now, look even closer and see if you can discover any natural or manmade feature that spans the plowed field and in a manner of speaking "connects" the distantly separated woodlots laying on opposite sides of the cropland.

The connecting link may be a fence with evidence of waist-high grass growing up around it, or a shallow drainage ditch used to facilitate irrigation or run-off rainwater. It could even be a distinct "edge" created where several hundred acres of soybeans are planted adjacent to several hundred acres of wheat or corn.

In any event, if a buck is spooked out of one of the forested areas and wants to chart an escape to the next closest forest region two miles away, or desires to travel from one forest to another far away in search of does, it's not likely he'll cross the wide open expanse in random fashion. He'll use a thoroughfare, of sorts, which in this case is the fenceline, drainage culvert, or the edge of diverse crops butting up against each other.

How would you scout and hunt such a location? Well, obviously, a lack of trees and other cover in cropland areas will require setting up in one woodlot or another and placing your stand in accordance with prevailing sign located there. Yet you'd also want to make every effort to be able to simultaneously be within shooting range of the "connecting link" between that particular woodlot and its sister cover located on the opposite side of the huge cropland.

When a mature buck is fully engaged in searching for does to romance, the time has come to rattle.

Picture a buck that has roamed far from his home grounds and suddenly hears the clashing of antlers in the distance. Instantly, the only conclusion he can come to is that two resident bucks have found a pocket of does, are battling for breeding rights, and perhaps if he rushes in and finds them to be subordinates he can do the breeding himself.

Or, if our hypothetical buck is on his home turf and hears the simulated sounds of two bucks going at it, his only conclusion is that immigrant bucks roaming for romance have infiltrated his domain and chanced upon his does. This is something he will not tolerate and he'll likewise rush to the scene to settle the dispute on his own behalf.

Unquestionably, a hunter's most important concern at this point is avoiding detection. When a buck responds to antler rattling, his sense of hearing has drawn him in, and as he approaches closer and closer he tries to make visual contact with the two other bucks his ears have told him are present. Therefore, a hunter's continued rattling may very well reveal his location.

"Once a buck has approached to within 100 yards, I stop rattling altogether," says my friend Will Primos, honcho of Primos Game calls in Jackson, Mississippi. "I figure the antlers have done their job, and now I don't want to risk having additional hand movements detected."

It's at this point that Primos switches to a grunt call that simulates the nasal-sounding tending noise of a buck trailing close behind a hot doe just moments before breeding. When a responding buck hears this sound, he is likely to think that the fight has been resolved, one of the bucks has retreated, the victor is now enjoying the company of the doe, and perhaps if he's of superior ranking that he himself can cash in big-time.

Admittedly, there's always the temptation to place a stand in such a manner that it overlooks a trail, scrape, or small food plot. Those are universal tactics that have worked for decades and will continue to work in the future. But strive to do your scouting in such a manner that you are also situated in close proximity to a well-defined travel corridor or other terrain feature deer may occasionally use during the course of their periodic long-distance travels from one place to another. And by all means, use your rattling antlers and grunt call.

Maybe the buck you'll end up taking will be one you've had your eye on for many weeks. Yet it may also be a lovesick deer that was just visiting from afar.

15   Still-Hunting Strategies for the Pre-Rut and Peak Rut

BY BILL VAZNIS

The expression "still-hunting" has always been one I have personally disliked, because of its vagueness and lack of spark. What's wrong with "stalking?" For me, that's the right way to describe sneaking slowly through the woods, pausing to look and listen, then sneaking on. "Still-hunting" doesn't say that at all. No matter, it's still a good way to hunt. For many hunters—gun hunters especially—still-hunting is not an option. It requires too much territory. Most hunters consider themselves lucky to find even a small piece of country where they are free to take a stand at a spot where they have a reasonable chance to see deer if they wait there long enough. But if you have the permission or own or lease a lot of land, then you'll find "still-hunting" to be a superb test of your woodsmanship and deer hunting lore. Here veteran writer, photographer, and bowhunter Bill Vaznis takes us through still-hunting at its finest, in the golden forests of autumn where great hunting takes place one step at a time.

Like a ghost, he appeared off to my right, head alert and looking in my direction. I stood transfixed, sure he could see me, and cursed myself for not being better prepared for the close encounter. Suddenly, the eight-pointer worked his jaw a couple of times and dropped his head back down to the forest floor, his white rack glistening in the early morning light.

He was feeding on acorns, as I suspected deer would be doing this morning on this ridge, and I congratulated myself for being in the right place at the right time. There was one small problem, however. I had to get an arrow nocked and come to full draw without him seeing me. Not an easy task, as only 12 yards separated our destinies.

Providence stepped in, however, as she so often does, and when the buck lowered his head a second time, I dropped to one knee and nocked an arrow in one fluid motion. Now I was ready to do the deed. I just needed a clear pathway for my aluminum shaft.

Suddenly the buck snapped his head back up, and again looked over in my direction. My heart, racing now to beat the band, was about to burst when suddenly the buck took a few steps forward and lowered his head once more. He was just being a buck, trying to catch a predator off guard. It almost worked.

I then made a fatal mistake. Excited at being so close to such a trophy, I quickly drew back my High Country Excalibur, picked a spot low and behind his near shoulder and released a shaft without noticing the pencil-thin sapling halfway between us. The arrow smacked that young oak dead center, sending the buck hightailing back along the ridge like the proverbial dog out of Hades. It was an exhilarating, but exasperating moment.

Still-hunting whitetail bucks with archery tackle is a boss way to bag a buck. It takes patience, but above all, it takes a plan. You just don't go out and start still-hunting without some sort of strategy. Indeed, walking patiently but aimlessly about the deer woods is most surely a recipe for tag soup by season's end.

Early-Morning Food Sources

During the pre-rut, bucks spend the predawn hours on patrol looking for the year's first estrous does. They are often out of their usual haunts by pink light, and as a result are late getting back to their preferred bedding areas. Indeed, seeing a buck an hour or so after sunrise is a sure sign the pre-rut is in full swing.

A good strategy now is to still-hunt known food sources that are off the beaten path. Not the edges of open alfalfa lots or even standing corn for example, but abandoned apple orchards, or ridges laden with acorns, hickory nuts and beechnuts that lie well above the valley floor.

These late morning food sources must offer plenty of cover in the form of thick tangles or uneven terrain, however, if you expect to catch a pre-rut buck off guard. You are not likely to catch a buck out in the open as you might expect to do later on when the rut really heats up.

Spring and summer scouting trips can help you locate these much-desired food sources. If you know the whereabouts of an apple orchard, or can find one on a topo map, check it out several times during the growing season to keep tabs on the upcoming harvest. And while you are there, make note of not only prevailing winds, deer trails, old rubs and browse lines, but also their juxtaposition to suspected nearby bedding areas.

Oak, hickory and beech ridges can be monitored in a similar manner. Simply peer through your binoculars at the uppermost branches on and off during the summer and see which trees have the best crops. This, and any knowledge of what particular trees the deer seemed to prefer in past seasons, will go a long way towards developing a still-hunting strategy once the pre-rut is underway.

Transition Zones

A second strategy is to still-hunt around and through a transition zone. These openings in the forest, once devoid of vegetation, are now likely to support finger- to wrist-sized saplings, raspberry and blackberry briars, goldenrod, staghorn sumac, dogwood, hawthorn and various grasses instead.

Old farmsteads are good spots to begin your search for these pre-rut magnets, which can be in the form of grown-over pastures and long-abandoned crop fields. Other good places to check out include dilapidated beaver dams, natural slides, clear-cuts and two- or three-year-old burns. The best part is that many transition zones can be found adjacent to a brush-riddled apple orchard, a transition zone itself, or mature stands of nut-bearing oak, hickory or beech trees.

The better transition zones are not in close proximity to active agriculture, however, but instead are located near or en route to a pre-rut buck's preferred bedding grounds. In fact, "good" transition zones can be a half mile to a mile or more away from an alfalfa lot or large cornfield in farm country, or a big woods feeding area such as the banks of a river or the periphery of a swamp.

Typically, a pre-rut buck will leave his daytime bedding area late in the day, and enter a transition zone to munch on goldenrod, leaves, various plant stems etc. There is plenty of cover here, and a buck feeling safe will linger here for some time. Then, using a ravine or even a nearby stand of open hardwoods as a conduit, he will time his departure so that he arrives at a large opening known to be frequented by other deer, especially family groups of does and fawns, at or near dark.

In the morning he will again pass through this transition zone, or another one nearby, and linger for a bit until bedding down soon after sunrise. He may even bed down in the transition zone. However, do not still-hunt these areas more than once or twice a week, be careful what you brush up against and always wear a cover scent on your feet. Fox or skunk seems to do the trick most of the time. Once a buck knows you've been snooping around, he will avoid that particular transition zone—often for the remainder of the season.

Buck Bedding Areas

As the peak of the rut nears, bucks will become more active, often leaving their bedding areas before sunset. They have got sex on their minds now, and glandular urges are beginning to take center stage. A careful bowhunter, skirting the periphery of known sanctuaries late in the day, can have plenty of action now if he plays his cards right.

There are some ground rules to bowhunting a buck's bedroom however! First of all, the wind must be in your favor. That sounds obvious, but there's no use pussy-footing in and around his bedding area if all you are going to do is scare him into the next county. If he hears you, sees you or smells you, he's history—and so are you.

To increase your odds of a shot, and lower his odds of learning what you at least smell like, wait for a windy day or a rainy afternoon. The wind will quickly dissipate your airborne stench, and the wet ground will eventually leach your odors into the earth. Either way, you should douse your boot pads or drag rag with real fox urine, and again be careful what you brush up against. The scent you leave behind can be more harmful than the odors that permeate the air.

The advantage still-hunters have over their treestand brethren is the ability to sneak in and out of areas that do not have large enough trees to ambush a deer from above. Patches of dogwood, hawthorn groves and young pine plantations, for example, are all good places to play peek-a-boo with an antlered buck, but do not generally exhibit the mature growth needed for treestand set-ups.

This still-hunting strategy does have its risks, however, but remember that once the rut is in full swing "your" buck will no longer be bedding in his usual haunts with any degree of regularity. He will instead be with one lady fair after another, bedding where they bed until the rut wanes.

Scent Trails

To get a shot at a buck, you have to be in the right place at the right time. One minute too early, or a couple of minutes too late, and the shooting opportunity will simply not present itself. Seeing a buck may get your heart pumping, but it will be only a "close call." But what about those bucks that cut your trail 15 minutes or a half-hour after you are gone? Is there anything you can do? In certain circumstances, yes! You can turn the buck around and into bow range by using deer urine as a lure.

A good choice during the pre-rut is a nonrutting buck urine. A buck that cuts your scent trail will change directions and follow your footsteps, believing his territory has been invaded by another buck. And he will likely do so in an aggressive manner.

An obvious second choice is a doe-in-heat urine. At first whiff, a passing buck will immediately put his nose to the ground, and follow the trail you have laid out in a direct and purposeful manner. To get the most out of your scent trail, however, you must plan ahead. It does little good, for example, to lay down a scent trail if you are going to still-hunt on the downwind side of a deer run, as it is unlikely any deer will cross your path!

A better strategy would be to lay down a scent trail in the late afternoon on the downwind side of a bedding area and then double back just before dark. Your goal would be to spread a urine trail perpendicular to expected deer traffic, not parallel to it. You would, of course, be still-hunting crosswind, but downwind of that scent trail.

Scrape Lines

Undoubtedly, my favorite pre-rut strategy is still-hunting along a fresh scrape line. Indeed, I have tagged several bucks in this manner including a nine-pointer that grossed in the mid-140s. I took that buck at 30 yards, but shots can be much closer. In fact, I arrowed a wide-racked seven-pointer at three yards one morning as he fed on acorns along a well-worked scrape line in upstate New York.

The best time to sneak along a scrape line is the very next time you expect the buck to return. You can generally determine when the buck will freshen his scrape line by examining nearby racks, rubs and the debris tossed to one side of the scrape. If debris is tossed towards a nearby crop field, then it is safe to assume it was made by a morning buck. He will likely return to the scrape line in the wee hours, whereas a scrape line coming out of a stand of thick pines would indicate the buck freshened the scrape line in the evening soon after he left his bedding area.

You must keep the line of scrapes in view as you are still-hunting. Last fall I caught a fat eight-pointer flat-footed as he worked his early morning scrape line. Unfortunately, I had wandered off to one side a bit to avoid a blowdown, and that's when the buck showed himself. I nocked a broadhead, but couldn't thread an arrow through all the brush. He quietly moved along none the worse for the encounter.

Grunt Tubes

One of the advantages of a grunt tube is that you can easily use one in conjunction with the previous still-hunting strategies. For example, I will periodically blind call when I think I am in the vicinity of a deer. You must be ready to shoot, however, on a moment's notice. I got caught flat-footed myself a few years back after I imitated a young buck with my variable grunt tube. Almost immediately a fat six-point buck stepped through the goldenrod and stood looking for me six yards off to my right. By the time I managed to nock an arrow, he wandered off.

You can also lure a buck that is about to walk past you into bow range. A single grunt of a young buck seems to work best, but you must call loud enough for him to hear you. If you get no response, call louder. Once you have him coming, nock an arrow and crouch down for the shot.

My favorite call, however, is a fawn bleat. I use it whenever I stumble in order to help mask my clumsiness. Fawns are always making noise in the woods, and any nearby deer will hopefully be relaxed by my renditions.

One year as I was still-hunting along the periphery of a bedding area, I heard a couple bucks sparring. They were less than 25 yards distant, but the vegetation was dry and noisy. However, I did manage to close to 12 yards or so and kill a yearling six-point with my recurve by intermittently blowing on my fawn call.

The Peak Rut Begins

It was still dark out as I locked the cab of my 4x4 and headed towards the top of a small hill about a mile away. I quickly circled a cut hayfield, and then slowed down to a crawl as I neared the crest of the hill.

I glassed the two fields below me, but it was still too dark to see anything of consequence. Finally, after waiting for the first pink rays of dawn to break, I spotted two, three and then six deer in one field, and at least eight more in the adjacent opening. One big deer especially caught my eye. I couldn't see a rack, but it was obvious that he was a buck by the way he was checking out the herd for a receptive doe. He soon disappeared into a grown-over apple orchard. The rest of the does then began to file out of the field in groups of two and three, heading nonchalantly towards a nearby bedding area. Sunup was still better than a half an hour away.

I glassed the fields and surrounding brush one more time, and then began still-hunting towards the orchard. I immediately jumped a couple of does that had snuck in from behind, and then a spike buck winded me. The deer were obviously on the move this morning, and if I took my time I felt my chances of a close encounter were excellent. I changed direction once more, and began to still-hunt crosswind along the edge of the abandoned orchard.

Ten minutes later I saw what looked like a deer's rack move in the goldenrod. I glassed the spot, and was shocked to see a fat nine-pointer bedded only 21 yards away. I immediately nocked an arrow, picked a spot and sent an aluminum shaft at his vitals. He leaped from his bed upon impact, and made a mad dash for safety. It was to no avail, however—he was already dead on his feet.

I can't think of anyplace I would rather be during the peak of the rut than still-hunting an abandoned farm with my bow and arrow. Frosty mornings and the smell of dead leaves help set the stage for the "moon of madness," a time when bucks go berserk as they search the countryside for a doe in heat. Indeed, it is a time when a bowhunter on the hoof can see as many as a dozen bucks together chasing after a single doe.

Bucks are not as predictable at this time of the year, or so we are led to believe. But if you think about the rut for a bit, there is a pattern to their behavior. Here are six still-hunting strategies guaranteed to get you a bow shot at a rutting buck his fall.

Look for Bucks to Be Where Does Are Feeding

Glassing a known feeding area and finding it devoid of does and fawns after first light is a sure sign the rut is in full swing. Resident females, harassed by every buck that crosses their trail, are already weary of the chase. The bucks nonetheless continue to patrol in and around these preferred feeding sites searching for a hot doe. Indeed, sometimes you will see racked bucks standing head erect and staring off into the distance, while at other times you will see them trotting brazenly across an opening, their noses to the ground like an old hound dog.

An excellent early morning and late afternoon still-hunting strategy is to sneak along the periphery of those feeding areas preferred by does, paying close attention to adjacent swamps, marshes, grown-over fields, abandoned apple orchards and those cover-rich conduits that lead to secluded bedding sites.

Check out those out-of-the-way drainages, creek beds and small fingers of brush that lead in and out of these feeding areas, too. Bucks that get lucky and locate an estrous doe often chase her into one of these small pockets of cover. They may bed down here for an hour or so, and even breed. Remember it doesn't take much cover to hide a pair of prying eyes.

Keep your eyes AND ears open. I have located a lot of rutting bucks by first hearing them push their way through thick brush, slosh across drainages and even jump over stone walls and barbed wire fences. If you still-hunt slowly and quietly, you may hear doe bleats, fawn bleats, tending grunts, sparring—even catch a buck and doe mating!

When bucks in rut are on patrol, they often throw normal caution to the wind, moving deliberately and purposely through all kinds of cover. Try to keep in mind that they are frantically looking for a doe in heat at this time of the day, not sneaking back to their preferred bedding areas.

Travel Routes Connecting Bedding Sites

Most does and fawns are well on their way to their bedding areas an hour or so after sunup. Now is the time to trail after them, so to speak, and still-hunt to one side of those travel routes that connect feeding areas to their preferred bedding sites.

Stick to the shadows, and look behind you on a regular basis. You never know when a buck will be coming along with his nose to the ground. I once had a yearling trot right past me within 20 yards as he sniffed his way up the same hillside. He seemed absolutely oblivious to his surroundings!

A popular feeding area may have a half dozen or more primary entrance/exit trails. Indeed, pay particularly close attention to those trails that are littered with doe and fawn tracks, scrape lines and buck rubs. Even though other scrape lines have long been abandoned, a line of pawed-out circles along a well-traveled doe route can be worth your while all season long—especially if there are several large rubs present.

You can try to still-hunt these more promising pathways one at a time, or you can still-hunt perpendicular to the entire maze, the way many bucks do when they are on patrol. In hilly country, ridges, plateaus, gentle slopes and the edges of steep ravines are all good routes to bump bucks as they try to intercept the trails of as many does as possible in the morning. A faint rub or scrape line may be all you need to discover the runway the buck is using.

Hunting Doe Bedding Areas

Another prime location to still-hunt rutting bucks is in and around a known bedding area preferred by family groups of does and fawns. Bucks from far and wide will arrive at all times of the day to search here for an estrous doe, giving the patient still-hunter a one-time look-see at bucks he never knew existed.

The best time to sneak and peak around a doe's bedding areas is in the morning right after a cold front has passed. Sometimes I like to start on the downwind side and weave back and forth through the thick stuff, stopping often to listen to the sounds of deer on the move. That doesn't mean that you shouldn't circle the bedding area, and then reenter the thick stuff once again. As I said, bucks will be arriving all day long during the peak of the rut. Although first light is best, you could almost as easily run into a buck at noon, making a doe's bedding area a veritable magnet for the region's best bucks.

Don't overlook those small pockets of cover adjacent to these bedding areas, however. Sometimes a doe will run here in an effort to shake an amorous buck, while at other times a buck will prod a doe into one of these holes in an effort to keep her to himself. Have you ever found a couple of big buck rubs in one of these pockets out in the middle of nowhere and wondered how they got there? Now you know!

One fall I casually glanced over at a small copse of aspens and was astounded to see a 140-class 10-pointer bedded under the branches. I immediately raised my Swarovskis, and saw a diminutive doe with six or seven satellite yearling bucks in attendance. I was flabbergasted, to say the least. I worked my way around the herd, but the doe split at the last moment, taking her entourage with her. I now make it a point to check every patch of cover adjacent to a doe's bedding area during the peak of the rut. You can never be too sure!

Connecting Routes

Where do you go after coming up empty-handed still-hunting a doe's security cover? That's easy! You do what any self-respecting buck would do under similar circumstances: Still-hunt directly to the nearest food source preferred by does, or the next hillside, swamp or stand of planted pines other family groups of does and fawns use as bedding cover.

And I mean directly! Bucks will sometimes take the most efficient route to the next doe-suspected hangout regardless of terrain features or available cover. This is one reason why we see bucks standing out in the open at midday. Look for new runways or a rub line that at first glance appears to lead nowhere special. This is a connecting route.

Generally, however, creek beds, drainages, hedgerows, fence lines, fingers of brush and stone walls receive the most rutting buck traffic in farm country. In the big woods, look for rub lines and natural terrain features to help you locate the buck's pathway. A line of old and new rubs along a ravine, for example, may indicate the connecting route of several bucks or a single mature buck, one that has been around for a couple of years and knows the ropes.

Using Scent Trails

A fifth still-hunting strategy for rut-crazed bucks is a scent trail. Bucks sniff out every track they come across, and will immediately run off after a doe in heat like a hound after a hare. Obviously, you'll want to use a quality doe-in-heat urine with boot pads or a drag rag.

Of course, you don't just lay down a scent trail haphazardly; you have to have a plan to increase your chances of a close encounter. One fall I watched as three bucks chased a doe out of a goldenrod field, and down along a ravine. Round and round they went, running and jumping after the doe like a pack of dogs.

I snuck down to the woods near the ravine, doused my boot pads with doe-in-heat, and then laid down a scent trail while still-hunting along the ravine some 25 or 30 yards from the edge. I caught one of the bucks bedded down, but he saw me first and high-tailed it to parts unknown taking the doe with him.

I decided then to circle around and still-hunt my scent trail by sneaking back along the edge of the ravine. I heard a grunt, turned around and saw a yearling buck bird-dogging my scent trail. I quickly nocked an arrow, and when he cleared the brush at 12 yards, I let a broadhead fly from my recurve. Much to my horror, the arrow sailed harmlessly over the buck's back—as did my second and third shafts (gulp!). That buck was so lovesick I could have hit him with a rock, and I doubt he would have cared. Now the fixins for a scent trail are always in my fanny pack.

Grunt Tubes

Another accessory a still-hunter should carry with him is a grunt tube. I hang several around my neck, store a few in my pockets and keep a reserve or two in my fanny pack. You can never have too many grunt tubes.

During the rut, I like to blind call when I am in cover I suspect harbors racked bucks. A single buck grunt may bring an unseen buck into range, but there are a couple of combination calls that work even better during the peak of the breeding season.

Try a doe-in-heat bleat followed by the tending grunts of a young buck. It tells an unsuspecting wild buck that there is a hot doe nearby, and that another buck, a buck he might be able to intimidate, will soon be breeding her. If he rushes in, he may be able to take over the action.

Or you can imitate a fawn bleat followed by the tending grunts from a young rutting buck. A fawn bleat during the peak of the rut tells an unsuspecting wild buck that the fawn's mother is nearby, probably about to be bred by the young upstart. Again, he should rush in so he can take over the claim.

See a buck tending a doe? If you can get in front of the doe, you might be able to call her towards you with a fawn bleat and a tending buck grunt. The doe may come to investigate, hopefully bringing the buck in tow. This combination brought in a doe to me with a 190-class behemoth right behind her a couple of years ago in Iowa. Alas, the doe caught my wind, ruining my ruse but confirming for me the fact that combination deer calls do work. Indeed, using a grunt tube during the peak of the rut can help you spell SUCCESS!

16   Where the Rut Really Happens

BY BOB MCNALLY

Climb that ridge during the rut and you'll find the best big buck hunting in your area.

When the rut kicked into full swing last October on our bowhunting lease, my oldest son Eric was in a familiar tree, on a familiar ridge side. He was seeing bucks regularly as they moved out of a beaver swamp bedding area. They'd work up an old logging road to the top of the hill, offering him a broadside shot as they passed his oak treestand on the ridge side near the top.

He shot a dandy six-pointer, and I met him late that morning to help track it. Curiously there was no blood trail, and the buck ran uphill following the shot. We looked for an hour, and found only a single drop of blood at the spot where the arrow hit him. With no shaft, and only faint tracks to give a slight indication of animal direction, it was more a matter of walking the hilltop and looking for a downed animal than hands-and-knees crawling for telltale sign.

As it turned out, the buck ran less than 100 yards, and piled up in a tangled thicket no larger than a bathroom, which we overlooked several times. But in searching the whole ridgetop area for Eric's deer I was stunned at how much buck sign had suddenly materialized in a place I scouted with him just two weeks earlier. After we'd set stands along the sides of the ridge we purposely didn't walk the area much to keep human scent to a minimum. So we had no idea the fresh rut sign had been made—and probably never would have known about it had we not been tracking his six-pointer.

There were at least 100 scrapes on the ridgetop, ranging in size from a basketball to a truck hood. There were uncountable fresh buck rubs, on trees ranging from pencil-thin saplings to cedars four inches in diameter.

The ridge is about 300 yards long, and is located in an ideal spot, with a deep ravine and creek on one side, and a clover- and ryegrass-planted open power line swath in the bottom on the opposite side of the ridge. The heavily-wooded ridge is loaded with white, red and water oaks, and is a natural magnet for deer moving from the creekbottom bedding area to highland acorns or to the power line grass. Does are thick along the ridge most all the time. So when the rut kicks in, buck action on the ridgetop is something to behold—as evidenced by the scrapes, rubs and crisscrossing new trails we discovered while searching for the six-pointer.

The abundance of scrapes and rubs that can be found on "ridges" isn't anything new to veteran deer hunters. But when I stumble across so much of it that

101

seemingly pops up overnight like I did last October while searching for my son's buck, it still amazes me how "ridge-oriented" rutting whitetail bucks can be. I emphasize the word "ridge," because a ridge in Florida or Kansas is a laughable "high spot" for a Pennsylvania or Western whitetail hunter. For example, I bowhunted last December on Mississippi's famed Willow Point, operated by Tara Wildlife in Vicksburg. Bucks were wildly in the rut, but scrapes and rubs were hard to find on the flat, bottomland river delta property until late one morning Bob Thompson and I went to inspect a spot where I saw several does walking across a flat, grassy area 200 yards from my daybreak treestand.

The ground was uniformly lush green, soft and pool-table flat, with occasional deer trails. I found the trail where the does had traveled, right on top of an ever-so-slight "rise" in the lowland timber. It was no more than a couple feet higher than the surrounding terrain—a river delta version of a "ridge"—and scrapes and rubs were everywhere. I hung a stand nearby, and had a number of "ridge-walking" deer within bow range, including several bucks. But none of Pope & Young size, which abound on Willow Point. Nevertheless, a "ridge" was still the rutting hot spot, even in a delta area that was extremely limited in terrain relief. I've experienced much the same thing in the low-country of coastal South Carolina, Georgia and on the desert flats of Texas. Locate a slightly elevated area or "ridge" with hardwoods, or thick cover like cedars, and if bucks are in rut, you'll find choice deer sign. It's almost guaranteed.

While ridgetops can have plenty of rutting buck activity, on many occasions I've found more deer sign on the sides of ridges. This seems to be most prevalent in rolling terrain, where deer can easily walk parallel along hillsides. In steeper ridge country, or in mountainous regions like the Rockies, West Virginia, Pennsylvania, New York, etc., the very tops of ridges or "ridge lines" seem to attract the most rutting buck sign.

In some areas, particularly the West, broad "benches" on ridgetops can be the ultimate gathering spots for bucks bent on mating does. Broad ridge "benches" frequently have parks or open grass areas, but the bulk of whitetail ridge rutting activity is along "edge" cover where mature timber or dense brush is adjacent to grassy parks—still on the ridge, but not in the wide open. Such mountain ridge whitetail hot spots are common in Idaho, Montana, even in parts of Wyoming and Colorado.

How to hunt ridges during the rut is a matter of choice, but well-known bowhunter and game call manufacturer Harold Knight prefers to set stand along trails leading from ridgetop scrape lines and bedding areas, which usually are in the thickets in nearby lowlands.

"Most rutting activity takes place at night, so if you're on a ridgetop, you'll likely not see bucks coming to check scrapes until almost dark," says the Tennessee archer. "During the peak of the rut bucks can be seen through the day, but for most bowmen, their best chance to ambush a rutting buck is picking off the deer as it heads to or from cover to scrape lines at daybreak and dusk."

I don't know that anyone knows for certain why bucks and does walk "ridges" during the rut, and, frankly, it probably doesn't matter—so long as hunters are aware of the phenomenon. However, in much of the country I bowhunt, ridges are where hardwoods are found, and where there are oaks and acorns there are does and yearlings. Find the does and you'll have bucks when the rut starts to rock. In the West, however, and in Northern pine and fir country, hill oaks can be comparatively scarce, but bucks still tend to travel ridges when testosterone levels rise in autumn.

Even in farm country where whitetails have learned to live in standing corn for safety and abundant food, when the rut sets in, bucks scrape and rub on slight ridges between fields. And timbered ridges afford great stand ambush sites for traveling bachelors with heavy sets of horns.

Locating low-relief ridges in flat country normally isn't much of a problem by using topographic maps or aerial survey photos. Even slight ridges often are a snap to find simply by observing tree lines. The tallest trees likely are on a ridge, or some type of "high spot." Scout 'em out and you might find enough rut sign to make your pulse rate quicken. I once located a hot scrape line along a woods fence between two Illinois cornfields. The corn was still standing—which was where the deer spent most of their time—but there was a scrape line along the fence that was incredible. The fence was the highest spot in the area, and essentially acted like a ridge. I hunted the spot for two days, saw a lot of deer checking scrapes, and missed a chip shot at a nine-pointer that was borderline P&Y.

Classic scrape lines on ridges are the ultimate buck calling cards for bowhunters. I've arrowed a lot of deer by hunting right over scrapes, and prefer a stand that can "cover" three or four scrapes, and hopefully see several others. But well-traveled bowhunter and Ol' Man treestand manufacturer John Louk follows a different ridge rut hunting tactic.

"I love bowhunting scrape lines on ridges during the rut," explains the Mississippi archer. "But I've learned to set stands 50 to 100 yards away from scrapes because a good buck's nose is working overtime—especially on an open hardwood ridge where a deer knows it's vulnerable. It's important to remember that a big buck doesn't have to come up to a scrape to check it. He can wind that scrape from a long way off. For years I mistakenly hunted too close to scrapes, and saw mostly does and small bucks which came to the scrapes. But big bucks running ridges stay back, they work a scrape line from well downwind."

This is important information to ridge bowhunters because wind direction from thermal currents vary a great deal in hilly country. Sometimes the air rises from a draw to a ridge crest, other times the opposite is true. So stand placement near scrape lines on ridges is crucial. It can require hunting "above" scrapes by 50 yards or more in the afternoon . . . a similar distance "below" scrapes in the morning. It all depends on wind direction.

When Louk locates a hot ridge with well-defined scrape and rub lines, he'll set several portable lock-on and ladder stands, hunting various spots according to the wind, and location of bedding areas from which he expects deer to appear as they check scrapes. Further, he's careful in his approach to a chosen stand so as not to spook bedded bucks or does. Sometimes it takes extra effort and a lot of walking to swing above or below a ridge and/or a bedding area to approach a scrape-line stand correctly. This is especially true in hard-hunted country; in places where bucks greatly outnumber does; and in the very early or very late stages of the rut when bucks are more wary than during the peak of the breeding season.

For this reason, ridge hunting over scrapes where wind is fickle is ideal for using climbing treestands. On more than one occasion I've worked into position to climb a ridge tree situated perfectly to a line of hot scrapes only to have the wind silently shift or suddenly notice hill thermals reverse direction. In such cases you've got to reposition your stand or you'll alert deer to your presence—especially the largest, oldest bucks with head gear you want to replant above your home mantle.

Well-known bowhunter Dick Kirby, owner of Quaker Boy Game Calls in New York, is a dedicated ridge hunter during the rut. But he's convinced the bulk of large, primary scrapes are worked at night by dominant bucks, so he usually places bow stands between ridgetop scrapes and bedding areas. The exception is immediately following inclement weather.

"Inclement weather can alter a nocturnal buck's scrape-checking routine, and this can be used to a bowhunter's advantage" he explains. "Every season during the rut, heavy rain or snow, or high winds can last through a night and this forces big, rutting bucks to 'hole up.' When this happens a hunter should be in the woods, on stand near a hot scrape, immediately when the weather clears and calms—especially if it happens at dawn.

"Foul weather at night alters a nocturnal buck's ridge rutting activity. So he's on the move again the moment the weather calms. Be on a ridge, near a scrape line, at that time and you can bet the biggest racks in the county are walking the high country looking for does in estrus. If you're not there you may have missed the best chance of the season for catching a dominant buck on a ridge scrape line during daylight hours."

Veteran hunter Brad Harris with the Lohman Call Company has used mock scrapes to draw dominant bucks to chosen hunting areas for years, and he says there's no better place to set a mock scrape trap for a big buck than on a hardwood ridge near a known buck bedding area.

"I've had excellent success making 'mock scrapes' to draw or pull bucks to specific ridge hunting spots where I can get good shots at them," says the outgoing Missouri hunter. "Bucks scrape along the same ridge trails, so I know where to make 'mock scrapes' from one year to the next. I make scrapes to attract bucks to places I can hunt correctly according to wind and cover. Also a 'mock scrape' can 'turn-on' a buck to scrape at a place before the deer naturally would on its own."

Harris makes a scrape simply by clearing a spot on the ground with a stick. Then he takes an actual "licking branch" from above a real scrape and places it above his "mock scrape." The licking branch has real buck scent, so it convinces deer the mock scrape is natural. Harris is certain to wear rubber boots, rubber gloves, and transports the sawed-off "licking branch" in a plastic bag—all to eliminate human scent.

Brad also touts the use of grunt calls and rattling horns when working ridges for rutting whitetails.

"Calling deer works well almost anywhere during the rut," he explains. "But doing it from a ridgetop is a natural place for a buck to expect another buck to find a doe in estrus, or for a pair of bucks to fight. Sound also carries a long way from a ridge, so you can 'cover' a much larger area for attracting bucks than you can way down in a bottom or creek draw."

Some very good whitetail bowmen I know still refuse to bowhunt ridges. They're so thicket, swamp and bottom oriented that they just can't leave the tangles for open ridge hardwoods. That's understandable to some degree, because most of the time the best place to ambush a buck with a bow is in or near his bedroom, which normally is in the thickest briar-infested tangles available. But when buck necks swell and does begin to sashay like New York fashion models, head for the hills, because that's where all the risqué action is happening. Be there with your bow, or be square.

Tactics at a Glance:

- Bucks in all geographic locations seem to be ridge-oriented during the rut.
- Even in farm country where whitetails have learned to live in standing corn for safety and abundant food, when the rut sets in, bucks scrape and rub on slight ridges between fields.
- Benches on ridgetops can be the ultimate rutting buck gathering spot.
- Ridge hunting over scrapes, where wind is fickle, is ideal for using climbing treestands.

Part Three
Super Strategies of the Experts

A pleasant stroll in the woods, or a few hours hunkered on a stand. That's what whitetail hunting is to many hunters. Sometimes they even bag a deer. The hunters in this section have given up on "wishing and hoping." Their game plans are built around strategies to make something happen. They will use every trick in the book to get the edge on a big buck, and if those stop working they'll be busy inventing some new ones. Get ready for some serious buck-hunting!

17   A Failproof Scent Strategy

BY ROGER BRISKI

This Wisconsin guide's scent tactic is so deadly it could change the way you hunt whitetails for-
ever. The author is a whitetail bowhunting guide whose amazingly consistent whitetail hunting
success prompted him to write this article and share with others the technique he has come to feel
is the ultimate whitetail hunting strategy.

Imagine having a dream where there's a herd of bucks standing at the base of your treestand! "Dream" is the right word, you say to yourself. Because that's the only place such a scene could ever happen!

Well, I'm here to tell you this dream can turn into reality. It now happens to me every year and started, literally, overnight.

The beginning occurred one early-autumn day when my father, brother-in-law and I stood in the woods all morning waiting for that elusive whitetail to pass our treestands. It was the end of September, and I had laid down a scent line of pure unconcentrated doe urine to my stand. I hoped it would pull a six-pointer in that I spotted a few days earlier.

After three hours of deer hunting, the only wildlife we saw were a couple of flocks of geese heading south and many gray squirrels scampering for acorns. Eventually, we abandoned our treestands and concentrated on collecting our limits of bushytails.

At dawn the following day, all three of us entered our same treestands and I immediately grabbed my grunt call and tried to entice in that six-pointer. After honking on my grunt call a few times, I noticed some movement out of the corner of my eye. It was the buck! He was moving fast to my treestand with his head close to the ground. He was grunting like a pig, and his nose was fixed to the doe urine trail I had left the day before. My arrow ripped through his rib cage and he lasted about 250 yards.

Again the following year, my brother-in-law came down the last weekend in September to do some bowhunting. We saturated our clothes full of doe urine and laid down scent trails to our stands. All day, the only things we saw were lots of sunshine and small game. About noon we decided to small game hunt the area and come back the next morning for more bowhunting. The next morning, before entering my treestand, I decided to sprinkle some brush in front of me with doe urine, hoping to lure in any passing bucks. Well, a few minutes passed, and I noticed a nice 10-pointer heading my way with his nose in the air trying to locate the source of the doe urine. He got about six yards away and my arrow made its way through his diaphragm and left lung. He dropped within 70 yards.

As I field-dressed the buck, I thought about where the deer first became visible and I remembered that it was the same area that we had hunted small game the day before. Well, then it hit me like a bolt of lightning—what had been happening to me when I used doe urine or doe-in-heat lures to attract deer.

These facts were very clear to me now:

After I had dispersed the lures in the woods, bucks were coming into the area at night, investigating the source of the scent, relentlessly searching for any prospective does and consequently staying all night until daybreak.

By the way, after I finished field dressing that 10-pointer, I decided to make a one-man drive through the area we had hunted small game the day before. I had a hunch that there would be another buck in the area. I knew that we stunk up the area with doe urine because we sprayed our clothes down with the stuff the previous day prior to deer hunting. While small game hunting, our clothes randomly brushed up against branches, and doe urine scent was inadvertently left as an attractant for any curious bucks.

Well, I made the silent drive toward my brother-in-law, and he developed a quick case of "Buck Fever" and missed a 10-pointer.

I've always used a lot of doe urine and after analyzing my earlier years of bowhunting, the deer action significantly increased the day after I used the lure. Since then, I've developed simple and innovative methods for hunting whitetails by the use of doe urine and doe-in-heat lures that have knocked down my scouting and hunting time from days to literally a few hours.

The number one principle factor behind these strategies and methods is the liberal use and radical distribution of doe urine or doe-in-heat lures the day before hunting and then returning to the area at dawn, the following morning, to hunt.

Deer Hunting's "Liquid Gold"

But, before we get into specific luring tactics I developed with doe urine, hunters should first examine the important role doe urine plays in whitetail communicative abilities, social behaviors and sexual activities. Then, they can realize how powerful of a lure this liquid substance can be—this "liquid gold" I call it.

Understanding basic whitetail social activities, hunters should consider an anthropologist's point of view. When I was a college student at the University of Wisconsin-Eau Claire, we studied which animals (in Wisconsin) resembled the human species in their behavioral and social traits. My favorite anthropology professor, Dr. Barth, claimed that coyotes seemed to be closest to the human race when it came to social behaviors and sexual activities. It has been shown that coyotes have a complex communicative system similar to humans.

But after studying whitetail social and sexual activities—and with respect to Dr. Barth's theories—I believe whitetails tend to resemble the human species more than coyotes. And, like humans, deer also have a complex communicative system.

Whitetails have been shown to communicate with a recorded 12 different vocalizations; plus, they communicate through body language, urine and scent glands.

Also, like humans, whitetails (mainly does) are very social creatures. Likewise, the most important whitetail social trait, deer hunters should remember, when luring deer is: "All whitetails seek the companionship of adult does."

I'm constantly preaching that bucks seek out does (sexual attraction), does seek out does (social attraction) and fawns seek out does (maternal attraction). And they come to each other not only vocally and visually but, also through the communicative ability of scent glands and urine (primarily doe urine).

Since deer have the uncanny ability to communicate with their urine, when a whitetail urinates, the spot where this happens is like a makeshift public bulletin board for other deer. Their urine (combined with glandular scents) may say many things: "I was here!" "Stay away from here!" "I'm horny!" or "Here we are!" When a deer urinates it tells other deer a lot.

Conversely, when hunters use doe urine as a lure, they're not only using it as an attractant for deer, but as a method to communicate with deer. Likewise, a large part of whitetail social and sexual activities are based upon the communicative abilities of doe urine. When a doe goes into heat its urine contains pheromones, a substance produced by does, that tell bucks she is ready to be bred.

How the Rut Affects Scent Tactics

Once we get a few cool nights and shorter daylight hours in September, look out: Bucks have a one-track mind—breeding. I have always contended that a buck's urge for sex is greater than his urge to eat, not unlike men. That's why whitetail bucks lose weight during the fall rut. They spend their time chasing does instead of eating. (Since deer communicate with their urine, bucks use their noses, their strongest sense available, to locate any does in heat.)

Most of the whitetail rut activities are done at night. Most rural farmers witness this each fall. They religiously drive by their fields several times a day and see little deer movement; but, then at the end of October, they'll walk the perimeter of the field only to find loads of scrapes and rubs. These were obviously made at night!

I also believe that with the significant rise in the number of bowhunters over the last 25 years, whitetails, trying to avoid human contact, are restricting their daytime movements, preferring to travel under the cover of darkness. I've talked with many hunters who will shine an area at night and see all kinds of bucks and does; then, to no avail, they'll return to the area to hunt only to find there's no deer to be had. (In large: Whitetails are interacting socially and sexually during the nighttime hours.)

The bottom line is since deer, under the cover of darkness, are engaging in social and sexual activities with the communicative abilities of doe urine, it makes perfect common sense that hunters, in order to make their hunting endeavors more productive during the day, duplicate whitetail activities with the luring (communicative) abilities of doe urine during the night.

Using MORE Scent Makes the Difference!

As a Wisconsin whitetail hunting guide, I've personally noticed two major problems that hunters have with lure applications. First, hunters don't use enough lure. Secondly, when they do use lures, hunters leave the area where they've dispensed the lure too soon, and in most cases the buck shows up after the hunter is heading home to watch football.

Remember, a whitetail's nose is a well refined tool. It's been documented that a deer can smell at least 100 times better than a human. I've even had bucks smell lure (doe urine) through 4 inches of snow.

Another aspect hunters should consider is how much natural deer urine is deposited in the woods each day. For example, say you have a small 40-acre patch of woods that you hunt. Each day, on the average, it is visited by nine deer (primarily does—in buck to doe ratios, does usually exceed bucks). Each deer urinates six ounces in the woods every day. Nine deer times six ounces equals 54 ounces of doe urine deposited in the woods per day. Fifty-four ounces times 365 days equals 154 gallons of urine deposited a year in an average 40 acres of woods.

That's why I'm constantly preaching, "The more lure the merrier." Hunters should liberally apply more lure (mainly doe urine) because they have to compete with the large quantities of urine the deer are naturally depositing in the area. Also, does, like humans, have their own makeshift toilets. If you are observant, you'll find that they will defecate and urinate in specific areas. These areas are called "core" areas. (Remember, deer communicate to each other through their urine.) I've observed these core areas, in my hunting area, to be about 10 to 15 yards in diameter and, because the deer are consistently urinating in the same area, the fine grass will be burned out. (Kind of like when your dog urinates in the backyard, the grass becomes burned out and nothing will grow there.) Remember, bucks under the cover of darkness are stalking the does and they frequent these core areas at night hoping to get lucky.

Not only do bucks check out core areas at night, they'll also investigate scent drippers and mock scraps, but, unfortunately, the bucks will investigate the source of the scent during the night, and then, within a short time, return to their normal rut activities, leaving the hunters skunked the next day, and the bucks long gone.

How to Implement Effective Scent Strategies

Fortunately, there is a solution to these problems of luring deer into my hunting area and keeping them there for a longer duration of time.

The day before I plan to hunt, I'll typically use a small, two-ounce squeeze bottle and radically apply large quantities of doe urine or doe-in-heat to trees, shrubs and the forest floor, in essence creating my own imitation (makeshift) core area which in turn will entice bucks into my hunting area that night. Because bucks will not be able to find any pattern of distribution with the lure, and because they're unable to locate the source of the scent, they'll usually stay interested in the urine-saturated area until morning. (By distributing some lure on trees and shrubs—waist high—not only will it aid in confusing the bucks, it will be elevated enough for any crosswinds to carry the scent for greater distances.)

In each application, I'll distribute one pint to a quart of unconcentrated doe urine or doe-in-heat in a 20 to 50 square yard area of a dense, thicker portion of my hunting land. (During lure distribution, I'll carry a quart of doe urine or doe-in-heat with me and fill the two-ounce squeeze bottle as needed.)

I recommend saturating the thicker, brushier spots in your hunting area for three reasons:

First, thicker, dense areas will physically hold more lure. By walking through the area, swinging my arm left to right, and vice versa, while squeezing the two-ounce squeeze bottle at the same time, I'm able to saturate 20 to 50 square yard areas very quickly and with no distinct pattern.

Secondly, bucks prefer to travel in thicker cover anyway, so luring them into the area poses no problem.

Thirdly, when I saturate thick, wooded areas, it decreases my chances of whitetails in and around the saturated area from spotting me while I'm on route to my treestand the following morning.

I also recommend saturating with doe urine or doe-in-heat minutes before sundown. This way your lure will be fresh during the nighttime hours. (As a general guide, I'll use doe urine the first three or four weeks of bow season. Then, anticipating prime rut, I'll implement doe-in-heat for the remainder of the season.) I'll return early the following morning and hunt near the lure, basically, just out of sight of the saturated area.

For the most part, bucks will stay in and around the saturated area for about 30 minutes after legal shooting time begins or until they realize it's getting too sunny for their liking. So, hunters should be up and at 'em and in their treestands when legal shooting time begins. (Since deer use the cover of darkness to their advantage when they travel, I've had my best luck hunting near saturated areas on cloudy mornings.)

I also recommend bowhunting from treestands 80 to 100 yards away from the saturated area. With the cover of darkness on my side, there's a lesser chance I'll spook any deer around the saturated area when I'm on route to my stand in the morning. Plus, 100 yards seems to be the optimum distance for any sort of grunting and calling. (As foliage decreases during the fall months, hunters should increase the distance between the lure saturated areas and their treestands.)

Whitetails usually exit the saturated area into the wind, so I recommend hunting from stands upwind from the saturated area. It's a little on the dangerous side, and I don't recommend that readers do this, but, before entering the woods, I've had my best luck saturating my clothes with the same lure used in the saturated area. If the bucks happen to smell me on route to my treestand, upwind from the saturated area, or on a down draft from my stand, they'll think I'm one of the does that urinated in the area and, combined with a couple of continuous purrs on a high-pitched grunt call, they will certainly think I'm a doe and head my way.

Calling and Rattling Not Working? They Will Now!

I've talked with many hunters who just have not had any luck calling or rattling in any whitetails. And when it came to using doe urine or doe-in-heat, many hunters haven't even tried the stuff.

Well, the bottom line is a hunter can't grunt or rattle in anything if there's nothing in the area to call in! To make grunting and rattling more effective, again, the day before you plan to hunt (at dusk), just saturate a 20 to 50 square yard-thick wooded area that's just out of sight of your treestand with a pint or more of doe urine. Return the next morning at dawn for some serious action. (In general: Doe-in-heat lures tend to be stronger smelling and more concentrated, so one pint or a little less distributed in a 20 to 50 square yard area is adequate. Pure doe urine lures are usually less concentrated, so I'll typically distribute two pints or more in a 20 to 50 square yard area.)

Don't worry about not seeing any deer. Just make sure you've practiced with your bow and you're in your treestand when legal shooting time begins. I've used this tactic over the last 10 years with such a high success rate that I've only had to return to my hunting area no more than two mornings before bagging and tagging. There have been many occasions where I've stood in my stand and observed not just one, but two or three bucks desperately searching the area for does in heat.

What's more, I'm able to entice deer into my hunting area from thousands of yards away. The luring tactic works so well that I often refer to it as corralling deer into my hunting area. Remembering that deer communicate through their urine and imagining that their noses are like stealth radar, when I saturate 20 to 50 square yard areas of woods (predominately thicker cover areas) with doe urine, it's like a group of does singing into a thousand watt P.A. system and broadcasting "Here, deer!" into all the land around me. Bucks residing in adjacent property I'm unable to hunt (posted land, game preserves or city limits) will investigate the areas saturated with urine or doe-in-heat and, more often than not, they'll stay at least until daybreak relentlessly searching for the source of the scent. (In general: Younger bucks—yearlings—will usually stick around the saturated areas for 30 minutes or longer once legal shooting time begins. Older, more-mature bucks will usually stick around no more than 30 minutes after legal shooting time begins or until they realize there's too much sunlight for them to be out in the open.)

The lure tactic works well when bowhunting rub lines, scrape lines, bottlenecks and staging areas. I already know that bucks (primarily older deer) are working these areas at night and splitting just before daybreak. It's just a matter of saturating a 20 to 50 square yard portion of woods with doe urine or doe-in-heat the day (at dusk) before I plan to hunt. Plus, with rub and scrape lines, there's always a prime spot that's just a little thicker, optimum for lure saturation. (As a general guide, I'll use doe urine for saturating areas in rub line, bottleneck and staging areas. I'll apply doe-in-heat to scrape line areas.)

In one instance, I was bowhunting in a 40-acre bottleneck which was surrounded by scrapes and had a heavily used deer trail that ran east and west through it. After a couple of morning hunting trips to the woods, I noticed that the deer were entering the area at night and splitting, just before daybreak, to a 180-acre plot of woods across an adjacent railroad track. So at quitting time, the last afternoon, I saturated a 50 square yard-thick area located at the east end of the woods with one pint of doe-in-heat.

Minutes before legal shooting time began, I returned to the woods the following morning and entered a treestand about 20 yards off the main trail on the west end of the wooded bottleneck. After nocking an arrow at legal shooting time, I reached for my grunt-call, and after three short grunts it took only seconds before a nice two and a half-year-old buck came prancing down the trail. After bagging the buck, I searched the woods for more deer sign.

Three Key Indications to Watch For

Then and throughout the years, I've used this tactic. I observed three things to be prominent after distributing large amounts of lure (doe urine or doe-in-heat) in the woods the day prior to hunting.

First, unless the area is hit with torrential rainfall, each 20 to 50 square yard area saturated with doe urine or doe-in-heat will be effective for luring deer for up to two weeks. So if you don't make it to your treestand the first morning after saturating an area with lure the previous day, because you forgot to set your alarm clock or your pick-up doesn't want to start, don't be afraid to hunt the area the second or third mornings.

Secondly, you'll notice a drastic increase in the size of scrapes in the area. I've noticed that some scrapes (community scrapes that are used by two or more bucks) will increase from four feet in diameter to an astronomical 10 or 12 feet. Obviously, if bucks in the area think a herd of does has suddenly gone into heat, they will instinctively and frantically work their scrapes.

Thirdly, you'll notice the main trails that deer (primarily bucks) are using during the evening hours to enter and exit the saturated areas turning into well-used mud paths. (Obviously, these scrapes and trails located near your saturated areas are the ones you should be bowhunting the following mornings after lure distribution.)

The luring tactic also works great for bowhunting high-pressure areas like public hunting grounds. If you've spent any time at all hunting in high-pressure areas like this, you probably have observed lots of prime spots loaded with deer sign like rubs, scrapes and well-used trails. But, because of the constant bombardment of small game hunters, whitetails trying to avoid human contact are forced into surrounding lands (posted land) during the daytime hours. Then, with no threat of small game hunters bothering them, whitetails (bucks) will return to public hunting grounds during the nighttime hours and resume normal rut activities.

In order to avoid as many small game hunters as possible, I'll try to hunt high-pressure areas during the middle of the week when most guys are at work. I'll usually arrive at the woods about two or three hours before sundown. This will give me ample time to do some preliminary scouting and find the optimum areas for lure saturation and treestand placement.

Adapting Scent Tactics to Gun-Hunting Seasons

In retrospect, the same lure applications used during bow season can also be implemented during rifle season, although bucks get real skittish once the shooting starts. So, I've found I'll get my best results implementing the lure tactic in larger wooded areas where there's low hunting pressure (200 acres or more). In Wisconsin, with over 500,000 hunters infiltrating the woods, getting access to larger low-pressure hunting areas can be tough.

To increase my chances of bagging Mister Big, I'll typically saturate a 50 square yard area at dusk the day before opening season. I'll saturate the thickest cover possible with a pint of my favorite doe-in-heat lure. Since deer get real edgy during rifle season, I'll try and reduce my chances of deer in and around the saturated area from seeing or hearing me while I'm on route to my stand the following morning by having my treestand no closer than 100 yards from the saturated area. (Remember, as foliage decreases during the fall months, hunters should increase the distance between the lure saturated areas and their treestands.)

While the most practiced method of rifle hunting is making deer drives, hunters should incorporate this luring tactic before making their drives. During the deer rifle season, the day before I plan to hunt (at dusk) I'll typically saturate 20 to 50 square yard areas in 40 and 80 acre wooded plots with doe-in-heat. Not only will bucks respond to the lure, but does and fawns will also respond to lure saturated areas. Deer, like humans, know that there is safety in numbers. Naturally, if a platoon of whitetails is trying to seek safety from the redcoats, they'll bee-line to thick, wooded areas that smell like deer once the roar of rifle season starts. I call these saturated areas deer SAFETY ZONES.

Obviously, these safety zones are defined by large deposits of deer urine, primarily doe urine. The bottom line is, "The more doe urine and doe-in-heat you saturate your woods with, the more deer your hunting party will drive out in the morning." Don't be surprised if your hunting party drives out 20 or more deer (does, bucks and fawns) in the morning. And don't worry about resaturating your hunting areas with doe pee. I've found the areas to be productive for up to two weeks; and in Wisconsin, one dose for every 40 to 80 acres is enough.

Test-Run Your Lures

All lures are not created equal. I've found this to be particularly true with store purchased doe urine and doe-in-heat lures. In most cases, the longer a lure sat on the shelf, the more aged and ammonia based it became. Although ammonia is a natural scent in the woods, whitetails will respond to all lures differently.

I recommend testing your lures before implementing them. I stumbled upon this years ago when, in order to cover my scent, I would apply an ounce of lure to the dirt, then scrape it around with my boots (it's kind of like making a mock scrape without the licking branch). Then I would walk to my treestand hoping to lure any passing bucks down my scent trail. And, of course, when I returned the next morning, I noticed the bucks in the area had entered the woods that night and left their footprints exactly in the middle of the scraped area. You can easily test your lures this way. By making a few mock scrapes in the soft dirt and applying an ounce of different lure in each one, then returning the following day to examine the scrapes, you will be able to see visual evidence of which lure will be most effective in your saturated areas the following nights. In one scrape, apply one brand of doe urine, and in the next scrape apply a different brand of doe-in-heat, etc. (The scrape that has the most deer tracks in it will tell you which lure is most attractive to the deer and will work best for saturating a 20 to 50 square yard area of your hunting land.)

As a general guide, if I plan to hunt a woods in September or October, I'll saturate 20 to 50 square yard areas with pure unconcentrated doe urine. Then, while anticipating prime rut being around the last week in October or the first week in November, I'll implement doe-in-heat.

Summing Up

"Doe urine, doe urine, doe urine." I can't say enough about it. This liquid gold is a valued commodity in my book. When I saturate a portion of my hunting area with doe urine or doe-in-heat, then return the following morning to hunt, and incorporate this tactic with other hunting methods, it enables me to see countless deer—on the average, about one buck every 90 minutes—from the nicest wall hangers to the smallest spikes.

Don't get me wrong: I'm not strictly a morning hunter, but I am a stickler for the use of doe urine no matter what time of the day I'm hunting. Also, I don't spend much time hunting over food sources like corn, bean or clover fields, because frankly, the deer are in control. Granted, a bowhunter will see an ample amount of deer, but waiting for a whitetail to walk in the right place at the right time can be very time consuming and more often than not, unproductive.

I advocate keeping an upper hand on the whitetails in my hunting area by controlling their movements and keeping them congregated in one place for a length of time.

"If you lure, they will come!" That's what I say to any hunter who only dreams of seeing more deer. Chances are you'll increase the number of bucks you see from one or two per week to an astounding 10 or 20 in a week, with the possibility of bagging a trophy. *For More Information, contact Roger Briski, Rog's Guide Service, P.O. Box 134, Altoona, WI 54720; 715/833-0256.*

Coyotes and Scent Lures: An Action-Packed Sideshow!

With falling fur prices over the last 18 years and the consequent reduction in the number of trappers, the population of coyotes in the U.S. has risen significantly. And with the high numbers of coyotes on the prowl comes the problem of feeding all those fur bearing "critters."

Not only do coyotes prey on small animals (their main course), they also include whitetails on their menu. Recent evidence has shown that coyotes will attack and try to kill healthy whitetail deer.

Coyotes have a keen sense of smell, which, I believe, is more sensitive and well-refined than whitetails'. They'll use their noses to locate any potential free lunches and zero in on any area that smells like deer. I've even shot a couple of deer with my bow, and after waiting a few hours before tracking, I've returned to the area only to find them munched on by coyotes.

I first realized how attracted coyotes were to areas of woods that smelled like deer when, years ago, I was hunting a creek bottom that I had saturated with doe-in-heat the day before. From my treestand that morning, I noticed a coyote entering and exiting the saturated area, relentlessly searching for any whitetails.

Since then I've documented some basic behavioral traits of coyotes and how they respond to areas of woods saturated with lure.

First, coyotes are somewhat attracted to doe urine and, on occasion, will investigate areas saturated with the scent. You can expect to see one coyote in every 10 morning hunting trips when using pure doe urine in your saturated areas.

Secondly, coyotes are really attracted to doe-in-heat scents. I say that coyotes are "head over paws" about the stuff. You can expect to see one coyote in every four morning hunting trips when using doe-in-heat in your saturated areas. Coyotes must think does in heat are more vulnerable, or possibly coyotes relate to the smell of doe-in-heat to blood. In any case, seeing coyotes 25 percent of the time during legal shooting hours when using doe-in-heat lures is a lot, since coyotes are notorious nocturnal creatures.

Thirdly, I've noticed that coyotes have a well-defined zigzag search pattern when investigating areas saturated with lure. Once a coyote catches wind of your lure, the general overall direction the coyote will zigzag through the saturated area will depend on the direction of the wind (fox also use the same zigzag search pattern when investigating saturated areas, but they pose no threat to whitetails).

For example, let's say the wind is out of the north. The coyote will more than likely start its search on the southeast or southwest corner of the saturated area. For example's sake, we'll say that the coyote will start the search on the southwest corner. The coyote will then travel straight north through the west side of the saturated area. After traveling straight through the west edge of this area the coyote (now on the northwest corner of the saturated area) will travel east about 20 feet and reverse its search to the south end of this area. After reaching the south end of the saturated area and not finding any deer, the coyote will move over another 20 feet or so to the east and reverse its direction back north through the saturated area. Coyotes will relentlessly search the saturated area with this zigzag pattern until they're satisfied there are no deer in the area to be had.

I believe that coyote populations have reached epidemic levels and too much coyote movement can be detrimental to the success of whitetail hunters.

Fortunately for deer hunters, especially bowhunters, and because coyotes use zigzag search patterns when investigating lure saturated areas, no matter where you have your treestand located, you'll probably get a decent shot at one of those canine creatures. (Check your state's hunting regulations. In many states it is illegal to hunt small game while deer hunting.)

And lastly, like whitetails, coyotes will investigate saturated areas for about 30 minutes after shooting time begins, or until they realize there is too much sunlight for them to be out in the open.

Roger Briski's Tactics at a Glance

Roger Briski's scent strategy calls for spreading BIG amounts of doe urine and doe-in-heat scents in the late afternoon of the day before his hunt. When bucks find the scent trails during their nighttime roaming, they will be unable to pinpoint the location of the does and, frustrated, will remain in the area searching until after daylight. Roger will be on his stand before first light, ready for action at legal shooting time. Bucks that normally would have departed the area before daylight will tend to remain for as much as 30 minutes after sunrise, stalking the scent trails in search of a doe.

18 Deer Calling's Fearsome Foursome

BY GARY CLANCY

Master these four calls, and you'll find yourself sweet-talking whitetails.

Researchers have been able to identify more than 20 different vocalizations used by whitetail deer. Luckily for you and me, we don't need to learn all of them to effectively call deer. In fact, just four will do fine. Learn how and when to use these four vocalizations, and you can call in bucks regardless of where in the country you hunt or when. And get this: You can do it all on one call! Here's the scoop on deer calling's fearsome foursome.

The Call That Does It All

Some calls have plungers like a trumpet. Others have a rubber band that you slip up or down on the reed to change the call's pitch. Still others rely on finger pressure. And there are even some that you can blow from either end or achieve different sounds by inhaling and exhaling. All of these calls fall under the category of variable-tone, or adjustable, grunt calls, and they are the most versatile deer calls on the market; the only calls you'll need to produce are the four vocalizations we are going to discuss. Hunter's Specialties, Lohman, MAD, Quaker Boy, Primos, Woods Wise, Rod Benson, Burnham Brothers and Knight & Hale all make adjustable grunt calls. I've used most of them. My favorite is the Tru-Talker from Hunter's Specialties. With this call, you simply use your trigger finger to depress a reed to change the pitch of the call. No other call I've used does the job of the Tru-Talker when it comes to making authentic-sounding buck grunts and doe bleats.

But no matter which brand you choose, it is to your benefit to practice with the call until you can make all four of the vocalizations covered in this article. Grunt calls are so easy to use that most hunters don't bother practicing with them as they do with turkey calls or elk bugles, and this is a mistake that will cost them opportunities at deer. It doesn't take nearly as much practice to become adept at making these four vocalizations as it does to learn to yelp, cluck and purr on a slate call, for example, but it does take some familiarization with the call.

The best way to learn to make the following four calls is to purchase an audio tape and then mimic the actual vocalizations produced on the tape. Or if you've spent a lot of time in the places whitetails call home, you've probably heard deer make all four of these vocalizations and will be able to reproduce them from memory without much difficulty.

The Contact Grunt

The contact grunt is a short, soft, singular, low-volume grunt that sounds like *uurrp*. Both bucks and does make the contact grunt, but bucks make it more often than does and are more responsive to it than does. The contact grunt has nothing to do with the rut, and it is not a verbal sign of aggression. In "whitetailese," the contact grunt is probably just a way of asking, "Anyone else around?"

When one buck hears another buck make a contact grunt, the first buck will often wander over to investigate. Luckily for us, whitetails are curious critters, and the contact grunt is one way that we can use this curiosity to our advantage.

I normally use the contact grunt on deer that are in sight but out of range. Typically, I will wait for a deer to stop before grunting at it, because it is difficult for a deer to hear a soft contact grunt over the sound of its own footsteps. Once I have the deer's attention, I don't call again unless it loses interest and wanders off line. Deer are not as adept at pinpointing the source of a sound as, say, a wild turkey or coyote, but they're not too bad, either. If you call to a deer after it's headed your way, you greatly increase the risk of being picked off.

When a buck comes to a contact grunt, he normally strolls in very relaxed. This is probably because, like I said earlier, there is no aggression in the call, so the buck is not expecting any trouble.

When hunting in the timber, I've used contact grunts to bring bucks right under my treestand for easy shots. But when hunting field edges, cut-overs, meadows or natural woodland openings, I've had problems with bucks coming to within 50 to 100 yards and then hanging up. The reason is that they know they should be able to see the other deer. This is where a decoy really shines; but if you're not using a decoy, resist the urge to call while a deer is facing your way. Just let the deer stand there as long as it wants. Eventually, it will decide to proceed, or it will turn around and walk away. If it turns to walk away, I immediately hit it with another grunt. About half the time, this will convince the deer to come closer for another look.

The contact grunt is used by bucks all year, but it is most effective early in the bow season. Once bucks start feeling their oats and preparing for the upcoming breeding season, the following three vocalizations are more effective than the contact grunt.

The Doe Bleat

I'll be the first to admit that for many years after I began calling deer, I had no time for a doe bleat. I know now that my shortsightedness cost me some opportunities at good bucks. There are times when a doe bleat used by itself is the most effective vocalization you can use. But most of the time I use a doe bleat to add authenticity to my tending and trailing grunts, which I'll discuss later. My theory on this is that anytime I call, there might be a buck just out of sight that happens to be a little reluctant to come into the sound of another buck grunting. Maybe the buck has had his butt kicked recently or perhaps he's been called in and shot at. Whatever the reason, I know that there are bucks that refuse to budge for a straight line of buck talk, but just can't help themselves when a few doe bleats are thrown in. The biggest buck I've ever taken with a bow ignored my best buck grunts, but turned on a dime and came marching in when I hit him with a couple of doe bleats.

There are "soft" doe bleats and "loud" doe bleats. Soft doe bleats are great for calming down deer or for getting the attention of a doe or fawn, but when it comes to actually calling in a buck, the loud doe bleat, which is often referred to as an "estrous bleat," is the vocalization to use. I've heard it said many times that the estrous bleat is a doe's signal that she is in desperate need of servicing. I'm not going to say this is never the case, but most of the times I've heard a doe use the loud bleat, she's been doing her best to get away from a hard-charging buck.

The loud doe bleat sounds more like a lamb than anything else. Try mixing in a few with your tending and/or trailing grunts, and see whether it makes a difference in your response rate. You can make a doe bleat on most adjustable grunt calls, or you can use one of those "calls in a can" like those made by Primos and Quaker Boy. Either works well.

The Trailing Grunt

This is the whitetail vocalization that many hunters have heard bucks make in the wild. The trailing grunt is the vocalization a buck makes when he is scent-trailing an estrous doe. Sometimes the doe will be right in front of the buck; other times the buck will be walking nose to the ground, trailing the doe.

Like the contact grunt, the trailing grunt is a short grunt, but the trailing grunt differs in that it is used in series and is louder than the contact grunt. It sounds something like this: *uurrp-uurp-uurp-uurp-uurp-uurp-uurp-uurrp-urp-urp-uurp-uurp.* When calling blind—with no deer in sight—I usually use a series of a dozen to more than 20 grunts, all the while slowly swiveling my head to give the impression of a deer on the move. Often I'll mix in a few doe bleats, as well. If I have a deer in sight, I call only long enough to get the deer's attention. Once I have its attention, I quit calling.

No two bucks act the same when trailing a hot doe. I've watched bucks trail a hot doe for hundreds of yards without uttering a single grunt, and I've watched others cover the same distance—sometimes on the same track—grunting each time a front hoof hits the ground. Maybe deer are like people; some just talk more than others. The good news is that because each buck is different, there is really no right or wrong way to make the trailing grunt. The only real mistake you can make is not to use this deadly call. I've lost count of the number of bucks I've called in with the trailing grunt. I do know that if I were forced to rely on only one vocalization for the rest of deer hunting, this would be the one I'd choose.

The Tending Grunt

Most magazine articles, books and videos on calling deer don't differentiate between the trailing grunt and the tending grunt, but I believe there's a definite difference between them and, more important, that other deer are aware of this difference.

The trailing grunt is uttered by bucks that are either scent-trailing does or sight-chasing does that won't stand for them. The tending grunt is, as the name implies, used by bucks that are tending an estrous doe. The trailing stage is over now. The buck is now tending to the doe, servicing her repeatedly and protecting her from other would-be suitors. A buck will tend a doe until she is no longer in estrus; then he will go off in search of another receptive female.

The tending grunt is very guttural, often long and drawn out, and often loud by whitetail standards. It is an aggressive call. I don't know how to explain it, but whenever I hear a buck make a tending grunt, it sounds like that buck is not a happy camper. Something has that buck disturbed, and he is voicing his displeasure. Sometimes it is because the doe is trying to make another escape. Often it is because another buck has shown up.

However, because there are as many variations of tending grunts as there are individual bucks, I cannot begin to tell you how you should make the call. I don't make the tending grunt the same each time I use it. Sometimes I go with a long, drawn-out *uuurrrrrrrrrrrrrrrrrrrrr,* more of a growl than a grunt, with a few doe bleats thrown in for good measure. Most often I opt for something like: *urrrrrpp . . . . uuurrrrrrrrrrrrp . . . . uuuuuuuuurrrrrrrrr . . . . uuuurrrr . . . . uuurrrrp.* Mix it up, experiment, have fun and remember: You can't make a wrong sound when it comes to tending grunts.

So get yourself an adjustable grunt call, practice until you can make these four vocalizations, and then get ready to enjoy your best season yet on whitetails. For more in-depth information on calling deer, check out Gary Clancy's most recent book, Rattling, Calling & Decoying Whitetails. *Autographed copies are available for $20 postpaid from Out There, 412 4th St. N.W., Byron, MN 55920.*

19   The Art of Seduction

BY BOB ROBB

Hunters who use buck grunts not doe bleats are forgetting one major fact: For most of the season, it's easier to seduce a big buck into bow range than to challenge him there!

In today's information age, whitetail hunters have been bombarded with a ton of information on deer calling. We're told that deer make at least 20-some different grunting sounds and are shown how to imitate them all. We're told that banging horns together during the pre-rut will bring bucks galloping to our stands. In recent years, virtually all deer-calling emphasis has been placed on imitating buck sounds during the various stages of the rut. When the timing is right and you find the right buck with the right attitude, these sounds can work magic. Then throw decoys and scent products into the mix and all of a sudden whitetail hunting is incredibly complex.

That's why, in recent years, I've gone back to using a small variety of simplistic doe bleats as my primary calling technique. You don't hear much about bleating these days. I guess it's too simple a technique in a high-tech world that wants more complex things. Yet it's worked well for me in different regions of the country, both in and out of the rut and in weather conditions ranging from really hot to bitterly cold.

Why Doe Bleats?

Grunting and rattling as the way to take mature bucks has long overshadowed doe bleating. In fact, most deer hunters believe bleating will only draw in does and small, immature bucks—which it will. At times, though, bleating can be the ticket to pulling a big buck to your stand when other techniques will not.

"Most deer hunters have no idea what a powerful tool a bleat-type call can be," said Jerry Peterson, president of call maker Woods Wise, Inc., and himself a very successful buck hunter who has been calling deer since the 1960s. "There's a time and a place to grunt and rattle, but if you are a one-technique person, you're restricting yourself to only 10 percent of the available calling opportunities," Peterson said. How so? "With today's super-long whitetail seasons, there is a ton of hunting open before and after the pre-rut and rut periods, when grunting and rattling are most effective. The addition of bleating, which deer may respond to all year around—including the peak breeding period—opens up a whole new world of calling."

During the 1999 mid-November peak of the rut, I was hunting with Heartland Outfitters in west-central Illinois's famed triangle of Brown, Adams and Pike counties when the weather set record-high temperatures daily. This turned the action for most whitetail hunters ice cold. Yet I saw racked bucks daily, including the typical 10-pointer I arrowed that gross-scored 180 Pope & Young points. My secret? Deer calling. That means I grunted them up, right? Nope. Instead I drew these bucks in with a series of doe bleats, in effect seducing, not challenging, them.

Does Grunt and Bucks Bleat

According to David Hale, half of the well-known Knight and Hale game-calling team, one misconception people have is believing that bucks make one basic sound, while does make another. "Let's start by categorizing what deer sounds do," Hale said. "First, contact-type calls are made by both bucks and does, from early life through maturity. The truth is that bucks and does share a common language. Bucks bleat as well as grunt, and does grunt as well as bleat. Both combine basic bleat, grunt and snort sounds, making small inflections in each, to give them different meanings in their common language." Deer hunters should remember that whitetails are social animals, and except during the rut, when bucks hate each other's guts, they all want to belong to a group. For example, researchers have identified a soft doe grunt as the call used by a doe to call a young fawn. "This same basic call, only louder, is the sound used by a mature buck as he pursues a doe during the rut," Peterson said. "The buck is still saying, 'Come to me,' but he says it with a more forceful inflection, more like 'Come To Me!' "

Variations of the Basic Bleat

There are several variations of the basic doe bleat, but they are so close in nature that trying to change the basic sound into another is often counterproductive. "Does are like bucks—they all make different sounds, depending on their personalities," Hale said. "I find that doe calling is most effective when you have isolated animals. If a doe is by herself, most of the time she is hunting for companionship. That's why when I use a doe call, I pretend I am a lone doe trying to call another deer to me. It might be I'm looking for another doe, but I might be looking for a buck, too." This is especially true during the pre-rut and rut periods, when a variation of the basic bleat that Peterson calls the "breeding bellow" can work wonders.

"The 'breeding bellow' is a high-to-low moaning-type sound, lasting almost a second, used when an estrous doe is trying to call a buck to her now, telling him she's ready for breeding," Peterson said. "The breeding bellow is an excellent choice for calling during the rut, because it is saying that a doe is ready to be bred, she will be receptive to a buck's advances and there are no other bucks tending her at the moment."

After Peterson explained the ins and outs of the breeding bellow to me, I gave it a serious try. Despite the hot weather, in six days I "bellowed up" four bucks, including the 180-inch deer I shot and a big 140-class eight-pointer that picked up my cameraman, Dan Larsen, and me in our tree before I could draw and release.

Matching Calls to the Stages of the Rut

Selecting the right call to match the various stages of the rut is important, too. Because the actual dates of the peak of the rut may vary from year to year in a given area, learning to "read" both the deer and the sign you're seeing will help you. Peterson's formula is simple: When the scrapes are active and most doe tarsal glands are white, the pre-rut is on. When the scrapes are abandoned and doe tarsal glands become black, the does are in estrus and the peak of the rut is on. He chooses his calls accordingly.

"A doe's tarsal glands are good indicators of the position of the rut," Peterson noted. Tarsal glands are located on the inside of a deer's rear legs, near the knee joint. "Early on, they're pure white. As estrus approaches, the center of the gland begins to get dark, with a lighter outer ring. That means the pre-rut is starting up. When the tarsals get completely dark and matted, the rut is on and is ready to peak. I use binoculars to help me see this and keep accurate field notes to track the activity."

Scrapes are important, too. "During the pre-rut, when only five to 10 percent of the does are in estrus, there are new, active scrapes everywhere," Peterson said. "This is an indicator that bucks are looking for, but not necessarily finding, estrous does. When the scrapes go cold, that tells you that bucks have begun finding hot does, and the rut is progressing toward its peak. When the scrapes are active and tarsal glands white, grunting and rattling will work best. But when the tarsals darken and the scrapes go cold, I use only doe calls."

At the end of October last fall in western Saskatchewan, the pre-rut was cranking up. Bucks were scraping like crazy and starting to actively rub. The doe tarsal glands were still white, however, and the bucks I saw up close and personal were just beginning to become interested in them, chasing and scent-checking every doe they could find in the hopes one would be in estrus early. When I saw this activity, I switched from grunting to doe bleats, with excellent results. I called up three bucks in the 110 to 130 class, but since I came to this big-buck Mecca looking for "Big Tobey," I never nocked an arrow.

Are Your Bucks Rattled to Death?

Given the number of bowhunters in today's woods, what are the chances a buck in your area has not heard more than his share of other hunters grunting and rattling to their heart's content? The odds are most of the bucks that have responded to this cacophony of sounds have either already been shot at or spooked enough that they might be a bit leery about coming in the next time. The survivors are deer that have been smartened up. Because there are so few bowhunters regularly using bleat calls, the odds are better that your calling will not spook these surviving deer right off the bat.

That's not to say that grunting and rattling are worn-out tactics that have gone the way of the rotary telephone. At the right time, they will certainly still produce lots of shot opportunities at bucks large and small. I know I'm not throwing my grunt tubes and rattle bags out the door just yet. Still, my bleat calls will continue to get the lion's share of attention. While grunting and rattling can work magic during a brief window during the pre-rut and rut, for all-season success nothing works like doe sounds.

20   Rattling's Best-Kept Secrets

*Minnesota whitetail expert Jeff Murray has never believed that rattling was only effective in
Texas, where it was originally perfected. And he has bagged the bucks to prove it!*

President Harry Truman's famous plaque on his desk read: "The buck stops
here." It would be nice if that timeless adage applied unilaterally to deer
hunters. Of course, it doesn't. Which is OK because near-misses and close
calls are what good deer stories are made of. Right? Not always! The best
stories involve hunters using grit and ingenuity to outwit elusive whitetails. So if
you're like me, you've probably had it with close shaves. You want to see more victory cigars than "coulda, shoulda" hunts.

Although we'll never get to 100 percent, there are some pitfalls hunters can
avoid to improve their odds. I could write a book on the subject (and, in fact, am
doing just that), but I'll limit the scope of this discussion to rattling. After all, who
doesn't have a heartbreaking rattling tale to tell? Simply put: No other hunting
tactic provides as many close encounters that start out rosy and end up discourag-
ing in a matter of moments.

Where to Rattle

Before I get to the cure for rattling's inherent shortcomings, I want to lay a foun-
dation for success. After all, there's no sense building on shaky footings.

First and foremost, hunters need to put themselves in position to score. Rattling doesn't work everywhere, according to top Canadian guide and outfitter
Terry Neely. "Up here [in Manitoba] rattling can be very effective because the
deer herd is pretty balanced," Neely said. "If we had, say, five or 10 does for every
buck, rattling would be a waste of time because there wouldn't be any competition
for receptive does. So you have to confine serious rattling to places where the
buck-to-doe ratio is balanced. I prefer even odds, but two does for every buck is
acceptable and certainly no more than three or four to one."

Southern deer hunters can certainly vouch for this. Unbalanced Dixie deer
herds not only strip hunters of the ability to use aggressive rattling tactics effectively, but rut lures and grunt calls are also less productive where deer populations
are out of whack. So if you have to travel a considerable distance to hunt balanced
whitetail populations, do it. Rattling will take on a whole new meaning.

Next, rattling is a tremendous long-distance call, but even though the sound carries far, it's pointless to rattle diligently where no bucks can hear you. This sounds elementary, but hunters often stumble over this rather simple rule.

Ironically, my all-time favorite area to rattle isn't a particular place. Sure, you want to pick a spot where bucks are likely to hang out during hunting hours, such as security cover, doe bedding areas and traditional travel corridors. But you can do a lot better, according to Neely. "A well-kept secret among accomplished rattle-hunters is doing everything possible to get close to a buck that's on his feet rather than one that's bedded down for the day," Neely said. "I mean, the difference is night and day. It seems a bedded buck gets into a sort of bunker mentality; he just doesn't want to budge once he's curled up and safety dominates his thinking."

"On the other hand, a buck on his feet is vulnerable, especially during critical periods of the rut. He may be heading directly for his bed when he encounters your [calling] session, but as long as he's up and around, you've got a good chance of turning him. Getting him within bow range is another matter . . ."

Ah, now we're beginning to narrow down the real estate. As mentioned, the three classic areas where hunters tend to set up are security cover, doe bedding areas and traditional travel corridors, but of the three, only two make sense—and only one of those is an odds-bust. Which one? The answer is travel corridors, with doe bedding areas being a close second. Learn to confine serious rattling sessions to where bucks move, and you'll call more of them in. It's that simple. Neely is 100 percent correct. This means any rattling strategy should be based on locating where bucks spend a lot of time coming and going, typically along natural funnels and terrain features between primary food sources and preferred bedding areas. It's a familiar tune, no doubt, but too many hunters overlook it as they seek to hunt near hot buck sign such as rubs and scrapes.

Don't overlook doe bedding areas, either; they're always good for a few well-chosen treestands. "I hunt doe bedding areas almost exclusively during the pre-rut," said Mike Bonner, a Kansas bowhunter with a dozen Pope & Young-class bucks on his wall. "I find that bucks can get real antsy waiting for does to come into estrus at this time of year. [The bucks] seem to know when it's time, but does don't always cycle when they're supposed to. One 'trick' bucks use to keep tabs on does is circling downwind of their bedding areas to scent-check them. Sometimes the bucks bust right in and kick up the does for a better whiff. It's real fun to watch; I've seen it many times. You just don't want to [set up] too close, or the does will relocate and you'll have to start all over."

Indeed, when does sense too much pressure they tend to bed in areas that are either more difficult to penetrate or deeper inside cover. Does, for the most part, don't bed as high as bucks, nor as far from primary food sources such as croplands or acorns; be careful when scouting doe bedding areas and err on the conservative side when determining where to locate.

Rattling several hundred yards downwind from these bedding areas works for the obvious reason that sooner or later a buck will show up. But rattling here, as opposed to areas where bucks are just completing their daily circuits, is trickier because you must be extra-careful with access routes. Go the proverbial (and sometimes literal) extra mile to leave doe bedding areas undisturbed.

A final option that's worked exceptionally well for me through the years is what I call "the corner-cutter." I've successfully rattled in bucks during the early fall, the fevered pitch of the rut and just after the rut when a blanket of snow covered the ground. Regardless of the time of year, bucks will take the quickest route to their destination from their point of origin. So all I do is figure out where bucks and does are bedding—which is never together, with the noted exception of a buck tending an estrous doe—and slip in between. Exactly where, however, depends on the topography. Invariably, I look for obvious terrain features that shape the way bucks travel. It may be a steep bluff or a river bend, the head of a deep hollow or a ridge point. If I've done my homework, I'll surely catch a buck off guard as he works overtime traveling between doe bedding areas to find a hot date.

I particularly like the corner-cutter option during the twin peaks of the rut—just before and after the majority of does enter estrus—because of the accelerated buck movement. Pick key funnels and let the bucks come to you. Of course, if you can double up, such as where two points come together or where a ridge separates two ravines, all the better.

Rattling Basics

Now that you're in position, it's time to call the right play. One helpful accessory is a grunt call. Many bucks have been rattled in just out of range and needed additional coaxing. Though bucks don't make "tending grunts" while duking it out, a timely grunt following a rattling sequence can make a difference. Start with an authentic-sounding call that can be adjusted for volume and tonality. Next, stick to the following rules:

- Never call if the buck is gaining ground.
- Never call if the buck is facing your direction.
- Never call the same way (tone, duration, intensity) every time.
- Always call if the buck is losing ground or interest.
- Always call louder if the buck appears to ignore your first attempt.
- Always call softer the closer a buck gets.

Recent additions to the trusty tending grunt merit further consideration. The snort-wheeze is a sound rutting bucks make when they're unusually aggressive. This is a "lure of last resort," as is the so-called aggravated grunt that can be either a bellow or a deep, elongated ticking sound. Before I get to the fine points of rattling, keep in mind the following. Always rattle:

- Regardless of the time of fall ("tickling" antlers is more effective apart from the rut than hunters realize).
- Aggressively during the rut, particularly during the pre-rut and post-rut "trolling" stages when competition for breeding rights is keen.
- Conservatively if you call in a lot of adolescent bucks; one could eventually peg you and blow your cover.

Never rattle:

- For "the heck of it." Always expect results and be prepared to shoot at the drop of a hat.
- At a buck facing your direction.
- At a buck traveling toward you.

Advanced Rattling Tactics

How skilled do you have to be to replicate a pair of bucks banging headgear? With two glaring exceptions, I believe that technique is over-rated. Last fall I had an experience while hunting with J&S Trophy Hunts in southern Iowa that showed that technique isn't everything.

I'd timed the rut just right and managed to score on a nice 5x5 in spite of unusually hot weather, which severely restricted daytime buck movement. But one evening in camp one of the hunters complained about "another hunter setting up too close" and "rattling too often." I had a hard time swallowing the notion that the outfitter, Steve Shoop, would compromise any hunter's chances. (Shoop has earned my respect as the best in the business.) So I asked a few questions.

"How do you know it was a hunter rattling and not real bucks fighting?" I asked.

"Because the guy was obviously using a set of those fake plastic antlers," snapped the hunter.

"Really?"

"No doubt about it. The sound was tinny, and it didn't let up all morning."

The hunter was dead wrong. I spared his ego by not telling him I was the closest hunter to him that morning and that I'd glassed a pair of bucks fighting off and on from dawn till almost noon. So the question begs: If this guy can't tell the real thing, how can he reproduce it?

This anecdote also raises another common stumbling block: Hunters simply don't rattle enough when the rut's on! Forget the standard advice that too much rattling will "give your position away." Baloney. Rattling is a natural sound during the breeding season. Besides, bucks aren't capable of reasoning. There's too much fighting going on around here; must be hunters trying to fool me. If you're going to rattle, rattle.

But rattling is more than banging a pair of main beams together. When I rattle, I mostly grind. Surely you've heard the stories of bucks "locking up" for extended periods, and each year bucks are found dead because they couldn't unlock their antlers. The fact is, when bucks go head to head, they mostly push and shove, with intermittent head-shaking. This is the sound you want to emulate, not just the initial crack of antlers. So make sure that grinding—twisting antlers together rather than smashing them—is your main goal.

In spite of all these precautions, however, chances are you'll end up rattling in a buck that stops short. This is especially common when bowhunting. The cause is as obvious as the cure. According to Pope & Young statistics, about 80 percent of all record-book bucks are harvested from treestands. As a result, most rattling sessions are done from above. This is a good start—but a poor finish.

If you rattle from a treestand, here's what usually happens. A buck picks up on the noise and either closes ground or circles—likely both. Because of your elevated position, however, the buck won't be able to pinpoint your exact location, so he'll hang up a comfortable distance away to wait for additional clues. A timely grunt call might help, but what the buck really wants to hear are the sounds made by rivals squaring off. After all, the main reason rattling can be so deadly is that bucks intuitively know they can often steal a doe when fighting bucks are distracted. Meanwhile, you're pinned in your treestand because any movement will tip off the buck.

The solution is doing a Mr. Bow Jangles impersonation. Bowhunter extraordinaire Mike Weaver taught me the value of dangling a pair of antlers tied together and suspended on a rope, then jangling them together. "Thanks to 'jangling,' " he said, "I arrowed four Pope & Young bucks that otherwise would have gotten away." For the record, that's four book deer in Weaver's amazing collection of 33!

Jangling works because it gives the bucks something to zero in on. But you must be careful when dealing with hung-up bucks. For starters, it's a good idea to store your antlers at the base of your tree rather than a limb at arm's reach. Rig up a rope from your treestand so you can dangle the antlers at ground level. Do most of your rattling from on high, each time returning the antlers to the ground, rather than the other way around.

A final trick is mixing the sound of rattling with that of rustling leaves; just let out more rope and "skip" the antlers on the ground. If the immediate area is bare earth, by all means import leaves—and you may just be able to rustle in a buck!

Rattling is one of deer hunting's classic mysteries. Although it isn't difficult to master, it sure is easy to screw up.

21　A Season to Remember

BY THOMAS L. TORGET

In 1996 Chuck Adams arrowed 12 Pope & Young-class trophies—far more than any bowhunter has ever tagged in a single season. The following spring Tom Torget interviewed Adams. Here's the remarkable story.

Every bowhunter shares The Dream: tag a Pope & Young-class buck, bull or bear. For most of us, however, that dream is all we will ever have. Truth be told, the average archer lacks the hunting savvy, shooting skill and bulldog determination usually required to generate the "luck" needed to achieve such a feat.

As an outdoor writer I've interviewed hundreds of successful bowhunters. I have yet to meet one who is harder-working or more determined to succeed in the field than Chuck Adams. If ever a man deserved the label "hunting fool," it is Adams.

His list of bowhunting accomplishments reads like no other. Adams is the first bowhunter in history to tag all 27 North American big-game animals, a feat he completed in 1990. His trophies include the current world-record mountain caribou, the former world-record Coues deer and the former world-record sitka blacktail deer. His trophy list totals an incredible 77 animals that qualify for the Pope & Young Club record book, far more than any other bowhunter.

Through his 32 years of bowhunting, however, no single season was as memorable as last year. Between July 17, 1996, and January 19, 1997, Adams arrowed 12 animals that qualify for the P&Y record book, a feat no other bowhunter comes close to matching.

"I have only one explanation for what happened," laughs Adams. "The stars were lined up just right for me! I never set out to do this, I didn't hunt more days than normal and I didn't hunt any harder than normal. I was just fortunate enough to have good shooting opportunities at mature animals all season long. It was a great experience and one that will probably never happen to me again."

Adams' season began in Colorado in mid-July and moved to Alaska, Quebec, Montana, Illinois and finally Texas in late December. He spent some 60 days stalking game on both public and private land, sometimes with an outfitter, sometimes not. We interviewed Adams to learn the details of this remarkable season to remember.

Tell us how your 1996 hunting season got started.

Adams: My first hunt was in northern Colorado with outfitter Phil Phillips. Colorado has the earliest pronghorn season and it's part of the state's "Ranching for Wildlife" program. The hunting is exclusively on private property managed for the state by outfitters like Phillips. The season opened July 13 and I planned to hunt five days.

Were you hunting from pit blinds at waterholes?

Adams: Yes. It was a very dry year in Colorado and the pronghorns were really flocking to the water. I've hunted with Phillips five times and I've killed pronghorns at waterholes and by stalking them. But I've never seen them come to water like they did that year. The hunting was absolutely terrific. I must have passed up 75 solid Pope & Young bucks that were within 20 yards of my blind before I finally shot one. I was looking for a big one and on the last afternoon of my hunt I shot a buck at 14 yards. He scored just under 72 inches, well above the P&Y minimum of 64. Pronghorn hunting is a lot of fun and it's great to get the hunting season started in July.

Where was your next stop after Colorado?

Adams: In mid-August my dad and I headed to Alaska for three weeks of hunting sitka blacktail deer. It was the third year that we've made the trip and dad and I really enjoy hunting and camping up there. Dad's 69 years old and he hunts with a .300 magnum rifle and we can hunt together because there's no separate bow season. We draw a four-mile radius around camp and he hunts inside the circle and I hunt outside. It works out great.

You've killed 19 P&Y-class Sitka blacktails, which is more than any other bowhunter. What is it that makes that species so attractive to you?

Adams: It's just fun to bowhunt on Kodiak Island in August. It's a great time of year up there because the brown bears are down at ocean level on the salmon streams. The deer are up high at 2,500 feet, so you don't have the conflicts that occur later in the season when many of the bears return to higher elevations. I like to spot and stalk and with four tags in my pocket I can do a lot of hunting. In the high country on Kodiak you can see for miles and I really like walking the ridgelines and spotting bucks with my binoculars and then stalking into bow range. I managed to shoot four bucks and all of them made the P&Y minimum of 65. I killed my first one August 18 and my last one September 1. Kodiak Island is notorious for bad weather any time of year and we were tent-bound a third of the time due to rain and fog. That's one reason I like to go up there for about three weeks.

How good were the bucks you killed?

Adam: I saw quite a few deer and I was picky about which ones I shot. One was the second-best Sitka deer shot during the last P&Y, two-year scoring period. It was a nice 4x4 that scored 101⅛. The Sitka deer really got hammered by the winters in the late '80s and early '90s and they're just now starting to come back. Compared to whitetails and muleys, Sitka are small-antlered deer. The P&Y minimum is 65, same as the Coues deer. So any buck that exceeds 100 is a very good trophy.

Your next stop was Canada for caribou?

Adams: Right. In early September I joined three friends from Easton USA on a bowhunt for Quebec Labrador caribou. I hunted with Peter Weaver, who's president of Easton, Randy Schoeck, Easton's marketing manager, and Mike Day, who works in personnel.

We hit the migration dead center. It was my fourth caribou hunt in that area and two of those trips were really tough because the animals were scarce and we really had to scratch to find bulls. Another year it was very good, but I found out last September just how good caribou hunting can be. I saw over 2,000 bulls in six days and I shot two of the best six that I saw. The other four I couldn't get to because they were too far away.

Were you hunting near water?

Adams: No, we didn't hunt on water. There were some lakes in the area but we were basically hunting tundra country. The first one I shot was 18 yards away. I spotted him coming toward me and jockeyed for position and got behind some rocks. The other one I shot at 35 yards. He was with 11 other bulls and he got off the migration trail and started feeding up a little draw. I managed to get within bow range and take him. Those were my two best-scoring Quebec caribou. One scored 363⅝ and the other scored 343⅜.

So it's still early September and you've already got seven record-book kills! Where to next?

Adams: Later that month I went hunting for mule deer near the town of Broadus in southeastern Montana. I really enjoy going after muleys because they're tough to bowhunt on foot, which is the way I like to hunt. And a trophy muley has such big antlers.

My buck last year was killed on the Keefer Ranch, which is outfitted by Rob Arnaud. They have about 6,000 acres of alfalfa fields on the ranch and the deer bed in the high country and come down to feed in the fields in the evening. The ranch takes 15 to 20 hunters each season and I'd hunted it the year before and took a real nice typical 4x4 with a 28-inch spread.

How long did it take you to locate a trophy muley?

Adams: Actually, that trip turned out to be one of my shortest hunts ever. On my first morning there I watched several good bucks leave the alfalfa fields and go into a patch of timber high on the adjoining mountain. They never came out, so I knew they'd stay there and work their way back down that afternoon. I picked out an area I thought they might move through and I guessed right. About 5 p.m. I saw this nice 5x6 buck coming my way and I managed to get into some thick cover and wait for him. When he stepped into an opening in the brush I let fly and I nailed him good. It was just one of those times when I played a hunch about where I thought I could intercept a buck and it worked out perfectly. He scored an even 158 and was a nice, high-horned buck. His rack wasn't very wide, but it had good mass.

Where to next?

Adams: My next hunt was for elk and it was also in eastern Montana. I was on public land and I hunted 12 days. The Montana elk season usually opens the first Saturday in September and runs to about October 15. I killed my bull October 10 and he was the second biggest bull I saw in almost two weeks of hunting. He was a heavy-horned 6x6 and he scored 305⅞.

Did you bugle him in?

Adams: No, and I don't think it's really feasible to call in a six- or seven-year-old bull that's been hunted hard. You can sometimes get him to answer your bugle, but he just won't come to you. I've found that I can bugle in younger bulls but not the really mature ones. What I do is locate them at a distance by glassing or calling and getting them to answer. Then I stalk them. That's how I got this one.

So now it's mid-October and you've tagged nine P&Y animals. Must be time to go after whitetails.

Adams: Exactly. I went to Illinois to hunt in November but I didn't have any luck. I hunted hard for a week and I passed up several bucks in the 100 to 115-class. But things just didn't work out and I never saw a really good buck. So it looked like my good luck might be running out. But then I went down to South Texas in late December and I got back on track again.

Was this your first bowhunt for South Texas whitetails?

Adams: I'd hunted down there once before in 1980 and had terrible luck, and I'd also hunted several times in the Texas Hill Country. One thing I've learned is that every deer in that state is absolutely wired! Hunting whitetails in South Texas is especially tough for bowhunters because the terrain is so flat and brushy and there are almost no trees that you can hang a stand in. Rifle hunting isn't particularly difficult, but getting into bow range is a real challenge.

The peak of the rut in South Texas is around the end of December. Is that why you went there when you did?

Adams: Yes. I arrived December 27 and planned to hunt for 12 days because that's when the biologists told me to expect the peak of breeding activity. Unfortunately, the weather was very warm when I arrived and the bucks just weren't moving very much. Daytime temperatures were in the 80s and I hunted through January 4 without seeing a single decent buck. The warm weather seemed to shut down any breeding-related movement during daylight.

You said it's impractical to hunt from tree-stands in South Texas. So were you stalk hunting or sitting in blinds?

Adams: I built several brush blinds in areas where I found good buck sign because stalk hunting with a bow is virtually impossible down there. The land is so flat that unless you're in a tower blind, you usually don't see a deer unless he's already close to you. It's not like hunting mule deer in the West where you can plan a stalk from several hundred yards away. Most rifle hunters in South Texas shoot bucks from tower blinds and they often take them at a considerable distance because they can see so far from those elevated stands. But for a bowhunter, a brush blind is really the only feasible way to go after South Texas deer. Even then it's very tough going.

Did the weather finally turn cold and get the bucks moving?

Adams: A big cold front swept through on January 5, and after that things really picked up. I shot a nice 10-pointer that afternoon at 30 yards. He scored 126⅝ so he made the book with a tad to spare over the 125 P&Y minimum.

Two days later, I was hunting a different spot and killed a second 10-pointer. That one was 37 yards away and his rack scored 142⅜. Two days after that I was in yet another ground blind and managed to fill my final Texas buck tag with a 10-pointer that scored 130⅞. That shot was 35 yards.

So you arrowed three P&Y whitetails in a span of just four days?

Adams: I got real lucky after the weather turned cold and the bucks started moving during daylight. Those were the biggest bucks I saw in 14 days of hunting and I was fortunate enough to get a shot at every one of them. Like I said before, it was just a matter of having the stars aligned just right. I'll probably never do it again because the most record-book animals I've killed in any previous single season was seven. But I always plan my hunts in areas where there's a potential for taking a real trophy because those are the animals I like to hunt. I'd much rather go home with an empty tag than shoot something small, so I usually plan on hunting several days or even several weeks. Last year something big showed up almost every place I went. The stars were aligned and things just worked out for me.

22   Instincts of the Game

BY JOHN E. PHILLIPS

Baseball and bowhunting have more in common than you would think. So Yogi would say:
"Ninety percent of the game is mental; the other half is physical."

As a big eight-point whitetail moved into bow range, Travis Fryman stood in his treestand and waited for the shot. Fryman, the shortstop and third baseman for the Detroit Tigers, recalled later that as soon as he saw the buck, his heart seemed to jump up in his throat.

"My adrenaline was pumping, and I could hardly swallow I was so excited. To get off the shot, I knew I'd have to collect myself and calm down."

To prepare for the shot, Fryman went through the same mental processes he always goes through before he steps to the plate to face major-league flame throwers.

"I closed my eyes for an instant and took a couple of deep breaths," Fryman said. "I looked at the line of travel I expected the buck to take. I tried to pick a spot to shoot where I thought I could place a good shot. Then I visualized taking the deer. I had to get my attention off the buck's head and his antlers and focus solely on the spot—a quarter size tuft of hair behind his shoulder—I wanted to hit."

Then Fryman only had to draw and shoot when the deer got into position. Fryman had learned that in bowhunting, as in baseball, he could rely solely on his instincts and the muscle memory he'd built up from hours of practice to shoot accurately without having to depend on any type of sighting device on the bow.

Before Fryman could launch an arrow, a squirrel fell out of a nearby tree and spooked the buck.

"I never heard the squirrel until it hit the ground and the deer broke to run because I was so in-tune to that spot on the deer where I wanted to place the arrow," Fryman admitted.

Why Dedication Is a Must

Traditional archery requires that type of concentration and dedication for success. According to Fryman, "You must be totally in tune to the spot you want to hit. You must be as focused as you are when you're watching TV while your wife's standing over you telling you the water pipes in the basement are busted and the house is flooding. Even though she may be screaming at you, you're not conscious of her presence because you're so focused on the TV game. I'm convinced that the ability to concentrate and focus are the key elements to being successful with traditional archery."

Baseballs, Bats, Recurves, and Longbows

For many years those who taught traditional archery used parallels of throwing or hitting a baseball to explain the body mechanics and mental processes needed by archers. But what if a highly trained baseball player who earned his living relying solely on his instincts, talent, training and muscle memory to . . .

- recognize a swiftly moving target and see the exact spot on that target he wanted to hit and
- throw an object an unknown distance to a small target where the trajectory of the object being thrown had to pass through an arc to hit the target accurately wanted to reverse the process?

Travis Fryman of Cantonment, Florida, who as a 10-year-old had begun hunting squirrels with his grandfather, asked himself these questions when he started shooting traditional archery. For Fryman, playing well in major-league baseball had represented the ultimate challenge for him as an athlete. Transferring those skills to his recreation of bowhunting became the ultimate challenge for him as a deer hunter.

Fryman has taken a number of big whitetails with his compound bow in years past. But in the last three years, he's also dedicated himself to traditional archery and shooting the longbow and the recurve. Fryman draws parallels between the sport of baseball and instinctive hunting and transfers the skills he's learned in baseball to hunting and shooting instinctively.

Eyes for the Game

To determine which way the seams on a baseball turn when the ball speeds toward home plate at more than 90 mph, you need the same skills you do to see a deer's ear twitch at 30 to 50 yards from your treestand. To calculate distance, trajectory and speed of flight to accurately place the arrow when a buck appears requires the same skills for fielding a ball hit between second and third base and making a quick throw at an unknown distance to get a runner out at first.

The ability to quickly identify what you see may mean the difference in getting a shot off at a buck 15 yards from your treestand or hitting a baseball as it streaks across the plate. Your ability to concentrate, whether at the plate or in your treestand, directly relates to how quickly you see the ball or how soon you detect deer movement. When you lose your concentration or begin to daydream, you won't see as many deer as you will if you remain totally focused on looking for deer.

"If you stand in the batter's box in a major-league park as a pitcher throws a fastball across the plate, more than likely all you'll see is a white blur," Fryman commented. "However, the more times you stand in the batter's box, the faster your eyes will adjust to the speed of the ball and the sooner you'll be able to see the ball as it comes to the plate.

"I've found the same to be true of hunting deer instinctively. The more time you spend in the woods, the quicker and easier your eyes will pick up movement like the twitching of a deer's ear. Once your eyes detect the movement, then you can see the deer accurately. I look for any part of the deer I can spot."

Good Form Is The Key

Once Fryman identifies movement as a deer, he goes through the same procedure he uses to hit the ball. He properly aligns his body in good shooting form to make an accurate shot just as he gets into the proper hitting stance to hit the ball.

"Executing good shooting form before you draw the bow is as important to the traditional archer's making an accurate shot as a major-league hitter's taking the proper batting stance to stroke the ball as it comes across the plate," Fryman emphasized. "If your body isn't in a good shooting position, you can't make an accurate shot with a longbow or a recurve."

Fryman also has adopted the idea from playing baseball to shooting a traditional bow that he catches the ball with his feet. As Fryman explained, "In baseball if you aren't in the proper position with your feet planted squarely and your body aligned properly, regardless of where you put your glove, you probably won't catch the ball. To be successful shooting traditional archery, you must do the same."

All-Season Spring Training

Fryman also mentions that a well-defined sense of hand-eye coordination will ensure your success as an instinctive shooter or as a highly skilled baseball player. But from where does that well-defined sense of hand-eye coordination come? Do you come into this world with it? Or, do you learn it?

Howard Hill of Haleyville, Alabama, one of the greatest instinctive shooters of all time, accomplished many feats with a longbow, including shooting an apple and a plum off a man's head.

"Although many people believe Howard Hill was born with a God-given talent to shoot the longbow instinctively," Byron Ferguson of Hartselle, Alabama, a trick shooter with a longbow on the TV program "American Shooter" on ESPN and TNN, reported, "what few people know is that Howard Hill practiced by shooting 100 arrows a day almost every day of his life. A well-defined sense of hand-eye coordination and the ability to consistently shoot accurately with a longbow or a recurve occurs when a man with talent works, trains and practices to develop that talent to its highest level of proficiency."

"A number of transfer skills involved in throwing a baseball helped me learn to shoot traditional archery accurately," Fryman said. "The ability to focus and concentrate on the target I wanted to hit, whether it was a first baseman's glove or the kill zone of a buck, required the same intuitive process."

When he's turning a double play from shortstop to second base, Fryman often will catch the ball, turn around and throw the ball instinctively to the second baseman's glove without going through the process of determining where the second baseman's glove is or having to aim the ball.

"Also, once I've practiced enough to feel comfortable with the bow and my ability to shoot it, all I have to do is point the bow where I know it should be instinctively," Fryman explained. "Then I let the muscle memory I've developed from my practice take over and shoot my bow accurately.

"To learn to shoot the longbow instinctively, you must do the same things required to throw a baseball accurately and quickly time and time again. You must train and practice until you reach the point where you can bypass thought action and rely totally on muscle memory to produce the shot you're attempting to make. A good instinctive shooter has the ability to pick the spot on the deer he wants to shoot quickly, tune everything else out of his mind and concentrate on that spot while in one fluid motion drawing and shooting the bow without aiming. When you practice the fundamentals long enough in any sport, whether football, baseball or archery, you can eliminate the thought processes required to execute an accurate performance."

Too, as Byron Ferguson observes, an archer who has shot a compound bow for years often makes the mistake of trying to aim the bow rather than point the bow when he picks up a traditional bow.

"The longbow is designed to be shot like a shotgun," Ferguson advised. "You simply see the target, point the barrel of the gun at the target and shoot. You don't consciously aim a shotgun if you're going to shoot accurately. But with a rifle, like a compound bow, you must aim it precisely to shoot accurately."

Fryman further mentions that a good infielder in baseball never thinks about what he does or plans what he'll do. His innate ability to react to the ball and make an accurate throw happens because of the repetitive, correct execution of the same skills for years.

Fryman believes that to become a good instinctive shooter you must practice consistently. Then the longbow or the recurve becomes a part of your body. Although Fryman has found he can take extended periods away from shooting the compound bow and then in a short time start practicing again and become reasonably accurate, he knows he must practice to consistently shoot the longbow or the recurve accurately.

Ball vs. Arrow Flight

As Fryman explained, "When you throw a baseball, you learn through practice and visual reinforcement how much force you have to apply to the ball to make it reach a certain point across an unknown distance at a specific time. The ball's flight has an arc to it. Even though you may throw the ball in a straight line, it still will go through some type of arc.

"And the same is true of shooting an arrow instinctively. To hit the target consistently, you have to subconsciously visualize how the ball or the arrow will fly as it goes up, over and drops into the spot you're trying to hit. That's why I think the traditional archer should use bright-colored fletchings to learn to shoot the traditional bow quicker. These fletchings will enable him to see the arc of the arrow and determine how much force he needs to use and where he should aim to hit the target. For a long shot, the archer will have to shoot the arrow higher to hit the target than he will if he's making a short shot."

For instance, compare what a center fielder does to throw a ball from the outfield to home plate and what a shortstop must do to throw the ball to home plate. The shortstop must throw the ball with less arc than the outfielder does to hit the same target at a different distance. The traditional archer must know how to adjust his bow to provide just the arc required to hit the target regardless of the distance.

Coping with Slumps

At times a major-league hitter will go through a slump and can't seem to hit the ball for some unknown reason. When Fryman hits a slump in baseball, he starts practicing with his recurve.

"I've learned that when I'm not hitting the ball as I should, I need to get my mind off hitting completely," Fryman explained. "The best way for me to do that is to go out in my backyard, shoot my recurve bow and free my mind. Then when I return to the ballpark, I can refocus on the game and hitting the ball and break my slump."

Traditional archers also occasionally go through slumps when they can't seem to hit targets and have no muscle memory.

"I don't practice bad habits," Fryman emphasized. "I believe you can train yourself to shoot inaccurately with traditional archery if you continue to shoot when you're shooting badly. I've found that to improve my ability to shoot, I have to lay the bow down and do something else for a day or two.

"I believe I either shoot badly or hit poorly because I start thinking and trying to make a conscious correction to an unconscious phenomenon. If you have to think to hit the baseball, the process takes place so fast that while you're thinking about what to do, you'll miss the ball.

"When I think about why I'm shooting poorly with my recurve and begin to adjust, then I'm attempting to retrain muscle memory, and I won't shoot correctly. For instinctive shooting to be instinctive, you must depend on your body to do what it's trained to do without going through a conscious thought process."

You can't learn to catch, throw or bat the baseball in only a week or two of practice. To play baseball well, regardless of the level of your play, you must practice until you can perform the skills required to make the play or hit the ball.

Fryman considers learning traditional archery exactly like learning to play baseball. If you can play baseball, you can shoot traditional archery. The more you practice the game of baseball, the better you'll play. The more you shoot traditional archery, the more accurately and consistently you'll shoot and the better archer you'll become.

23　The Art of Seeing

BY JAY CASSELL

They say that some fool once asked Stevie Wonder, "What's the worst thing about being blind?"
The talented, and obviously patient, Stevie is said to have replied, calmly, "Not being able to
see anything." Well, some hunters who have no problems with their vision really can't see
very well when they get into the whitetail woods. This malady is far more widespread than
you might think, as Jay Cassell explains here, along with some suggestions for possible cures.
Jay is a bowhunter and card-carrying whitetail addict who writes about the outdoors as often
as he can but more often can be found editing books like this one for The Lyons Press. He is
editor of the book The Best of Sports Afield, *and in fact served as Features Editor of*
Sports Afield *for several years.*

I t was one of those cold, gray November days that typify deer season in the Northeast. The temperature was hanging at 32°F, it had been drizzling since dawn, and all the trails had turned to mud.

I had slipped into the woods well before sunrise, planning to spend the morning in one of my tree stands. Sitting still on my plastic milk crate, I watched fog drifting up the hillside from the river below. The woods had become dripping wet as the drizzle gave way to rain, and my only hope was to see a deer skulking like an apparition past my stand, in view one second, gone the next. With this wetness I'd never hear one coming.

At 11:30, I gave up on stand-hunting and went back to the cabin. I had a leisurely lunch, took a quick nap, and was back in the woods by 1:30. My plan was to still-hunt for the rest of the afternoon, ending up on a rocky ledge that overlooked a well-used deer runway at the far side of the Catskill Mountain property.

It was raining lightly, and the temperature had nudged into the low 40s. I was moving slowly and was still within sight of the cabin when I felt as if I were being watched. Scanning to my left, I stared at a dense grove of hemlocks without altering my pace. Eventually, I made out a form behind some branches and tree trunks. Yes, there was definitely some sort of horizontal line in those trees that somehow looked out of place.

I kept moving, slower, as I eased my Golden Eagle bow off my shoulder. Now I could make out four or five horizontal lines. Concentrating, I recognized the outline of two deer ears, little satellite dishes, pointed in my direction. A dark nose, some sets of eyes, a glint of antler . . .

I stopped, and the hemlocks erupted. By halting, I had let the deer know that I was onto them. Five white flags, 40 yards away, went bouncing away from me.

The buck, a small one, was shielded by another doe. No shot, even if I had wanted one.

The lesson here is always to look, no matter where you are. Hunt from the minute you leave your cabin or car, as deer can be anywhere. And don't just look ahead; let your peripheral vision go wild. Inspect anything that seems even remotely out of place. Don't stop if you think a deer is there, either, since it will know something is up. It's almost like pheasant hunting: If you keep walking, birds will let you go right by without moving. If you stop, they get nervous and take off. The same applies to whitetails.

An hour after that encounter, I was way off trail, moving cross-country through a stand of hardwoods. This is the kind of hunting I enjoy most of all: moving slowly and silently, following my feet, letting them take me along the natural flow of the terrain.

I was seeing a lot of deer sign now; and while I couldn't really tell if the droppings were fresh, because everything in the woods was so wet, I was in an area that I had seen deer enter before.

There were ledges dropping down 40 yards in front of me, and I moved toward them cautiously, using rocks and trees to break up my silhouette as I approached. Fog rolled off the ledges, misting my eyeglasses. I was surrounded by gray and black forms, vertical tree trunks, horizontal rocks, a dim sky at the edge of my view. Except for the sound of a distant stream, everything was quiet.

Moving to the lip of the first ledge, I crept behind a tree and carefully peeked over the edge. Nothing. I waited five minutes, then picked my way through some rocks, down onto the ledge. It was maybe 20 yards across, and I moved across it slowly, again breaking up my silhouette with trees and boulders. This time, when I peered over the lip, three does were right there, almost in front of me, pawing in the leaves for acorns. Their dark bodies looked almost surreal in the dim, foggy light. I didn't move, and eventually they worked their way out of sight, not even suspecting I was there. Though there hadn't been a buck in the group, I felt good, knowing I had snuck so close to deer, unnoticed. I was also pleased that I hadn't spooked them; if they had gone tearing off through the woods, flags up, snorting and crashing, any buck that might be nearby would know that something was wrong and take off, too.

I generally like to move when the woods are wet, and sit on stand when the woods are dry and noisy. Wet weather in many ways evens your odds with deer. Yes, your ability to see far in the woods is greatly diminished when it's foggy and rainy, but so is the deer's. They're not going to see you from far off, so you have a greater chance of sneaking up on them. The next time another hunter tells you he's not going out because of the rain, don't follow his lead. You know better.

While rainy days can give you the advantages of closer stalking and easier spotting (you can look for dark silhouettes instead of various parts), they can also put you at a disadvantage by dimming colors. Everything is gray, especially as the afternoon begins to wane, making you less likely to see a brown body, or even a white flag, in the woods.

Sunny days present a different set of problems. If you're heading into the sun, you're practically blinded; while if the sun is at your back, your shadow or silhouette is going to give you away in many situations. Plus, with the sun streaming down and casting a checkerboard of shadow and sunlight across the forest floor, you have to look for parts of deer: flicking ears, glinting antlers, horizontal lines of backs or stomachs, swishing tails, ears pointed in your direction, with the two beady eyes and black, round circle of nose in the middle. On sunny days, I find it easier to spot deer early and late, when the brown body colors and full silhouette are more likely to stand out.

I ended the day out on the ledge, my original destination. I sat on my insulated pad with my back against a tree and my bow across my knees. I had a perfect view of a major game trail below me. By 3:30, it was already getting dark. The walk back to the cabin—a good three miles—was going to be an adventure.

One reason a lot of hunters don't see deer is that they move, fidgeting, shifting their bows or rifles, scratching their noses, rotating their heads from right to left to right like tank turrets. I didn't do any of these. I was warm and comfortable, and had no reason to move. So I didn't. Wearing a black-and-gray camo suit, gloves, Trebark hat and headnet, I blended into the woods.

But nothing came down the trail. With darkness setting in, I was about to get up when I heard a slight thump close by. Then I heard a twig snap under some weight. Rotating my eyes, keeping my face hidden by my collar, I saw a deer leg within 15 feet of me. It belonged to a doe, shuffling her nose under some leaves, looking for food. There were four other does with her, all moving across the forest floor like phantoms, making virtually no noise in the gathering darkness. As I sat there, motionless and with the fog keeping my scent pressed down, they all walked right past me, moving along the ledge, one coming within 10 feet. Then they were gone, and all was quiet. I remained still for 10 more minutes, then reluctantly admitted to myself that hunting, for this particular day, was over.

With darkness almost complete, rain starting to fall heavily, I started to get up. That, of course, was when a deer snorted from right behind me. Then the deer turned and, through the dark, I watched as its white flag went bouncing off into the blackness. Because it had been following the group of does, it was probably a buck. If only it had come 15 minutes earlier!

Knowing how not to move is an important step toward seeing more deer. It's something you have to work at, though. You have to force yourself not to fidget, not to make little movements; and you have to make yourself concentrate on looking for deer. Letting your mind wander, thinking about things you're going to do back at work, or at home, clouds your concentration. I've done it more times than I care to admit. It's human nature. You're sitting there in the woods, and you start daydreaming, and all of a sudden 15 or 20 minutes have gone by. And when you dissect that time period, you're hard-pressed to remember what you saw.

If you're daydreaming, you're not watching the woods and you're not listening to the sounds. And that's when a buck will slip by you. You're thinking about something, a buck enters the edge of your peripheral vision, and is gone in 10 seconds, on his way to who knows where. You didn't even see him because you weren't totally focused on looking for deer.

If you can see out 100 yards or farther as you still-hunt your way through the woods, do it; your eyes will pick up everything between you and that focal point anyway. In thick stuff, look for anything that shouldn't be there, anything that appears different or a bit out of place. In bad weather, look for shapes and forms. In sunny weather, look for brown, or for parts of deer in the sunlit kaleidoscope of the forest.

It's easy to walk through the woods and not see deer. People do it all the time, much more than they realize. But walking through the woods and seeing deer most of the time is a talent. And it's something you can learn, that you can teach yourself, because the deer are definitely there. You just have to pay more attention.

Part Four
All About Treestands

The old bromide that says, "Deer never look up," has been proven to be untrue. That still does not change the fact that using a treestand is Strategy Number One in most bowhunters' bag of tricks. Here's how the experts go about it—effectively and safely.

24   Perfect Perches

BY THOMAS L. TORGET

Still unsure about what treestand style is right for your brand of hunting? Let the author's experience help you sort through the myriad of choices.

I'm old enough to remember making my own treestands. I used ½-inch plywood, angle iron, heavy chain and toggle bolts. Each stand took two hours to build and—it seemed—two hours to install. Though these garage-built creations surely would have earned low grades in Engineering 101, they served my purposes. I needed multiple stands for multiple hunting sites and I couldn't afford the price of a half-dozen store-bought stands.

Back then, there were surprisingly few treestand manufacturers. And frankly, much of what they offered was little better than what I could craft myself. So if I had to do it all over again, I would.

Few segments of the hunting equipment industry have changed so much in 20 years as treestand design and construction. With few exceptions, today's products are far superior to anything available in 1980. Engineering is better. Materials are better. Attention to detail is better. And today's stands are far more comfortable, safer and easier to install than their predecessors. While prices have edged higher, there still are quality stands available for less than $100. And a huge selection of more feature-laden models is available for $150 to $250. Given that a superior-quality treestand will last many seasons, purchasing two or three is a sound investment in safety and comfort. And the safer and more comfortable you are, the more effective hunter you'll be.

The two most popular styles of treestands today are fixed-position (or hang-on) stands and climbing stands. Use of ladder stands is growing nationwide and tripod stands, long popular in the south, are gaining converts outside of Dixie.

Each stand style has its advantages and disadvantages. **Fixed-position stands** are the least-expensive because they require the least amount of material. They work well in almost any hunting venue and are a perfect choice for areas that lack straight-trunk trees. A fixed-position stand requires use of a supplemental climbing device, such as a climbing ladder or a set of screw-in or strap-on tree steps.

Climbing stands are two-piece units that allow a hunter to move up and down a tree while in the stand. They can be put up very quickly, usually in less than five minutes. On average, climbers are heavier and more expensive than most fixed-position stands. And they're a poor choice for hunting in areas that are full of crooked trees or trees with multiple low branches.

A **ladder stand** is essentially a fixed-position stand attached to a lightweight ladder. Because installation and removal is a simple task, ladder stands are popular with hunters whose physical condition is less than ideal. Not long ago, most ladder stands were quite heavy, often 50 pounds or more. That made transport into and out of the woods a chore. Many of today's models are much lighter, with a few weighing less than 25 pounds.

Tripod stands have long been popular in the south and southwest, particularly with rifle hunters. Bowhunters in these regions also use tripods when hunting locations that lack large trees. Tripod use is growing among bowhunters in the midwest and east, but the south remains the region where tripods are most popular. Like ladder stands, tripods are more cumbersome and heavier than fixed-position and climbing stands. But tripod setup is quick and easy and a tripod can be positioned virtually anywhere as long as the ground is level.

Beginning in the late 1980s, treestand makers responded aggressively to consumer demand for lighter weight models. Entire product lines were redesigned. Lighter materials were introduced. Platform and seat sizes shrunk, then shrunk some more. The race for lightness continued and, by 1994, several fixed-position stands weighed less than seven pounds, making them lighter than some accessory laden compound bows of the day.

Meanwhile, treestand consumers who had demanded these featherweight platforms were learning the truth of the adage, "Be careful what you wish for, because you just might get it." Bowhunters discovered that sitting—or should we say crouching—in a treestand too tiny to allow anything but minimal movement was, quite frankly, an awful way to spend the day. With knees in their faces, leg muscles cramped and butts turned numb, bowhunters decided enough was enough. The new rallying cry to treestand manufacturers: "Give us comfort!"

Once again, entire product lines were redesigned. Platforms grew longer and wider. Seat sizes expanded and padding was added. Seat heights on some models could now be adjusted. Other seats swiveled. Foot rests were added to some models. But while the new emphasis was on roominess and comfort, the mass weight of most stands did not rise substantially. Lightness is still important to many bowhunters and manufacturers understand that a comfortable stand weighing 12 pounds will outsell a competitor's comfortable stand that weighs 18 pounds.

Obviously, safety has always been a major concern of treestand manufacturers. No manufacturer wants his customers injured while using his products and he sure doesn't want the hassle and cost of dealing with lawsuits. Several manufacturers recently formed a trade association to help bolster the emphasis on safety and to encourage the use of the highest-quality materials in treestand construction. Known as the Treestand Manufacturers of America, the organization has adopted a rigorous testing program to ensure uniformity in product strength and safety. To earn TMA certification, each treestand model must pass a series of engineering tests to confirm its strength and load capacity. Only then can the treestand be marketed as having been TMA-certified.

"When a hunter bought a treestand in the past, he had no assurance that it would perform as advertised," notes Ray McIntyre, president of Warren & Sweat

Manufacturing. "And while the majority of manufacturers have always produced excellent stands, a few companies were hurting the reputation of the industry by turning out poorer-quality goods. So many manufacturers decided to develop a uniform set of engineering standards that could be used to test the safety and reliability of individual treestands and related products. We organized the Treestand Manufacturers of America to establish an engineering-based testing system. Testing will include all stand styles and related products such as tree steps and ladders, safety belts, harnesses and so on. Only when a product has passed these engineering tests can it display the TMA certification logo. If the entire effort saves just one life, it will be well worth it."

So which treestand design is best for you? Hang-on or climber? Ladder or tripod? In answering those questions, consider these factors:

Factor #1: Your personal hunting style. Some bowhunters like to set up multiple treestands prior to opening day and rotate their activity among those sites. Others studiously avoid hunting the same location more than once, believing it's best to avoid any possibility that nearby deer might pattern their comings and goings.

For the bowhunter who moves constantly, a climbing stand is usually the best choice. A climber allows you to always set up downwind of deer trails. With a fixed-position stand, however, a shift in wind direction can render a location useless for hours or even days. With a climber, you can set up in just minutes and can do so anywhere there's a straight-trunk tree. Discover a hot deer crossing in early afternoon and you can be hunting it minutes later. If it works out, you can return the next day. If the site is a bust, you're not "stuck" there because you invested 30 minutes or more setting up a hang-on stand.

Factor #2: Your hunting terrain. While climbers provide maximum flexibility, you can't use them everywhere. For example, climbing stands are of little value in my home state of Texas because of the scarcity here of straight trees that don't have an abundance of low-hanging limbs. I could use a climber to ascend to five feet or so, but then I'd likely encounter a pair of five-inch limbs. Setting up at an elevation of five feet isn't the best way to fill a deer tag.

Even if you bowhunt in the midwest, south and east, your hunting location may be filled with trees sprouting lots of low-growing limbs. Or perhaps trees that lean more than you'd like. In these situations, a fixed-position stand works very well. You can attach a fixed-position stand to a very crooked tree, so long as the trunk has at least one three-foot section that's essentially vertical. Many towering oaks in Texas fit this description and I've sat in a bunch of them perched comfortably on a fixed-position treestand well above the sight-line of passing whitetails.

Sometimes deer travel through areas with few or no trees suitable for either a climber or fixed-position stand. Locations near water holes often fit this description. Another example: A corn or soybean field may be surrounded by brush or young trees that leave no opportunity to use a conventional treestand. This is where a tripod stand works wonders. Tripod heights vary from six to 16 feet and the lower stands often work better for the bowhunter. Ladder stands are an alternative to tripods in those areas that have trees of suitable size and shape.

Factor #3: Your age and physical condition. Installing a fixed-position stand 15 to 25 feet above ground requires more than a little strength, flexibility and co-ordination. As hunters from the baby boom generation age and soften, the appeal of this exercise dims. Any hunter who's seriously overweight, has a bad back or other physical limitation should probably avoid using fixed-position treestands. A climber, ladder stand or tripod is a more practical choice.

Today's climbing stands are far easier to use than their predecessors of the early and mid-1980s. Memorize the procedure for the model you're using and practice with that stand several times (near ground level) before taking it to the woods. Used correctly, a modern climber is an extremely safe product. But it's easy to use it improperly if you don't study the instructions carefully and practice the procedure. No two stands are identical. So don't assume you know how to use your new one because you know how to use your old one.

Ladder and tripod stands are especially appealing to older hunters and those whose physical condition isn't what it used to be.

Factor #4: Your budget. Treestands are like other hunting gear: there's no such thing as "too much." But everyone must live within his budget, which means you may need to forego the most feature-laden stand and opt for a more inexpensive model. There are plenty of excellent fixed-position stands available for $100, climbers for $200, ladder stands for $175 and tripods for $200. Personally, I'd much rather own three "Chevy" treestands than one "Mercedes-Benz" model. The extra features that come with top-line stands are nice and usually worth the extra expense. But because having multiple stands in multiple locations is the key to successful bowhunting, that will always be my focus. It's hard to do that if I have just one or two stands.

Treestand Choices of the Pros

Paul Vaicunas: "During the peak of the rut I try to stay in my treestand the entire day," says Paul Vaicunas, National Sales Manager for Game Tracker. "That's not possible unless my stand is extremely comfortable. The Ol' Man Vision climbing stand is an excellent choice for extended hunting sessions because the mesh seat is so comfortable. It's my number-one choice among climbers."

When using a fixed-position stand for an all-day hunt, Vaicunas opts for the Big Foot model offered by Rivers Edge Treestands. "It has a huge platform and a two-inch padded seat that's extremely comfortable," he says.

Earlier and later in the season, when whitetails are focused on feeding rather than breeding, Vaicunas likes to stay mobile and therefore selects stands that are lightest in weight. His favorite is API's Baby Grand, used with Game Tracker's Ultra-Lite Climbing Sticks.

Chuck Nease: "My favorite style of stand has changed as I've grown older," says Chuck Nease, president of Custom Shooting Systems. "In my early bowhunting years, I really enjoyed using climbers because they allowed me to keep moving and gave me tremendous flexibility. But as I began focusing on trophy hunting the past few years, I've used climbers less and fixed-position stands more."

Nease's favorites are fixed-position stands offered by Loc-On and Summit Specialties. "I like to scout for likely ambush sites and hang these stands well in advance of when I plan to use them," he says. "I often install them in September and don't use them until November. A fixed-position stand is perfect for this style of hunting."

Nease still uses climbers now and then. In fact, it was a Summit climber that he used in 1996 when he arrowed a 10-point West Virginia whitetail that scored in the 150-class. "I had planned to hunt from a Loc-On fixed-position stand that day, but decided to let a friend use it instead," he says. "I carried my Summit climber to a spot where I knew the acorns were dropping heavily and it paid off when this huge buck came along and stepped into bow range. That's one of the key advantages of a climber: it lets you move quickly into an area where the action is hot that day."

Greg Sesselmann: "I prefer fixed-position stands for most of my hunting because they're usually quieter than climbers and I just feel more solidly locked to the tree when I'm in a hang-on stand," says Greg Sesselmann, president of Scent-Lok. "Personally, I find ladder stands a bit too heavy and cumbersome for me. Tripods are also heavy, but they're sometimes necessary in places like Texas."

Sesselmann's favorite fixed-position models are the Lone Wolf Treestand and the Baby Grand from API Outdoors. He enjoys using these stands in combination with climbing sticks because portable ladders are so easy to set up and they don't damage trees.

Sesselmann says he prefers positioning his stands as low to the ground as the surrounding terrain allows. "I like to hang them on a split main tree with heavy cover behind me to break up my silhouette," he says. "And whatever stand style I use, I'm always certain to wear a climbing belt and safety harness. The two I like best are from API Outdoors and Fall Woods. They're both excellent products."

Treestand Accessories

In addition to one or more treestands, today's bowhunter should look into the following essential accessories:

- Safety harness
- Climbing ladder
- Bow holder
- Tree steps
- Pull-up rope
- Limb pruner
- Reflective trail markers
- Folding hand saw

A ladder stand is an excellent choice for the older or overweight hunter who prefers the security of having his platform attached to the climbing ladder.

Screw-in or strap-on tree steps are still a favorite of many bowhunters who use fixed-position stands.

Lightweight climbing sticks and ladders make it easy to install and remove a fixed-position treestand.

With a climbing stand, a hunter can set up quickly in a new area and thereby take advantage of changing conditions.

Several factors must be considered when deciding which style of treestand best suits your hunting terrain and individual preferences.

25 The Bowhunter's Treestand

BY BILL BUCKLEY

For bowhunters, not any treestand site will work. But it also doesn't have to be perfect. Here's how to determine what will suffice and what won't.

Not all treestand setups are bow-and-arrow friendly, a fact many archers learn the hard way when they hunt out of the same stand they used the previous gun season. That's because moving a bow into shooting position requires a lot more motion and maneuvering room than shouldering a rifle. And since its killing range is significantly less, and holding it at ready until a buck steps clear of brush infinitely more difficult, there's no choice but to make your move only when the deer is close by. Then your every movement or noise can make or break the hunt.

Truth be told, the most important part of selecting an effective bowhunting stand isn't predicting where the deer will pass, but evaluating a specific stand site once you do and deciding if, with a few alterations, it will be good enough. That's not always easy, since rarely will you find the right tree in the right spot. Like The Rolling Stones say, "You can't always get what you want, but if you try sometimes you get what you need." And for bowhunting, if you focus on adequate concealment, economy of movement, and good shooting clearance, you'll get what you need.

You've probably discovered by now that climbing up a tree doesn't guarantee deer won't see you. And it's not just because they're wise to hunters in treestands. Their peripheral vision happens to be outstanding, so even when they're close they can still spot you if you move at the wrong time. Also, the farther away you can see them approach, the more opportunity they have of seeing you. Which is why, when you pick a stand site, you've got to picture how exposed or hidden you're likely to be. That means paying attention to sunlight and shadows, making sure there's adequate background and side cover immediately around the stand, and that there's screening cover between you and where you expect to draw on the deer. We'll assume you've already determined the prevailing wind direction and are only considering downwind or sidewind sites.

Because most areas with high deer traffic have at least a few different trails running through them, you can't predict exactly where a buck will approach your stand. That said, should a deer approach from any direction but head-on, placing your stand in a lone tree with no branches to screen your outline will have you sticking out like the proverbial wart on the witch's chin. And every time you move, any deer within sight will spot you. That's why searching for a stand location should begin with an eye toward blocking your outline.

Background and side cover are especially critical on clear days, when sunlight highlights everything it strikes and then casts shadows. Given the sun will be low at dawn and dusk—peak periods of deer activity—any shadow you cast won't hit the ground immediately below you but will reach well away from your perch. Then it's not just that sunlight-rimmed form of yours you have to worry about concealing, but also the giant shadow extending 50-plus feet away, moving every time you do. Don't think cautious deer don't cue on moving shadows. They do.

Finally, screening cover between you and the buck is essential to your success. Those branches and leaves behind your treestand might keep the deer from detecting you when you're sitting still, but to stand and move your bow into shooting position requires more cover to go unnoticed. The closer that cover is to the deer, the better it will block his angle of view, and the more time and opportunity you'll have to draw your bow while his head is behind a tree trunk or bush.

With those basics in mind, it's time to evaluate stand sites in your deer woods. Obviously, the thicker the woods, the easier it is to stay hidden (if for no other reason than the deers' vision will be obscured the farther away they are), while open woods call for much more discriminating setups. And chances are your hunting ground has a bit of both. Should you find a good funnel where the topography concentrates the deers' travel routes through an area of thick vegetation with small openings, you'll have the best of both worlds: cover and natural shooting lanes. So concentrate your search there.

But for the sake of illustration, and since nature rarely provides us with ideal situations, let's say you've scouted relatively open ground and have found a place where two heavily used trails converge. Unfortunately, being a mature woods, the trees next to the crossing don't have branches low enough to block your silhouette. So your next option is to look for trees growing close together, where if you place your stand in one of them, the others will block your outline from the sides. A cluster of three or four trees is ideal, but even two could suffice. And if one of the trunks also happens to fall in the shadows of the other trees, you'll be all the better hidden if you place your stand there.

Let's say, however, that no matter where you scout along the two trails, you can't find any promising sites close by. Then it's time to look farther off the side of the trail. Your shooting accuracy will limit how far you can stray, but suffice to say, the greater it is, the better your chances of finding a tree or trees with adequate background cover. Even if you can't, moving farther away from the trails will achieve two important advantages: You'll have more trees and vegetation between you and the buck to screen your movements if you ultimately have to settle for a bare tree trunk, and the deer won't be focused on you but along the trail directly in front of him. In fact, because deer tend to scrutinize what's directly ahead of them, it's never a good idea to place your stand on top of a trail, even when there's plenty of outline-blocking cover. Place your stand at least 15 yards to the side, with 20 being better, unless no other options exist. And in some open woods, it might take 30 yards to escape a deer's notice.

Staying out of sight isn't the only reason to avoid setting up close to a trail. The deer will be less likely to hear you shifting around or drawing your bow. There's also less possibility of the deer jumping the string. That's why soundproofing your stand and bow is critical to making any setup successful. What good is a well-hidden stand if a squeaking hinge or bow rest sends the buck into orbit?

To avoid unpleasant surprises, make sure every joint of your stand is lubricated and that the platform doesn't make popping noises when you shift your weight. If it does, tighten every bolt and screw you can find. Should it persist, then have someone else try their luck, and if nothing works, get rid of the stand and buy a different manufacturer's product. A lot of squeaks and pops can be avoided by making sure the stand contacts the tree bole solidly and evenly at the base of the platform. If there's any play when you shift weight from one side of the platform to the other, almost any stand will produce deer-spooking noise.

Also sound-proof your bow, which at the very least means using string silencers and whatever material is necessary to prevent an arrow from squeaking against the rest as the bow is drawn. It's also smart to cover the window and shelf of your bow with thick, sound-deadening moleskin. Then, should the arrow fall off the rest, it won't make a loud clanking noise it otherwise would. If it turns out you're having trouble soundproofing your bow, take it to a qualified archery shop.

Lastly, be sure to sound-proof your tree and clothing. If rough bark catches on your jacket every time you move, it's bound to make a grating noise when it comes time to stand for a shot. Either quietly rub the bark smooth or bring a spare camo shirt and wrap it around the trunk where your back makes contact. You can tie it in place with the sleeves. Speaking of sleeves, if they swish or make other noticeable sounds when you draw back, wear something quieter. In a still woods, a deer at 20 yards will pick up any unnatural noise you make.

Regardless of how much screening cover your stand has, the less you have to move—both to watch for approaching deer and to get into shooting position— the better, because as long as the wind's favorable, the only thing left to give you away will be motion. And what direction you hang your treestand has everything to do with keeping head and body movement to a minimum.

Some bowhunting experts advocate facing your stand away from the direction you expect the deer to come. The theory is that the deer has to walk past you before you can draw and shoot. Then he can't detect you move. For people with lots of self control, this setup might work dandy. But if you're like me and want to peek every now and then for incoming game, so you're not caught off guard, all this arrangement will do is force you to twist around frequently and awkwardly, making way too much motion and giving you a sore neck.

Much better is to point the stand roughly perpendicular to where you hope to arrow the buck. Then you won't have to turn your upper body and strain your neck to watch for deer, nor shift around to shoot. If you're right-handed, for example, set up so a buck coming from in front or right of you will walk slightly past your tree before you shoot. Should he come from your left, or slightly behind you, then you'll have a broadside shot when he's even with your tree, again without any twisting in your seat to shoot sitting down. If you have time to stand, you'll already be facing the right direction. Movement is then kept to a minimum and you won't have to shift your feet, minimizing the possibility of your stand creaking.

Limiting movement also means either keeping your bow in your hands at all times, even when resting it on your lap, or in a bow rack that attaches to the front of the treestand. If you make the mistake of hanging it on a branch or spare tree step, you'll quickly realize that grabbing it takes too much movement to avoid being detected.

Finally, a good bowhunting stand has to have adequate clearance, not just for shooting lanes so your arrow won't deflect off branches, but up in the tree so you can swing and draw the bow without raking, or being restricted by limbs.

While having lots of shooting lanes sounds great, remember that only two or three are necessary, provided they're wide enough so the deer doesn't have to stop in exactly the right spot and you don't have to thread an arrow through a tiny opening. Shooting lanes should have enough room for a deer to take a few steps and still offer a shot, and any branches running through the middle of the lanes, especially those small enough to go unnoticed in dim light, should be removed. But be careful not to overprune, particularly if you're planning to hunt that stand soon. If, after you've cleared lanes, the woods looks like a logging crew just came through, the deer will surely notice. They'll also pick up on all that human scent you've just spread around. A good rule of thumb is to alter the immediate area as little as possible while still getting by.

As for good clearance up in the stand, don't get carried away with blocking your outline if it means you don't have enough room to stand up for a shot, you have to shoot from an awkward position, or you can only shoot in one direction. Deer have a habit of showing up where they're not supposed to, and if you can't shoot in a couple different directions, your odds of downing a buck are halved. If need be, bring a folding saw and cut away intrusive branches. But if you have to cut away lots of branches, then consider lowering or raising the stand. That will disturb the woods far less than a major pruning job. What branches you do remove, however, can usually be propped against other branches to the side of the stand to further block your outline. Otherwise remove them from the area after you've finished.

Also be sure to clip off any branch your bow or arrow might touch as you're easing them into position for a shot. If you find yourself having to weave the end of the arrow around various twigs, there's a good likelihood of the arrow getting knocked off the rest at the worst possible moment. When a buck comes in close, your attention will be on him, not on your arrow tip.

Most important, if there's any question of being able to draw or release your bow without it or your drawing-arm elbow touching a branch, be sure to find that out before a hunt, not when a buck is standing broadside before you. A bow limb that contacts a branch upon release will kick out and throw off the shot. And if you can't come to full draw without contorting your body, you probably won't get a consistent anchor or release, likewise sending the arrow off-target.

Those are some of the many reasons archers have to choose their stand sites with more care than rifle hunters do. Bowhunting being a close-range sport, success often hinges on tending to the smallest detail. Still, don't expect to find the perfect treestand site every time you go searching. And don't think you must have one to kill a deer. You may not get what you want, but with some forethought and effort you can usually find what you need. That's what makes bowhunting such a challenging and rewarding sport.

Anchor Points:

- Bowhunters would do well to avoid using their rifle stands during bow season. Few stand sites are ideal for both seasons.
- Bow-drawing clearance is at least as important if not more so than clearing shooting lanes. You'll never get to full draw if your equipment continually makes contact with limbs.
- Stand positioning on your tree is critical. Take the cover into account and play the percentages on where deer will approach and where you want to shoot.
- Soundproof everything including your treestand. Moleskin is a great sound-deadening material.

26   He Hangs 150 Stands a Year

BY JOHN WEISS

If you want to perfect your stand-placement strategy, learn from chief guide Larry Frasier who puts hunters on giant whitetails every year.

On my farm and lease lands in southeastern Ohio I routinely have in place about a dozen stands ready and waiting for opening day. The reason for that many stands is because I know in advance that I can usually count upon several relatives or friends showing up on the spur of the moment and not having the time to do their own scouting.

Admittedly, for one person to maintain that many stand locations is a major undertaking. Or at least, so I thought until I became friends with Larry Frasier about five years ago. Frasier is the boss guide for western Kentucky's famous Deer Creek Outfitters, which has a reputation for consistently putting hunters onto some of the biggest bucks taken every year in the Bluegrass State.

The operation, situated on 5,000 acres of prime whitetail habitat, is managed exclusively for bowhunters and blackpowder enthusiasts by veteran deer hunter Tim Stull. Moreover, just one of Larry's responsibilities is situating the approximately 150 stands (gasp!) necessary to accommodate the lodge's many hunters every year.

"It's a tireless job but it's highly rewarding when a hunter takes the biggest buck of his life from one of my stands," Larry beams. "It also has been an incredible learning experience that should provide a wealth of insight that can benefit any hunter no matter where he lives or pursues whitetails."

The last time I visited Deer Creek I picked Larry's brain about some of the finer points of stand placement.

Question: Larry, what's your number-one objective when placing a client on one of your countless stands?

Larry Frasier: I look at it from the standpoint of being a long-time hunter myself. If I showed up at a commercial deer hunting lodge I'd want the assurance that the stand a guide placed me on was fresh, not burned out from being occupied by dozens of other hunters in the weeks before my arrival. I'd also want the confidence that my stand has the potential of providing not only the biggest buck of my life but maybe even a record-book candidate.

Q: What if you put a hunter on a particular stand and he later says he doesn't like that stand?

LF: That's understandable because stand characteristics are a personal matter and each hunter has his own acquired preferences. A hunter may tell me that a given stand is so high it makes him feel uncomfortable, or that it's in tight cover and he prefers longer-range coverage, or that it overlooks a feeding area and he'd rather be in a travel corridor. But whatever the reason, if he doesn't have the highest confidence in his assigned stand I'll quickly move him to another fresh stand elsewhere. And I'll keep doing that until he's satisfied, even though I myself know every stand has great potential for producing a big buck.

Q: Are there any times when you'll pull a hunter off a given stand and relocate him even though he likes the stand and wants to remain there?

LF: Absolutely! Every morning when our hunters are having breakfast I have a confab with my guides and the first thing we discuss is the wind direction. At many of our stand locations, wind direction is critical and if it's not just right I won't risk ruining that stand by putting a hunter there on that day. This is why everyone who hunts on their own should also have numerous prepared stand sites to choose from each day.

Q: Are there any other reasons for pulling a hunter?

LF: Well, another consideration is how many times the stand has been occupied. I've learned that hunting a given stand more than two days in a row allow deer to pattern coming-and-going hunter activity and quickly burns the stand out. Beginning on the third or fourth day, it's wise to rotate to another stand.

Q: So all of this is why it's necessary for you to hang an average of 150 stands a year?

LF: Yep. When I move a hunter to another stand I want him to have the confidence he's in virgin territory and no one else has just come off that stand.

Q: Why has the entire western Kentucky region become such a hotbed of big bucks in recent years?

LF: Primarily because there is a wide diversity of rugged escape cover interspersed with agricultural operations. This is a land of flooded timber, bogs, swamps, meadow, and mast-bearing hardwood ridges which provide deer with ideal habitat and a year-around cornucopia of good eats. Plus, at Deer Creek we also offer superb quail and pheasant hunting, so we have hundreds of acres planted to row crops, grain crops, and legumes which the deer also utilize while having easy access to nearby security zones that are too nightmarish for hunters to penetrate.

Q: I understand your trophy management program is paying off big-time.

LF: Yes. We don't allow bucks to be harvested unless they have a minimum eight-point rack with a minimum 16-inch inside spread. Last year our hunters passed up shots at over 300 bucks! The bucks that have been harvested in our area frequently score 150 Boone and Crockett points or better. The largest bow-kill to date scored 183 and the largest blackpowder buck scored 199⅞.

Q: Let's more specifically look at some of your stand placement tips that will benefit hunters no matter where they deer hunt.

LF: First, I leave my stands in place all winter. This allows deer to become accustomed to their locations. Then I pull all of the stands in the spring and relocate them just before the next season opens. This keeps the deer guessing. They never know where a hunter may be perched. However, some general areas are such regular producers that when I relocate a stand it may be only 100 yards away from where a former stand was hung the previous year.

Q: So clearly, you use nothing but portable stands?

LF: Absolutely! Many outfitters around the country build permanent wooden stands which their clients occupy all season long, year after year. Eventually, they become doe and small-buck stands. If you want to consistently see big bucks you must use portables exclusively and regularly move them around.

Q: Do you prefer one type of portable stand over another?

LF: I mostly use fixed-position chain-on or strap-on stands and screw-in tree steps because, compared to climbing stands, you make far less noise climbing into your stand and you leave far less scent on the tree trunk each time you climb in and out of the stand. If a hunter wants to use a climbing stand, I suggest that it be attached to the base of the tree trunk the evening before his scheduled morning hunt and that it be completely sprayed down with one of the scent-neutralizing sprays on the market.

Q: What's one of the most important elements in deciding where to place stands?

LF: The type of hunting that's being done! If it's bowhunting, you're pretty much dealing with undisturbed animals, so being in the vicinity of fresh sign is critically important. Therefore, stands should be located overlooking scrapes, feeding areas, or heavy trails leading in and out of thick bedding cover. But during the firearm season, deer are under intense pressure and restrict most of their feeding and rutting to after dark. Now, sign isn't as important and you need to switch. Forget scrapes and feeding areas and hunt funnels, bottlenecks and escape corridors.

Q: If you could pick your two most favorite stand locations to bowhunt and gunhunt for the rest of your life, what would they be?

LF: That's easy. One stand would be in a funnel connecting a feeding area and a bedding area. The other would be a staging area where thickets meet hardwoods because this is where bucks spend most of their time chasing does and sorting out their differences with other bucks.

Q: Is there any particular time of year you prefer to hunt more than another?

LF: Yes, I definitely prefer to bowhunt the late season, well into December. Deer activity levels are high then, yet human activity levels are low, and that's a combination that provides lots of action.

Q: Why are deer activity levels high then, especially considering the cold and the fact that the animals have been experiencing hunting pressure for the past several months?

LF: You'd be surprised how quickly deer recover from hunting pressure, especially when cold weather requires them to fuel their furnaces with more food than any other time of year. In most regions of the country, deer want to herd up in the winter. And since food sources are becoming fewer and fewer, this means you can expect to see big groups of deer feeding in the same places. I've seen bunches of 50 to 60 deer in a few clover fields that were still green. When deer are concentrated like that, and especially if there is a dusting of snow on the ground, it's easy to find the trails they're moving along from their bedding area to the food source.

Q: In using this approach, what's your best personal buck to date?

LF: I'm still looking for my first Booner. My best bow-kill is a heavy nine-pointer that scored 152 Pope & Young points.

Q: Do you have a second rut in western Kentucky?

LF: Yes, and that also plays right into my consideration of where to hang stands. If you want to take a big buck, you have to be hunting where the does are. And as I just mentioned, the does will be tied to the few major food sources still remaining. So it's all very simple. Find the food, find the does, and you'll be right where the bucks are.

Q: Do you hang stands right at the food source, say along a grain field or clover field?

LF: No, because like any other animal, when deer are on their feeding grounds, which usually are in the open, they're on radar alert for danger lurking around the perimeter edges and this increases the chance that you'll be detected. In hanging a stand for late-afternoon use, I like to set up on a trail as much as 125 yards back from the feeding area, preferably where there is a lot of heavy cover where deer like to mingle around before traveling the rest of the way down to the feeding area at dusk.

Q: What about a stand reserved for morning use?

LF: I also like to be 125 yards back from the feed source but where numerous trails converge into a major trail leading to a bedding area, usually on higher ground such as a steep hillside or the side of a ridge.

Q: What time frames do you recommend your hunter/clients spend on stand?

LF: In the morning, I like to see them on stand a full hour before daylight and ask them to remain on stand until at least noon before climbing down and returning to camp for a break. Late in the day I like them to be back on stand by 3 o'clock. But all of this changes when the first or second rut is in progress. Now, I strongly encourage them to pack a lunch and remain on stand all day because many of our biggest bucks are taken between noon and 2 p.m.

Q: Aside from choosing the wrong location, what are the two most common mistakes bowhunters make when placing a stand?

LF: The first mistake is not getting high enough. This is especially important late in the season after the leaf drop when a hunter in a tree is far more conspicuous. Now, you must be 25 to 30 feet off the ground. If you don't like to be that high, pick a tree that has multiple trunks or lots of low limbs to help break up your outline. The second mistake is setting up too close to sign such as a scrape or trail. You must be back away, at least 25 yards. The worst-case scenario would be a stand that is situated too low on a limbless tree and too close to the sign. In this type of situation a mature buck will pick you off every time.

Q: What if a deer winds you, snorts, and then runs off. Do you advise relocating the stand?

Only if the deer obviously sees you. Otherwise, since there's so much human activity everywhere in the outdoors, I wouldn't relocate a stand just because a buck scented you, although I'd probably rest that area for a week or more.

Q: Do you have any advice about getting into and out of a stand?

LF: Yes! Once you've patterned deer and know where they're bedding and feeding and the trail they're using to go back and forth, don't throw all your hard work out the window by walking right through the feeding area to your stand. And don't walk along their trail, either. Always take the long way around to reach your stand because if you bust the deer you intend to hunt and send them high-tailing you'll have to start all over and repattern them elsewhere.

Q: Earlier you mentioned the importance of spraying a scent-neutralizing agent on a climbing stand. Do you take other scent precautions?

LF: Yes, I recommend hunters spray the same odor eliminator on their clothing. If it's not too cold, I also suggest wearing knee-length rubber boots, even when gun hunting. Otherwise, leather boots and your lower pantlegs will leave human scent on cover when hiking to and from your stand, which is just one more element that will allow deer to pattern you.

27   Super Stands

BY MICHAEL HANBACK

Any one of these hot all-season stand set-ups can make this deer season your best ever.

There are few guarantees in deer hunting, but I bet you one thing. Strap on a safety belt and hang high in the following treestands, and you will see lots of whitetails glide by below. Better yet, there's a good chance you'll get the drop on an old, hip-swiveling buck with a big chunk of bone on his head.

I devised the "Big 4" strategy in the rolling hills and hollows of Virginia where I live. In recent years I've taken my act on the road and hunted from minor variations of the stands in Missouri, Mississippi, Kansas, Kentucky and other states. The setups are universally effective. Tweak them to the habitat you hunt and I, er, guarantee you'll have success this season.

1. The Mast Stand

In early bow season scout for deer trails that wend out of clover pastures, food plots, crop fields, burns, rights-of-way or any low-grass openings where whitetails clinging to late-summer patterns feed and mingle. Spray on some scent killer, pack a treestand on your back and follow those paths back into the surrounding woods and thickets. (Use your head and don't walk on deer runs; parallel them from a safe distance to minimize your man-smell.) Sneak around in widening arcs out to 300 yards or so (probe any deeper than that and you might bump bedded deer). Just what are you looking for? Simple. Mast trees dropping the first fresh fruit of fall.

Zero in on white and red oak acorns, which everybody knows are the staples of whitetails across much of their range. But don't overlook isolated pockets of persimmons, crabapples, wild grapes, honey locust, pokeberries and the like. Deer love to fatten up on soft mast when they can.

In any given region family units of does home in on preferred mast once it ripens. Coming to "hot" trees from virtually all directions, all those does and fawns leave secondary trails that, if you look closely, often resemble spokes on a bicycle wheel.

And what about the bucks? In mid-September and early October, they become reclusive and hang out in the woods near mast ridges, flats and bottoms. As they gobble acorns and soft fruits and make early contact with the does they'll breed in a couple of months, mature deer blaze signpost rubs and rub-mark their travel corridors between bedding and feeding areas.

Evaluate the terrain, foliage and prevailing breeze. Then pull the stand off your back and hang it in one of two places: downwind of "wheel spoke" doe trails near mast trees; or along a shiny rub line in the vicinity of signpost rubs.

Climb into the perch in early afternoon. An hour or so before sunset, does, fawns and immature bucks may parade into view. The deer should stop to nose and paw the mast, acting as natural decoys for a mature buck that might show up later. After a while, the animals might proceed along a main trail to the open feeding area (that field, food plot, etc. a couple hundred yards away).

Around dusk, you may hear deer running deep in the woods. Stand up and get ready! More does, along with a good buck, might roll into the mast. If the does pause to nibble acorns or mushy fruit, the buck will too, perhaps offer a shot. If the does then move toward the field or plot, the buck may follow but odds are he will stage right there before ghosting into the primary feeding area after dark. Either way, you might fly an arrow at a big-racked deer in the last wisps of shooting light.

2. The Strip

This set is dynamite anywhere crop fields, pastures, woodlots and mid-size forests are interconnected by brushy fencerows, ditches, stream bottoms and bands of trees. Come to think of it, that's 75 percent of the whitetail habitat in North America!

Strips that link deer feeding and bedding zones are easy to find. Simply walk a piece of country and mark obvious linear covers on your topographic maps and aerial photographs. Then scout for tracks, trails, rubs and scrapes. Strips that concentrate traveling whitetails are typically pocked with a mother lode of sign.

In my experience, a moderately wide strip of woods is best to hunt. It's small enough to neck down the travels of deer, yet large enough to provide an array of treestand options with good cover. Play the wind, read the buck sign and hang a perch as you would when hunting any wooded area.

Whitetails slipping between two sizeable blocks of cover often cling to narrow ditches, fencerows and the like. Trouble is, these strips may have only one or two trees (if any at all) large enough to support a fixed position or climbing stand. Set your perch as high as possible in the best available tree. Wear camouflage (with a fluorescent orange cap or vest in gun season) and don't move around too much. Never hunt this setup when the breeze or thermals are the least bit wrong. Old deer that walk flimsy strips of cover are ultra-spooky. If they bust you, the gig is up.

Strips are excellent places to ambush bucks on bed-to-feed patterns early in the season. But my favorite time to employ Setup 2 is late in the pre-rut. Big deer often lay rub lines and scrape lines in linear covers, then cruise the strips as they prowl around to check the estrus stage of various pockets of does.

3. The Forest Funnel

In big woodlands, say 500 acres or more, whitetails don't wander mindlessly around the woods. They stick to funnels and bottlenecks (the best ones are laced with cover) when sneaking between feeding, bedding and breeding areas. Terrain funnels come in literally hundreds of shapes and sizes across North America. But regardless of where you hunt, hang treestands in these four places. I can almost guarantee you'll see deer—not only early in the season, but throughout the peak—and post-rut phases as well.

- Creek bottom with finger ridges. Let's see, there was a gnarly nine-pointer in Virginia, a good eight in Missouri and a seven-pointer with tall tines in Mississippi. I shot those bucks last season from stands set where two or more ridges petered out into wending creek bottoms. Anytime you can hunt this type of setup, do it! Ridge bases and creeks (or rivers, sloughs, oxbow lakes and the like) are typically rimmed with cover and pocked with deer tracks, rubs and scrapes. They form three- or four-sided funnels that squeeze lots of whitetails within bow or gun range.
- Saddle: In mountains, deer use obvious saddles as shortcuts between points. And in rolling hills and even flatlands, does and bucks sneak through little cuts and depressions that make their travels easier. Play the wind and set up near a shallow saddle when you can.
- Edge: Pines meet hardwoods, cedars border second-growth saplings, alders rim aspens . . . you get the picture. Bucks are notorious for traveling edges, where they love to rub and scrape along the way. When bowhunting, hang a stand in the dark, dense edge of pines, cedars, etc. That's where big deer like to walk, and you'll be well hidden in there. When hunting with a scoped rifle, slug gun or muzzleloader, set up 50 to 100 yards away and watch for a buck running a sign-blazed edge.
- Head or foot of a hollow: When you're hunting along and run across a deep hollow, ravine or ditch in the woods, you probably stop and think, "Why walk down into that thing, and then back up the other side, when I can skirt it?" Deer seem to rationalize the same way. Scout for doe trails and single sets of three-inch buck tracks around the head or foot of a major terrain break. Hang a perch where the tracks are fresh and the wind is right, then watch for bucks skirting an obstacle and slipping within shooting range.

4. The Overgrown Field

In Alabama one December, I sat in a stand and watched eight tall, porcelain-white tines weaving through a maze of broom sedge, honeysuckle, briars and saplings below. As I raised my rifle and tried to scope the buck's shoulder in the cover, rack and all disappeared. The deer bedded down before my eyes!

Is there an overgrown field like that in your hunt zone? If not, what about a tangled cutover, burn or gas right-of-way? Any place with cover head high to a buck is a prime bedding ground. After a long night of feeding and mingling with does, a big deer often sneaks out into a "dirty" field and curls up with his back to the wind. If he smells, sees or hears danger approaching, "see ya," the buck slips away like a rabbit through the thick stuff.

Scout the edges of overgrown habitats for doe trails and buck tracks, rubs and scrapes. Check for narrow, twisting trails gouged out into cover. Then play the wind and hang treestands strategically along the perimeter. What if a buck disappears into cover before you can touch off a shot? After an hour of sitting on the edge of your seat, burning holes in the thick stuff with your binoculars and scope, you still cannot pick out the deer. You get this uncontrollable urge to climb down and stalk him. Big mistake!

You must remember that from ground zero, tall, tangled cover looks totally different than it does from 20 feet in the air. It's tough to pinpoint where a deer is bedded. And even if you have the wind, it's damn near impossible to sneak up on a buck in thick, noisy brush. I learned that the hard way on the Alabama hunt I mentioned earlier. I shinnied down from my stand, tried a fancy stalk, spooked the buck and ruined a prime bedding area to hunt!

Don't mess up like that. Hang in your stand and continue to glass. In time the deer might stand up to stretch and look around, offering a quick shot. Or you might nail the buck as he skulks out to feed later in the afternoon.

I find that many mature bucks stick to woodland thickets early in the season, then move out to bed in overgrown fields, cutovers and the like as the rut approaches and then explodes. This in many cases positions the testosterone-addled deer between the feeding and bedding grounds of several doe units. Pressured, weary bucks naturally hang in the nasty covers deep into the post-rut.

28   Ernie's Stand

BY BOB MCNALLY

How one stand produced three Pope & Young bucks and several misses in just four years. Here's why Ernie Calandrelli's stand is tops.

I t was 1996, and champion turkey caller and veteran deer hunter Ernie Calandrelli knew his "timing" was perfect. It was early November, the whitetail rut was underway, and calm and cold weather had settled into the area. Calandrelli was also certain that the central-Iowa farm he was hunting was a premier spot for buster bucks.

The 1996 bowhunt was the first fall trip Calandrelli had made to the 590-acre farm. He'd come at the invitation of the owner, who he'd met during the previous spring's turkey season. When hunting toms on the Iowa farm, Calandrelli had seen plenty of buck sign, including giant rubbed trees.

While scouting only 50 yards off a field edge, Calandrelli stumbled across a pile of big-buck sign—and it was fresh. Trails and tracks crisscrossed everywhere beneath a tangled buck-brush canopy. Then he saw plenty of droppings and nearby tree bases that had been rubbed heavily by bucks. The trees were as big around as Calandrelli's forearms, which are impressive in their own right.

The bowhunter located a natural funnel beside a field ditch where the wind was perfect. He placed a portable stand in a giant cottonwood, with limbs large enough to perfectly conceal him 20 feet up. The stand overlooked the ditch and a number of crossing deer trails. Buck scrapes and rubs were everywhere, and because the stand was sandwiched between a fresh-cut cornfield and a broad, open pasture, he could easily get a shot at any deer skirting the fields, traveling the ditch or using the crossing trails.

Upwind of the field corner, to the northeast, was a dense hardwood area. Deer were using the ditch and wooded corner for cover as they moved about to feed in the corn. Bucks were obviously cruising the area looking for hot does.

Calandrelli hunted the ditch the first afternoon and didn't see a deer. Not one. He started second-guessing the spot, but decided to give it a little more time. The next morning he was having doubts as he climbed into the stand in the 25-degree weather.

An hour passed, and he saw no deer. After two hours, Calandrelli was angry with himself for not scouting harder and finding a more sure spot. That's when movement in the ditch caught his eye. It was a dandy eight-point buck with a large body and heavy rack. But instead of staying in the ditch and moving into the wind toward Calandrelli, the buck turned to walk into the corn. The deer was 80 yards away, and Calandrelli was sure he was leaving the area, so the bowhunter grabbed his Quaker Boy grunt call and softly blew it several times.

Instantly, the buck stopped, threw up his head and tested the wind. Then he turned back toward the ditch and moved quickly toward the giant cottonwood. Calandrelli had just enough time to stand, turn quietly toward the deer, raise his bow and wait for the buck to offer a shot. At 40 yards the buck stopped, alert, looking around and checking the wind. The deer appeared nervous, and Calandrelli sensed he was about to leave. Figuring he'd better try a shot, he raised his bow, drew, settled a sight pin behind the buck's shoulder and released. The shaft sailed low, missing the deer cleanly, and the buck bolted through the ditch, disappearing into a distant thicket.

The miss was devastating. Calandrelli was so mad at himself that smoke practically filled the air from his fuming. He believed he'd lost the best opportunity he'd ever have for a quality Iowa buck. He sat in the stand dejected, figuring to bide his time until midmorning, when he'd break down his stand and gear and scout for another spot. But then something made him glance down the ditch, and there he could see a huge deer rack coming his way—following the same path the eight-pointer had taken.

The hunter stood, nocked an arrow and watched in amazement as the deer came toward him like a laser beam tracking a target. When the deer was 70 yards out, Calandrelli made another low, reassuring grunt call, and the buck continued his beeline to the hunter, nose to the ground like a setter tracking a quail. The whole time the buck was walking toward Calandrelli he was grunting, low and slow, and this gave the hunter the shakes like he'd never had before.

Apparently, the larger buck was tracking the smaller eight-pointer, and when Calandrelli made a final grunt call, the bigger buck turned from the smaller deer's trail and walked straight toward the hunter. At 17 yards the buck offered Calandrelli the shot he'd been hoping for, so he drew, aimed, released and watched his arrow pass completely through the deer. The threeblade Thunderhead Spitfire did its job, and the giant buck fell within sight, traveling only 51 steps.

It took three men to load the whitetail onto a four-wheeler to get it out of the woods. The deer had a field-dressed weight of 260 pounds, with an estimated live weight more than 300. His 10-point rack gross-scored 147 Pope & Young points, easily qualifying for the record book. This was the first P&Y buck for Calandrelli, who had more than 50 bucks to his credit. The deer's main beams each measured more than 22 inches and had heavy mass, yet the rack seemed small on such an enormous body.

The Iowa farm was a proven giant-buck producer, but Calandrelli had only just begun to understand how remarkable his spot was.

He slated the first two weeks of November 1997 to hunt Iowa and nearby Missouri. His plan was simple: Hunt the Iowa farm in the mornings, then drive 20 miles to Missouri for the afternoons. (It was the last week of the Missouri bow season—just prior to the gun opener—and a prime time for rutting bucks.) Both spots were near the camp he was staying at in Missouri. If he arrowed a Missouri buck, he'd shift all his efforts to Iowa, where bucks were also rutting. Once the bow season ended in Missouri, he'd focus completely on Iowa, where the season runs well into December.

The plan went well, with Calandrelli arrowing a nice eight-pointer in Missouri the third day. So he hunted the Iowa farm every morning and afternoon, determined to find a buck better than the huge 10-pointer he'd shot the previous year.

Every time he sat in his cottonwood stand, Calandrelli saw deer—plenty of does and small bucks. He was also seeing lots of coyotes cruising the ditch near the field/woods corner. He was convinced that if coyotes and does were regularly walking the ditch line near his stand, so would traveling bucks when the peak of the rut began to make them throw caution to the wind.

The fifth morning was perfect, with frost on the ground and no wind. Coyotes yodeled at sunrise. And from first light Calandrelli saw deer—mostly does and yearlings, but a couple of small bucks checking scrapes a scant 20 yards away.

Finally, at midmorning, he caught movement in the ditch and saw an enormous deer with a blocky, muscular body that could only belong to a buck. The deer stopped in a tangled thicket, almost disappearing in his perfect camouflage. Calandrelli strained his eyes to see the buck's head, and when he did he almost fell out of his stand. The buck was enormous—even bigger than the previous year's. He had 10 massive points, and his neck was swollen to the size of a bull's.

The buck was 60 yards away, looking and listening. When he turned his head away from Calandrelli, the hunter positioned himself for a shot, then grunted softly with his Quaker Boy call.

The buck spun his head in Calandrelli's direction and came quickly.

At 30 yards the deer stopped in a thicket and turned, at which point a small opening to his chest showed through the cover. In one smooth sequence Calandrelli drew, held and loosed his arrow. But midway to the immense buck the arrow struck a twig and the shaft vaulted harmlessly over the buck's back.

The monster wheeled and dashed away down the ditch.

"I've shot a lot of bucks, and some huge ones that have scored over 150 inches," Calandrelli said. "That deer was a perfect 10, and easily would have scored 160 inches. Easily!"

On the last day of his 1997 hunt, Calandrelli arrowed a 130-inch nine-pointer. It was a great buck by any measure, but only a consolation prize considering the buck he'd missed.

The 1998 hunt was similar to 1997's, but Calandrelli was determined to arrow a buck of the caliber he'd missed the previous fall. He passed many bucks from his now-favorite cottonwood stand, some of P&Y caliber, but he stayed focused on a true trophy with an outsize rack. He finally saw the buck of his dreams one afternoon as he walked to the stand. On the edge of the cornfield, at 2 p.m. in the bright sun, a buck stepped out of the woods to work a scrape. Through strong binoculars, Calandrelli watched the perfect 10-pointer he believes would have scored 170-plus inches. Standing just 100 yards away, the buck pawed the ground, then slowly ambled straight away, entering the far woods directly where his stand hung in the cottonwood.

Timing, he though dejectedly. Being on the right stand at the right moment is what bowhunting is all about.

Before the 1998 hunt ended Calandrelli had missed another 135-inch 10-pointer from his stand. The buck had been running after a doe on the far side of the ditch and had stopped for a moment while crossing the ditch. Calandrelli had grunted, but the buck would come no closer. He took a shot, and the arrow sailed wide.

That's when Calandrelli decided to use a doe decoy, which he did this past fall.

This past November was unseasonably warm. Bucks were late coming into rut, but when they did they went bonkers chasing does. Calandrelli was on stand one cold, calm morning when he saw movement across the ditch. It was a heavy-weight buck that was looking directly at the doe decoy stationed five yards from the base of the cottonwood. Using fishing line tied to a real deer tail mounted on the decoy, Calandrelli made the tail twitch in a lifelike manner. That's all it took, and the bowhunter tagged another monster from his stand. This one was a nine-pointer weighing an estimated 280 pounds and scoring an impressive 137 P&Y points.

By any measure, Calandrelli's Iowa cottonwood stand is phenomenal, and he'll surely be in it again this November. In only a handful of sessions during four years, he has arrowed three P&Y bucks with a combined weight of more than 700 pounds and antlers measuring more than 400 inches! And he's missed and seen bucks even larger.

"The place has everything a bowhunter could possibly want," Calandrelli said. "First, it's in Iowa, which is without question one of the best places in America for heavy, older, genetically superior bucks with large racks. Second, it's on private land, which doesn't get hunted too much and the deer are pretty much left alone before the rut.

"The stand location also is picture-perfect. Cut corn is a key because of its food value, plus it's surrounded by heavy woods and brush, so there's plenty of bedding cover. The back corner of the cornfield is far from a main road [nearly a mile], so few people and no poachers are likely to disturb the spot.

"Another important part of the location is that the prevailing north autumn wind is almost always blowing perfectly away from the timber and out into the pasture, so bucks checking the area don't smell me. I'm fortunate enough to hunt whitetails in many places in many states through fall and winter. I've had great hunts in lots of spots, but that Iowa bow stand may be the single greatest archery location I've ever seen.

"And to think it all happened because I met an Iowa farmer during a turkey hunt who'd never shot a gobbler. I guided him and his grandson to big toms one day, and from that moment on I had a bow deer spot to hunt that every archer only dares to dream about."

Why Calandrelli's Stand Is Tops

1) Food: Corn is the big draw, because this is Iowa. But pastures near the corn are important, too, as are the hardwood buffers between the pastures and corn, where oaks bear acorns.

2) Cover: The timbered creeks, CRP and briers in the timber make for ideal safety zones and bedding habitat.

3) Funnel: Calandrelli's stand is located in the corner of timber adjacent to the cut corn and pasture, where deer funnel their walking patterns to stay in cover as they work from bedding and feeding areas. This funnel is ideal for primary fall/winter north-wind direction.

4) Rarely hunted: Calandrelli's stand is on private property and is a good half-mile walk from the nearest farm road and more than one mile from the nearest hard road. All adjacent farms are private, and each landowner respects the rights of the others, so trespassing is never a problem. Human intrusion onto the farm is rare.

5) Good approach: Walking into Calandrelli's stand from the west allows a hunter to disturb few deer. By walking in through the pasture and the corn, Calandrelli is also able to keep his scent away from deer travel areas.

6) Rut Magnet: When the rut starts, bucks looking for does habitually cruise the trails near Calandrelli's stand. The necked-down funnels concentrate bucks, so it's just a matter of time before a good one wanders by.

29　Five Steps to Ultimate Concealment

BY BILL BUCKLEY

Whether you bowhunt from a treestand or at ground level, the problem remains the same: How can you stay hidden from game well enough to get a killing shot?

When I first moved out West, I lived next door to an elk guide. Like many hunters he bragged about his hunting prowess by degrading his quarry's intelligence. "Rutting bulls are dumb," he said one day. "In fact, you don't even need camouflage to bring them in close. Only elk hunters who don't know how to hunt need camo."

Listening incredulously, I could only remember the countless times a cautious bull elk had pinned me down immediately after coming into sight—despite my thinking I was well hidden. That conversation occurred in late summer, and the following September I looked out my window as the guide's truck pulled in front of his house. Out he stepped after returning from a hunt, not only wearing a full suit of camouflage but face paint as well. No doubt camo gloves were stuffed into his pants pockets. So much for dumb animals and ignorant hunters.

I've also read lots of articles by various hunting "experts" who preach that whitetails have all sorts of supernatural powers and can only be fooled by superhuman effort.

Thankfully, for those of us who still hunt for enjoyment, the truth is most animals are neither stupid nor supernatural. You can dine on bean-sprout burgers and wash yourself until your skin hurts—it won't kill you. But hunting doesn't have to be that way. Yet neither can you waltz haphazardly around the woods without suffering consequences. As the saying goes, you're operating in the animals' world, and they have the benefit of living there 24 hours a day. They notice subtle changes in their environment.

So what does it take to be a successful hunter and keep from being detected? Mostly common sense, thank goodness. All you need to do is follow these five rules of hunting and you'll stay hidden from the most discerning eyes and still get off a killing shot. For a whitetail hunter, that's what ultimate concealment is all about.

1. Be All That You Can Be

No, we're not talking about joining the Army. We're talking about your camo wardrobe and how it needs to match the varied habitats you hunt. You may not want to hear this, but your favorite camo could be letting you down; you could be sticking out like the proverbial sore thumb. That's because, in any given situation, not all camouflage is equal.

An easy way to judge your camo's effectiveness is to tack your hunting jacket or shirt against the types of trees in which you place your stand or by which you stand or kneel, then step back 50 to 70 yards and take a look. Sounds pretty elementary, but most hunters take for granted that good camouflage will work anywhere. It doesn't—nor should it be expected to—and this test will point it out. If your camo's tone is significantly lighter or, more typically, darker than the background, it will stand out sharply, particularly to a deer's eyes. Think how much more it will show up with a person inside it instead of pressed flat against a tree.

You'll also notice, if the pattern is tight, how it begins to block up as you step farther back. It will begin to look more like a solid color. This may not be bad as long as that portion of your body remains tight to a tree, but the camo will stand out against a more mottled background of other tree boles, branches, and leaves. It will clearly show your human form.

Experiment a little, pinning different camo patterns to different backgrounds and you'll soon realize one might work well with oak trees, for instance, but not with pines. Another might disappear in brush but appear black against marsh grass or standing corn. In other words, unless you hunt identical surroundings for all your bowhunting, you'd better own a varied wardrobe. Luckily, there are so many great patterns, especially looser ones—like Mossy Oak's Break-Up and Shadow Grass, Realtree's All-Purpose patterns, Skyline's Apparition, Backland's Full Benefit—that you can literally match any background you want. Even the old standby, woodland camo, has its place.

You can often take a giant step toward ultimate concealment by becoming a cross-dresser. Forget the high heels and lipstick, just mix and match your pants and jacket with the most prevalent background. For example, a tree-bark patterned jacket with leaf-patterned pants might work best for a treestand hunter who spends most of his time sitting. The pant's looser pattern will blend with the surrounding woods while the jacket's bark pattern will match the tree trunk you're leaning against. The same might work best for ground blinds if you mostly kneel or sit. The opposite works best if you plan to stand against a tree, where your lower body will blend with the tree trunk, your upper body with the branches and foliage. Whatever you wear, try to match your background. Choose a setup that best matches your camo when you plan an ambush. If you've tested your camo against different backgrounds, you'll know precisely what to look for.

Blending into your background also necessitates wearing hand and face camo. Nothing stands out in the woods like a pale face or the flash of bare, moving hands as you raise or draw back a bow. Treestand hunters can avoid messy face paint by wearing a face mask as long as it doesn't interfere with their release. But for hunters who cover lots of territory, camo paint is the only practical solution. Masks are too hot to wear while hiking, and I've been caught more than once trying to get my mask into position when a buck suddenly showed up and stared me down.

Lastly, your equipment should be properly concealed. Spray with a flat, earth-tone paint anything on your bow that shines. Bow-sight housings, stabilizers, even arrow rests can give you away if they reflect sunlight. So will broadheads. I dull the shine of sharpened blades and reflective ferrules with an indelible black magic marker. Not attending to these small details could cost you a shot.

2. Think Sideways

That's right: Think sideways for stand placement, silhouette and shine control, scent control, and calling and you'll remain undetected and get more shots than ever.

For the sake of explanation, let's assume you've come across a deer trail winding from a swamp through some woods to a nearby cornfield. Big tracks are carved deeply into it, and all you have to do is find the right stand location and the buck is yours. Where do you set up?

First you need to establish the prevalent wind direction. Obviously, you don't want your scent blowing right to the buck. Yet if you pick a stand where the wind normally blows from him to you, he can't smell what's ahead of him. He'll either use a different trail that gives him a more favorable wind or wait until dark to move.

Ideally, the prevalent wind cuts sideways—perpendicular or quartering—to most of the trail. Why? Because the buck still thinks he can smell danger ahead, yet he can't smell you. You'll then have more potential stand sites at your disposal. If the prevailing wind does blow from the cornfield to the swamp, look for a sharp-enough turn in the trail where you can set up on the downwind side and your scent will angle away from the trail. He'll feel safe moving during daylight hours, and you won't be detected. Either way, setting up so the prevailing wind blows sideways or quartering will give you the best chance of having the buck move past your stand most days of the week.

Now let's say you're able to narrow down your stand site to three locations. Two are 20 yards off the trail, one a lone tree and the other a tight cluster of four trees. The third spot is a multi-trunked tree not five yards from the trail. Any one could give you the shot you want, but one gives you a great advantage. It's the group of trees 20 yards to the side of trail. Not only won't the buck be looking directly at it when he comes down the trail, as with the tree five yards away, the four tree boles will help block your silhouette no matter what angle he approaches your stand. The single tree will only block your full outline if he walks either directly toward or away from you, not from the side. Of course, if the lone tree has branches and foliage on either side of your stand, it too will prevent the buck from seeing you. The main point is to envision how you'll stand out from all sides.

Sunlight can also severely compromise your concealment. In a perfect world it will always be at your back and in the buck's eyes. But, even then, unless there's enough foliage to keep you in shade, any movement you make will catch the bright light and will cast shadows on the ground. Either one will readily spook a deer. Before you settle on a stand site, consider how the sun might creep in from the side and highlight your movements as it moves across the sky. If you'll be lit up like a Christmas ornament during prime hunting time, either create a screen of foliage using prunings from clearing shooting lanes or find another spot.

Hunters trying to ambush game from ground level should pay special attention to where the sun's heading, since being on the game's level amplifies the chance of being spotted. In 10 minutes the sun can move enough to turn a perfect shady stand—shade is a hunter's best ally for staying hidden—into a spotlight where any move you make will be instantly detected.

Lastly, thinking sideways grunting up a buck can sometimes distract him from pinpointing your location. Animals have the uncanny ability to determine a sound's precise point of origin. If you point the grunt tube directly at a buck or bull every time you call, he'll come in looking directly at you. Throw your calls in various directions, however, or to the side where you have the best shot, and you'll often turn a low-odds situation into a sure kill. It will also sound more natural, since animals rarely face the same direction when calling repeatedly.

3. Hear No Evil, See No Evil

That's what you want your quarry to think, which means you've got to keep noise and movement to a minimum. Remember back to all the deer you saw last season. How many did you suddenly notice just standing nearby, oblivious to your presence? Probably not many. Most deer you detected by hearing their approaching footsteps or by seeing movement in the brush. And that's exactly how animals lock on to most hunters.

Careless movement will render even the best camouflage useless, although if you've set up with sufficient screening cover to your sides you don't have to stay statue-still. And who can? The good thing about hunting is that it isn't war; you won't give away your company's position and condemn your fellow soldiers to death if you're caught swatting a mosquito or picking your nose. Still, your success will hang on your ability to keep movements to a minimum. Scratch that itch, but do it slowly, keeping your hand tight to your body and only after having scanned the woods for game. Shift your weight to get comfortable and to keep your legs from falling asleep, but again easy does it. Few treestands come with comfortable seats, and that's the principal reason hunters squirm on their stands. So find a thin cushion and strap it to your stand's seat upon arrival (if it's loose it might fall off). You'll reduce unnecessary movement by 90 percent.

Noise is often harder to control, but you can reduce it substantially by attending to a few details. First, even if you go to your stand an hour before you expect deer to start moving, stillhunt your way to it. Walk softly and stop often to survey the woods ahead. If it's dark, use your ears to detect deer ahead of you, and stop until they've moved out of the area. Few things kill a stand site like does blowing alarm snorts.

Your clothing must also be quiet, as should your bow. Avoid nylon and Dacron outer clothing, as well as any material that grates against itself when you move into a shooting position and draw your bow. If the back of your jacket catches on tree bark and makes noise, tie an extra shirt around the trunk before you sit down. And if your bow squeaks or your arrow grates against the rest, fix the problem before it costs you a shot. The same goes for a bow that makes a loud vibration noise upon release. If the buck jumps the string, what good have all your other precautions done? Also check your stand for squeaks and popping noises as you shift your weight. They'll draw a deer's attention like lightning.

4. Envision the Shot, But Easy Does It

As a teenager I once found the ultimate ground blind: an immense hollowed-out tree trunk big enough to stand in and only 15 yards from a well-used deer trail. Sure enough, an hour after setting up one morning a doe stepped into view, broadside, totally unaware I was there. I raised my bow confident I was about to kill my first deer. Until, that is, my elbow bumped into the back of the hollow and I couldn't get past a quarter draw. I leaned forward, gaining an inch or two, but still couldn't get the string anywhere close to my anchor point. The doe finally walked off, and I'd learned an important lesson: Keeping well hidden is only part of the equation; you still need to get off a shot.

Over the years I've hunted many stands where I could get a shot but only through one narrow shooting lane or by contorting my body in awkward positions. And I've let a lot of what should have been easy shots pass me by. I've also ruined excellent stand sites by making sure I could get a shot in almost every direction. I'd prune so many shooting lanes it looked like a logging crew had swept through the area. Then I'd never see a deer walk within range.

The truth is, many stand sites look like perfect ambush points, but only by erecting your stand and envisioning the shot can you tell their real potential and glaring flaws. If you can't get into shooting position and draw your bow unimpeded, and without having to snake your bow past limbs even after a little pruning, try raising or lowering the stand. Failing that solution, find another tree. If the stand is fine but cutting shooting lanes requires extensive pruning, don't count on hunting the stand any time soon. The deer need time to get used to the changed environment, and you've just spread your human scent all over the immediate area.

As hard as it may be to accept, the ultimate stand site doesn't offer you complete immunity from being spotted, nor does it promise you to an unimpeded 360-degree shooting range. It's a compromise that balances a few key shot openings with enough intervening cover to draw your bow unnoticed and get off a killing shot. The sooner you know when to leave well enough alone, the better you'll blend in effectively as a hunter.

5. Don't Overindulge

If moderation is the key to a happy and productive life, it certainly is a major key to ultimate concealment. Even with the best-laid ambush, over-using a particular stand will quickly whittle down its effectiveness. The standard rule of thumb for stand hunting states that your best chance of killing a buck from each location is the first time you hunt it. With each successive visit your chances diminish. That's because every time you walk to and from a stand, you leave scent on the ground and on any vegetation you contact. The deer take note, and when they associate that area with human scent they'll start avoiding it. To preserve each stand location's effectiveness, use it sparingly and have other stands set up elsewhere.

A good strategy is to keep scouting your hunting territory throughout the season. Not only will you find new and exciting stand prospects (and not overuse the ones you have), you'll also keep tabs on changes in deer movement that naturally occur due to the animal's breeding cycles and forage supplies. You might even locate a much better spot to hunt.

Wherever you take a stand, how you maximize its potential depends on having respect for your quarry's keen senses and being able to overcome them. That begins with matching your camo to the stand site, then tailoring each stand to hide your form, scent, and movements. You don't have change your lifestyle or go to ridiculous extremes to conceal yourself from game. All you need to do is follow these five steps and you'll be well on your way to a successful bow season.

Tactics at a Glance:

- A good test of camo effectiveness is to tack it to a tree in your hunting area. Step back 30 yards and see how it blends.
- Open patterns work better than tight patterns.
- Sound-proofing gear and clothing is the ultimate camouflage.
- Hide well, but you must still be able to draw your bow.
- Don't overuse your stand sites.

Part Five
Those Magnificent Muleys

Believe it or not, there used to be a time when many writers found themselves more or less apologizing for loving to hunt these big western deer. "Muleys Aren't Easy!" was a frequently heard theme as the writers tried to improve the muley's standing as a hunting challenge. These scribes took us along on exciting hunts in both mountains and down on the plains and river valleys as they sought to prove that the muley was as worthy as the whitetail when it came to rating game animals by degree of difficulty. That all started to change in the 1970s as quality mule deer hunting began to become about as rare as four aces in hunting-camp poker. Today, the quest to bag a big muley with a bow is no less difficult, but it is possible and represents a hunt worthy of any bowhunter's planning and effort, as you'll soon learn right here.

30   Big Bucks with a Bow

BY DWIGHT SCHUH

The best way to take a trophy-rack mule deer? Believe it or not—it's with a bow! Here's why!

I f you asked me, "What's the best way to take a big mule deer buck?" I'd say, "Bowhunting." "Oh, come on," you say. "Everybody knows rifle hunters kill a lot more big mule deer than bowhunters even dream about."

Indeed, rifle hunters do take more, as record books and hunting surveys show. But I doubt that they *see* more, and that's the key point: To take big bucks, you have to see them. That may seem obviously trite, yet the main reason most of us, whether rifle *or* bowhunting, never collect big mule deer is that we never see them. That's why bow seasons offer so much. You'll see far more big mule deer during bow seasons than at any other time.

That's because most western bow seasons take place very early or late in the fall. As a whole, general archery seasons in the West open from mid-August through early September, when mule deer have migrated to high country, either alpine mountain basins or high-desert rimrock ridges and sagebrush plateaus. With scant cover here and little hunting pressure, deer spend much of their time in the open, and you'll see more bucks than most rifle hunters ever dream existed.

At the other extreme, some states hold November and December bow seasons. At this time, bucks are in rut, which means they're more active than normal, and heavy snow generally pushes them down onto wide-open winter ranges. So, again, deer are highly visible. As I've said, to kill big bucks, you have to see them, and bow seasons at the head and tail of fall are the times to do just that.

Optics for Muley Country

You've probably guessed by now I consider big buck hunting a visual affair. Indeed it is, and you must have good optics. I've used a variety of binoculars from 7x to 10x, and for all around hunting from timber to tundra I'd take 8x. Some serious mule deer hunters prefer 10x, which are good for desert and alpine hunting. But they do magnify hand movement considerably, a bothersome trait when your hands are shaking from fatigue or excitement. And they're a bit much for close-range viewing in timber or brush.

Here are two important points about binoculars. One, don't buy miniature binoculars (an objective lens smaller than about 30mm), because the small objective (front) lenses restrict light and dim your view, a big handicap at the prime dawn and dusk spotting periods. Two, buy quality. Many cheap binoculars will give you a hangover headache to end all hunting trips. Remember, to spot big bucks, you'll spend several hours a day looking through binoculars. Your entire hunt depends on them, so buy the best you can afford.

Along with standard binoculars, optics in the 15x to 30x range for judging heads and spotting deer at distances of 2 to 3 miles or farther are needed. A high-quality 20x scope covers most situations very well. The problem with any scope is that viewing with one eye for hours can strain your eyes. For prolonged spotting, big binoculars can be better. Set on a tripod so they're absolutely steady, 15x binoculars can be the ultimate spotting gear. I've used a Steiner 15x80 for several years with excellent results, and Zeiss makes a popular (and expensive) 15x60 that some serious hunters use almost exclusively.

Great optics do no good if you don't use them. Once you reach your hunting country, sit down and walk with your eyes. You may spend four, five or six hours a day just looking. To see big bucks, you have to look, long and hard.

Hunting Techniques—First: Stand Hunting

Okay, so what do you do after you see them? I would suggest four ways to put your spotting to work. No single method is better than another. You have to analyze your hunting conditions to decide which will work best for you at the moment.

The first is stand hunting. For years this has been "the" method for trophy whitetails, but it can be just as good for mule deer. Like whitetails, mule deer follow remarkably predictable patterns. The only difference is that, in open territory where they can wander freely, you'll rarely find enough concentrated sign to read these patterns. So instead, you read the patterns by watching the deer.

In Colorado's San Juan Mountains, my friend Bob Robb and I found a group of seven bucks. At night they would feed onto the open tundra above timberline, and during the day they'd work downhill into the timber to bed.

Not one morning went by that we didn't spot the bucks. At first we tried watching them to set up a stalk, but invariably they disappeared into heavy timber where we couldn't find them, or they bedded where we couldn't stalk them successfully. After five days of observing these bucks we finally came to: "Those bucks are following the same pattern, day after day." Consistently they passed through a chute between two rock outcroppings and into a timbered basin. With only one day left to hunt, we took ground blinds near the chute. The bucks came by on schedule, but they drifted just out of range and we didn't get a good shot. If we'd had more time we could have fine-tuned our stand locations and probably taken a buck. The movements of those deer were very predictable, an ideal situation for stand hunting.

Jay Verzuh, a Colorado outfitter, takes many bowhunters each fall, and they average 60 to 70 percent success on mule deer (compared to 25 percent statewide). Verzuh attributes this high success to the use of treestands. "Eliminating treestands would cut our success in half, at least," he said.

Verzuh and his guides find treestand locations by scouting with binoculars and scopes. Early in the morning they locate deer out feeding, and they watch as these animals filter into aspen groves and other bedding grounds. Observation over a period of days reveals movement patterns, and Verzuh places stands accordingly, most commonly on trails between bedding and feeding grounds.

Hunting the same country year after year may give Verzuh an advantage over the average hunter, but he believes anyone can do the same thing if he'll take time to scout. "Most hunters don't find good locations because they think they're wasting precious time by watching deer through binoculars," he said. "Nothing could be further from the truth. That's how you find out where to put your stand."

The Ambush Drive

A second hunting method could be called the "ambush drive." Actually it's a form of stand hunting, but with a couple of twists. One, you need somebody to push deer to you. If there are lots of other hunters around, you can let them unknowingly drive for you. But during most bow seasons you won't see many other hunters, so you need a partner to work with you.

Two, you must know the deers' escape routes. Mule deer normally follow paths of least resistance to escape danger—cuts through rims, saddles in ridges or hilltops, chutes between rock slides. You often can pick these out just be studying the terrain, but you can find them more reliably, again, by observing deer. Anytime you see spooked deer, watch them carefully. They'll follow their favorite escape route, and chances are good they'll do exactly the same thing time after time. That's the key to placing your stand.

One December, a friend and I tried stalking several bucks on a desert foothill. With crunchy snow on the ground, we made too much noise and the bucks spooked out well ahead of us and marched single file out of sight through a saddle at the top of the hill.

The significance of their escape didn't strike us right then because all we could think about was the blown stalk. But a couple of days later, when we spotted the same group of bucks back on the same hillside, we got to thinking. "The snow is still too crunchy for any kind of a stalk," we agreed. "But we know where those bucks will go if we spook them. Wonder if they'll use that saddle two times in a row?"

To find out, my friend gave me an hour to circle around the hill and come into the saddle from the back side. I took a stand there under a juniper tree as my partner slowly walked up from below. The plan worked. To elude my friend, the bucks headed straight for the saddle, and the closest walked by me at 10 yards.

The Ambush Stalk

I call a third proven method the "ambush stalk." In a sense this is a combination of pure stalking, discussed in more detail below, and stand hunting. Although you're looking for an ambush point, you don't need a driver. Rather, you observe deer in their natural feeding and movement patterns, and then you immediately stalk into position to intercept them as they feed along.

Again, observation is the starting point. You must locate and watch deer from a distance long enough to figure out what they're doing and where they're going. And then you must analyze the terrain and vegetation to plan a good stalking route and ambush point.

Harold Boyack, perhaps the most successful mule deer bowhunter in the West, likes this approach.

"I love steep canyon country where I can see across and watch a buck's movements. My method is to spot a buck and to watch long enough to chart where he's going," Boyack said, "Then I hurry around and intercept him. I like a buck coming to me because he won't be as alert as when he's bedded.

"It's also easier to get a good shooting angle this way. I can plan my ambush in just the right place so the buck must present a good broadside shot as he comes by."

For two days in Colorado, Boyack watched a buck feed low in a creek bottom at night and then work up through some cliffs just after dawn to bed high during the day. As this pattern developed one morning, he hiked above the buck and took a stand on a cliff. Before long the deer came through and stopped broadside, 12 feet away.

Using this approach extensively, Boyack has taken some huge bucks. One non-typical, with a score of 232⅝, ranks No. 4 in Pope & Young records. A 40-inch typical monster he took in Utah is one of the largest bucks ever taken by an archer.

The Stalk

A fourth method for big bucks, and the one I've personally used most, is the "stalk." This approach differs from the first three in that you're working on a stationary, rather than moving, buck. In most cases, that means he's bedded. That's an advantage because it eliminates the guesswork of predicting a buck's movements. Once you've seen him bed, you *know* where he is.

As in the other three methods, you start by watching for feeding deer at first light in the morning. But when you've spotted a buck you want, you wait for him to bed for the day. You may have to move around to keep him in sight, but you stay back, undetected, until he's settled in for the day, generally 9 to 10 a.m.

Then you make your move. At first you can move quickly, and getting within 100 yards or so should be fairly easy, provided you're out of the deer's sight. It's the last 100 yards that can be tough, because there you're within the buck's most acute sensory range. It's this stage that separates bow from rifle hunting. As always, scent is your No. 1 concern. You must approach from downwind. Period. That's your only guarantee against being smelled.

That leaves the deer's sight and hearing to overcome, and you do that with Slow Movement. If you move slow enough (and wear camouflage), a deer won't see you, even in the sparsest cover, and he won't hear your slight, deliberate movements. (On crunchy gravel and other noisy footing, I often stalk in socks the last critical yards, which reduces noise immeasurably.) If you take enough time, you can consistently get within 40 yards or less of bucks, even in the most open country.

Under some conditions, it can be easy, but commonly you'll have to sneak and crawl for hours to get close. One December I'd glassed for a couple of hours one morning with my 15x binoculars when, about 9 o'clock, I saw an antler under a juniper tree a mile away. The buck was already bedded for the day. The weather was warm and sunny, and a steady breeze was blowing uphill, perfect for stalking.

Moving fast, I stayed out of sight behind a low ridge and got within 100 yards of the deer in 20 minutes. But from there on, things slowed down. The only cover between me and him were sparse sage and knee-high rocks. Slowly I crawled up behind one of the rocks, 40 yards from the buck and sat down to wait. That seemed a good place to shoot from, but the range was a little long, and besides, the buck lay on the far side of a juniper tree, shielded by limbs. For a half-hour I sat there, analyzing, and finally I decided it would be possible to get a clear shot from much closer range. It would only require circling around to shoot from the other side of the tree. Simple, no?

The crusty ground was noisy, so I took off my boots and pulled on an extra pair of wool socks to pad my feet. Then I moved into the open above the deer. As long as he looked straight away, I crept ahead; any time he turned his head so he could see me with peripheral vision, I stood still and waited. During the entire time, I was within plain sight of the buck.

For two hours I inched along, eventually circling 180 degrees above the buck, never more than 40 yards from him. Now he was wholly visible, presenting a clear shot. I started to crawl down behind a big rock 10 yards from him but decided against it. At such close ranges, I tend to panic. So I stayed back and shot from 20 yards. The arrow hit him midchest, and he ran less than 100 yards. He was an old buck, later aged by a biologist at nine years, and his rack measured a shade wider than 30 inches. I may be exaggerating to say bowhunting is the *best* way to take a big buck. But with the right approach, it's one way that works.

31   Muleys Aren't a Mystery

A veteran of stalking the big-racked bucks of the west, the author doesn't believe miracles are needed for success.

If someone had advertised a "beginner's class for muleys" before my first trip West, I would have signed up faster than a senior citizen signs up for a free sample of Metamucil. Muleys were mystical to me. Heck, I was used to those deer with the large, flagging tails.

Muleys were deer of the open prairies as well as the high mountains. They were deer equipped with radar ears and long, bounding escape leaps. They seemed so foreign to this teenager from corn country. They could just as well have been from Africa for all I knew about them and their habits. How could any hunter ever take one with a bow and arrow?

Those are the thoughts of a nonthinking, testosterone-laden, hyperactive teenager. Too bad I had not been blessed with the experienced mind of a Metamucil drinking senior citizen. Like my 70-year-old, set-in-his-way, grandpa, I would have taken on mule deer with an approach that fit my routine. Remember, they are still just deer.

So all of your experience centers around whitetails? Mule deer seem as foreign to you as Mongolia? If you happen to be fretting a Western mule deer and wondering if you're up to the mule deer ways, read on. Muleys are not mystical deer. Nope, they are just deer with the word "mule" preceding their title.

Although not as widespread as whitetails, mule deer cover an expansive chunk of Western real estate. This is the type of real estate that serves as backdrops for John Wayne movies. Their range extends from just south of the Arctic Circle in Yukon Territory to Mexico. Mule deer researchers argue today on how many subspecies of mule deer exist, but it is accepted that at least three main subspecies, maybe more, do exist, not including the two separate subspecies of blacktail deer. Some researchers argue whether they are distinct subspecies or just the same species more adapted to their ecosystem.

The most widely distributed is the Rocky Mountain mule deer. The other species are divided between desert mule deer from both the California and Mexican coasts and interior desert mule deer, again from California and Mexico.

We do know for sure that both Sitka and Columbian blacktail deer are separate subspecies. The Columbian blacktail deer makes its home along the Northwest coast of North America and the Sitka deer lives primarily in southeastern Alaska. Still, the majority of hunters target the more widely distributed Rocky Mountain muley.

According to Valerius Geist in the book "Mule Deer Country," mule deer are recent newcomers to the earth, geologically speaking. According to Geist's research, they are actually descendants of whitetail deer twice. And for you trivia buffs, the whitetail deer is the oldest deer species in the Western hemisphere.

Are you now beginning to scratch your head, thinking if these critters are related to whitetails, and twice at that, you might be able to outsmart them? Read on.

Making its appearance nearly four million years ago, Geist theorizes that whitetail deer spread throughout North America, finally populating the Northwest coast of North America and eventually evolving into the blacktail deer. Remember that little bit of information. It's the first way mule deer are related to the whitetail deer.

That little whitetail deer side trip to the Northwest took a million years alone. Approximately 10,000 years ago, a change took place in the animal kingdom that included the extinction of many varieties of herbivores and carnivores. With less competition and a changing habitat scene, both whitetail and blacktail deer expanded their populations and range. Eventually, they met, settled down and had babies. Presto, the creation of the mule deer and the second way muleys are related to the whitetail deer.

With all the cloning flap going on these days, it's interesting to note that mule deer DNA is almost identical to whitetail deer DNA. On the other hand, the whitetail and blacktail deer were very far apart according to Geist's information.

"If the mule deer runs on whitetail deer mitochondria, then it means that all mule deer are descendants of whitetail deer mothers and blacktail deer fathers," states Geist.

Before things get too technical, let's just finish with the statement that blacktail deer and whitetail deer successfully hybridized to form the mule deer. That's something that only has chance happenings in nature and about 10,000 years ago, the mule deer was the latest deer to arise and successfully populate North America.

When you compare whitetail deer to mule deer, you quickly see significant physical differences. Mule deer are larger and blockier than the average whitetail. A typical mule deer buck weighs about 175 pounds, whereas a whitetail deer weighs in at 150 pounds. Of course, subspecies and regions cause weight differences. Just in case you get into a round of Double Jeopardy and the category is mule deer, the highest recorded weight of a muley was 475 pounds . . . a real hog!

It's those ears that give away a mule deer. It was named mule deer because their ears resemble those of a mule and the large ears actually serve two purposes. First, mule deer spend most of their life in open country and need to hear at longer distances. The larger ears cup the sound and gather it better. Secondly, the large ears may actually regulate body heat, especially for desert mule deer. As the deer rests in the shade, blood cools as it courses through vessels in the ear, and assists in cooling the deer's body as the cooler blood continues through the body.

Other than the large ears, mule deer have a thin, black-tipped tail and a white rump. Its masked face also is a dead giveaway, especially with a mule deer's dark winter coat. Just remember one thing. When you screw up and bump a muley, its tail won't be waving goodbye like a whitetail, but its springing escape will definitely tell the tale.

We've now linked muleys to whitetails and shown that, physically, they differ, but how do their habits differ? It's the habits that will form much of your bowhunting gameplan anyway. Instead of covering mule deer habits through the seasons, let's focus on one season, the fall, as if you couldn't have guessed.

Like whitetail deer, mule deer reside in bachelor groups in early fall. For the hunter, this is a definite advantage in locating bucks. In prairie areas, hunters often locate bands of bucks by scanning lush feeding fields like alfalfa, prairie hay fields and harvested small grain fields. High in the mountains, finding muleys is a different story. There, a hunter needs to concentrate glassing efforts on lush valleys or alpine slopes. And whether high or low, muleys require water. Seeps, springs, reservoirs and even stock tanks provide water.

All of these locales provide options for either stalking or standhunting. For the first-time hunter coming from a whitetail background, early fall is the time to stand hunt.

Stand hunting is relatively new to the mule deer bowhunting scene. It's only been in recent years where enough hunters have watched muleys closely enough to see their subtle patterns. A good friend of mine in Montana does 90 percent of his mule deer bowhunting through the use of stands and in recent years his clients have experienced 80 percent success.

I often think of mule deer as chickens wandering around a barnyard. They seem to stop and feed wherever and whenever, but if you watch them long enough, they end up somewhere predictably.

Mule deer play that same chicken game. Their casual style often has them roaming while feeding and choosing bedding sites in scattered areas. But if you watch close enough, they do have favorite feeding and loafing areas.

And, as they get closer to their final destination, whether it be a feeding or bedding area, they often follow routine trails. The problem is that they may only follow a certain pattern three out of five days. Then again, patience is the name of the game in bowhunting.

One large prairie buck I had patterned, generally bedded in the shadows of a shale slide each morning. Because I only had weekends to hunt, I generally found him one out of two days bedded in the shale slide. Getting close to him was another story as his early October bedding partners kept a watch on nearly every access point to the shaded location. About the time I thought I was in bow range, a pesky young buck would blow out of a hidden washout. The location and numerous buddies saved that buck's hide.

Thinking back, I would have been much smarter to play the waiting game. By identifying prevailing winds and watching their entrance to the bedding area from afar, I could have located a stand site. Then, instead of stalking and bumping them in the morning, I would already be lying in wait as they returned from feeding to bed.

As days grow shorter, so does the circle of guy friends a mule deer buck likes to have around. Again, mule deer are similar to whitetails in which the mature males begin to show their dominance and have little tolerance for lesser bucks.

As the rut begins, mule deer exhibit behavior many whitetail hunters will recognize. First, they spar with rival bucks in a playful, almost teenage-like tussle. Muleys and whitetails spar with brush, or horn brush as some refer to it. In both species, this serves not only as a means of releasing aggression, but many researchers believe mule deer use it to locate one another. After thrashing the brush, a buck will stop and listen, then travel and do it again until he hears a reply. Then, he'll seek out the possible contender.

Over the years, I have rattled in my share of mule deer, both intentionally, and by accident. During the 1996 Montana hunting season, I rattled in four mule deer bucks in three days. What's so amazing about that? Well, I was rattling for whitetails at the time. I'd have one or two whitetails circle in and inevitably, a muley would come bounding in, hair standing on end and nostrils flared. Keep this in mind as an alternative to stalking. And in traditional muley country, don't just rattle antlers, thrash the brush. You may end up staring down a wide-eyed muley.

As does begin coming into estrous, both species of bucks lip curl or flemen. This behavior is used to taste or smell the air and locate does in heat. It also serves as a time saving measure so bucks don't waste precious time courting does not in estrous.

Both mule deer and whitetails urinate on their tarsal glands and rub them together. This serves as a way to communicate using the olfactory senses. In layman's terms, "I stink, therefore I'm tough. Leave me alone." But mule deer take this a step further and it is the reason they do not make ritualistic scrapes like the whitetail deer.

Whitetail deer paw at the ground creating a dirt circle, then urinate in the middle of it. He is in essence, leaving a calling card of urine as an advertisement for does. The mule deer carries his urine on his body like the elk and the larger ungulates. Geist believes this may be due to the large area a mule deer covers compared to a whitetail deer.

By the peak of the rut in mid-November, the mule deer bucks have established their dominance and moved down into the valleys with the herds of does. The larger bucks are kept busy defending groups of does from smaller, satellite bucks looking for action. If you did plan on hunting rutting muleys with a whitetail stand-hunting game plan, you probably won't have much luck. At this time of year, muleys wander even more randomly than in early fall. And since mule deer don't scrape like whitetails, placing a stand would be even more difficult. During the rut, mule deer are best hunted on foot, or by stalking.

At this time of year, a good hunt usually starts on your butt with quality optics. Scanning basins and mountainsides for a buck's location, then noting their behavior and how many companions accompany them, is the basis for this technique. If too many does surround a buck, making a stalk can be next to impossible. Usually locating a loner buck with a single doe is best since you only need to hide from two sets of eyes and not 20. Noting a buck's behavior is also crucial. If a buck is staying in one area and chasing a doe, that sets up a great opportunity for a stalk. Whereas, if a buck is wandering by himself, or following a doe, it can create a more difficult scenario by having to keep up with a moving buck and formulate a stalk at the same time.

A mule deer buck may wander miles searching for does. Once you can establish their route, a stalking ambush is possible, if you have the legs and lungs to keep up. Several years ago, I spied a mule deer traveling across a prairie basin and made mental note of his direction. A peculiar antler configuration easily identified this wanderer. After thoroughly hunting this one area and not interested in the wanderer, I drove my truck around to another prairie pasture nearly four miles away and guess what I found? Yes, that same buck, traveling in the same direction at the same pace. I'm not sure how far that buck traveled, nor whether he has ever stopped.

Whatever you do, don't stop your plans for a mule deer hunting trip because you've spent your whole life hunting whitetail deer. Any hunter with enough experience can tackle another species. By investing time in researching mule deer behaviors and characteristics, you can begin formulating a plan before ever leaving. And remember one thing, a mule deer's closest living relative is the whitetail.

32   The Monster Man of Mule Deer

BY MICHAEL PEARCE

A revealing profile of master hunter David Bainter, a true legend among mule deer chasers.

Last October 17, six hours of walking in Indian-summer heat were starting to wear on bowhunter David Bainter. Conditions were hardly ideal, as most trophy mule deer hunters would see it. In addition, the western Kansas countryside was still a tall carpet of uncut crops. The small draw that Bainter was walking was surrounded by unharvested corn and milo fields—perfect places for a mule deer buck to bed and never be found.

Bainter was moving slow when he got "a feeling."

"It's hard to explain," he said, "but most people know what I'm talking about. I just had this feeling that something was around. I slowly turned my head, and I could see this buck bedded about 60 yards away, in the shade of a plum thicket. I squatted right down. I could tell he was a pretty good buck, but I wanted to know just how big."

Bainter studied the buck's rack with binoculars, and the more he looked, the more he liked what he saw. "I could tell he was pretty wide," Bainter said, "with about a 190-inch net typical main frame plus a few extra points. I figured I'd study him a little more, then maybe try to get him."

Few North American mule deer hunters—gun or bow—can comprehend why Bainter said "maybe." After all, a true trophy mule deer is largely regarded as the toughest animal to take on the continent. Spend enough money, and you can expect to take a monstrous elk from a Southwestern Indian reservation. Make a few trips to Canada or some Northern high-fence operation, and you can expect to kill an impressive whitetail.

But big mule deer are becoming a thing of the past, thanks to shrinking habitat, competition with elk and overharvesting in many states. A buck that's at or near Boone and Crockett minimums (190 typical, 230 nontypical) is the Holy Grail of big-game hunting, and Bainter wanted to study such a buck before trying him with a bow? To know Bainter's history is to know why.

A lifelong hunter from Norman Rockwell-kinds of Kansas towns, Bainter began bow hunting in the early 1980s. Like most who enter the sport, he was at first happy to arrow almost any mule deer buck. As the decade wore on, however, he began to set his sights higher.

"There was a time when I'd have loved to take a 160- to 170-class mule deer, which we have quite a few of," Bainter said. "But it's only natural for someone to want to get better year after year. I started passing up a few of those and began seeing some even bigger deer. They got me fired up, and I set my sights a bit higher."

Bainter remembers the day, in January 1992, that pushed him totally over the trophy-hunting edge. "My brother, Joe, and I were out coyote hunting when we came up on this herd of 10 mule deer bucks," he said. "Of those 10, five were nontypicals—and some were pretty darned impressive. With gun season over, we knew they'd be around the next fall."

The Bainters bowhunted for those bucks the next fall and saw some dandies, but they never got a close shot. However, their luck changed the following year, on October 30, 1993.

"We went back and worked that same pasture," David said. "We'd done a lot of glassing and saw a lot of deer, but nothing I'd have called a shooter. Then as we were leaving and driving down the old dirt road, we drove by an old farmstead, looked over and there he was, standing at the edge of a windbreak with three does. He wasn't 30 yards away, and it was sure obvious he was a big nontypical."

Rather than slow down, the Bainters continued down the road, parked out of sight and hatched a scheme that had the brothers still-hunting in from different directions.

David used a ditch and thick weeds to sneak within 30 yards, where, to his amazement, he missed the kind of opportunity he'd dreamed about for years. But rather than dwelling on the failure, he continued his efforts.

"When I missed, the buck went right up through the middle of the windbreak, and I was jogging right behind him," Bainter said. "I figured, if I could stay close enough, he'd eventually turn and look back, like they often do, and I'd get another chance." Sure enough, the buck stopped about 100 yards from where he'd started, paused and turned to check his back trail. Bainter was already at full draw and delivered a fatal shot.

To say Bainter's buck was a trophy would be like saying Shania Twain is a woman. The great buck carried 27 scorable points, with a 167-inch main frame and nearly 80 inches of nontypical points, including multiple brow tines and four drop tines. All in all, the buck netted 245⅞ nontypical inches, easily putting it in both the Pope & Young and Boone and Crockett record books! In fact, the buck took second-place honors after Pope & Young's 19th measuring period.

Bainter wasn't bold enough to plan on "bigger or nothing" the following years and tagged a 160-class muley in 1994 and a 28-inch 3x4 in '95. His 1996 buck was a 140-class whitetail that he still-hunted during a heavy snow.

But he did find some bruiser mule deer bucks still hanging around his hunting grounds and missed a makeable shot at a 250-class buck and a long shot at the buck of his dreams. "He was really something," Bainter said. "I mean really. We figure he had a 210 frame and would net out at around 280 nontypical. It was a long shot, and I just missed."

By then Bainter was into year-round scouting, and he found himself looking at some very impressive deer in the summer of 1997. "We were out looking around and saw a couple of big bucks in a bachelor group," Bainter said. "Even though it was only mid-June, one of them was pretty wide. I knew he was probably already more than 30 inches. We recognized him as a buck that had been on the neighbor's property the year before. The neighbor wouldn't let us hunt him because he had a boy that was after him."

Bainter checked on the buck from time to time, always keeping his distance. "In early October I found him bedded by a windbreak and got a good look at him from about three-eighths of a mile. I went ahead and tried to figure out what he'd score. It looked to me like he had about a 185-inch frame and enough nontypical points to score about 220. He was wide, definitely more than 30 inches. I figured I'd give him a try sometime."

Sometime came later that month, when a nasty blizzard hammered most of western Kansas. Nineteen inches of snow fell in one day, and all roads were impassable. "I went ahead and called my brother and told him we should take the snowmobiles out and see what was up," Bainter said. "I was curious to see what had happened to our pheasant population. We were mainly just going to look. We didn't even take our bows."

But while out on their look, the Bainters spotted the big mule deer buck in the bottom of a draw, not far from a shelterbelt. "I saw him first, then showed him to my brother," Bainter said. "The buck eventually moved off into the windbreak. We waited quite a while, and he never came out the other side. I asked my brother, "Well, what do you think?"

He thought as most serious hunters would have, and the Bainters made the cold ride back to town, got their equipment, formalized a plan and rode back out. As it had been with other big deer, the plan was for both hunters to slowly still-hunt toward each other, hoping one could either slip into bow range or push the buck past the other.

Bainter circled wide through a wheat field and got glimpses of the buck bedded in the trees. He was still 35 yards from the deer when the buck stood, stretched and looked in his brother's direction. "I knew he had to come by somewhere where I could get a shot," Bainter said. "I kind of figured he might loop out through the open, but instead he came right back through the middle of the trees. I picked an opening and shot as soon as he stepped into it. He wasn't but 12 yards away, and I got a good double-lung hit on him."

The buck was as wide as Bainter had predicted, stretching a tape to 32⅝ inches. His main frame netted a tad better than 180 inches. "He looked the same until I got up to him and I saw he had two more long points on the back I hadn't been able to see before," Bainter said. "I told my brother I thought they'd put him over 230. He scored 234⅞. At the time, it really didn't hit me that I'd taken two Boone and Crocketts or just what kind of accomplishment that was."

According to most, taking two B and C mule deer in the same decade is akin to winning the lottery twice. No other bowhunter has accomplished the feat, nor has any other gun hunter in recent times!

Still kind of aw-shucks about the deal, Bainter hunted hard in 1998 for another good muley. "I didn't get anything monstrous, but I'm spoiled," he said. "I know there are a lot of hunters who'd be slobbering all over themselves for the kind of buck that I killed. It was a 160-class, and it did have a 29-inch outside spread."

Bainter went into last fall with as much enthusiasm as ever, having seen some nice bucks and heard about a few others. In fact, he was looking for one particular trophy when he got "that feeling" while still-hunting that warm October morning.

"I just held my ground and stayed squatted down," Bainter said. "He acted like he kind of knew something was there, but he wasn't overly alarmed. After about 20 minutes, he kind of relaxed, then got up and started hooking the brush and rubbing his antlers on a few trees. I could tell he was kind of curious, though. He kept working his way closer, little by little. I kept figuring he'd cut out to one side and either head to the crops or try to circle around and wind me."

After 45 minutes of cat-and-mouse in the draw, the muley was within bow range. When the buck dropped his head as he walked between two wild-plum thickets, Bainter came to full draw. When the buck reappeared in the open and stopped, Bainter made the 35-yard shot, and the buck was quickly down.

The buck was basically a big 7x7, with a main frame of 186 inches. With roughly 19 inches from four nontypical points, he nets 206⅞ P&Y inches. The buck ranks well up in the prestigious Kansas Top 20 for nontypicals.

"He wasn't as big as those other two, but I realize they're pretty amazing mule deer," Bainter said. "I've been very fortunate. I already have my eye on a couple for this fall. They didn't get taken during rifle season, so they should be around again, only bigger."

In these days of celebrity wannabes, Bainter is a breath of fresh air when it comes to his secret for taking big mule deer. "The most important part is to live where they can grow this big," he said. "A lot of it is the management of the Kansas Department of Wildlife and Parks. Our mule deer are pretty vulnerable, and they've protected them pretty well. Sure, genetics is some of it, but you can overharvest genetics real easily.

"And you have to put in your time. That starts with scouting and ends with hunting hard. No matter what the conditions, you have a chance if you're out hunting, and you don't if you're sitting around the house. A lot of times I'll ask someone to go when it's hot or the crops are still standing, and they won't because they don't figure the hunting could be any good. It's a matter of being out there as much as you can."

It's only right that the man who puts in an amazing amount of time has taken some of America's most amazing mule deer bucks with a bow.

Part Six
Big Game—the Ultimate Challenge

This is where things get real interesting, as the game becomes much, much bigger and hard to bring down. The element of danger enters into the equation now, with unpredictable grizzlies and black bears capable of making a charge that will make your bowhunt more of an adventure than you bargained for. In addition, the high mountains, remote tundra barrens, and northern swamps where game such as elk, caribou, moose, and sheep thrive present challenging terrain and a full agenda of weather not seen in travel ads. The time has come to crank up the level of your game several notches. Read on to see if you're ready.

33 So You Want a Moose?

BY JUDD COONEY

Colorado bowhunting expert Judd Cooney is very familiar with the malady known as "moose fever" and has been working on a cure in forests ranging from Canada to Alaska. Here he points out some unexpected complications in encountering the game animal every bowhunter would love to bag.

Ha! There's nothing to this moose calling," I thought to myself, as I watched the black blob of a moose suddenly appear at the top of the timbered ridge 100 yards above where I knelt. It was my first evening in northern Alberta and I was about to have an "up close and personal" encounter with a Canada moose. Great way to start a hunt!

Fifteen minutes later, the black blob hadn't moved and I had exhausted every bit of my moose calling vocabulary several times over trying to get the reluctant animal to come my way. I was beginning to wonder if maybe this moose hunting/calling was going to be a bit tougher than I first thought. There was no way I could stalk closer because of the blob's position above me on the ridge.

I eased the binoculars out of my jacket and up to my eyes just as the "moose" moved a couple paces along the ridge and suddenly mutated from a moose into a prime black bear! No wonder it wasn't seriously attracted to the mating call of a cow moose.

I snatched my ever-present predator call from my upper jacket pocket and five hackle-raising and tension-filled minutes later had called in and arrowed a gorgeous black bear at a distance of FOUR YARDS! Not a bad way to start a moose hunt!

The following morning was spent getting the bear back to camp and taking care of the hide and meat. Later in the afternoon while Terry Raymen, our guide, finished taking care of the bear hide and salting it down, George Fotiu, my hunting partner, and I took the two Suzuki 4-wheelers and headed down the sandy logging road to do some photography, scout for fresh moose sign and explore the countryside. The area had been burned over some 15 years earlier and most of the rolling hills were covered with dense stands of almost impenetrable new growth jack pines up to 10 feet tall. Most of the numerous small lakes nestled in the valleys and pockets of the hills had patches of unburned mature pines bordering them and there were scattered strips of mature pines that offered ideal places for calling moose "up close and personal."

The following morning found George and me moving quietly down the sandy logging road to a place we had located the previous evening. Terry stayed back a couple hundred yards or so where he could get a wider view of the surrounding country.

George and I set up in the middle of a strip of timber at the top of a ridge overlooking a long narrow lake. The lake was in the center of a flat depression and bordered by open muskeg marsh, willows and strips of timber. A real "moosey looking" spot.

I had been calling for 15 minutes when I caught the first faint grunts of a bull moose. Almost immediately I picked up the bull's wide, white antlers flashing in the willows on the far side of the lake. When the huge bull came to the edge of the lake he hesitated for a few minutes grunting and raking brush and then plunged into the icy water and headed our way. Before swimming completely across the lake, another bull almost as big busted out of the brush, trotted to the edge of the lake and also started swimming our way. There was no doubt about my taking the first bull—his antlers were wide and seemed to spread forever as the monstrous animal weaved his way through the dense jackpines at the base of the hill. I figured there was a good chance both George and I would fill our licenses if both bulls kept on their present course.

Fifteen minutes later, I had lured the lead bull to within 25 yards and put an arrow into his vitals. When he pounded back down the hill toward the lake, the other bull must have thought he was getting charged and about to get his butt kicked so he took off for parts unknown.

Little did I realize at the time that the bull I had killed was going to be the new Alberta Provincial record with a score of 192 points. I did know that I had one of the most challenging and largest of North America's big-game animals on the ground one heck of a long way from camp. Thank goodness for 4x4 4-wheelers.

During the next eight days, George, Terry and I called in eight more bulls and George missed a bull with his bow that might have been even larger than the one I killed. He finally ended his hunt by taking a very good bull with my .270 Winchester. My calling lured the bull across one-half mile of sparse jackpines that glowed golden in the early morning sunlight. While we were photographing George's downed bull, another trophy size bull showed up and stalked back and forth within 20 yards of us for 10 minutes trying to figure out what was going on with his buddy and why there was still a cow moaning in the area. A truly fantastic ending to an already great hunt.

The key to an exciting and successful Canada moose bowhunt is to do everything in your power to book your hunt during the peak of the rut when the bulls and cows are fully engrossed in the throes of breeding. In Canada, the rut usually takes place the last two weeks of September and the first week of October. As with all rutting seasons whether for moose, elk or whitetails, the weather is a big factor and can be the most unpredictable element of your hunt.

All hunting for Canada moose by a nonresident from the Lower 48 must be done with the services of a licensed outfitter. There are a number of excellent outfitters in each of the moose-producing provinces and a letter to the provincial Department of Natural Resources requesting a list of licensed outfitters will give you a good starting point. All of the Canadian provinces have the potential of producing record-class bulls but the province of British Columbia is the leading producer of trophy bulls, followed by Alberta. The further north you travel in the provinces, the closer you get to the dividing line between the Canada moose and the Alaska-Yukon moose and the larger the Canada subspecies bulls are going to be. When trying to book a hunt make it clear to your outfitter that you want to bowhunt during the rut and book accordingly.

Bowhunting for the gigantic Alaska-Yukon moose is equally as challenging and exciting and you don't necessarily need an outfitter to bowhunt them legally.

A "do-it-yourself," Alaskan moose bowhunt can be the bowhunting experience of a lifetime. Whether this experience is one with pleasurable memories or a nightmare depends on how well you do your homework and plan and outfit your trip. Alaska is an exciting place to bowhunt but it is a land where mother nature still rules and if you don't play by her rules you can get in too deep in mighty short order.

Several years ago, a couple friends of mine went on a "drop camp" fly-in moose and caribou bowhunt. The day they were flown out and dropped on a small lake was perfect. They saw lots of caribou in the vicinity and a couple of record-class bull moose within stalking distance of the lake campsite. From that point on their trip turned into an Alaskan nightmare. The next seven days were spent under the most miserable conditions possible, and they were lucky the weather finally broke on the eighth day and the plane was able pick them up or they might have been in an even more serious, life threatening situation.

It rained almost constantly during the week with winds in the 30 to 50 mph range. The bowhunters' tent was not designed to stand up under these extreme conditions and the vicious wind blew water right through the fabric. After the first day, their sleeping bags and most of their clothing was soaked and there was no way they could even begin to build a fire to dry things out during the entire week-long disaster. One or both of them had to stay in the tent and hold it down to keep the violent gusts of wind from blowing it out across the tundra. There clothing consisted mostly of cotton and twill camo pants and shirts which did little to maintain their body heat or shed water. The plastic rain ponchos they had brought along were quickly shredded by the brush and winds and did little to protect them when they did try to venture out and hunt. To top it off, with the constant soaking, all the feathers fell off their arrow shafts leaving them with nothing to shoot at a moose or caribou if one would have ventured within bow range of camp. Great hunting experience, if you survive it.

My advice for your first Alaskan moose hunt would be to hire a good outfitter and learn the ropes. Alaska has a large number of competent outfitters who produce record book moose on a regular basis. You can get a list of outfitters by scanning bowhunting and other outdoor magazines and contacting the Alaska Department of Fish & Game in Juneau. Start your trip planning well in advance of your hunt to give yourself plenty of time to research prospective outfitters and find the one that will best fill your wants, needs and budget.

My first Alaskan moose hunt took place on the north slope of the Brooks Range where the tundra stretches for miles and miles broken occasionally by alder and willow-filled creek bottoms.

I was hunting with a buddy from Texas who was on his first Alaska bowhunt and wanted to concentrate mainly on caribou while I was moose hunting. Our outfitter, who is no longer in business, had one of his guide/pilots fly Victor and me about 100 miles out onto the tundra and drop us onto a rocky expanse of creekbed near an area they had previously spotted several trophy size bulls.

Alaska is a huge expanse of wild country and while many hunters think that this vast wilderness is overrun with big game animals, such is not generally the case! You can fly over miles of tundra country and not see a single game animal. However, when you find the right pocket of timber or brush-lined creek bottom it might be loaded with critters of all types.

Such was the situation with our camp. While we were setting up our Eureka Storm King tent we saw several herds of caribou and had a cow and calf moose watching us work while the sky overhead was constantly filled with family groups of white-fronted geese. Since we couldn't hunt until the following morning we spent our time making sure our camp was snug and comfortable. Good thing, cause the next morning there was snow on the ground and ice covering the edge of the creek and numerous tundra pools.

Vic went downstream after a herd of caribou while I headed upstream toward the thicker brush hoping to run into a moose. At this point in time I didn't know a darn thing about moose calling and it's probably a good thing cause I might have gotten run over by an irate bull in the throes of passion.

I had covered less than half a mile, easing through the ballbearing rocks and boulders of the creekbed, when I glassed a huge, snow-covered bull bedded in the willows at the edge of a dense alder thicket. About the time I spotted him he got up, shook the snow off and started meandering through the brush feeding. I spent a frustrating three hours trying to get closer but the brush made stalking a tough proposition. He finally disappeared into the dense brush. If I had only known how to imitate a cow, I probably would have had him in my lap in short order.

Later that morning, I walked up on another Pope & Young bull, misjudged the range and shot under him. I spent the rest of the day following him through the alders and willows trying to get close enough for another shot. That long-legged monster would walk casually into a thicket and I would run like a madman to cut the distance, but when he reappeared he always seemed to be the same distance away. Finally, late that afternoon four miles from camp the bull cut out across the open tundra headed for another creek bottom that was several miles away and I gave up. I'm glad I didn't get him down that far from camp. That would have been one of the stupider things I had ever done bowhunting.

When I got back to camp at 10 p.m., totally exhausted, Victor had already given me up for dead. He had hit a good bull caribou just across the creek from camp so the following day was spent finding it and packing the head, hide and meat back to camp and resting up for the following morning's moose hunt.

Vic and I left camp at 5 a.m. and by 6 a.m. we were still-hunting a step at a time through the thickest part of the creek bottom. This jungle-like area was a maze of moose trails and the whole place stunk to high heaven with the musky aroma of rutting bulls and horny cows.

This is humongous country, but when you look down in the muddy trail and see a rather large grizzly track with water still seeping down from the edges it sure seems crowded in a hurry. Up to that point, Vic had our trusty back-up shotgun slung over his back and was carrying his bow in hand. I glanced back after we passed the grizzly track and he now had the bow slung over his shoulder and the shotgun in his hand. I don't know what concerned me more, the thought of a grizzly in front of me or a nervous, shotgun toting Victor behind me.

About that time, a slight slurping sound off to my left in the brush took my attention off both Vic and the bear. I froze in position and slowly eased my head around and found myself staring at a huge bull moose bedded not 15 yards away. The minute we made eye contact things happened! The bull lurched to his feet quartering away from me as I jerked my 90 pound Pro-Hunter to full draw, picked a spot behind the massive shoulders and released, all seemingly without pause. The blaze orange vanes disappeared just behind the bull's ribs and a split second later, the bull disappeared behind the dense screen of brush. The crashing and splintering of wood lasted for a few seconds and then the only thing I could hear was Vic's panting and my thumping heart.

That ornery bull managed to find the only hole in the tundra before he expired and died belly down in the shoulder-deep depression. After four hours of butchering and two days of dragging meat-laden 10 x 20 truck inner tubes a mile down the creek to camp, Victor swore he would never, ever, go moose hunting again! Me, I like bowhunting an animal the size of a small building that sports a truly awesome set of antlers, provides hundreds of pounds of steaks that melt in your mouth and responds to calling like a runaway express grunting every step and plowing over everything in it's path. Yessir, that first moose hunting trip is liable to addict you forever, or make you take up golf or bowling!

34   Grizzlies with a Bow

BY BOB ROBB

From his home base in Alaska, Bob Robb doesn't have to go very far to take on a variety of big game with his bow. But his pursuit of the mighty grizzly tops his list of hunting adventures and challenges.

I can think of several things that are safer than bowhunting grizzly bears. Putting out oil-well fires. Driving a cab in New York City after dark. Riding bulls for a living. Especially the bull riding. After all, when riding a bull you only have to stay on his back for eight seconds.

I vividly remember the last time I was within bow range of a grizzly bear. It was a brilliant fall day, the leaves deeply colored and the sky a deep, cloudless blue. I was crouched behind some thick brush on the banks of a small feeder stream plugged with salmon. It was hard finding a place to walk on the bank without stepping on either a dead coho, a big bear track or a pile of fresh bear scat. As the eight-footer splashed toward me, the 10-pound salmon dangling from his mouth looked as small as a toothpick. When the breeze shifted and he caught my scent, he whirled like lightning and raced downstream, water gushing from under his feet and scattering squawking seagulls like bowling pins. I remember thinking three things at that moment—Rats, there goes my chance; I'm sure glad he ran that way; and wow, that was the longest five minutes of my life. I was trying to be cool, but my hands had a slight tremble to them and my knees were feeling as if I'd packed moose meat for two days—uphill.

Together with the polar bear, the huge coastal brown bears of Alaska and the interior, or mountain, grizzly bear of Alaska and western Canada are the strongest, fastest, meanest predators on the continent. Big brown bears will weigh well over 1,000 pounds, with some approaching 1,500 pounds or more. The mountain bears have to make their living in a tougher neighborhood, without the thousands of salmon that brown bears eat each summer and fall. Thus they weigh substantially less, on average, with a big one weighing 650 to 750 pounds. There are exceptions, of course. I once shot a mountain bear with a rifle in Alaska's Wrangell Mountains, hundreds of miles from the nearest salmon stream, that squared an honest nine feet, one inch and weighed probably 900 pounds. Two of us could barely roll him over for the skinning job.

Strong? I've seen where bears have mowed downed trees that had to weigh several hundred pounds to get at some food source. They've been known to rip doors off cabins, and can knock over a 55-gallon drum of fuel without breaking a sweat. They're also lightning fast. Scientists will tell you they can outrun a race horse. And we haven't even begun talking about their legendary bad attitude. When they get their dander up, these bears turn into the devil himself.

All this is a round-about way of saying that if you've ever thought about bowhunting grizzlies, you might want to reconsider. It isn't for everyone.

Since I moved to Alaska in 1991, I've spent a lot of time around grizzlies and brown bears, both as a hunter and observer. I've taken several with a rifle, been with a half-dozen friends who have done the same and helped a couple of guide friends take clients grizzly hunting. A couple of years ago, I finally put it together and shot a grizzly with my bow. It was something. I did it on a one-day, on-your-own hunt. Sounds like no big deal, right? Well, before that came together, I had tried very hard to get a quality shot at a bear. I tell people my bow bear was the one-day hunt that took four years. Here's what happened.

When I finally put it all together, it was almost too easy. I was bored that spring day and decided to drive up the one paved road leading in and out of the coastal Alaska town I live in, stopping to periodically glass the adjacent mountains for bears. Spotting black bears is pretty much a daily occurrence, and every now and again a grizzly shows up. That day things happened in a hurry. I hadn't been parked 20 minutes when I spotted a bear moving along a steep mountainside, then lie down in the warm spring sun. It was a grizzly, and a nice one. I knew the mountain well and how to get up above the thick brush line without ripping my clothes off. I didn't hesitate, grabbing my bow and pack and heading off at a dog trot before starting the climb.

I was by myself, once again proving that I am not the world's smartest guy. But in less than two hours, I was where I wanted to be when I relocated the bear. He was up feeding now, heading in my general direction, maybe a half-mile off. With the afternoon thermals wafting upwards, I climbed a bit more, then used a screen of brush as a makeshift blind as I vectored towards him. As if on a string, the bear ambled along until he was right below me, seemingly without a care in the world. I had taken a laser range finder reading on a stump near where I thought the bear would walk—35 yards. As he moved behind some brush I drew, and when he cleared and passed just in front of the stump I settled the 30-yard pin on the upper third of his chest, let out a little air and released. The carbon shaft blew right through him. He roared, standing the hackles on the back of my neck at full attention, spun around and raced off down the slope. He didn't go 100 yards before piling up, graveyard dead. The .375 H&H magnum I'd hauled up the hill "just in case" was nothing more than extra weight added to the 100 pounds of wet hide, head and paws I packed down to the truck.

It had been a long time coming. I let out a war whoop that would have curled Custer's hair.

Packing my .375 is something I never look at as a nonessential item. It's a Remington Model 700 from their Custom Shop, featuring a lightweight synthetic stock and stainless-steel metal work that I sent off and had the barrel cut down to 20-inches and added a muzzle brake to and designed as a bowhunting backup rifle for my Alaska adventures. Though it weighs about eight pounds loaded, it's something I feel almost naked without. Here's why.

In 1993 a buddy and I were bowhunting fall bears on the Alaska Peninsula. Skiffing along a lake, all of a sudden there he was, swimming across the water. At a mile it looked like a basketball floating in the water. By the time Bo got the skiff to the beach, the bear had disappeared into the thick brush. We both thought he would head for a nearby stream that was choked with sockeye salmon. I grabbed both my bow and my .338 and headed off at a trot while Bo secured the boat. The plan was for me to relocate the bear, wait for Bo to show with his .375, then figure out our next move.

That changed in a hurry when, 100 yards inside the brush cover, I found the bear. He was rolling on his back in some tall tan grass, smelling for all the world like the rotten fish he'd been rolling in all summer long. The wind was perfect, I had some cover, and I thought, "Why are we here?" So I chambered a round in the .338, put it on safety, moved to within 30 yards of the bear and nocked an arrow. I figured that when he stood up and turned broadside I'd let him have it.

When he stood up, though, he looked right at me. How did he know I was there? I can vividly remember his eyes locking with mine as his head started to sway back and forth and he popped his teeth. I didn't move a muscle. When he took a step toward me, then put his head down to sway it again, I slowly let go of the bow string and grabbed the rifle. When he threw his head up and bounded forward, I must have reverted to my old quail shooting days. When he was 10 yards away, I threw the rifle to my shoulder and fired in a single motion, then rolled onto my back and got as ready as a person can get for the mauling I knew was an instant away.

Nothing happened. It was as quiet as the proverbial church mouse, and I stayed in the fetal position until I felt the earth pounding. Then Bo hollered, "What the heck happened?" Somewhat dazed, I raised up and looked around. The bear lay dead 50 yards away, my snap shot having luckily taken him through the throat, breaking his neck. He never knew what hit him.

I was fine until we walked over to look at him. I'm not sure how much he weighed, only that the two of us could not roll him over to start the skinning chore. I had to sit down and get control of myself before the sharp knives went to work. Later, the hide squared nine feet, four inches. Remember how Grandpa used to tell you about the fish he caught, and how big they were between the eyes? I measured this bear between the ears. It was 12 inches from inside ear tip to inside ear tip. His hide, including skull and paws, weighed 157 pounds on a certified scale before it was fleshed out. He's a dandy bear, but that shot kept me from hunting them again for the next four years.

It was then I learned rule number one: Never, ever attempt to stalk a grizzly or brown bear unless accompanied by someone backing you up with a large-caliber rifle. Make sure he knows how to use said rifle and has the nerves and presence of mind to stand in there and get the job done if things get, as the British are wont to say, a bit dicey. Your petunias just might depend on it.

My friend Jim Boyce is one such man. Jim is a whale of a hunting guide, an ex-special forces guy with Vietnam experience, and someone who can keep his cool when it gets interesting. Coupled with his bear-rich Southeast Alaska guide area, I knew I had to say yes when he invited me down one fall week to try and arrow a brown bear.

Boyce hunts up small salmon streams that run through the thicker than thick old-growth Tongass National Forest. The stream we were hunting was covered up with bear tracks, but unfortunately it was a strange fall in all of Alaska—the salmon were late. Without fish to draw the bears to the river and hold them there, they were scattered all over the steep, timbered mountainous country. It was tough hunting.

The game here goes like this. In the early afternoon, you hike a mile or two upstream, looking for fresh bear sign and pools of fish over which you can set an ambush. Because big bears in this area rarely show themselves before it begins to get extremely late, you end up trudging back to camp in the dark. And it gets very, very dark on the banks of a timbered stream in the Tongass. Which is fine. You have a head lamp, you know the way and it's relatively flat walking.

Except that after dark, "the bears own the stream banks," as Boyce told me. One pitch-dark night as we were walking back, we learned that lesson hard. Our lamps found three sets of bear eyes, obviously a sow and a pair of cubs. (Point to ponder—there are few things on earth scarier than a sow grizzly with cubs, after dark. Take on the sow or six Hell's Angels in their local bar? I'm thinking I'd have a small chance with the bikers, only because I could probably outrun them.) The sow walked her cubs into the safety of the brush, then came back and charged.

Fortunately we had the river between us, and she stopped on the far bank at about 10 steps. I was well armed—my bow—but Jim had his .375, so I tucked in behind him and made sure my light stayed on the bear. He fired two "get-outta-here" shots into the water in front of her, but she didn't even blink. I think that was when I said something like, "Golly gee, I hope this very nice lady decides to go see how her children are doing. Please go away." After what seemed like an eternity, she growled and huffed off, leaving us wondering just how quickly we could get back to camp and the comfort of the brandy bottle.

In college, I had a class that told us all about risk/reward ratios and how one needed to balance the risks of any endeavor against the potential rewards. Bowhunting grizzlies is a lot like that. Is there a risk? You bet. Are the rewards worth it? After playing the game for a while, I'd have to say that, for me, the answer is yes. The key to tipping that ratio in your favor is to become intimate with your bow-and-arrow setup, learn to shoot it well under tough field conditions and pick a partner (in the case of the nonresident, that means an outfitter and guide) you feel comfortable riding the river with.

Win, lose or draw, it's an adventure that will teach you a lot about yourself. And one you'll never, ever forget.

Alaska Grizzly Hunting Trip Facts

SEASONS: Both spring and fall hunting are allowed. Spring hunts occur in April and May, while fall hunting runs September and October.

BAG LIMIT: One bear every four years in most units of the state (in a few units, the limit is one bear every year).

LICENSE, TAG FEES: Nonresident hunting license, $85. Grizzly or brown bear tag, $500.

HUNTING METHODS: No baiting or dog hunting is allowed. Most grizzly hunting is spot and stalk hunting, although in some cases treestands and/or ground blinds set along salmon streams are employed.

CLOTHING NEEDED: Varies by season, hunt area. Generally speaking, fleece or wool outerwear for quiet and warmth, if wet; good hiking boots and ankle-fit hip boots; high-quality rain gear (I use a packable Gore-Tex rain suit from Whitewater Outdoors all year in Alaska, with great results); warm gloves and hat; wicking long underwear (Thermax, Capilene, etc.); warm wool or synthetic socks. In Alaska, cotton clothing is a formula for hypothermia.

HUNTING EQUIPMENT: The best 10X binoculars you can afford, plus a quality spotting scope and small camera tripod. Large daypack to carry hunting gear and spare clothing. Your outfitter will send you a specific gear list tailored to his camp's needs.

BOWS AND ARROWS: The most important thing is being able to place your first arrow in the boiler room at 40 yards and under, from a variety of field-shotting positions. Alaska has a minimum arrow weight requirement of 437.5 grains (1 oz.). Broadheads must have at least a ⅞-inch cutting diameter. (Mechanical broadheads are legal.) No electronic devices may be attached to the bow, and no scope sights are allowed. Because hunting bush Alaska is hard on equipment, you're best served by a simple setup that can take some tough field abuse. And bring a spare everything.

GUIDES: By law, nonresidents must hire a licensed guide to hunt brown/grizzly bears, Dall sheep and mountain goats in Alaska, or hunt with a resident who is second degree of kindred.

HUNT COSTS: Costs vary, but in general terms, coastal brown bear hunts range from $8,000–$13,000. Interior grizzly hunts range from $6,500–$8,500. Also, interior grizzlies can often be added to the bag on mixed-bag hunts for a trophy fee. For More Information: Alaska Department of Fish & Game, 333 Raspberry Rd., Anchorage, AK 99518; 907-267-2347; fax 267-2433; on the Web at www.state.ak.us. A complete list of Alaska hunting guides is available for $5 from Alaska Dept. of Commerce & Economic Development, Division of Occupational Licensing, Box 110806, Juneau, AK 99811; phone 907-465-2543.

35   Black Bear Challenge

BY GARY CLANCY

Veteran Minnesota outdoor writer Gary Clancy isn't about to tell you that hunting black bears with a bow is as dangerous and difficult as taking on grizzlies. But he's here to say that this kind of hunting will keep your nerves on edge any time you're willing to give it a try.

I'll admit it sounds easy. Climb into a stand overlooking a pile of grease-soaked oats laced with a few old donuts and sit back and wait for a bear to waddle in for a free dinner. No problem right? Well, yes and no. If you really don't care if the bear rug in your den resembles the hide off of a black Lab, then no, shooting a bear is not going to be much of a problem. But if you are looking for a REAL bear, then listen up, because big bears, like big bucks, rarely come easy.

My first lesson in this truism took place on the third evening of my first bear hunt. My friend Kurt von Besser and I were hunting deep in the endless bush country of northern Canada. This vast region supports a tremendous population of black bears and since the area is very sparsely populated—and most of the people who do live in the bush could care less about hunting bears—the bears here tend to live long lives. This is precisely what it takes to grow really big bears. Although it was my first time bear hunting, I was no stranger to black bears. Back when I was growing up in Minnesota, bears were not even classified as big game animals. In fact they were looked upon as pests because of their penchant for raiding garbage cans and for occasionally breaking into an abandoned summer cabin in search of food. Bears were numerous at the open garbage pits which were common in those days and tourists who had come to the land of 10,000 lakes on vacation loved to sit in their parked cars and watch the bears sift through the debris. So I will admit that when Kurt and I went on that first bear hunt, my heart really was not in it. I was expecting it to be too easy. So I made up my mind right from the start that I would hold off for a big bear, a bear that would at least qualify for entry in the Pope & Young record book.

Even though I was fairly familiar with bears in the wild, I had never really studied them. I went to the library and checked out books on bears. I read all of the magazine articles on bear hunting and questioned friends who had been on bear hunts. Then I went to our local zoo and spent hours just watching the bears to get a feel for judging the size of the bears. My biggest fear was that I would get so excited that I would shoot the first bear to come along, which is often, a small one. I knew, from having talked to a lot of hunters and a few outfitters, that this was commonplace on bear hunts. I was determined that I would not allow it to happen to me. By the time spring arrived in Minnesota where I live, I felt that I had learned all I could from books, magazines and the bears at the zoo. I knew that a big bear would appear to have short legs, or put another way, a big bear's body is close to the ground, while a youngster shows a lot of daylight under his or her belly. I knew that if the bear I drew down on was not six feet long or longer from nose to tail, odds were good that the skull would not measure up to P&Y standards. I knew that most full-grown sows topped off at about 5½ feet. I knew that rounded, stubby ears that appear to be too small for the head are a good sign and that pointy, big ears, like those on a police dog are a definite sign that I was looking at an immature bear. And I knew that a short, blocky nose on a big, round head was good, but a long, pointed snout on a small, elongated head was bad.

When the three feet of snow in my backyard melted I got out bow and arrows and set up some targets. I shot from the deck on the back of our house so that I would have the feel of how to make the shot from a treestand. I knew from having spoken with our outfitter that all stands were within 25 yards of the bait, so I concentrated on that range and closer. By the time I packed my bow and arrows for the trip I could hit a 50-cent piece every time. Each of the six "hunting arrows" had been spun and re-spun to make sure that each was perfectly straight. Fletching and nocks were inspected. My broadheads were surgically sharp.

My first evening on a bear stand was memorable because I never saw a bear. I know that sounds crazy but let me explain. You see, even though I had prepared well for the hunt, I still expected the hunt to be very easy. As it turned out, I spent the first evening sitting still as stone perched in a jackpine while a bazillion skeeters and black flies tried to extract the last drop of Irish blood from my body. I waited for a black ghost to emerge from the swamp but did not see a single bear. That was the first indication that maybe this whole bear hunting thing was not quite as easy as I had thought it to be. This notion was reinforced by the fact that twice during that first evening I had heard a bear or bears back in the bush, but could not see them. I suspected that the wind, which was swirling that evening had betrayed my presence.

The next morning, as we discussed stand options over breakfast, I was surprised when the outfitter, a young, former bush pilot named Tim Hastings, suggested that I hunt the same stand again that evening. I knew that Tim prided himself on having so many stands in place that some get hunted only one or two evenings per season, so why would he want me to return to a stand in which I had not seen a single bear? So I asked him why. "Come with me and help bait this morning and I'll show you, eh"?

So I spent all morning and the early afternoon driving rutted logging roads and humping Duluth packs full of bait and five-gallon pails of grease into bait sites. At each site, Tim inspected the sign. Tracks, scat and "bear trees" are the best sign when it comes to determining the size of the bear or bears hitting a bait. The front foot is the best indicator of a bear's size. Most tracks are between four and five inches wide across the pad. Only tracks with a pad width greater than five inches attract the attention of Mr. Hastings.

Because bears are eating machines, they leave behind a lot of scat. Don't worry, you won't confuse bear droppings with the scat from other critters. Just trust me on that one. Droppings from average-sized bears will run an inch to 1½ inches in diameter. A big boar will be in that two-inch diameter and up range.

"Bear trees" are trees that have been bitten and rubbed by boars, probably as a way of marking their territory. Most of this activity takes place in late May and through June, which is the peak breeding period for black bears. The size of the tree marked and height at which the bite occurs are good indicators of a boar's stature and size.

The stand I had hunted the evening before was one of the last baits we visited that day. As we hiked into the site carrying heavy packs and five-gallon pails, Tim suddenly stopped and pointed down at a track in the soft mud. It was the largest track I had seen all day, probably six inches across the pad. Tim just looked at me and arched his eyebrows.

At the stand site we dumped the contents of our packs into the 55-gallon barrel chained to the tree so that the bears could not drag it off and poured the used cooking oil over the bait and the ground around the barrel. Then Tim wandered off a little ways and when I heard him whistle softly I walked over and found him kneeling in the grass, bear scat in his fist, only this time, his fingers and thumb were an inch shy of touching. "Giant *%*&*, giant bear, eh," he said. I just stood there and dumbly nodded my head. We had seen a lot of bear scat that morning, but nothing even close to this size.

Then Tim walked over to leg-thick tree, which showed the unmistakable sign of having been marked by a marauding boar. I took a picture of him standing next to the tree, his arm outstretched, his fingers just barely touching the shredded bark where the bear had clamped his powerful jaws and bitten down.

We left then and hiked back to the truck. Like most men who make their living in the bush, Tim is not much of a talker. Probably comes from going long stretches with no one to talk to. So I instigated the conversation. "Thanks for taking me along this morning," I said. "I know now why you want me back on that stand this evening." Tim just grinned.

I would like to end this story by telling you about how I returned to that stand and killed the giant boar that had left behind the huge tracks, droppings of epic proportions shall we say and the shattered bear trees, but that is not how it happened. As the title of this story say's bear's ain't easy. Instead, it happened like this.

When I slipped over the lichen-carpeted granite outcropping which loomed up behind the jackpine in which my stand was situated, I had a good view of the bait and even though it was only midafternoon, there was a bear already on it. At a glance I could tell that the bear was a juvenile, so after watching for a few minutes to make sure that there were no larger bears around, I walked to the jackpine, tied my bow to the pull-up rope and began to climb to the stand. The little bear, which had his pointy head jammed in the hole in the top of the barrel, was so busy scarfing up the grease-soaked goodies within that he never knew I was around until I scraped up against the raspy hide of the jackpine. The little bear, probably assuming that the noise had been made by a larger bear, jerked his head from the barrel, conking his noggin on the barrel in the process and went galloping off into the swamp. In the real world where Disney does not rule, little bears make fine meals for big bears.

As the long shadows of late afternoon lengthened, I heard a splash somewhere out in the swamp. It was not a splash like a beaver slapping it's tail or a moose plodding through a beaver pond, but rather the kind of soft splash a bear's foot makes—kind of a muffled sploosh. I heard another sploosh a moment later and then, later still and much closer a stick cracked. Bears do move very quietly thanks to their large, soft feet and soft fur. Many hunters claim that you rarely hear a bear before you see it, but I'd guess that I have heard at least half of the bear's come to the bait before I saw them. Hearing the bear first is an advantage, because the adrenaline rush is not quite as great if you know that something big and black is about to appear. I'm convinced that fewer hunters would make mistakes by shooting small bears if they heard the bear first and had an opportunity to compose themselves before the bear made an appearance. Anyway, if I did not have excellent hearing, I would consider wearing a Walker's Game Ear on bear hunts over bait just to provide myself with this slight, but important advantage.

The bear that materialized was a good one. Six foot easy. Big head, short nose, stubby ears. From my elevated position there was no daylight beneath the bear's belly. This was a good bear alright, but it was not the bear that had left the sign which had impressed even Tim Hastings, a man who has killed or been instrumental in the kill on hundreds of bears.

As the bear got down to the business of grabbing a paw-full of grease-soaked potato chips from the hole in the barrel and then licking his paw clean before scooping up another mitt full, I went through considerable mental anguish. Here I was on my first bear hunt and posing perfectly in front of me was a P&Y shoo-in. If I did not shoot the bear, and this would prove to be my last opportunity at a good bear on the trip, I would kick myself all the way home to Minnesota. On the other hand, if I did take this bear, I would always be left to wonder about the other bear, the bear that Tim referred to as a "magnum bear." Even in remote country, only a very few boars ever attain magnum status, Tim had told me. I was still engaged in these mental gymnastics when the boar at the bait made up my mind for me. The bear suddenly quit feeding and stared intently off into the swamp. I had heard nothing, but evidently the bear had. He stared for a long time and then made a circle of the bait before returning to his former position. On the far side of that circle a rub the size of a serving platter was plainly visible on his otherwise thick, black coat. The rub was much too large for a taxidermist to repair, so I made up my mind then and there not to shoot the bear. I learned another lesson there.

The bear with the rub hung around for an hour. A smaller bear joined him and I was surprised when the big boar allowed the smaller bear to feed with him. About a half-hour before dark both bears stopped eating and again stared off into the swamp. When the two bears turned and left the bait, I knew that something was going to happen. "The really big bears," Tim had told me, "nearly always come in right at last light, eh."

There was a long, narrow, natural grassy opening stretching out into the swamp. I suspect that at one time it had been one heck of a beaver dam. That slot was my only peek into the swamp and it was up that narrow avenue in the fading light of an early June evening that I watched what I thought was a sow and her cub stroll towards the bait. About 60 yards out, I detected something odd about the sow. The front legs appeared bowed as if the load were too much for them and the head, which swung side-to-side in grizzly fashion, looked as if it would have trouble fitting inside a bushel basket. "This is one big sow," I thought to myself.

As soon as I had the thought, the lead bear abruptly sat down. The second bear loomed over the sitting bear. When the standing bear took it's huge head and attempted to nudge the sitting bear back to it's feet, the sitting bear whirled around and slapped the big bear up alongside the head. One of the bears—I still don't know which—let out a bellow which made the little hairs on the back of my neck stand straight. And then it hit me like a Mack truck. What I was looking at was not a sow and her cub, but a full grown sow, probably in heat and the "magnum bear" which had left the outsized sign at the bait. My right leg began to shake, like it does sometimes when something really exciting is unfolding and for the first time all evening I did not notice the swarms of insects searching for an opening in my bug-proof head net. My total focus was on that giant bear. When it got dark, my total focus was on getting out of there without running into that giant bear, because unexplainably, he and his lady friend had not moved since she had first sat down.

Kurt killed a nice P&Y boar that evening and so did two of the four other hunters in camp for the week. Tim was up half of the night skinning the three bears. It was afternoon before I had a chance to fill him in on all of the details of the previous evening. "Mind if I sit with you this evening," Tim asked, "I would sure like to get a look at that bloody magnum bear before you put an arrow in him, eh." I assured Tim that he was welcome to share my stand anytime and later that afternoon we climbed back into the jackpine.

That evening brought a parade of bears. The rubbed boar came back and I was pleased with my judging skills when Tim agreed with my assessment of the boars size from the previous evening. Then bears started showing up like blowflies on a roadkilled skunk. By the time it was full dusk, over a dozen different bears had visited the bait. Several of them were very nice, but none even approached the size of magnum. Then at last light, off to our right, where the swamp gave way to higher ground and the undergrowth was not so thick, we saw him. He was dogging a sow, probably the same one he had been with the previous evening. He looked like a black Volkswagen Beetle. When Tim got excited I knew that we were looking at one very special bear. But once again, the big bear did not make the mistake of visiting the bait and darkness forced us to retreat and leave the bush to the bears for the night.

The next evening Tim was not able to sit with me. I saw a dozen or more bears once again, but no sign of magnum. And then I was down to my last evening. Even though I knew that it could mean going home without a bear, I vowed to hold off until the final bell for a chance at the giant bruin. The wind was again in my favor that evening and bears came to the bait from about four o'clock on. As usual the rubbed boar was one of the first to arrive. He was still on the bait when about a half-hour before dark another large boar emerged wet to the withers from the swamp and cautiously approached the bait. The two boars circled each other, checking one another out and when they stood up eyeball-to-eyeball, I could see that the new arrival was several inches longer than the rubbed boar, which made the new arrival a very good, bear to be sure. I thought there was going to be a battle royal, but there was not. Both bears dropped to all fours, the rubbed bear walked off into the swamp without so much as another glance at the larger boar and the bigger bear got busy wolfing down some bait. For 10 minutes the big bear fed while I listened and strained my eyes for any hint of the magnum bear's presence.

With only minutes of shooting light left, the big bear at the bait, which had been laying down and eating, stood up and presented me with a picture perfect slightly quartering away angle. I knew that the odds of the magnum bear making an appearance in the few remaining minutes were slim, so I came to full draw, made sure that my single pin was slightly above the horizontal middle of the bear's body and in line with his off shoulder and released. It's always magical when the fletching disappears right where you are aiming. The bear crashed off into the swamp for 50 yards, thrashed around a few seconds and died.

Bears aren't easy, but they sure are exciting!

Important Gear

Besides your bow and arrows, you should have a daypack in which you can carry the following:

- Packable Gore-Tex rainwear.
- A complete Bug-Out System.
- Two flashlights with spare batteries.
- Camera.
- Water.
- Snacks.
- Extra jacket or sweater.
- Skinning knife and steel or stone.
- You may also want to carry your video camera and a small tripod, since hunting bears over bait is an excellent opportunity to capture the hunt on film.

36   Black Bears: Up Close & Personal

BY JUDD COONEY

Whoever said that black bears aren't dangerous never hunted the isolated woods of the Canadian wilderness!

Larry was darn glad he'd traded his normal footwear of knee-high rubber boots for his steel-toed firefighter's boots for pulling treestands, particularly when the raging bear grabbed his foot and chomped down. Larry Gardiner and Michael Bates are partners in Black Bay Outfitters in far northern Saskatchewan, where they concentrate on guiding trophy spring bear hunts in some of the best bear country in Canada. Their bear hunt is the next thing to a fly-in hunt, without the plane. Black Bay's comfortable camp is a 45-minute boat ride from the outpost village of Isle a LaCrosse on a huge lake with the same name.

Larry was born in the area and lives from the land, hunting, trapping, guiding and fighting fires. He grew up around black bears and has dispatched his share with everything from a .22 rifle to bow and arrow. Larry has great respect for the bear's tremendous strength, stamina and survival instincts. Until last year he'd never had a serious run-in with black bears, but according to his brother he evidently upset the bear gods, 'cause things changed.

Larry's first encounter came while he was looking for blood after one of the hunters took a shot at a bear. Larry was crawling through an aspen thicket checking a well used bear trail for sign when he heard another hunter behind him. When he turned around Larry found himself face-to-face with a 300-pound black bear—at 10 feet! The bruin had his ears laid back and was in the process of taking another stealthy step when Larry jumped up hollering. Taken by surprise in mid-stalk, the bear backed off and disappeared into the dense undergrowth. When Larry emerged from the woods at the boat landing, he was carrying a 10-foot bear pole.

A week later Larry was packing a box of pastries to a bear bait and walked head-on into a monstrous black that met him with flattened ears, raised hackles and popping teeth. As the bear advanced, Larry shoved the box of goodies in his face and beat a hasty retreat. Fortunately the bear had a discerning appetite and opted for the doughnuts over a stout, stringy outfitter. When Larry told the story back at camp, he quickly earned the nickname, Dancing With Bears.

Several days later I was perched in a treestand overlooking the same bait when the enormous bear walked under my treestand and stopped near the bait to survey the surroundings. There was no doubt about his size as I eased to full draw and sent a Phantom-tipped Gold Tip shaft through his chest at 15 yards. He made it all of 30 yards before piling up for good and ended up being the largest black bear I've ever taken with a bow, scoring 20¹³⁄₁₆.

Larry's confrontations didn't end with the last hunters leaving camp. Several days after the final hunter had departed, Larry was pulling treestands when he encountered his third cantankerous bruin. He had just started to climb up to a stand when a large bear came bounding out of the brush and came for him with deadly intent. He knew a serious bear when he saw one and lunged up the climbing sticks as fast as he could climb. The aroused bear was right on his heels. As Larry reached the stand and vaulted onto the platform, the bear grabbed his foot and bit down. During much of the previous weeks, Larry had worn rubber boots to facilitate getting in and out of the boat. Fortunately, for climbing and pulling treestands he'd switched to his steel-toed, firefighting boots. When the bear clamped down on his boot, it got a mouth full of steel and leather rather than rubber and meat. Larry quickly kicked the bear in the side of the head with his other boot and discouraged it enough to make it drop back to the ground. He quickly discovered the reason for the bear's anger when he spotted two cubs in a nearby tree.

For the next two hours the furious female kept Larry precariously treed. His slightest move brought her raging up the tree, snapping and popping her teeth in uncontrolled anger. After three nerve-wracking hours, the cubs finally descended, and, with their aggressively protective parent as a rear guard, disappeared into the dark timber. After the third black bear encounter in as many weeks, Larry finished pulling treestands toting a can of pepper spray and a shotgun loaded with buckshot!

Black bears generally aren't considered dangerous game, but after almost 40 years of dealing with them the only thing I know for certain is black bears are totally unpredictable. In my experience, black bears with minimal human contact or confrontations are the most unpredictable.

The bears that inhabit isolated areas such as northern Saskatchewan have virtually no contact with humans and consider themselves "Boss Beast." A black bear in some ways is more dangerous than the grizzly when it comes to bear-human encounters. Playing dead may work with a grizzly, but when a black bear goes on the attack it doesn't back off until you fight it off. If a black bear gets you down, it won't quit until you're dead, and then it will likely make you its next meal or two.

Northern Saskatchewan consists of thousands of square miles of uninhabited bush country with a thriving black bear population that rarely encounters the human predator. When I first started hunting black bears along the shores of Isle a LaCrosse lake, I couldn't believe the audacity of the bear population. We had bears walking through camp at midday, seemingly unconcerned, and one of the largest bears we took that first year was taken within 100 yards of our main camp, where we literally had a tent city.

My first Saskatchewan bear, a huge male, came into a new bait the second night I sat on the stand. I'd watched a gorgeous blond male work over the bait the first evening, and judging by his skittish actions as he watched the surrounding brush, I knew he wasn't the dominant bear in the area. He was almost record-book size, and I spent that night and the next day mentally debating whether I should take him if he presented himself with such audacity the following evening. The long silky fur of his prime hide shimmered golden in the late-evening light. He was one of the most beautiful bears I had ever seen and would be tough to turn down a second time.

I was in the stand early the following evening, and within an hour I caught the movement of a black shape 100 yards through the timber. A few minutes later a huge black bear strolled nonchalantly into the bait-site clearing and moved directly toward my treestand. He stalked back and forth below my stand, popping his teeth for several minutes. About that time the blond bear appeared on the far side of the bait, and the black lost interest in me. He charged the interloper and ran him into the brush. When he returned to the bait he paused long enough to give me a broadside shot at 15 yards, and I ended his bad-attitude problem permanently. From that point on I had a whole different attitude about hunting these north-woods reclusive bears.

My first face-to-face encounter with a mad north-woods bear came shortly after I watched a client arrow a huge bruin on a bait. I was perched in a treestand right behind the client and saw his arrow hit the bear high in the shoulders. I knew the hit was marginal at best, but took the blood trail hoping for the best. Two hundred yards into the dense spruce timber I spotted the bear lying against the roots of a downed tree about the same time he saw me. He lurched up and started my way, ears flattened and hair on end. Since I was totally unarmed, I decided discretion was the better part of valor. I had to hold back a bit on my retreat to keep from passing my short-legged client. That bear made it obvious we had better not take Saskatchewan black bears for granted.

All of our clients were given a choice of carrying the potent 10% pepper-spray canisters or a 12-gauge shotgun loaded with #4 copper-plated buckshot to the stand with them. During the four seasons I ran the bear camp, we had one or more bowhunters each spring who had close encounters with surly Saskatchewan bruins, and it added a whole new dimension to bowhunting them.

On another occasion I sent a young bowhunter from Iowa to a bait where we'd previously seen a few Pope & Young bears. He'd already passed on several good bears and was holding out for a record-book bruin. I warned him there was a sow with three cubs hitting the bait and gave him pepper spray to take to the stand with him.

Shortly after getting into the stand, the bowhunter saw a large black bear easing toward the bait. He got his bow off the hanger and was ready for a shot when three bouncing balls of fur appeared behind the approaching bear and headed toward the bait. He was in the process of hanging his bow back on the hook when one of the cubs caught the movement and with a squall headed for the nearest tree, followed by its two siblings.

Following my advice, the bowhunter spoke to the alert sow to let her know he was there. At the sound of his voice she charged his tree and started up after him, huffing and chuffing as she clambered up. The spooked bowhunter already had his pepper spray in hand and gave the mad momma a dose from less than five feet. The bear fell out of the tree, rolled on the ground and proceeded to climb the tree adjacent to his treestand. When she got level with him she reached across the open space and got another hefty shot of the orange-colored spray from the thoroughly panicked bowhunter. Once more she hit the ground bawling and squalling, and as the bowhunter radioed his guide to come and get him the hell out of there, the bear again came up his tree fully intent on mayhem. For the third time the bowhunter sprayed the bear and put her back on the ground. This time she'd had all the pepper she could handle and bolted for the tall timber, followed closely by her cubs.

By this time the guide had the boat on the beach below the treestand, and the hunter decided he'd had all the bear bowhunting he could stand for one evening and headed for camp.

I spent 25 years guiding and outfitting spring and fall bear hunts in Colorado and rarely ran into an overly aggressive bear that wasn't aggravated by hounds or wounded. Saskatchewan bears are different. They have little to fear from the wolves and smaller predators in their domain, and many have never encountered humans and therefore have little fear of them. The high population of uninhibited bears in the northern part of the prairie province makes a close encounter with an insolent Saskatchewan bruin a distinct possibility.

This past spring Louis Dodaro, an avid bowhunter from Pittsburgh, encountered just such a problem. He was hunting a well-hit bait along the shore of the 40-mile long lake and was inundated with bears his first evening on stand. He saw seven different bears, including a monstrous, luxuriously pelted male that would make P&Y with room to spare. The big bear was a bit more cautious than the younger bears and stayed out of bow range. The second night on the stand the parade of smaller bears continued, and Louis patiently awaited the big one's arrival. Several medium-sized bears walked unconcernedly to the base of Louis's tree and gave him a close once-over from 15 feet.

One of the bears bedded down at the base of another tree 10 yards from Louis while a second worked over the bait. Louis was enjoying the show when suddenly all hell broke loose. The big bear came charging out of the dense brush popping his teeth and groaning at the trespassers on his bait. The smaller bears broke for the woods in a panic. Breaking branches and scraping sounds behind him took the bowhunter's attention off the scene below in short order. Louis spun around and found himself face-to-face with a 200-pound bear at less than five feet. With the speed of a fast-draw artist, Louis jerked up his pepper spray and loosed a blast at the bear, spraying the tree and his bow at the same time. The bear instantly slid back down the tree and rolled around on the ground, bawling and squalling his displeasure while Louis tried to get his tongue unstuck from the roof of his mouth and his heart back in his shirt. Nothing like a sudden "up close and personal" black bear encounter to add zest to a Saskatchewan bowhunt.

Bowhunting black bears with an attitude adds a whole new dimension to your bowhunt, and there isn't a better place in North America to indulge yourself than tangling with the surly bruins of northern Saskatchewan.

37   Bears over the Border

BY BILL VAZNIS

Looking for a great black bear hunt? The Canadian bush should be your destination.
Bill Vaznis is just the man to get your hunt started.

Black bears are the number two sought after big game animal, just behind caribou, for American hunters visiting Canada. The Lower 48 has some big bruins, but the bulk of North America's biggest bears are in the boreal forests of southern Canada.

Here is a rundown of some of the best black bear hunting now available. Keep in mind that bagging a trophy bruin is never a sure thing, and that bag limits, legal weapons, methods of chase and other regulations vary widely from one Province to the next. Therefore, always consult with the appropriate game department before going afield.

Northwest Territories

According to wildlife biologist Adrian D'Haunt, there is very little research on black bears in the territories, but the black bear populations are assumed to be stable.

However, we do know they are common in the boreal forests, and they are also occasionally sighted on the open tundra. Most bears are black, with a tan muzzle and a white "V" on the chest, and although a big male may tip the scales at over 400 pounds, there are no known NWT bears in either of the record books.

"The highest densities of black bears," added D'Haunt, "continues to occur along the Slave, Liard and Mackenzie River systems. Even so, most blackies are taken by sport hunters who stumble upon a bruin while they are out after moose or caribou."

For more information on hunting big game anywhere in the Northwest Territories, contact Northwest Territories Tourism, PO Box 1320, Yellowknife, N.W.T. X1A 2L9; 1-800/661-00788.

Yukon

Conservation officer Ryan Leef indicates that there are about 10,000 black bears in the forested regions of the southern Yukon. "According to our latest harvest figures, bear hunters tagged 91 black bears in '96–'97, which is about average. We only sell 200 to 300 tags a year.

"About 70 percent of these bears are bagged in the spring," added Leef. "Any river with open side hills or with south facing slopes is worth hunting. Try the Teflon River or the middle reaches of the Yukon."

Yukon bears are not generally big in body size or skull size which is due primarily to the fact that the habitat is not very productive. Nonetheless, all bear kills must be reported and the skulls submitted for study. Baiting is not legal in the Yukon. Neither are crossbows.

For more information on all the hunting opportunities in the Yukon, contact: Tourism Yukon, PO Box 2703, Whitehorse, Yukon Y1A 2C6; 403/667-5340.

British Columbia

According to Information Officer Norah Laity, "There are 120,000 to 150,000 black bears distributed equally about the province. The population is generally stable, although poaching remains a problem in some areas."

Latest available figures (1996), indicate 14,981 residents harvested 2,825 bruins whereas 2,614 nonresident hunters tagged 1,240 bears.

There is a two-bear limit in B.C. but baiting is not legal. Although many bruins are tagged as the opportunity arises, most bears are taken by design using the spot-and-stalk method. I have had success calling bears to within bow range in B.C. I used a predator call while hunting with outfitter Ken Robins.

One of the continent's real hotspots is Vancouver Island where outdoor writer Jim Shockey, well known for his big buck exploits, now runs a bear/steelhead camp on a 4,000 square mile tract located at the island's northern tip. Body weights on the island hover between 300 and 500 pounds!

The Kermode's bear, an all-white black bear, is fully protected with absolutely no hunting allowed. For a complete list of guides and outfitters, contact: Dale Drown, General Manager, at the Guide Outfitters Association of British Columbia, 250-7580 River Rd., Richmond, British Columbia, V6K 1X6; telephone 604/278-2688, fax 604/278-3440.

Alberta

According to Harold Carr, big game management coordinator, there are about 48,000 black bears in Alberta. "Nonresident hunters are more serious about bear hunting, and are therefore much more likely to tag a trophy bear."

Why do so many big bears come out of Alberta? "We have a hard working outfitting industry, a lot of bear habitat and an extended age structure with many older bears in the population," Carr said.

Alberta is definitely trophy bear country. The province has good numbers of mature black and color-phase boars residing in both active farm country and untouched wilderness. But best of all, the bear population is well managed with a two-bear limit.

My friends and I have arrowed several 400-pound-plus bruins in farm country just north of Edmonton with Eric Grinnell's Silvertip Outfitters, and in the deep wilderness sections of central Alberta with Bob Heyde's Homestead Outfitters.

All bear hunters must also purchase a $24.45 wildlife certificate. It is, however, no longer necessary for bowhunters to indelibly print that number on their arrow shafts. Crossbows are illegal for hunting.

For additional information on all the hunting opportunities in Alberta, contact: Alberta Tourism, Vacation Counseling, 3rd Floor City Center Building, 10155 102 St., Edmonton, Alberta T5J 4L6; 1-800/661-8888.

Saskatchewan

Saskatchewan estimates its black bear population to be about 30,000. There is a spring and fall season, but according to resource manager Rob Tether, "85 percent of the bear hunting takes place in the spring. Look to the fringe areas between provincial forest and agricultural farm lands for the best hunting."

Success rates for average bears is quite high, and nearly all well-stocked bait stations see plenty of action. The bigger bruins however come a little harder. It pays not to shoot the first bear if you are looking for a bomber bruin.

Please note that official spring bear hunting attire is now based on weapon of choice. That is, all firearm hunters, including muzzleloaders, must wear a complete outer suit colored scarlet, bright yellow, blaze orange, white or any combination of these colors. The cap may be any of these colors except white. Archers can stick to camo.

In addition, crossbows are not considered a bow and arrow, and cannot be used during the archery season.

For more information on all the hunting opportunities in Saskatchewan, contact: Tourism Saskatchewan, 1919 Saskatchewan Drive, Regina, Saskatchewan S4P 3V7; 1-800/667-7191.

Manitoba

There are an estimated 25,000 to 30,000 black bears in Manitoba, and most of these are jet black. However, a larger sample size of harvested bears now indicates that a small population of color-phase bears seems to be concentrated in the bottom third of the province.

"Recent province-wide success rates for residents is 25–30 percent," says Hank Hristienko, big game technician, "while nonresidents enjoy a 70 to 75 percent success rate."

If you are looking for a trophy-sized boar, and they are scattered all about the province, it's best to do your homework and book with an outfitter like Jack Smith of Canadian Wilderness Outfitters or Tim Hastings of Hastings Brothers Outfitters. They specialize in big bears.

There is a one-bear limit in Manitoba. Hunting with dogs is illegal. The blaze orange requirements of a hat and 400 square inches are not in effect in the spring.

For additional information on hunting all of Manitoba's big game, including a complete list of lodges and outfitters, contact: Travel Manitoba, Department 20 7th Floor, 155 Carlton St., Winnipeg, Manitoba R3C 3H8; 1-800/665-0040.

Ontario

There are conservatively 75,000–100,000 black bears in Ontario, and according to biologist Maria de Almeida, "about 7,000 are harvested each year." Success rates for nonresidents and aliens is nearly twice that of residents presumably because all nonresidents must hire the services of an authorized outfitter or tourist establishment before stepping afield.

Latest stats (1995) indicate nonresidents take about two-thirds of the harvest with an estimated 49 percent success ratio. The northwest and central sections of the province are the most productive due to more natural food sources.

Baiting and dogs are legal, but there are some restrictions on dogs during the spring season. A dog entering Canada from the United States must have a certificate indicating the dog has been vaccinated against rabies during the preceding 36 months.

For additional information on all the hunting opportunities in Ontario, contact: Ontario Travel, Queen's Park, Toronto, Ontario M7A 2R9; 1-800/ONTARIO.

Quebec

There are an estimated 60,000 black bears in Quebec, and according to biologist Helen Jolicoeur, the highest black bear densities are found just west of Montreal in the southwestern portion of the province.

There is, however, good bear hunting throughout the province, and if you like to fish for pike, walleye and brook trout, Quebec should be high on your list. I hunted Le Domaine Shannon last spring for example, and although the big bears were not moving much due to heavy rains, the trophy fishing was excellent. Le Domaine Shannon will refund $1,000 CN or offer another trip if no bears are spotted at the bait.

Research has shown that spring is the best time to pursue Quebec bruins. They are easier to bait then, there are fewer people in the woods and the boars are moving greater distances due to the upcoming mating season. In the fall, black bear hunting overlaps with both the deer and the moose seasons.

For more information about hunting big game anywhere in Quebec, contact Tourism Quebec, C.P. 20 000, Quebec, G1K 7X2; 1-800/363-7777.

New Brunswick

"About three in 100 bears tip the scales over 350 pounds," says biologist Kevin Craig. "The province record was taken in the fall of 1991. This 17-year-old bear had a live weight of 690 pounds.

"We now have one license valid for three seasons—the traditional spring season, a 'bow-only' hunt in September and the general firearms season in October/November, with a bag limit of one bruin per calendar year," adds Craig.

However, in order to spread out and limit the bear hunting pressure, some licenses have been allocated directly to outfitters, others are available in a random draw which can be done over the telephone. Any remaining licenses can be purchased by telephone or in person on a first come basis. All nonresidents must hunt with a licensed guide who may or may not be an outfitter.

Officials don't usually say where the bigger bears are located, but most of the outfitters work the St. John, Miramichi and Tobique River Valley Systems with good success. However, there is less hunting pressure and good numbers of mature bruins (hint!) in the north central portions of the province, too.

Crossbows and hunting with hounds is illegal; there is no orange requirement in the spring. For more information about all the hunting and fishing opportunities in New Brunswick, contact: Tourism New Brunswick, PO Box 12345, Fredericton, New Brunswick E3B 5C3; 1/800-561-0123.

Nova Scotia

Nova Scotia remains the "sleeper" of the Maritime Provinces due to extremely light hunting pressure, and a healthy population of jumbo bruins. Several bears have been killed recently tipping the scales between 350 and 500 pounds; these bruins were between 10 and 20 years old.

According to wildlife officer Vince Power, "nonresident interest in bear hunting is increasing, even though hunting is only allowed in the fall. Success rates can drop a little each autumn, however, whenever there is an overabundance of natural foods like apples and mountain ash."

Baiting and snaring is legal, dogs are not. There is a no spring season, but a fall hunt could easily double as a preseason scouting trip for the upcoming whitetail opener.

For more information, contact: Department of Tourism and Culture, PO Box 456, Halifax, Nova Scotia B3J 2R5; 1-800/341-6096.

Labrador/Newfoundland

Biologist Shane Mahoney estimates that there are now 10,000 to 12,000 black bears on the island of Newfoundland. In Labrador, the bear population is said to be "very numerous" according to biologists.

Black bears are thought to have been isolated on Newfoundland for more than 10,000 years, and as a result they may have evolved into a distinct race of super, predatory bears. Indeed, black bears feed heavily on moose and caribou calves taking up to 40 percent of all moose calves and 15 percent of all caribou calves. In some herds, bears may also be responsible for up to 40 percent of adult caribou mortality.

I bowhunted Newfoundland with Ray's Hunting and Fishing Lodge, and encountered many bomber bruins, including several that ranged in weight from 350 to 675 pounds. I eventually tagged a P&Y boar whose estimated live weight was 425 pounds.

Hunting seasons vary, but there is a two-bear limit in Newfoundland. Crossbows are not legal for hunting.

For additional information on the trophy bear hunting now available, contact: Department of Tourism and Culture, PO Box 8730, St. John's, Newfoundland A1B 4K2; 1-800/563-6353.

38   Bulls of the Big Tundra

BY BILL VAZNIS

*On the wind-swept treeless tundra where the caribou thrive, bowhunters find the endless fasci-
nating challenges of spotting and stalking. Here's what it's like in the land of the Northern
Lights when the herds are on the move.*

Have you ever wanted to step back in time and see what the world was
like 50 years ago? One hundred years ago? What about right after the
last ice age? What was the hunting like back then? Indeed, what was it
like to bowhunt a pristine wilderness teeming with wild game?

This may surprise you, but we can step back in time, so to speak, and
bowhunt a land that in many respects remains unspoiled by the hand of man. I am
not talking about a national park or some 1,000-acre, private set-aside parcel
stocked with fenced-in game, mind you, but an area encompassing hundreds of
thousands of square miles where the only sound you will hear, outside the occasional drone of a float plane, is the wind. And where the herds of wild animals are
so extensive their numbers rival that of the Serengeti.

I'm talking about caribou hunting, of course, from the wooded regions just
north of the U.S.-Canadian border through the taiga and onto the treeless tundra
of the high Arctic. This region in general, and the treeless tundra in particular, remains so wild that caribou, wolves and in some cases polar bears still live out their
lives without ever seeing a human being, never mind sniffing one. This is truly the
land that time forgot.

Caribou Grand Slam

Taxonomists and those that study wild critters tell us there are at least nine and
maybe as many as 27 subspecies of *rangifer tarandus* roaming the world, but at present only five are recognized by the Pope & Young Club. Ironically perhaps, the
boundaries for these five subspecies are based on geography, not biology.

For example, the only place in the world where you can tag a Woodland
Caribou is on the Island of Newfoundland. Biologists will tell you, however, that
"woodies" can be found sparingly in many wooded areas across the southern portions of Canada and as far north as the Mackenzie Mountains in the Northwest
Territories. The minimum archery score for record-book entry is 220, but the
archery world-record bull had 23 points and scored a whopping 345⅞. Dempsey
Cape tagged it in 1966 near the Victoria River. There are presently 89 Woodland

Caribou entries in the 5th Edition of the Records of North American Big Game (RNABG).

For the records, Mountain Caribou are found in British Columbia, Alberta, southern Yukon and the Mackenzie Mountains of the Northwest Territories. They can be found in the high country along with black bears, grizzly bears, elk, wolves and moose, and can often be hunted in conjunction with one or more of these big game animals. The minimum P&Y entry score is 300 with the world record arrowed by Chuck Adams in 1995 near Divide Lake. His 26-point NWT bull tallied 413⅞, only the second Mountain Caribou to score over 400. There are currently 83 entries listed in the RNABG, plus several velvet specimens not yet ranked.

The most famous caribou in North America is probably the million-strong Quebec-Labrador variety located, you guessed it, in the provinces of Quebec and Labrador. The first time I bowhunted caribou back in the early 80s, it was nothing to see herds of 5,000 or more animals crossing a river or moving through a remote valley. Although the dynamics of that herd have changed since then, it is still possible on occasion to see thousands and thousands of animals in a single day.

The minimum P&Y entry score is 325 with the current world record arrowed near the Tunulik River in Quebec, in 1984, by Carol Ann Mauch. Her 29-point bull scored an amazing 434⅞, one of 16 that now tally over 400. Quebec-Labrador is the second most popular caribou among trophy hunters with 443 record-book entries, plus several velvet bulls not yet ranked.

The largest-racked caribou are undoubtedly the Barren Ground Caribou or Grant's Caribou found only in Alaska, northern Yukon, Saskatchewan, Manitoba and Ontario. These tall-tined and long-beamed animals are very, very impressive. The minimum archery entry score is 325, but the current world record is a 37-point bull arrowed in 1984 near Lake Clark, Alaska, by Dennis Burdick. It scored 448⅞! There are 444 entries in the RNABG, plus several arrowed in velvet that are not yet ranked; 31 bulls tally 400 or better.

The last of the big five is also the newest member to the Grand Slam club. Located basically on Baffin Island and the mainland of the Northwest Territories, the Central Canada Caribou, a.k.a. Central Canada Barren Ground Caribou, travels in herds that rival those of Quebec, but unlike his eastern cousin, the Central Canada Caribou is more predictable in its migration routes. The minimum entry score is 325 with the world record arrowed by Al Kuntz in 1994 at Humpy Lake. This 24-point bull tallied 420⅞ and to date is only the second bull to be listed with a score above 400. There are 162 archery entries in the RNABG, including several velvet bulls not yet ranked.

Booking a Hunt

According to license sales, caribou are the most sought after big-game animal for sportsmen visiting Canada. And for three very good reasons. One, a white-maned bull is a stunning critter whose antlers are rivaled only by that of a moose for their size and majestic appearance. Two, most arctic hunters agree that caribou meat is unrivaled, with even moose steaks coming in a distant second. And finally, caribou of any subspecies make an excellent target for bow benders due to their numbers and overall body size.

Once you have been caribou hunting with a bow, all other big game hunting pales by comparison. Indeed, there is nothing in North America that compares to the cry of the wolf pack on a foggy morning and the sight of several thousand high-racked bulls pounding across the tundra in your direction.

So how do you go about booking a hunt? You can start by telephoning the Canadian Tourism Commission toll free at 877-8-CANADA (877-822-6232) and asking for information packets on the province(s) you wish to hunt. You can then visit some of the outfitters mentioned at winter/spring sportsmen's shows scattered about the country. Just as you would with any outfitter, if you do not know someone who has hunted with that operation in the past, it is wise to ask lots of questions and to check references. You might not care, for example, if your tent is heated, but you might want to know if the nearby terrain is suitable to bowhunting with a recurve or long bow.

You can also book through a reputable booking agent such as that offered by Cabela's or Wes Vining at the Trophy Connection (307-527-5506). This will help ensure a quality experience. Expect to pay between $2,500 for a semi-guided, do-it-yourself trip to over $4,000 for a personalized, one-on-one, fully-guided tour, not including license fees, trophy fees, camping fees, air fare, motel/hotel rooms plus tips and gratuities.

You will probably also have to purchase some specialized equipment you don't already own, like a durable bow case, quality binoculars and Gore-Tex rainwear. And if you are successful, and many caribou hunters are allowed to tag two bulls, full-shoulder mounts will run you an additional 500 clams apiece. Caribou hunting is without a doubt one of the more expensive one-week hunts.

When is the best time to book? If you are after a bull in velvet, take a close look at the last two weeks in August; otherwise, book the first two or three weeks in September.

Archery Tackle

Any bow and arrow that is set up for whitetail deer is sufficient for caribou. Even though caribou are thin-skinned animals, I prefer cut-on-impact broadheads like the 100-grain Satellite TNT and the Phantom 125, but replaceable-blade heads like those from Bruce Barre, Thunderhead and Muzzy are excellent choices, too. As far as bows are concerned, compound users who can poke a bull's-eye out at 50 yards will appreciate a multi-pin setup and flat-shooting arrows, but traditional aficionados will have little trouble getting shots under 20 yards if they bide their time, I've arrowed caribou between 10 and 40 yards.

The two most important pieces of equipment you need, however, are 10- to 12-inch waterproof boots, preferably leather to help protect your ankles from sharp rocks and uneven terrain, and a quality binocular. Footware from Rocky, LaCross or Cabela's is always a good choice, as are binoculars from Nikon, Burris, Swarovski, Leica or Zeiss. However, due to the amount of glassing you can expect to do each day, leave the minis home and spend as much as you can afford on a medium- to full-size pair. My Nikon 8x32 Superior Es fit the bill perfectly.

Camouflage is your next concern. You have a pick of two general patterns here. A shadow-based camouflage, such as Mossy Oak's Break-Up, is a dynamite choice for sneaking about on the open tundra. A gray-based pattern, such as Jim Crumley's original Trebark, is a good alternative due to the number of rocks and rocky outcroppings on the tundra. Or you can mix and match these patterns for good effect, too, as you spot and glass across the treeless terrain.

Tundra Tactics

There are four methods commonly used by bowhunters to tag a 'bou on the tundra. The most popular is spot and stalk. Hillsides overlooking treeless basins, rocky outcroppings and high points adjacent to known crossings are all good places to spend at least part of the day glassing for wide-racked bulls. It is not unusual to see small herds of five to 50 animals slowly working their way across the barren landscape from these various vantage points.

The mature bulls, the bulls with the best racks, often sport white manes that are clearly visible from quite a distance. In fact, herds of big bulls can sometimes be spotted two to 10 miles in the distance, giving you plenty of time to get ready or plot a course for interception. Shots, however, can be difficult, depending on how close you can stalk. Fifty yards is about average.

Ambushing bulls at preferred crossings or along natural bottlenecks, however, can give you shots at point blank range. I once had a bull so close I could have almost touched him. Being that close and then watching him come unglued when he saw me was one of the highlights of that trip.

Caribou often use the same trails to navigate across the tundra as those caribou that just preceded them, lured on by the presence of interdigital scent. Thus, fresh tracks and droppings on well-worn trails are good areas to set up for the next herd of migrating bulls. Saddles between two high points, brush-choked lake crossings and the shorelines around the tips of ponds and lakes are all good places to hide in ambush.

Sometimes, however, the best-laid plans go awry. A distant herd of bulls can suddenly switch course and trot past you well out of range. The same goes for ambush sites. A careless cough, a sudden change in wind direction or even a shiny face can all cause a herd of white-maned bulls to turn away. A guide, however, can sometimes swing upwind of an approaching herd and then put on a mini-drive pushing a good bull past you and within bow range. The shooting can be fast and furious, though, with little time for yardage estimation.

My favorite tactic for tundra caribou is undoubtedly still-hunting. Taking advantage of land contours and available vegetation, while sticking with the shadows, can make for an action-packed day on the tundra. Unlike still-hunting for whitetails, there are many caribou on the tundra, and if you fail to get a shot at one bull, there is always another racked giant in the next basin for you to test your skills.

My best still-hunting bull to date was a Central Canada Barren Ground bull taken while hunting with Moise Rabesca at Camp Ekwo in the NWT. Under Moise's watchful eye, I managed to shoot the B and C bull at 25 yards as he loped past me through a patch of willows. The 100-grain Satellite TNT passed completely through the bull, striking a rock on the far side and leading Moise and me to believe I had missed him clean. Much to our surprise, the heavy-beamed bull traveled less than 100 yards, as I recall, before topping over. He later scored 360⅜, placing him in the number 27 slot in the RNABG.

Camp Ekwo

I arrived in camp the day Al Kuntz loaded his new world-record bull into a float plane for the long flight home. Ironically perhaps, the hunter who helped Kuntz load that bull was Don Hotter, who would within a few days rifle another huge bull at Camp Ekwo. Hotter's bull eventually scored 433⅜ on the Boone and Crockett scale, making it the new world-record bull with a firearm.

Two record-book animals from the same camp is unheard of, but wait, it gets even better. Two years later, in 1996, Randy Rollera blasted the new world record with a muzzleloader from Camp Ekwo. Roller's bull scored 378⅜. However, it was only listed officially in the record books for two weeks before an even bigger bull was tagged with a muzzleloader at Camp Ekwo. That's right! Blackpowder hunter James Nelson's central Canada barren ground bull tallied 385⅜, bumping Rollera's bull to second place. Imagine that—four world-record caribou from the same camp!

Conclusion

Bowhunting Tuktu on the tundra can still be a timeless experience, giving you some idea of what it was like to traipse about in a wilderness setting hundreds and even thousands of years ago. Things are changing in the North Country, however. Diamond mines, new hunting camps and the ever-increasing numbers of human visitors are changing the look and feel of the tundra. Don't wait until you retire to book a hunt—book it now while you can still enjoy it. Time is, after all, of the essence.

Field Judging Caribou

It takes plenty of experience to field judge any subspecies of caribou accurately. The first thing I look for when picking out a trophy bull is a white cape. A brown-colored bull is usually a younger animal. Next, I look for a set of antlers that looks bigger than the body and appears to have plenty of mass. This, too, is the sign of a mature animal.

I then zero in on symmetry. View the bull from as many different angles as possible. A difference in beam length, for example, can easily drop the score out of the record books.

I then look closely for two 12- to 15-inch symmetrical points per side at the tops, as measured from the bottom of the beam, not the top like a whitetail, and heavy (five-inch) palmation. Keep in mind that only two points per side count under B and C and P&Y rules.

The length of the main beam is next on my list because it can account for 25 percent of the total score. Look for beams that bend back over the body, then curve out and up before hooking forward over the face. The more curves the better! Double shovels, both the length and width, are also important. A second shovel is counted as a bonus; its absence is not considered as a deduction.

The bez tines, the second point growing from the main beam, lie just above the shovels. There is little variation among the better bulls; they are all about 20 to 22 inches long, and the width measurement is not taken for B and C and P&Y. If you see a bull with long points on the top, long main beams, and double shovels but short bez tines, shoot him as he is undoubtedly a record-book bull anyway!

39   Moose Mayhem

BY LON E. LAUBER

*During a colossal battle of two titan moose, the author was able to arrow a top-10 P&Y bull!
Here's an account of the hunt.*

Bowhunting monster moose can be intimidating to the uninitiated. But
grabbing the bull by the antlers, so to speak, is part of the adventure.
There are, however, some preliminary chores to tackle before stepping
into the swampy Northland moose call home. Neither my hunting partner, Phil Lincoln, nor I had much moose hunting experience prior to this trip.
Regardless, with nine months of research, generous advice from three local
hunters and high-dollar phone bills, we were ready.

Alaska-Yukon moose are built like Clydesdales and can sport antlers the size
of a porch swing. To sustain such a colossal creature, moose need immense country.
That's why they thrive in the vast Alaska wilderness. However, as sure as paper
comes from trees, where you find moose you'll find wolves and bears too. When
bowhunting, one must be attentive of bears and act accordingly in their territory.
Wolves aren't really a threat to humans but they sure are lethal to moose. If I had
half the slyness of *Canis lupus,* I'd really be deadly. For me, seeing a wolf is the spirit
of raw nature.

On our September wilderness hunt, my lanky-legged partner, Phil, and I
were fortunate enough to see wolves. "There's a wolf, there's another one," Phil
said, while poking his right index finger against the plane's window. The pilot spun
the plane in a tight doughnut for a closer look. We located seven of the wild ca-
nines before moving on. They were all cigar-ash gray or lighter. Some were almost
white. Currently, these wolves contrasted against the darkness of the autumn, boreal forest. However, for the eight months of winter in northern Alaska, they are
well suited. In the scheme of things, seeing the wolves from the air was just the
pollen on the flower.

We continually saw moose, 39 in all, during the hour-long bush flight.
Nothing pumps me up more at the start of a hunt than seeing abundant game
from the air.

The pilot deftly maneuvered the aircraft onto a tiny crescent-shaped lake.
The plane glided in with the grace of a honker. Quickly, we piled out and stepped
on to the lumpy, soggy tundra. The pilot's landing was much softer than his attitude. "You guys will have to carry your gear over to the river from here. It can't be
more than a half mile," he belched. "I gotta get out of here before this weather

231

keeps me here with you guys." After reconfirming our pick-up time and destination, the banana-colored plane vanished into the mist.

For just a moment I felt sick to my stomach. It happens each time a bush pilot abandons me in isolated country. That's when the gravity of a wilderness hunt sinks in. "Phil and I are truly on our own," I thought. "We'll have to endure whatever this harsh environment hands out." As the volume of the plane's mechanized hum faded, I was engulfed by the deafening silence of the wilderness. For the next two hours, as we lugged our gear to the river, we heard nothing but the wind.

In a dank drizzle we pitched our tent that would be home. I lit the Coleman Apex stove to manufacture supper. The one-burner was situated over a bed of dried, pelletized moose nuggets.

"Cooking over moose droppings is a good omen," I thought. After dinner, we organized our belongings for the following day's adventure. Alaska state law forbids hunting on the same day you're airborne. So, instead of hunting that evening, we hiked out for a look-see. Less than a football field's length from the tent, we stopped. Not because we saw anything particularly interesting, but we were gasping for air.

"These tussocks are a pain to walk in," Phil said.

"Yea, and you never get used to them no matter how much tussock-walking you do." I huffed. For the unknowing, tussocks are your leg's worst nightmare. They are milk-jug-sized bumps of grass growing haphazardly betwixt the other mosses, lichens and grasses that comprise tundra. Occasionally one can step between tussocks. Usually though, they torque ankles and knees while disrupting your cadence. It's ten times worse than walking a train track. Somehow, moose take it in stride. In the fading light we caught our breath and glassed for Alaskan waterhorse.

Quickly, I spotted a mature bull across the river. He was meandering across a slope dotted with willow patches. Then he evaporated into a draw. "See that rocky outcropping on top of the hill and behind the gully that swallowed the moose," I said while pointing northwest across the river. "I think we should be on that point at first light tomorrow morning. What do you think?" I asked Phil. "That sounds good," he replied. "It'll give us a commanding view of our entire hunting area. From up there we'll get familiar with this river drainage."

The Play Begins

Exhausted from the lengthy trip, I fidgeted myself to sleep. Shortly, I found myself dreaming of monster bulls like the ones seen from the plane. All too quickly, the annoying computerized beep, beep, beep of Phil's wristwatch alarm pulled me from a slumbering sleep. It was 5:10 a.m. Rising before the sun is paramount to moose hunting success. Moreover, we had an icy river and a mile stretch of tussock-filled tundra to cross before reaching our vantage point. In our enthusiasm, we made the hike in less than an hour.

My haunches hadn't even established wrinkles from the rocky tundra before Phil said, "There's a moose, and it's a big bull." I whipped up my 8x30 Swarvoski's and located the giant almost instantly. He was a tremendous bull with approximately 65-inch wide antlers. However, it was the length and height of his antler palms that were most impressive. This monarch was hotly pursuing his girlfriend. They were all over the mountain. When moose are "courting," it's a gamble on where they might end up. From a mile away there was nothing we could do except watch the ritual. The bull nosed up behind her but she wasn't willing to submit. She'd ward off his advances by whirling around or ambling off. Shortly, she led our trophy out of sight. We weren't too concerned because their behavior provided a low percentage opportunity for a bowhunter. Anyway, it was early on the first day of our hunt. We continued glassing. Moose were everywhere. This was truly enticing and surprising.

Most moose habitat can sustain one legal bull moose for every five square miles. Prime moose habitat will hold three to five moose per square mile. And, I was told by a biologist, there were places in our hunting area supporting up to 14 moose per square mile. This must have been one of those spots. We saw 13 moose on the first day. Six were mature, rut-crazed bulls. Ironically, all these wall-hangers walked upriver.

Upstream was the predominate direction the bulls traveled the entire hunt. Like clockwork, we'd locate moose each morning and evening. If it was a single bull, he'd be strolling upriver in search of a cow. Later, we asked a more experienced moose hunter if there was any reason for this upstream pattern. He told us they were just walking into the wind to find a receptive cow. Once Phil and I stopped to think, it made sense. Almost the entire hunt, the wind was blowing with the river's current. This same upriver roaming ultimately led us to my bull.

The Plot Thickens

Late one evening while glassing from a willow and alder-choked ridge above the river, I noticed the unmistakable gleam of moose antlers. "There's a bull. Quick, Phil get the scope on him," I said. Phil pulled the spotting scope out of his pack. In seconds he was peering at the bull with 25X glass. "Oh Lon," Phil said, "he's got unbelievable brow tines!"

"Let me see that big boy," I said. Briefly I glanced through the scope. The bull's antler bases were the size of a baseball bat and they arched down from the weight of the palms. The antler paddles extended way past the massive shoulders of this monster bull. And, like Phil said, his antlers had heavily palmated brow tines with six points on each side. I'm sure his antlers spread at least 65 inches, maybe 70. In a few seconds I was convinced. "That's the kind of bull I came to hunt," I said. "Phil, you stay here and give me hand signals if I need them, okay." Momentarily, I was on my way.

My stomach felt like I'd just been pulled over for speeding. My mouth was dry as the desert too. Regardless, I was loping down the hill hurdling blueberry bushes and stumbling in the tussocks. I'm certain I looked silly but at that point I really didn't care. Meanwhile, the massive bull moose was across the river ripping a willow bush to shreds with his antlers. He was unaware of our closeness. A steep bank thick with brush bordered the river. I struggled down and through the Alaskan jungle desperately needing a decent spot to cross the river.

Two-hundred yards downstream, I began wading. With my juices pumping, I barely noticed the chilling water. Hurriedly, I poured the icy brine out of my boots. More methodically, I wrung out my socks. Shivering with excitement and my waist-deep bath, I looked toward Phil with binoculars. He was preoccupied with the moose. I could see him glued to the scope. It was pointing farther up-river. I hustled ahead trying to locate the bull. When I eased into the clearing where the bull had demolished the willow, I couldn't find him. Shortly, Phil noticed me. He gestured the bull was farther south and across the river. I also determined from Phil's signals that I'd better hustle.

Immediately I trotted after the bull. As luck would have it, the river meandered back in front of me. If I wanted to kill this bull, I had no choice but to brave the current again. I waded out in the icy swiftness. Then I dove in. With my bow in hand, I did the side stroke in Olympic fashion. I wanted that moose. Unfortunately, by the time I had hauled my shivering, weary body out of the drink, Phil waved me off. The bull was gone.

I was stripping down to wring out my clothes when Phil caught up with me. Together, we twisted the remaining river out of my clothes. Good thing for polar fleece and Capilene, they dry out quickly. Chilly and bummed, we hiked up-river toward camp.

We hadn't covered a couple hundred yards when our ears were filled with the indisputable, hollow sound of moose antlers clanking together. Phil and I stared at one another in pleasant disbelief. We were off in a flash. Quickly, we determined the bulls were (of course) on the far side of the river. At first we tried calling them across with a series of lustful cow moans. At the time we didn't know they were battling for the love of two long-nose cows watching nearby. I must admit though, after calling, the war became more furious. We crossed the thigh-deep river and trotted toward the brawl. Neither of us bothered to empty the water out of our boots this time.

It was easy to find the struggling monsters. Trust me, the results of 3,000 pounds of fighting moose flesh doesn't go unnoticed. The bulls were flattening trees like a steam roller ironing toothpicks. With fiery eyes and mucus flying from their nostrils, the bulls battled on. Meanwhile, the two cows watched like tennis match attendees. They swung their heads toward us and then back to the bulls and so forth. The cows were very aware of our presence. However, since the masters didn't seem to mind, they just stood there and gawked.

Instantly we identified the bull on the left as the one I'd just been stalking. Since I'd originally spotted him, it was my choice. "I'm gonna take him," I said. Phil concurred, "Okay, but wait until they stop fighting before you shoot." At this point in the confrontation, you could have sent a parade through the area and these bruisers wouldn't have noticed. During a pause in the fracas, I drew my Browning Maxim and picked a spot. When it felt right I released. The Phantom-tipped XX78 2215 arrow disappeared through the dark hair behind the bull's massive shoulder. It flashed through his rib cage right where I was aiming. Amazingly, the bull only flinched upon the arrow's impact. He just kept fighting. Seconds later, his knees buckled. With the hunger instinct of a scrappy boxer, the other bull tore into his dying opponent. Sensing his eminent victory, the other bull slashed at my trophy moose with reckless abandon.

My bull tried to maintain his footing and continued fighting, but it was useless. Even after he stumbled to the forest floor, the monarch lifted his head and kept fighting. In less than a minute this bull lost the challenge and his life. My emotions were as mixed as a milkshake in a blender. On one hand I was thrilled with my shot placement and taking a trophy moose. On the other hand, I felt truly remorseful for reducing the king of the woods to a pile of meat and antlers. The day I no longer experience mixed emotions like that, is the day I'll quit hunting. Meanwhile, the other bull had an inaccurate sense of authority. He continued to trounce my dead moose. First it was an antler-to-antler thrashing. Then he began jousting the limp carcass. Hair was flying everywhere. Phil and I screamed and clapped our hands to shock him back to reality. He was so engrossed in his glory that our sounds fell on deaf ears. Finally, Phil said "Let's howl like wolves." At this point I'd try anything to save what was left of my moose. "Let's give it a try," I said.

With two extremely nervous cow moose jeering at us, one monster moose on the ground and another bull nearly as large only a stone's toss away, we began to howl. It took a few "ah woos," but finally the bull snapped out of his trance. He literally shook his head in disbelief. With one grunt and a whirl, he was off. The cows followed.

Phil chose not to shoot the other bull. It was late evening and we still had more than a week to hunt. Besides we had a three-quarter-ton of work sprawled at our feet. Plus, considering the bounty of moose thus far, Phil was sure he'd get another crack at a good bull. He was right.

Each day, Phil had a chance at moose. With a rifle it would have been easy. With a bow, more effort was needed. Considering our lack of experience with moose hunting, the calling techniques we employed worked flawlessly. Every bull located and set up on was called in. Phil either passed them up or a high-percentage bow shot wasn't offered.

Phil Takes Center Stage

Five days after killing my bull, Phil's quest for a bow-bagged bull was about to gel. That morning, we overslept. It was 8 a.m. when we finally dragged our weary, moose hunting bones out of the tent. "I think we should skip breakfast and hustle up to our glassing hill," I suggested. "Maybe we can find a bull before it gets too late." We hurried through the forest and up the brushy hill. After seven minutes of trying to keep pace with my spry partner, I stopped for a breather. Naturally, I turned toward the river. Once again, the telltale flash of antlers betrayed the bull's presence. He was less than 100 yards from our riverside camp. Phil and I raced back down the ridge. After a quick analyzing session, we set up to call. With a previous record of luring in six bulls on six tries, I was quite hopeful with the situation at hand.

With our tried and true litany of raking a stick in the brush, grunting like a bull, and moaning like a cow, we proceeded. I did the calling. Phil made himself scarce near the edge of a marshy meadow below me. After one short calling session, the bull headed our way. Occasionally, I could hear him grunting. But that was only between my ear-thumping heart beats. Even though I wasn't going to shoot, I was polluted with excitement. Also, I could see the trees and brush parting as the bull and his antlers forged our way. Once, the bull stopped and stared toward Phil for a couple minutes. "Oh, no," I whispered to myself. "The wind must have shifted." Slowly, I turned away and produced one seductive cow moan. It worked. He was coming in! The bull plodded through the understory. He stopped less than 20 yards directly in front of me. I could see his eyes searching for the cow he'd just heard. I had selected my calling location perfectly. I was well concealed. Meanwhile, Phil had come to full draw when the moose stopped. However, some willows blocked a clear shot at the bull's vitals. With my eyes only, I looked at the moose, then at Phil holding at full draw, and then back again. "This must be how those two cows felt when I shot my bull," I thought. It felt like an hour before the bull walked forward but I know it was only seconds. When the moose stopped in the clear, Phil shot.

I did not see or hear the arrow coming. All I heard was the arrow passing through the moose. The bull winced and bolted. He stopped only seven yards uphill from me. Now, I could see the entrance wound right behind the bull's shoulder. I looked at Phil. We traded smiles and gestured thumbs up. The bull was dead in less than 30 seconds.

Time for Praise

Phil's moose was slightly smaller than mine, but any mature moose is an awesome sight. His antlers spread 53 inches. I must applaud Phil for being so steadfast under tension. He made a great, double-lung pass-through shot after holding at full draw for so long. Moreover, I truly respect Phil for his sensible decision in not shooting the large bull fighting mine. If we had two monsters to butcher—starting at 7:30 p.m.—it would have been a very long night indeed. Phil may have taken a smaller bull in the end but he's a bigger man for his actions. I wouldn't have behaved with such prudence if I were in his hip boots. However, there must have been a greater plan in the works. Because of Phil's forethought, we had more hunting time. In the process we learned volumes of moose hunting doctrine.

The Final Scene

With more than a thousand pounds of moose meat and all our gear in one raft, we started the 33-mile float. With just a few inches of freeboard, the raft just barely stayed afloat. These were the longest, coldest four days of my existence. Sitting motionless for hours on end in subfreezing temperatures is not my idea of fun. If it weren't for the perils of river rafting we'd have been bored to tears. However, the power of the river's current and weight of the raft drifted us into all kinds of trouble.

Once we got sucked under a tree that had fallen across the river. Like the fingers of a biology-class skeleton, the sweeper clawed at us with no sorrow. Mostly, we made it past unscathed. The raft remained airtight. However, a few bends down the river, I noticed my bow was missing! The sweeper had stolen my Browning Maxim. I'm sure it's nicely preserved in that Arctic river. Luckily, we were finished hunting.

It's humbling to contend with the rigorous standards Alaska demands of bowhunters. It's not impossible. It just takes extensive research before the hunt. Remember, the moose hunting experience is secondary to planning.

40   Eighteen Days with Elk

BY GARY CLANCY

If you're like most bowhunters, the hankering to hunt elk will soon hit—and hit hard.

If you're like most bowhunters and have chased deer around with your stick and string, the hankering to elk hunt is sure to hit. It's hit me numerous times, and during the fall of 1994 I was fortunate enough to spend 18 days hunting elk. No record I'm sure, but not bad for a flatlander from Minnesota. It was the year during which I learned the most about elk and how to hunt them. I was into elk on all 18 days and there is not a better teacher of elk hunting know-how than the elk themselves. If you've got a hankering to bowhunt elk, or maybe you have been hunting them without much success, come on along and I'll share what the elk taught me during my 18 days in their classroom.

This has been the most difficult lesson for me to learn. Most of us from "back east" bowhunt primarily whitetail deer. Rarely does it pay to become aggressive with a whitetail. In fact most whitetail hunters work very hard at selecting stand locations where the deer will come to them. But elk are different than whitetails. And even though there are times when it pays to be patient, most of the time being aggressive will pay bigger dividends. On the long drive from our Minnesota homes to the mountains, my hunting partner and I talked of many aspects of elk hunting, but I kept coming back to being aggressive. Finally Larry said, "Man, you're really hung-up on this being aggressive thing aren't you. You must have used that word 100 times since we left home."

"I think I'm trying to convince myself," I laughed. "I figure that if I talk about being aggressive enough maybe when the time comes to get aggressive I'll make the right moves instead of holding back like I've done on past hunts. I'm convinced from my own experiences and from talking with a number of really good elk hunters that not being afraid to get right in the face of a bull is really important."

Of course, you are going to blow a few chances by being aggressive, but not nearly as many opportunities as you will lose out on by pussyfooting around elk as if you were stalking whitetail. Let me give you a prime example of just the type of aggressive behavior I'm talking about.

For an hour I had followed the bull up the side of the mountain. The 6x6 was going to bed and as lone bulls often do when calling it a night, this one was voicing his displeasure at once again suffering the frustration of not finding any willing cows during his long night of carousing. The problem was he was not frustrated enough to succumb to my pleading cow calls nor angry enough to charge in to a bugle. I was doing my best to get ahead of the bull in hopes of ambushing him, but even though the bull was only walking, his long strides were allowing him to pull away from me. I had that sinking feeling a hunter gets when he is so close but yet knows he is losing. My rubbery legs and burning lungs were pleading with me to give up the chase. And then I heard the bull thrashing a juniper just ahead. The words of Corky Richardson, one of the best elk guides in the southwest screamed in my head, "When you've got a bull raking, don't dillydally," Corky had told me.

So I sucked up as much of the thin air as my sea-level lungs would hold and sprinted 50 yards up the mountain to where I could see the top of a juniper tree gyrating wildly in the thin mountain air. When I burst around the side of a pinion tree, there stood my bull, hind legs slightly spraddled, his antlers buried in the branches of the defenseless juniper. He was so close I could smell the rankness of his urine-soaked belly. Two steps to my right and I would have enough of an angle to slip an arrow into the bull's vitals. I made the two steps, drew back the 70 pound Matthews Solo-Cam and was just ready to release when the bull suddenly pulled back from the juniper. In that instant I knew that this was not the bull I had been chasing all morning. Still, I had the 5x5 dead to rights and the temptation was great to let the arrow go. However, my decision made, I eased off as smoothly as possible, but the bull caught the movement, turned to glare at my fully camouflaged figure standing five yards away, whirled and went charging down the mountain. I sat down in the rocks for a long time and let the shakes subside.

O.K., so it was the wrong bull, but only by being aggressive had I placed myself in position for the shot.

The same is true for calling. Sure you can get a bull to talk back to you every time you bugle from the far side of the canyon, but so what. Rare is the bull who will go out of his way to kick some butt. The closer you can get to a bull, the more effective both bugling and cow calling will be.

Night Patrol

Except during the very peak of the rut, it is common for bulls to bugle frequently at night, but to be closemouthed during the day. In those areas where hunting pressure is a significant factor, bulls learn to clam up once the sun breaks even during prime breeding time. The elk have taught me that they will answer my bugles with reckless abandon at 3 or 4 a.m., but flat refuse to so much as grunt to the same bugle once it is daylight. That is why I now consider the most important two hours of the "day" to be the two hours of darkness prior to dawn. It is during this time that I can locate the bulls which I will hunt when shooting light arrives.

Where whitetail deer are abundant, you can bet that every woodlot has a few resident animals that call that place home. But even where elk are found in good numbers, it is possible for large expanses of habitat to be devoid of elk. I've spent enough time hunting in places where elk were not present. That is why I'm willing to give up a couple extra hours of much needed shut-eye and crawl out of a warm sleeping bag in the inky black to go off in search of bugling bulls.

Whenever possible I use forest roads and a vehicle for my predawn bugling missions. This method works great in the southwestern elk states of New Mexico and Arizona where a maze of logging roads on public land make penetrating good elk country easy. Typically, I like to drive one-quarter mile between stops, bugling two or three times at each stop and listening for answering bugles. If I get an answer I jot down the location on a map or punch in the coordinates on a handheld GPS unit. Night bugling will work in backcountry areas which must be covered on foot, but of course the limited amount of country you can cover will limit the number of bugling bulls you can expect to hear.

Team Calling

Although my hunting partner and I normally hunt alone morning and evening, we often get together at midmorning for a few hours of team calling. Our method is quite simple. We find a place where we are convinced there are elk, probably a place where we have either seen elk, or heard elk during our predawn bugling runs. We climb to the highest ridges and split up 30 to 50 yards apart, each of us finding a place that affords good cover, but not so thick that it impedes getting off a shot. I like to kneel on a seat cushion, squatting back on my heels. After a summer of practice I'm confident of my shooting ability from the kneeling position, but more importantly, if an elk does come to the call, I don't have to make any unnecessary movement to get into position. Once settled I'll start cow calling and Larry will chime in with either more cow calls or very often the higher pitched mews of a calf. We call back and forth for a few minutes, wait about five minutes and then call again, giving each position 15 to 20 minutes before moving on. Cows respond well to team calling and since the rut is in progress during archery elk seasons, it is not uncommon for the cows to drag a bull in with them. That is exactly what happened when Larry and I spent a clear, windless morning team calling a long ridge in an area where we knew there were elk, but where our morning and evening efforts had so far proved futile. It was 10:30 when we silently split up, Larry dropping just over the crest of the steep spined ridge, while I hunkered in front of a clump of immature pines. Three cows responded to our calls and came up the steep hillside toward my position. I quit calling not wanting the cows to pinpoint my location. Larry and I have hunted together for a long time and he knew that when I suddenly quit carrying on a conversation that something was up. Larry kept calling which focused the attention of the cows on his position. The cows were only 15 yards in front of me and I had about given up on a bull being with them. Suddenly there he was, stepping majestically onto a little rise 25 yards to my left. I swiveled my body on my knees, drew and released. Double-lunged, the bull crashed off down the mountain and piled up.

Team calling is the best method I know of for bringing in bulls during that midday lull when most hunters are back in camp napping.

Waterholes are obvious locations for a treestand, but many hunters don't bother to bring a treestand along unless they are hunting semiarid habitat where waterhole hunting is common. That is a mistake.

Even where water is plentiful, prime wallow areas may be in short supply. While wallows are not as dependable as waterholes, a wallow that is being hit regularly is certainly worth a sit or two. And hey, let's face it, elk hunting is physically grueling. After a long day of chasing up and down the mountain, sitting for a couple of hours on stand is a welcome respite.

Trails are another good bet for a treestand. Especially where elk are feeding on agricultural land, usually hay fields, it is often possible to locate the main trail the herd is using and hunt effectively from a portable.

Larry and I took four stands on our 18-day hunt and wished we had taken four more.

Don't Forget to Rake

No, I'm not talking about your front yard. I'm referring to the most overlooked means of communicating with a bull elk. In these days of call-shy bulls it is not only common to encounter bulls that will not come into your bugling or cow calling, but will even refuse to honor your best calls with a reply. As every elk hunter knows, it is darn hard to stay in contact with a bull if he won't mouth off every so often to let you know his location and direction of travel. That is where raking comes into play. Bull elk just love to destroy young pine and spruce trees. When a big bull starts working that headgear up and down the trunk of some hapless sapling, baseball-thick limbs snap off like toothpicks. Maybe they do it to strengthen neck muscles or maybe they are just showing off for the cows. Raking may simply be a display of frustration. Whatever the real reason for raking, there is no doubt that raking is contagious and that is what makes it such an effective tactic for staying in contact with a bull. When one bull hears or sees another bull raking a tree, almost invariably he is compelled to thrash a sapling of his own.

So next time you lose track of a bull, don't give up until you try raking. Grab a good stout limb and beat the heck out of tree trunk or log. Really go at it, you can't make too much noise. Odds are good that if there is a bull within hearing he will start to rake as well, betraying his location to you in the process. And when you hear that bull raking what are you going to do? That's right, get aggressive and go right at him.

Odor Control

1. Rig up some kind of shower. In a semi-permanent camp you might luxuriate beneath a generator powered makeshift shower, but even in a backcountry camp a collapsible bag-type shower holding five gallons of water will get the job done. As a last resort take a quick dip in that ice cold creek or clean up with a spongebath. Always use an unscented soap. If you don't bathe forget about the rest of this sidebar.

2. Put on clean clothes each day. I've met many elk hunters who hunt in the same clothes for a week. They smell worse than a rutting bull. If I can smell them, imagine how they must smell to an elk. On backpack hunts, carry two

sets of everything. Wear one and wash the other in a scent free soap and hang to air dry.

3. Use an odor destroying liquid spray such as NO-ODOR several times each day, paying special attention to groin and head.

4. Dust feet liberally with NO-ODOR II and sprinkle in boots each morning. NO-ODOR II does a super job of absorbing odors. I like to carry a change of socks in my fanny pack and slip into a fresh pair at midday.

5. Whenever I take a stand for elk, I do all of the above, plus don a Scent-Loc suit. I've learned the hard way that the folks at Scent-Loc provide a hood with the suit for a reason. Not wearing the hood decreases the effectiveness of the suit dramatically. All of this attention to scent control takes time, but I guarantee, it is time well spent.

41   Are You Tough Enough for Pronghorns?

BY MARK KAYSER

There's nothing easy about antelope hunting if you're crazy enough to chase them with bowhunting gear.

Deciding on whether to sit and wait for antelope, or to actively stalk them, armed with a bow, is like deciding whether to run the Boston Marathon or participate in a weekend volksmarch. If your idea of training is mowing the lawn, you may want to rethink your fall archery antelope hunting plans. For a true answer to your dilemma, don't consult a psychic. Instead, have your own out-of-body experience. It's cheaper and less humiliating than waiting until an outfitter gives you mouth-to-mouth. Odds are they wouldn't anyway.

By taking a step back from yourself and examining your weaknesses and strengths, you'll find the answer to your archery antelope dilemma: should I sit or should I stalk?

The most important consideration is your physical shape. Can you handle a stalk hunt in antelope country? Most macho hunters look at the rolling sage and prairie country and say, "Heck, it's as flat as my hometown golf course . . . no problem," maybe, maybe not.

First, antelope hunting takes place early in the fall and that means summer-like temperatures. In prime antelope states like Montana and Wyoming, temperatures in the 80s and low 90s range are common well into September. Exhaustion and muscle fatigue invade a body considerably quicker in hot weather and even quicker in an out-of-shape body.

Secondly, antelope country may not look rough, but antelope can cover a lot of country, meaning high mileage for your footwear. Reports have shown that an antelope can easily average 30 mph for seven miles or more. Try and keep up with that during an 80-degree day.

If the long hike doesn't get you, the short belly crawl might. Somewhere during a stalk, you will need to get down on your hands and knees, even on your belly, and squirm along the ground to shorten the final distance. You will now become personally acquainted with the prairie, especially the hardy and sometimes hidden, prickly pear cactus. Those memories will stay with you long after the hunt . . . imbedded in your mind and knees.

Oh, did I mention God's little creatures? There are a few animals who do not appreciate trespassing on their homeland. In western and southwestern antelope range, it's not uncommon to see rattlesnakes, or hear one buzzing in a nearby sage bush. Out West, a common phrase is "don't trust anything because it either bites or pricks you."

So a Lazy Boy in a blind is beginning to sound good? That isn't as easy as it sounds either. The most common blind for successful antelope stand hunting is the pit blind or blackout blind. This type of blind is completely covered to create shadows inside and shroud the hunter in darkness.

Of course, unless you are paying an outfitter to have a blind waiting, you have at least one hard day's work ahead. That includes digging a pit in cement-hard clay and fashioning a roof. You will also need several days of research to locate where antelope are watering or traveling for a successful ambush site. Now that the blind is finished, are you prepared to spend all day in a windless blind in sweltering heat? Hey, never mind the heat, do you even have enough patience to idly sit all day in wait for a buck? Sometimes antelope may water at another locale, or the buck you desire may have found a doe to breed.

And those creepy things you can encounter on a hike also may find their way into your blind. Rattlesnakes seek out shaded daytime resting spots making your pit blind a prime target. Finding a resting rattlesnake under your chair can be the ultimate test of your patience.

Antelope Facts

If you've never tackled antelope before, or if it's been awhile, there are a few things you should know about these open-country speedsters. Antelope are not a true antelope at all, but rather a sole remnant of a uniquely North American horned mammal that existed for nearly five million years. Before man's modern appearance in the West, antelope were estimated to number nearly 40 million animals. Pioneers, homesteaders and market hunters drove the animals to near extinction by the turn of the century. Fortunately, antelope have a high reproductive rate and with the aid of conservation groups, they've made a dramatic comeback. That's good news for hunters because antelope are a unique challenge.

You've undoubtedly heard this before, but antelope have terrific eyesight. Although it's impossible to determine their exact power, biologists often equate their eyesight to a 10X binocular. If you have a 10X binocular handy, test your eyesight compared to using the binocular. You'll see why antelope miss little movement in their open country environment. And as I stated earlier, they are remarkably fast. On flat ground, antelope have been clocked at 60 miles an hour making them North America's fastest animal.

Antelope communicate in several ways including the fluffing of their rump patch to warn of danger. This signal can be seen over two miles away. Antelope are also very vocal. Does and fawns use the common bleat and mew to communicate. Both does and bucks use a high-pitched snort to also warn of danger. A unique vocalization, only recently made aware to the hunting public, is the antelope bugle. This high-pitched series of snorts is now used as a decoying aid.

Are you still removed from yourself and thinking about the best technique for you to tackle antelope? Let's review the popular tactics and why they might work for you.

Stalking

If you seek out hunting challenges, nothing can match stalking antelope on their turf. Remember what I wrote about an antelope's eyesight and their speed? Combine that with open country barely suitable to hide a blacktail jackrabbit and you'll have a challenge tougher than getting an animal activist to wear a fur coat. A few have risen to the challenge and overcome the formidable traits of the prairie speedster, including South Dakota bowhunter Bob Barden.

When meeting Barden in his home turf, a dentist office, polite and easygoing would seem an appropriate description for him. Yet, he's better described as a seasoned stalker who consistently scores on trophy antelope.

Barden has been pursuing game with bow and arrow for 40 years and is an associate member of the Pope & Young Club with several book antelope bucks to his credit. Actually taking an antelope is not as important as the personal challenge.

"For me, the biggest benefit of stalking is that it makes antelope hunting more interesting. You're always seeing new country and not bored by looking at the same terrain," says Barden.

Being in good to excellent shape is a must and Barden knows that firsthand after more than one failed stalking attempt turned into a 10-mile hike. Knowing your hiking limits and carrying plenty of water and snacks is mandatory. Good optics also play an important role in locating antelope before they spot you. My personal binocular is a Pentax 8x42, but I've also used Bausch and Lomb and Zeiss products with nothing but praise for all three brands.

For a successful stalk, Barden scouts for country that sports plenty of rugged, broken terrain and a healthy pronghorn population. This allows him a better opportunity to sneak into bow range of an antelope and it offers concealment when drawing an arrow. Some areas are just not conducive to successful pronghorn stalking.

"Some of the large sagebrush flats in Wyoming and large prairie pastures you find in South Dakota don't offer enough terrain to hide, but with the right amount of ridges and washouts, a person has a good chance of getting into position for a shot," claims Barden.

In fact, Barden feels getting close is fairly easy compared to the final draw and release. Antelope, like all ungulates, have their eyes protruding from the sides of their heads allowing them more than 300 degrees of viewing safety. For all practical purposes, the only time it won't detect movement is when it's looking away or preoccupied while sleeping or eating. That's when Barden makes his final move.

"Over the years, I discovered the best way to take a good antelope buck was when he is alone and bedded in rough terrain. The rough terrain allows me to sneak closely with little chance of spooking him and his being alone allows me to draw when he isn't looking without another animal spotting me," states Barden.

Finding lone bucks for stalking is generally better early in the archery season before bucks band together with a harem of does. Most western archery antelope seasons open in July or August and close during the October rifle season. Time of day doesn't seem to matter much, but Barden admits most of his kills came between 10 a.m. and 2 p.m.

An early-season hunt in 1992 ended with Barden tagging one of South Dakota's best antelope bucks. From a distance, he viewed a good buck bed atop a ridge. Then, using gullies, he approached to within good archery range. Slowly peering up from his hideout, he waited until the buck turned his head, scanning for danger straight away and giving Barden the cue to shoot.

Decoying

For those who like short stalks with modified stand hunting involved, antelope decoying may just be your answer. Modernized by pioneering South Dakota bowhunter Mel Dutton, antelope decoying seemed to stir the decoying craze now afflicting whitetail and even elk hunters. Having learned firsthand from Dutton, I, too, have been afflicted with decoying and use it almost exclusively when chasing these oversized prairie roadrunners.

Unlike stalking, which can take place most anytime during the archery season, decoying works best during the period of the rut. In the western United States, the antelope rut begins in early September and ends in late September, peaking about September 15.

Visualize antelope as prairie elk. Like elk, antelope gather a harem of females for breeding and aggressively defend the harem from other males, otherwise known as satellite bucks. Antelope even have a dominant "bugle," like elk. I remember the first time Dutton introduced me to bugling. He had not developed the call for it yet and taught me using my mouth. Within a few days, I had successfully called in a buck to the decoy. It was amazing!

So how does decoying work? The best method is to use a decoy imitating an immature buck with horns six to eight inches tall. Next, locate a herd of antelope with a dominant buck cruising the perimeter looking for pesky satellite bucks. Like stalking, a hunter will need to use available cover to move within 150 to 200 yards of the herd without any of the animals seeing your approach. Wearing leather chapped clothes, or tough Cordura, is a must to deter cactus from ruining your tender body parts.

Now, slowly raise the decoy and get ready for a charging response from the dominant buck, or a slow game of bluff. Whatever, it's best to have an arrow on the string in case the buck decides to charge. In my experience and Dutton's, decoying seems to work about 30-50 percent of the time. When the buck does come in, let him approach as close as possible, and as he turns to walk parallel with the decoy, slowly rise, draw and release in a steady, fluid motion.

If you have a partner you wish to hide, use another decoy imitating a doe. This can irritate a dominant buck even further as he believes a subordinate buck has stolen a doe from the harem and is holding her hostage. I think that's what they think anyway. If this sounds exciting, wait 'til a buck antelope is making dust trails toward you at 55 miles an hour. Montana outfitter Doug Gardner, of Powder River Outfitters, near Broadus, advertises decoying as an option on his archery antelope hunts. At times, he'll incorporate a morning of decoying to break up the monotony of sitting in blinds all day. That was my plan during a 1996 hunt with him, but a Pope & Young antelope buck visiting my waterhole blind ended that plan.

Stand-Hunting

If the other two techniques have you breathing hard by just reading about them, take a sigh of relief. Hunting antelope from blinds, whether elevated or on the ground, is one of the most successful techniques and requires little in physical stamina.

As I just stated, while hunting with Powder River Outfitters, my intentions were to sit in a blind early in the day and decoy the remainder of the day. I had never hunted antelope from a blind and wished to get the experience. Unfortunately, my experience was all of three hours. A Pope & Young buck sauntered in with a herd of does offering me a 30-yard shot and a chance to end my hunt early. Needless to say, the next four days we chased deer as my antelope buck hung in the cooler.

If you go on an outfitted hunt, the outfitter should have the blind in place. Otherwise you will need to decide whether to dig a pit blind, use a portable above ground blind, or find a tree, or windmill overlooking a waterhole to place a treestand. That will be the end of the physical demands on your body.

Although Wyoming outfitter Jerry Murphy utilizes any technique a hunter requests, sitting in blinds near waterholes are where 90 percent of hunters end up. Murphy operates High Plains Outfitters with partner Merv Griswold near Gillette, Wyoming, an antelope warehouse if there ever was one.

"I recommend blind hunting to anyone who feels they are not capable of a strenuous walk or crawl. Let's face it, stalking or decoying is a tough hunt," claims Murphy. "My experience proves hunting from a blind to be a far more successful way to take a buck, especially a buck of trophy caliber. I don't think there is any antelope that can't be killed at a waterhole."

Although a few outfitters have access to windmills for elevated stands, they do work favorably since antelope were never programmed to look above for danger. By far, most guides and experienced hunters use pit blinds or ground blinds near waterholes. Whether using a recessed, darkened pit or a manufactured cloth blind, be sure it provides complete darkness inside. Waterholes work best for blind locations since antelope require water every day and water in the West is generally sparse. On the other hand, food sources are everywhere and travel routes may vary throwing off a travel route ambush.

"We use portable burlap blinds with three shooting windows per blind," says Murphy. "Even if a buck or group of antelope moves to another waterhole, we can move the blind or, more likely than not, we already have another blind in place."

Murphy strongly recommends placing blinds early, though, to make sure wary bucks relax in their presence. Even so, he knows he can watch a group of antelope for a day or two and confidently place a blind to intercept the antelope on the third day.

One wouldn't think there would be a negative to hunting from a blind, but if you get frustrated by waiting in line at a McDonald's, you may not have the patience to sit in a blind. Murphy feels far more antelope spook from seeing nervous hunters peek from their blind than from getting their scent. He recommends hunters wear a face mask or paints, and keep their viewing to a minimum. He also doesn't allow hunters to wander from the blinds and personally drops off and picks up every hunter with a truck so antelope don't associate the blinds with human activity.

If being chauffeured to your hunting locale in an air conditioned truck sounds like a tough hunt, I'd pick sitting in a blind as your archery antelope hunting choice. Otherwise, make sure you're in shape. You don't have to be in marathon-quality shape, but definitely in shape for what may end up being a volksmarch across the Western prairies.

42 The *Almost* Complete Elk Hunter

BY DWIGHT SCHUH

When the words "bowhunting pros" or "bowhunting experts" are mentioned, the name of Dwight Schuh will always belong at or near the top of the list. As an editor, Dwight calls the plays at Bowhunter *magazine. As a writer, his byline has appeared in practically every major outdoor magazine, and he has authored several books. Dwight is at home bowhunting anywhere, but perhaps his favorite hunts of all have taken place in the remote high country of the Rockies.*

The knob was isolated and desolate, the haunt of lonely elk hunters—and big, lonesome bulls. Giant juniper trees with their alligator bark and heavy green limbs shaded out all undergrowth and formed a virtual cave. I moved quietly and slowly, awed by the sense that an old bull, a bull that had evaded hunters for years, might be lurking nearby, watching me.

I didn't see the bull, but I did find evidence of his existence. There, under a tree, ghostly white in the dim shadows and dusty juniper duff, lay two elk antlers. One side had been gnawed apart by rodents, but the other side was whole. I picked up the antler. It was heavy. Adding up the tine and main-beam lengths and the incredible mass of the antler, I figured the bull would score at least 370. This was the bull, or the kind of bull, I'd come here for. Even though the sheds were a year old, the bull could still be here, hidden in the vast desert. Finding the sheds gave me anticipation, hope.

And it wasn't just finding the shed. You see, after accumulating preference points for six years, I'd drawn a tag in one of Colorado's limited-entry units. With tightly controlled permit numbers here, some bulls *had* to be growing to old age. Additionally, other hunters had reported seeing big bulls here, and a local had told me two Boone and Crockett bulls had been taken in this very area. The potential was here.

Thus, my goal was to see—no take—one of those bulls. What would it require? I'd never done it in the past. That's because I've never really been a trophy hunter. I just love hunting elk, and when bulls have got in my way, I've dropped the string, figuring an average bull hanging in camp was worth more than a giant bull in the woods. For me to get a bull like the benefactor of those sheds, that would have to change. I would have to become a complete hunter.

Most obviously that meant learning to pass up average bulls in favor of big ones. And to do that, I would have to come to a point where killing an elk was no longer important to me. It seems a bit ironic that in order to kill an elk, you have to *not care* whether you kill an elk. But to be a complete hunter, a hunter of big bulls, that's what you have to do.

I would also have to change my tactics. Most seasons I've called in numerous bulls but rarely any giants, and that probably relates to technique. In 1983 I wrote a book called *Bugling for Elk*, which describes this approach: You roam and bugle until you get an answer from a bull. Then you move in on the bull, hide, and begin bugling, cow calling and raking a tree to entice the bull within range. Since that book came out I've written many stories and been in two videos along the same theme. Additionally, articles and books by other writers, as well as most new videos on elk hunting, have portrayed a similar approach.

Mind you, I'm not knocking it because the method has always worked. However, used alone it's a one-dimensional approach that limits a person's potential, especially for taking big bulls. That's because the biggest bulls, the herd bulls, more often than not will run *from* rather than *to* calling.

Also, in some areas bulls simply won't respond well to calling. Many videos you see today were made on private ranches with lots of big bulls and few hunters, and indeed standard calling works there. It also works as well as ever on remote public lands where bulls have had little human contact. But in areas pounded by hunters, where bulls have learned that calling can be bad for their health, they stay away.

That's why a complete hunter must be versatile, analyzing conditions and situations and using the best methods at the moment. In different cases that could mean spotting and stalking, stand hunting, subtle calling, ambush. That's what I planned to do to take a megabuck—become a complete elk hunter.

The season opened August 30, and for the first couple of days, I spent my time hiking long distances to learn the area—that's how I found those sheds on the lonely knob—and sitting behind 15x binoculars, looking for elk. One afternoon I saw 13 elk, 11 of them bulls, three of those six-points. None was huge, but that concentration of elk, along with the sheds, convinced me this was a good place to start.

No rain had fallen for several weeks and under the eternally blue sky and blazing sun, temperatures were up to 80 degrees every day. Two mornings in a row I'd got five-point bulls bugling, but given the conditions I felt the best approach for a big bull would be taking a waterhole stand.

A friend had told me of a spring in this area. The spring wasn't shown on any topographic maps, but glassing a deep draw, I saw some aspen trees in the bottom and dropped down to explore. Sure enough, among the aspens were three small ponds fed by a seeping spring. I got a treestand from my truck and put it in a scrubby little pine, the only suitable tree within range of the spring. I'd planned to hunt there that afternoon, but with a swirling wind, I decided to go exploring rather than taking a chance on having an elk smell me here.

The next afternoon, with a steady up-canyon breeze, I was in the stand by 2 p.m. The sun was blistering for the first couple of hours, but in late afternoon it dropped behind a ridge, bringing cool relief—and quick action. Right at 5 p.m. a little five-point showed up and drank and then stood knee-deep in one of the spring pools. He stuck his head under water and swished it back and forth and then, for 20 minutes, splashed water onto himself with his front hooves.

At 6:30 a bigger bull came down from the shaded hill to the west. My first impulse was, *Aha, here comes a keeper. Get ready.* He was a five-by-six, a decent bull, and in most cases, grist for my bow. He marched by 30 yards away, right to the spring, and drank long, and then he lay down in one of the pools, groaning like an old man in a hot tub, a picture of ecstasy. After 10 minutes in the tub, he got out and raked a tree near my stand for a while and then grazed around me for an hour. Despite the temptation, I shot only my camera. To finish out the fine evening, a spike came in about 7:30.

As I continued to hunt the spring each afternoon, I hunted by glassing and calling each morning. One day, as I climbed to the top of a rim in the dark, I heard a bull far out across a tableland. At first light, using binoculars, I could see a six-point and three cows in the distance. As in the past, I was tempted to try calling him in. But given the sparse cover here and the fact that he had cows, I figured pulling him within range was unlikely. Stalking seemed better suited to this situation.

I dropped below a rim and raced to get in front of the elk. Before I could get into position, the cows appeared from the trees, 80 yards ahead. Then the bull charged into the open toward the cows, head down like a snake. The cows scattered. Then, with determined fury the bull attacked a clump of sage and plowed up dirt and rocks with his antlers. The cows went back to grazing, and when they'd fed past me, I crawled toward the bull, using a bushy juniper for cover.

I'd got within 30 yards when he realized his ladies were getting away and walked after them. As he stepped into the open, I drew and aimed at his heart. He stopped and looked at me. I started to release. In the past he was a shooter. But not right now. I let down and the bull ran.

Over the next few days, similar scenarios occurred numerous times. I came within a few yards of ambushing a nontypical bull, a definite shooter; had two new bulls visit the spring; and bugled a five-point within 20 yards. Overall I felt good about my results. I'd hunted carefully and had adapted, using techniques that seemed right for the conditions, and the result had been seven bulls within range. Was I being too picky? Or was I finally becoming a complete-enough elk hunter to kill a big bull?

After eight days, rain started falling, often in torrents, leaving puddles in every rut and pothole. The bulls I'd been seeing dispersed, and hunting over water was futile. So on the 10th day I moved to a new location, low country where juniper cover gave way to sagebrush, the fringe of elk habitat, where few people would hunt and big bulls—I hoped—would hide out. Just before dark I parked under an arching juniper tree, and as the drizzling rain turned into a downpour, I sat under my truck canopy and heated a can of Dinty Moore Beef Stew for dinner. Then, with rain pounding the canopy, I crawled into my sleeping bag.

Rain fell most of the night, but by daybreak it had let up. As I walked up a sloping ridge in the dim morning light, weaving through the big junipers, the humid air smelled fresh like air-dried clothes. Water droplets glistened on the grass and shrubs. Whoa. I loved it.

For an hour I'd poked around, calling, when I came to a point overlooking a flat bisected with alternating bands of sage and juniper like stripes on a zebra. I sat down to glass. Through my 8x binoculars, I saw an elk. He was far away, maybe two miles, just a tan speck. But he was definitely a bull, a good one, with long, even tines. I couldn't tell how big he was for sure, but he was worth a closer took. He and his half-dozen cows were feeding up a long juniper string. I watched them for a half-hour until they went over a saddle out of sight.

With wind from the south, I circled north to cut them off. But before I was halfway to the elk, the storm clouds began breaking up and the wind shifted. I cut back to the south, nearly running now, and had gone a mile when I realized the wind was swirling every which way. No good. I walked back to the truck for breakfast and sat there, thinking. Sometimes waiting, doing nothing, is the hardest part of elk hunting. But sometimes it's the most critical. I *had to* wait until conditions were right.

By 10 a.m., the sky had cleared, and a steady, cold breeze descended from the north. It felt good. The hunt was on.

I crossed a deep draw and climbed onto a juniper ridge south of the elk. They had gone out onto a vast flat of dense junipers where I would never spot them to plan a stalk. So I crept along, cow calling softly. Maybe the bull would answer. For a half-hour I heard only the sighing wind. Maybe the elk had gone out of the area.

But, then, from maybe 300 yards out, I heard a light groan. It had to be the bull.

Now what? With all the rain, hunting him on water was out, and in this juniper jungle, stalking within range seemed a slim possibility. Aggressive calling might work, but with those cows, he most likely would run away. Maybe passive, subtle calling would be best.

On the sandy ground, my canvas shoes were light and quiet as I probed through the thick trees, listening, thinking, sensing. How far was he? Was I getting too close? What was he doing? These weren't questions of doubt, just caution, and I tingled with the thrill of pitting my stealth against the bull's senses and instincts. With the chill north wind steady in my face, I felt confident, almost invincible. Guessing he might be 100 yards away, 200 at most, I found a good hiding place under a big juniper and knelt in the sandy soil and got comfortable. No hurry. This could be a waiting game.

Very lightly I mewed with a mouth diaphragm, just one little squeak. The northern breeze hissed through the rigid juniper needles, the only sound. I felt a rising impatience. The old me. The incomplete elk hunter. I want to call, to force the action, to get an answer. *Be quiet. Listen. Be patient.*

Five minutes go by. Ten. The bull groans. *Aha, there you are. You did hear me.*

Ten more silent minutes creep by. Tension grows. Doubts. *Be patient.*

Then movement. There, in the black-green limbs. Polished ivory. Oh, he's beautiful. But as he comes toward me, now within 30 yards, I can see he's not the king of this unit, not the depositor of those sheds, not *the* bull. *Complete elk hunter? Pass him up. Keep searching. Killing an elk must mean nothing to you!*

The bull stops behind a big juniper, his eyes probing. Continuing on, he clears the tree and stops 15 yards away, broadside, looking beyond me. A blend of tan and brown and ivory, he virtually glows in the darkness of the trees. This moment is why we all hunt elk.

Friends, I must confess. After more than 25 years of elk hunting, I have not come to a point where killing an elk is no longer important to me. As I stood over the fallen bull, I had no regrets. In fact I felt a certain triumph. For 11 days, I'd forsaken one-dimensional elk hunting by staying flexible and adapting to conditions, and I'd hunted carefully, waiting until wind and other variables were just right before making any moves I couldn't remember ever having hunted any better, any more complete. And this was my reward.

But as I took off my pack and dug out my knife and game bags, the thought of those giant sheds momentarily flashed through my mind. And I had to concede that this beautiful bull lying at my feet was about 100 antler-inches shy of that standard. The complete elk hunter? Almost.

43   Sheep and Caribou Double

BY LON E. LAUBER

*Guts, stamina and darn good glass are just a few hunter attributes needed for a caribou–Dall
Ram combo. Are you ready?*

One of the beauties of bowhunting Alaska is the very real chance of encountering multiple big-game species on the same hunt. Since there
are about a dozen species to choose from when hunting this great
land, it would be impossible to pursue them all on one hunt. However, it is a viable option to hunt Dall sheep and barren-ground caribou on the
same Alaskan adventure.

Four of us did such a trip with good results. We flew out of Fairbanks and
into the Alaska Range mountains. The trip was scheduled for the last week of August (sheep season opened August 10) and the first week of September (caribou
season opened on September 1). This time frame allowed us a full week to concentrate strictly on sheep before caribou season opened. Here's why the dream of a
sheep and caribou combo trip is in your reach!

One may think caribou live in flat country, which at times they do, and
sheep live in cliffs, which sometimes they do. However, there are a lot of sheep that
inhabit the rolling hills near steep cliffs. Moreover, caribou favor this rolling country as well. What draws both species to this intermediate range is lush food. This
in-between land usually lies between a few hundred feet in elevation and 4,000 to
5,000 feet high. The grasses, forbs, mosses and lichens that collectively create tundra is highly nutritional and keep both species in the open where they feel safe.

For the caribou this intermediate habitat is mostly out of brush. These open-
country dwelling nomads prefer the wide open space. I've actually witnessed caribou, on numerous occasions, literally skirt around brushy draws, even if it made
them travel an extra mile or more. I'm not saying barren-ground caribou won't
mill through brush because they do. Apparently though, they have learned that
large expanses of brush often harbor predators like wolves and bowhunters. Thus,
they are more likely to avoid brush or nervously rush through it. Neither of which
are conducive to bowhunting. Additionally, caribou have survived through centuries by outrunning wolves. Thus, if they can detect their nemesis with at least an
80-yard buffer they can outrun the predator.

Now, I bet you're thinking, if caribou are in wide open spaces and try to
maintain an 80-yard buffer, how can I get within bow range? Well, with a little
map studying and patience, you can frequently catch them in the natural folds of

the country. Yes, the country is open and mostly void of brush but it's not all pancake flat. There is no better approach to bowhunting open country than undulating terrain that keeps you out of sight until you're in bow range.

Basically, the same holds true for Dall sheep. These golden-horned white monarchs actually prefer less severe country with good food—as long as there are rugged escape cliffs nearby. For the bowhunter, this can work in your favor twofold. First, that same undulating terrain discussed with caribou applies for sheep. Second, when the sheep move between the cliffs and more gentle feeding areas, a bowhunter can ambush them and score.

Take for example the ram I killed on the trip explained in the beginning. We split up into two pairs. Mark and Rich headed off into a different drainage than Craig and me. Our plan was to meet back at base camp along the river in four or five days. With a bivi sack, lightweight sleeping bag, a little freeze-dried food and a frame pack, we hoofed it up a feeder stream drainage to the north. Walking up stream drainages such as this one is fairly easy walking. Sometimes though, you have to fight a little brush and do some boulder hopping. After several hours of hiking we had reached what we felt was a good spot for bowhunting sheep. This particular drainage had lots of ravines, cuts and gullies bulging with luscious tundra. Moreover, the upper reaches of this canyon were nearly vertical with rusty orange striations in the rocks. Once again the rolling food plot close to the safety of cliffs was a natural magnet for sheep. Shortly, we glassed up three really nice rams chewing their cuds in the cliffs far above. While there was no apparent way to get on these rams, it was reassuring just to know we were hunting in a productive spot.

Craig and I pressed on; hiking a short ways and then sitting down and glassing carefully in all directions. Realize this broken terrain can gobble up a sheep and keep it out of sight in spite of the openness. Thus, gaining a slightly different perspective and glassing the same country is the only way to discover the critters. Case in point: One evening while stump shooting, or in this case, tundra-clump shooting, a flash of white burned the corner of my eye while at full draw and aiming at a fiery patch of tundra. I let down, pulled up my binocs and was stunned to see a full-curl ram just a few hundred yards away.

"Craig, there's a ram right there," I whispered. "Let's slowly sit down and see what he does." The nonchalant ram casually fed down the hill, across the stream in which our bivi sack camp was located and began to mosey up a steep yet narrow cut. "This is perfect," I said, "I'm gonna hustle over there and see if I can take it in the cut." Off I went, scurrying like an arctic ground squirrel dashing for its hole to escape a golden eagle. As I neared the ravine, the ram had fed into, I slowed to catch my breath and quiet my approach. Oh, that's another benefit of hunting in this type of terrain. Usually, the tundra is moist, soft and as quiet to stalk in as shag carpet in slippers. Thus was the case here. I eased to the lip of the gully as silently as an owl in flight. Much to both of our surprise, the ram fed up my side of the cut and nearly bumped into my hunkered down form. At 17 yards, it stopped, turned broadside and stared at me out of shear curiosity. Slowly, I drew my bow and settled my 20-yard pin (as settled as I could with a radically pulsating blood pump exploding in my chest) and zipped an arrow into the white ram. With him being less than 20 yards and down hill, my arrow impacted higher than I wanted. It did clip the main artery under his spine and shortly, I was admiring a nice Dall ram.

He wasn't a monster by any stretch of the imagination, matter of fact, the last time I looked, he was the second smallest ram listed in the Pope & Young records. Regardless, I was beaming with pride and so was Craig. I can still remember the enthusiastic congratulatory bear hug from Craig. He'd hunted Alaska extensively and knew just how monumental this archery achievement was. I believe he was just as happy for me getting this ram as if he'd taken it himself.

That night, back in my bivi sack, the endorphins and adrenaline coursed through my weary body to the point where I couldn't sleep. However, my restlessness afforded me the opportunity to witness one of the most spectacular northern light shows I've ever seen. The green and rose-colored light danced and flickered across the starry sky for hours. I felt as if the Aurora display was a sign of approval from the "Big Bowhunter In The Sky."

Craig helped me pack out the ram (six miles) and finally we made it to base camp. Rich and Mark stumbled into camp with similar results. Rich had arrowed a nice ram after an exciting ambush. Apparently, Rich caught the ram on its way out of the feeding terrain back up to the cliffs. He hustled up and around and caught the ram just before it disappeared into the cliffs.

Hopefully, the point learned from these two bow-killed sheep is the importance of mobility. Shooting a sheep with an arrow is not like whitetail hunting from a treestand. At times you have to make snap decisions, and literally sprint to an ambush spot to get a shot. Obviously, being in top physical form is paramount to success in this environment. Also, these successes illustrate the importance of using the broken terrain to hide the hunter's approach.

Since Rich and I had filled our sheep tags and caribou season was not yet open we putzed around camp. With valid sheep tags still burning their pockets, Craig and Mark headed out for sheep again. And in a few days they returned with a third ram that Craig had taken. Realize 75 percent success on Dall sheep is respectable in anyone's book.

By now, September 1 and the opening of caribou season was upon us. Rich and I had glassed up a small band of bulls the night before the opener and we "camped out" near them. At first light we eased up a gently inclining ravine and located the bulls promptly. There were only two problems. One small problem and another bigger problem. One, the caribou were grazing in a totally unapproachable location. It was too flat and too open. Nothing to do but wait for them to feed into more bow-stalkable terrain. The second problem and much greater dilemma was two rifle hunters moving up toward the caribou.

There was nothing we could do but watch their hunt unfold. Shortly, the caribou caught the hunters' scent and became nervous. The 'bou became curious, but unlike whitetails, held their ground. They downed the nicest two bulls in the bunch and the remaining tundra trotters left the scene. Since we were up high and had a good vantage point, glassing for more caribou was the only logical thing to do.

Later, we glassed up two mature bulls—way on the other side of the valley—at least two miles away. At that distance we couldn't make out antler tine detail but with a spotting scope we could tell that one of the bulls was a dandy. "If we can make out antlers from here, he's got to be a nice bull," I said. "What should be do?" I asked Rich. "Well, let's just watch them for a while before committing to such a long hike," he replied. The bulls just stood there for more than an hour. So off we went. We hustled down the ridge, waded a knee-deep, glacier-fed stream and then worked back up through the brush and into the basin where we'd last seen the two bulls. They'd moved and bedded down on a stretch of open tundra with no chance of a bow stalk. Once again, there was nothing to do but wait.

With both sheep and caribou, the waiting game is a large part of success. It's kind of like a giant chess game. You make a move and then patiently wait for your opponent's move. In this case it was two bull caribou. In late evening the caribou made their move and similar to a sloppy chess player, overlooked their opponent's next move, the bulls fed off the flat and close to another gully. I slithered into the gully undetected, jogged around a 200-foot-high ridge and waited for them to feed into range. Luckily, they did and I shot the larger bull at 45 yards.

This particular stalk started at about 8 a.m. and I finally shot the bull about 7 p.m. Realize all-day stalks are not unusual when hunting this way. Actually, I've had to wait for several days for an individual ram or bull to make a mistake by wandering into ideal bow-stalking terrain. Another aspect you may be curious about is why I made the stalk on both the ram mentioned early in the story and the caribou just mentioned. Before each hunt we lay the ground rules to avoid confusion or hard feelings. Since locating game in Alaska's huge expanses is so crucial to success, we agreed that he who sees the critter first gets first crack at him. On this hunt, I was the one who first located both the ram and bull. Trust me, over the course of a two-week trip all parties get their share of stalking opportunities—if you spend the time glassing that's necessary for this type of hunting.

Anyway, back to the hunt. After hauling out the meat and antlers of my caribou, Rich and I headed out on another bivouac skirmish to see if we could get him a caribou. Meanwhile, Craig and Mark continued to hunt sheep for Mark and caribou for both of them. There were lots of close calls but no one else connected on this hunt. Regardless, three sheep and one caribou is not anything to snivel about.

When planning your Alaskan bowhunt don't overlook the possibility of a two-species hunt. By selecting the right part of the right mountain range you too can experience the adventure and challenge of a sheep and caribou combo hunt.

Planning Your Double On Tundra

For Alaska residents, this type of trip is quite easy, just study the maps and assimilate data provided by the Alaska Department of Fish and Game to locate a good combo area. For nonresidents, it's actually easier logistically but quite a bit more expensive. Understand, nonresidents are required by law to have a guide to hunt Dall sheep. Thus, your chore is coming up with the money and researching a quality guide willing to arrange a sheep/caribou hunt specifically for a bowhunter. Contact: Department of Commerce & Economic Development, Division of Occupational Licensing, P.O. Box 110806, Juneau, AK 99811-0806; (907) 465-2543.

Now for trip planning. I'd recommend at least 10 days of actual hunting time for a two-species bowhunt. You'll also need a few days of travel time to get to and from the Northland and a couple more to fly out for the hunt. Be sure to communicate effectively with the guide on how the hunt will unfold. You want to know how you will arrive at the hunting area. If it's by horseback, you may be able to take a few more luxury items than flying in a Super Cub. Likewise if a larger float plane or river raft is used, one can pack more comfortably.

Realize the weather in late August and early September can vary between 0 and 60 degrees F. Pack layered and hydrophobic type clothes like Micro-Tex, Hush Hide or Saddle Cloth. I've had excellent results with clothing from both Browning and Cabela's. When hunting the wilderness, the right clothes can literally save your life. Don't scrimp here. Also, the right boots can make or break a remote hunt. During the fall I practically live in LaCrosse or Danner boots depending on the terrain.

For archery tackle I strongly believe in shooting the most accurate and forgiving setup instead of the fastest bow. Especially with the availability of laser range finders like Bushnell's Yardage Pro Compact 600. In the last couple of years, I've used the Yardage Pro 400 to range the distance to most all of my successful shots. I'm currently using a Browning Backdraft one cam bow at 70 pounds with 2213 XX75 arrows and Thunderhead 100 broadheads. This setup is forgiving, accurate and produces enough punch to effectively harvest sheep and caribou. Starting to plan an Alaskan hunt 18 to 24 months ahead is none too soon.

Tactics at a Glance:

- On archery tackle, use the most forgiving and durable equipment.
- Use terrain features like stream drainages when putting on a stalk.
- Grasses, forbs, mosses and lichens are preferred food sources of 'bou and are what draws them to open areas.
- Caribou often avoid brush due to the predator-in-the-bush factor.
- Sheep will beeline for cliffs to avoid danger.
- Trip essentials: binocular, spotting scope, bivi sack, sleeping bag, freeze-dried food and the like.
- An Alaskan hunt should be planned 18 to 24 months in advance.

Part Seven
Gearing Up—How to Choose and Buy What's Right for *You*

Entire books can be written, and are being written, on this subject. And while this is a book on tactics, these chapters on gear will supplement your new hunting game plans and help you put together bowhunting rigs that won't let you down.

44 Bowhunting Equipment's
10 Greatest Myths

BY BILL BUCKLEY

Every bowhunter's entitled to his opinion about archery gear, but don't you believe everything you hear.

For many aspiring bowhunters, ending up with the right equipment is a long and expensive journey. And it begins innocently enough. You're at the range or in an archery shop when the conversation inevitably rolls around to bowhunting tackle. Being a relative beginner you listen to every word being said, hoping to find out what's the deadliest equipment money can buy. Although the guys may disagree on what broadhead is best or what draw weight is necessary for deer hunting, the fact is they get their bucks each season. Or so they say. They have to know more than you do, so you eagerly catalog every pearl of wisdom they let slip. Then, for the fifth time in less than a month, you decide to buy a different arrow rest or broadhead, or tune your bow a different way.

Oftentimes the advice is good. But just as likely you'll be pointed down another path of despair to hunt with a bow-and-arrow setup that is improperly matched, poorly tuned, and deadly only to your confidence as a hunter. That's because you've fallen for yet another lie about bowhunting equipment.

To keep you going on the right track, here are some common misconceptions to remember as you prepare for the next hunting season. Knowing them won't ensure you'll bag a wallhanger buck. But if you do get a shot at one, you can be confident you'll have the right equipment for the job, and that you didn't spend a fortune to get it.

Lie #1: "The Guy Behind the Counter Knows Best"

In a perfect world the person selling you archery equipment should know what he's talking about (especially if you're buying something based on his advice). Unfortunately, that's not always the case. When I bought my first compound bow, the sporting goods salesman told me how important heavy arrows are to penetration—and the heavier the better. A willing disciple, I returned home with two dozen arrows so over-spined that they couldn't shoot straight from my bow. They also had such a round-house trajectory that even a slight error in range estimation would result in a clean miss. A year later a bowhunting friend told me what arrows to buy, but that was $60 and two missed shots down the line.

The fact is, many sporting-goods salesman know just enough about archery gear to be dangerous with your money. Their recommendations, though well-intentioned, may not be founded on solid knowledge. That's why, generally speaking, you're much better off buying a bow from a store specializing in archery gear.

Unfortunately, not all archery shops are equal, because you still have to rely on the guy behind the counter. Most archery-store salesman are avid bowhunters who know more about bows than you and I ever will. Yet one archery "pro" sent me off on my first elk hunt with a new bow that shot arrows every which way but straight. He'd placed the arrow rest over a half-inch to the left of where it should have been, even though he swore he'd tuned it properly. That same dealer sold me a rest so flimsy that it bent everytime I touched it. When I complained about bow noise, he told me bow noise didn't matter, as long as a deer was in range, the arrow would hit it before the deer could react. Anyone who's had a deer jump the string knows that isn't true.

So what's a beginner looking for sound advice supposed to do? First, talk to any bowhunters you know and read as many magazine articles you can about archery equipment. You'll be given a lot of conflicting advice, but at least you'll have a basic understanding of the different kinds of archery gear available to you. Then visit every archery shop in your area. If you're looking for a new bow, test-shoot as many as you can and note which ones feel the most comfortable.

How a dealer treats you is a good indication of the value of his advice. If he lets you test a number of bows and is willing to spend whatever time is necessary to help you find what you need, trust him. If, on the other hand, he immediately tries to steer you into having a certain bow, or treats you like a moron who's wasting his time with a lot of meaningless questions, bail out immediately. You won't end up with the equipment you need. A good rule of thumb is as follows: The cockier the archery-shop pro, the less he knows. That also applies to your fellow shooters at the archery club. Some people love to talk, but you don't have to listen to them.

Lie #2: "Buy from Catalogs and Pawn Shops and You'll Save Big Bucks!"
It's true you'll probably spend more money for a bow and arrows at the local archery shop than from a discount house. Most bow dealers can't compete with the volume sales the catalog companies rely on, or with the cheap, used equipment pawn shops sell. Unfortunately, though, in most cases the salesmen are not knowledgeable about archery gear, have never bowhunted, and are only interested in making a sale—whether it's right for you or not.

Archery-shop pros, on the other hand, are as much consultants as they are salesmen. They want to keep you as a customer for years to come, so good ones will make sure you leave with a good bow-and-arrow setup. Most importantly, you'll be able to test-shoot bows before you buy one, with the archery pro assisting you all the way. You'll know what you're getting long before you plunk down your hard-earned cash.

Bill Lewis works at The Archery Center in Bozeman, Montana, and pays attention to his customer's needs. He says the No. 1 equipment-related problem he sees is that many hunters' bows don't fit them and their gear is incompatible.

"A lot of folks come in with bows of the wrong draw length and arrows that are way too long, don't match, or are improperly spined. Or they might have a short bow with an overdraw, yet shoot with fingers—a combination that rarely works. Usually they've been given these bows or have bought them at a pawn shop. What they don't realize is that a bow has to be set up for the individual. What's good for one bowhunter may be totally wrong for another one, especially if they aren't physically similar."

Do yourself a favor and buy your bow from a qualified archery dealer. You may pay a little extra up front, but that buys you a lot of good advice and prompt service if you decide to alter your bowhunting setup later on. And chances are you'll save money over the long haul.

Lie #3: "The Heavier the Draw Weight, the Faster the Arrows"

It makes sense, and is true to a certain extent, which is why so many bowhunters go afield each year with bows that are way too heavy for them.

Crank up your bow's draw weight, while still using the same shafts, and your arrows will fly faster. The problem, however, is that the heavier draw weight will probably require an increase in arrow spine for your bow to shoot well. Then you could very well end up with heavier, slower arrows.

Arrowhead weight affects speed too. A 125-grain head, for example, will fly 5 fps slower than a 100-grain head on the same arrow. And it will probably require a more heavily spined arrow in order to fly well, further decreasing arrow speed.

Differences between bows will also determine how fast they propel an arrow. A 60-pound longbow, for instance, doesn't store as much energy as a 60-pound compound, so it won't shoot an arrow as fast. What wheels a compound has also determines the energy it stores. In general, cam wheels store more energy than round wheels, resulting in greater velocities with arrows of the same weight.

Still other factors come into play. For instance, the longer the draw length on a bow, the longer the "power stroke." Hence more energy is transferred to the arrow for greater speed. Of course, a corresponding increase in arrow length might require going to a heavier spine value, thus increasing arrow weight and decreasing velocity. Bows with shorter limbs recover faster than longer-limbed bows, also creating more speed. However, they may cause excessive pinching for fingers shooters with long draw lengths and thus be impractical for some bowhunters.

In other words, there are many considerations aside from draw weight that affect arrow speed. If you want to gain more speed but can't easily handle a substantial increase in draw weight, consider using a lighter head or lighter-spined arrow that will still fly true. Or you can go to an overdraw, which will significantly reduce your arrow length and spine weight, and thus the overall weight of the arrow.

Lie #4: "Cam Bows Are Faster and Therefore Better for Hunting"

In general cam bows are faster than round-wheel bows. They store more energy, which is transferred to the arrow for increased velocity. What many archers don't know, however, is that this greater energy oftentimes requires heavier-spined arrows to produce good arrow flight. Take my two bows as examples. One is a Hoyt Pro-Force Hunter, which has round wheels; the other is a Pro-Force Extreme with cams. Using the same 28-inch 2213 arrow shafts, the Pro-Force Hunter shoots arrows at 232 fps set at 66 pounds. The Pro-Force Extreme, however, won't shoot well over 58 pounds of draw weight, producing velocities of only 214 fps. In order to shoot the cam bow at the same draw weight as my round-wheel bow, heavier-spined arrows are needed.

There is one more trade-off for the increased energy you get from cam wheels: bow noise. In general, cam-wheel bows are noisier than round-wheel bows; that's because they are less efficient in transferring that energy to the arrow. The less energy that's absorbed by the arrow, the more is sent throughout the bow in the form of vibration. And vibration is the chief culprit of bow noise. Another part of this equation is that heavier arrows absorb more of a bow's energy than lighter ones, which helps deaden bow noise.

So what does this mean to bowhunters? First, radical cams mated with light arrows might send arrows at blistering speeds, but the resulting noise could spook game into jumping the string. Second, a modified cam might be a good compromise if you're looking for a fast bow with only moderate noise. Your best bet is to test a number of different manufacturers' bows and wheel designs to see what gives you the optimum balance between velocity and low bow noise. Remember, what works on the range might not be to your advantage in the field.

Lie #5: "Heavier Arrows Penetrate Better, so They're Deadlier"
Penetration is measured in foot-pounds of kinetic energy, and it's determined by arrow speed and weight. Shot from the same bow, heavy arrows generally penetrate better than lighter ones. That might lead you to believe you're better off hunting with them. Like most bowhunting gear, however, there are trade-offs, and the big one here is arrow speed. For every five grains of arrow weight, there is a corresponding 1 fps increase or reduction in velocity. Shooting a heavier arrow may give you greater penetration, but it will fly slower with a rounder flight trajectory. This isn't a problem if you can accurately judge distances shot after shot under all kinds of conditions. But who can? Misjudging by five yards the distance to a deer standing 30 yards away could cause a low or high hit using a moderately flat-shooting bow. With heavier arrows you're apt to miss the deer completely. Then all that penetration potential is wasted.

More important is figuring out how much kinetic energy you need to kill certain animals cleanly. The general rule of thumb is over 40 foot-pounds for deer-sized game and over 50 foot-pounds for elk. Then, reviewing the arrow shafts that will fly well from your bow (consult an arrow chart to see your options) you can decide which one gives you the best compromise between penetration and trajectory.

My Pro-Force Hunter with 2213 shafts produces more than 55 foot-pounds of energy. The heaviest shafts I could shoot at my draw weight of 66 pounds are the 2117s and 2216s, both weighing 62 grains more. However, for the 12 fps I give up going with the heavier shafts, I gain less than 1 foot-pound of energy—hardly worth the resulting loss in trajectory. In this case the heaviest shaft is not the deadliest, and for your bowhunting setup the same will probably be true.

Lie #6: "Big Broadheads Kill Faster Than Smaller Ones"
The broader the cutting surface of a broadhead, the more damage it will do upon entering an animal's vital organs. Unfortunately, the problem with many wide

heads is hitting the game's vitals. That's because the wider a broadhead is, the more it tends to plane or veer off target.

If your bowhunting setup shoots wide broadheads straight and true, stick with them. But if it doesn't, don't be afraid of trying other heads. Hunting with broadheads that plane badly increases your odds of wounding game, not killing it cleanly. In general you'll get better arrow flight with heads of 1¼- to 1⅛-inches wide. And as long as they're sharp and your aim is true, they'll kill an animal plenty quick.

Lie #7: "Broadheads Come Razor-Sharp from the Factory"
Despite the warning label on every box of broadheads, they aren't necessarily razor sharp when you take them out. If they're of a cutting-tip design, you can be assured they're not nearly sharp enough for hunting. Make sure you have a good sharpening system designed specifically for broadheads, because without one your bowhunting gear will be more of a game crippler than a game getter.

If you use replaceable-blade broadheads, there's a far greater chance the blades are ready for hunting. I've rarely found fresh-out-of-the-box blades to be less than razor sharp, but I have upon occasion. That's why you should always test your broadheads' sharpness. An easy way is to push each blade sideways along your forearm; if it shaves off hair, it's plenty sharp. You can also run the blades sideways across a thumbnail. If it digs in and hangs up, it's sharp.

Lie #8: "Cutting-Tip Heads Penetrate Better than Replaceable-Blade Heads"
Broadhead design fuels plenty of debates at any archery club. Many archers would say cutting-tip heads penetrate easier than round- or chisel-pointed (replaceable-blade) heads. And they'd be right, provided each head was equally sharp. That's because a cutting-tip broadhead, like the Bear Super Razorhead or Phantom 125, begins cutting through hair and hide the instant it hits the animal. Round- and chisel-pointed heads have to push through most of the hide before the blades make contact, and that causes some initial resistance.

So where's the big lie? It's in many bowhunters' perceptions that because they use a cutting-tip head, their arrows will automatically penetrate well.

Let's face it: Most of us sharpen our broadheads right before the season opener, then take them in and out of our quivers throughout the fall. The only time we're apt to resharpen them is after we've shot an arrow.

I use cutting-tip broadheads for much of my big game hunting, but it's amazing how quickly they can be dulled simply by taking them in and out of the quiver. Every time I set up on an elk or sit in a treestand and nock an arrow, my broadheads' edges get duller. Unless I resharpen them after four or five times out of the quiver, they're useless for hunting.

Replaceable-blade broadheads are much easier to maintain. Once they become dull, simply remove the old blades and insert new ones. Then you're back to razor-sharp status. You can also greatly assist the penetrating potential of chisel-pointed heads, like Thunderhead 100s and 125s and Wasp broadheads, by filing the points' flat surfaces. This creates sharper edges where they meet and helps the point cut through hide instead of just pushing through it. That's why these heads penetrate better than those with round points.

Given that most cutting-tip heads are relatively dull out of the box, and replaceable blades are usually razor sharp, many archers are better off hunting with the latter. Unless you have the right sharpening equipment to maintain a sharp edge on a cutting-tip head, it's not going to penetrate nearly as well as heads with easy-to-replace blades.

Lie #9: "The More Hi-Tech the Accessories, the Deadlier the Bow"

Many bowhunters think that the more complicated their hunting equipment, the more effective they'll be in the woods. Unfortunately, that's not necessarily true. Various hi-tech gadgets that are supposed to make you a more successful hunter sometimes end up ruining a hunt.

Some bulky shoot-through rests have so many adjustments and metal parts sticking out that they're easily knocked off kilter. Other rests are so delicate they bend from normal use. Fancy sights are another disaster waiting to happen. If they're not highly visible and sturdy, they'll eventually fail you. Too many sight pins can also hurt you in the excitement of shooting at game; there's a good chance you'll inadvertently use the wrong one.

What all this means is the simpler you keep your equipment, the better. A gadget might look cool on your bow, but will it make you a better hunter? It may work fine on the shooting range, but what about under real hunting conditions? Before you spend a lot of money accessorizing your bow, determine what you truly need to be an efficient hunter and leave it at that. The fewer accessories you rely on, the less likely your bow will let you down.

Lie No. 10: "Once Your Bow's Ready to Hunt, It's Fine for the Whole Season"

Actually, I've never heard a bowhunter say this, but from the complaints I hear after every season, most archers must believe it. It goes hand in hand with the apparent belief that you can stop practice shooting once the season begins.

One friend once complained that his peep sight moved on him, causing him to miss a giant bull elk. If he'd shot his bow every day he hunted, using blunt-tipped arrows matched to his broadheads, he'd have known something was wrong long before the elk showed up. Another friend's sight was slightly bent after a fall, yet he never test-shot his bow before he muffed an easy shot at a whitetail buck. I once missed a big whitetail because my flimsy arrow rest got knocked out of position. And I can't even count the number of times friends have spooked deer and elk because their bows squeaked when they drew back.

The fact is, everything from your sights and rests to your arrows and broadheads can get damaged or altered over the course of a hunting season. And hunt-killing bow noise can crop up any time. That's why it's so important to check your equipment in between hunts and shoot your bow to make sure everything's operational. Then you can have absolute confidence in your equipment and your shooting, both of which are critical to your hunting success.

45   A Sight for Sore Eyes

BY JEFF MURRAY

Bow-mounted scopes have come a long way and can significantly increase your ability to shoot under dim conditions. But there are major factors to consider. Here's what one bowhunting expert found out.

The evolution of archery dates back many centuries, but recent times have radically altered the way man uses a bow to fling an arrow. For example, it only took a few decades to go from cedar arrow shafts to aluminum and now carbon. Perhaps even more extreme is how today's archers aim. While a small cadre of "stick bow" devotees continue to hunt and shoot instinctively without any sighting device, the vast majority of modern bowhunters rely on a sight pin or a combination of such pins.

Now even that could be changing. The vast latest craze in on-the-bow accessories is the dot scope, or "scope" for short. Advantages outweigh drawbacks, proponents say, forcing today's archers to once again reevaluate personal favorites.

Why Scope 'Em?

"The main advantage to this type of sight is its ability to eliminate a peep," says Chris Hamm with HHA Sports, Inc. "With proper technique, a peep is extra baggage because it won't improve accuracy. In the case of our new Eclipse sight, by lining up the two fiber-optic pins and centering them in the round sight window, you get the same effect as a peep. The benefit for hunters is significant: the ability to shoot in low-light conditions where conventional sighting systems fail. Moreover, the large sight window [1½ inches] is superior to a pin-peep combo in that the entire vital area of an animal comes easily into view."

Besides enhanced visibility, another major benefit of eliminating a bowstring peep is improved arrow velocity. Bowhunters in the know do everything they can to squeeze every ounce of kinetic energy from their bows, but surprisingly few realize the impact of a peep: If you rely on a bowstring alignment device such as rubber tubing, you'll lose as much as 15 feet per second. That's equivalent to loosening both limb bolts of your bow two to four full turns!

Noted ESPN television personality Tom Miranda is a scope fanatic who shoots a different design, the Bracklynn Hi Tech Bow Scope Mount System. "It really performs well for me," he said. "It's incredibly durable and can withstand the rigors of worldwide travel—from mountain goat stalks and brown bear hunts in pouring rain to bush-plane junkets to caribou camp. And the Bracklynn yardage dial system easily calculates arrow trajectory out to 60 yards. But the most important feature is the sight's rifle bar that adapts the scope mount to iron sights. This allows me to shoot with both eyes open to get pinpoint accuracy with solid shooting form."

Why is shooting both-eyes-open such a big deal? Because Miranda, like many archers today, battles one of the sport's most perplexing obstacles. "I'm a right-handed archer, yet I'm left-eye dominant," he said. "This used to drive me crazy; I almost gave up archery. But my Bracklynn rifle-bar setup saved the day and put the fun back into shooting a bow."

The Major Players

Scope sights vary considerably in design and cost. HHA's Optimizer-Life Eclipse, alluded to above, does not project a dot electronically as most other designs do. Instead, this sighting system resembles an open gun sight. The five-inch scope houses two vertical .030-inch fiber-optic pins that are about four inches apart. The closest pin to the target is green, the one nearest the shooter is red; simply line up the front pin with the rear pin, and when the green pin is fully blocked out, you're on target. A sight light is also included for extra-low-light conditions.

The mount is machined aluminum anodized in flat black and comes with a lifetime warranty. An adjustable "radial arm" with an arm lock knob can be adjusted for distances out to 65 yards, yet is slip-proof and vibration-proof. Additionally, the sight accommodates most quivers (shims are included). Weight is about 11 ounces.

A highly sophisticated dot scope, EOTech's second-generation HOLOgraphic Sight Model 520 is vastly improved from the introductory model I scoped out back in 1998. For starters, the 520 is more compact. It's also much brighter and has improved battery life (powered by two type-N alkalines). Plus the price has dropped from $459 to about $299.

The 520 I tested featured a microwindage adjustment setting and an internal range-estimation system in the sight window (parallel bars placed on the back and belly of a deer approximate distances from the shooter). The 520 does not come with a mount, but HHA's Optimizer-Lite Plus mount proved to be a satisfactory marriage, although the two in combination is fairly heavy.

The 520's most distinguishing characteristic is the sight window: a red dot inside two rings. This arrangement gives instant feedback on shooting form. If the dot is centered inside the rings and the rings are perfectly concentric, alignment is true and hand torque is minimal. Any slight variation of the bow-hand position immediately alters the placement of the dot and rings. For instance, if the dot and inner ring are positioned toward the right edge of the outer ring, you're likely putting too much pressure to the left, or outside edge, of the grip (for a right-handed shooter). This feature alone is an excellent training aid for beginning archers, since it shows what the shooter is doing, as well as how hand position can affect arrow flight.

According to EOTech, their hologram—that projects a three-dimensional reticle pattern in space at two distances—significantly enhances accuracy. It's the same principle that makes sights on a rifle more accurate than those on a handgun. Simply stated, a longer sight radius means better aiming.

Leupold, known for superior rifle scopes and binoculars, makes an outstanding dot scope, the Leupold/Gilmore Red Dot Sight. It's constructed of the same aircraft-quality aluminum (6061 T-6) as the company's rifle scopes, making it one of the most rugged and dependable available. But what really separates the Leupold/Gilmore sight from others is its exceptionally bright resolution; 11 different brightness settings are available, so eye relief shouldn't suffer regardless of how far the target is or how dim lighting may be.

Aimtech makes the mounting bracket Leupold currently recommends. It's lighter than other mounting systems, but its elevation adjustment isn't quite as handy as, say, HHA's Optimizer-Lite Plus.

Several years ago, Hesco incorporated a low-level radioactive substance, tritium, with their Meprolight sight pin. When combined with fiber optics, this basic technology is transformed into a hunter-friendly scope sight—the Mepor 21 Targeting System. And because the fiber-optic ring situated along the rim of the scope is powered by tritium and not by a battery, it projects a red dot that isn't considered an electronic device. Hence, it's Pope & Young Club acceptable.

The Scopemate 2, made by Bowmasters, fit the Hesco sight well enough to accommodate my new Mathews Q2, but I had to do some serious jury-rigging to center the dot. (I suspect mounting scope sights will be a common problem, given the many riser configurations on today's spiraling bow models.) Although the Mepor 21's illumination is not adjustable, it seemed to perform equally well in bright light and low light, but overall clarity of the sight window was noticeably less than the top-performing Leupold/Gilmore.

Testing the Sights

I just had to field-test the more promising models to see what the hoopla was all about. After all, if I'm going to switch from my trusty fiber-optic multiple-pin sight, I better not rely on second-hand smoke and mirrors. My hands-on tests turned up some interesting insights.

For starters, these scopes are relatively heavy by current standards. Fortunately, bow weight has been reduced drastically in recent years, thanks to machined risers and lighter limbs and components. Nevertheless, better plan on at least doubling bow weight at the middle of the riser if you take the scope plunge.

I also discovered that mounting a bow scope is a lot more complicated than mounting a conventional pin sight. The typical pin system, for example, relies on a pair of bolts to secure it to the riser and, in most cases, two more bolts for adjusting windage and elevation. In stark contrast consider the EOTech 520: Two bolts for attaching to an L-bracket which, in turn, takes two more bolts to attach to a plate which takes two more bolts to attach to HHA's mount and two more for attaching to the riser. Two, four, six, eight . . . that could be a headache! The point is, solidly securing a scope so it doesn't jostle out of position isn't any different from attaching and maintaining a precision scope to a rifle. If you don't cut any corners, you should be able to enjoy trouble-free operation in a variety of conditions, as Tom Miranda attests.

Another revelation quickly surfaced after launching a pair of arrows: You may not need a peep sight (one won't hurt), but you will need some kind of bowstring aid to reproduce a consistent anchor point. A kisser button, typically positioned on the bowstring so it lines up with the corner of the mouth, is a tried-and-true option. Also, you'll need to get used to centering the bowstring just to the right of the dot (for right-handed shooters).

Some additional considerations:

- For some archers, the added weight of these sights might require modification in aiming technique. For instance, if you've gotten into the habit of drawing your bow well above the target before settling into position (a common practice when drawing too much weight) you'll need to change your ways. Begin the draw with the scope aimed dead on the intended line of arrow travel. The sooner you settle in, the sooner you can release the shot and the more you can avoid fatigue and shaking.

   Anticipate mounting problems. Because mounting systems must be purchased separately from scope manufacturers—and because no two bows are exactly alike—I strongly suggest working with a local pro shop rather than ordering parts by mail order. Then you'll know if every bolt fits and every notch lines up before cash is exchanged. If the nearest professional archery shop is a considerable distance away, at least discuss mounting instructions for your particular bow model with technical representatives from the scope and mount company. Don't take anything for granted.
- Practice shooting with both eyes open from the very first shot. You may be more accurate on the target range with one eye closed, but a recent turkey hunt to Nebraska taught me that two-eyed bowhunting with a scope is more effective in the woods.
- Although it's possible to adjust for distance—out to 60 yards or more—with a radial-arch-type mount, it's wise to get used to shooting at a single calibrated distance. Depending on bow poundage, arrow weight and the species hunted, your preferred setting will probably range from 15 to 30 yards. This semi-instinctive approach helps hone range-estimation skills and ingrains arrow-trajectory compensation. Look at it this way: You'll be more effective when you have to get off a quick shot, yet if time permits you can always "dial in" the required yardage.

- Once you lock onto an accurate elevation and windage adjustment, secure all bolts with proper lubricants (some are designed for metal, some for plastic; never mix the two). Scribe all settings with a permanent marker.
- When you arrive at your hunting destination, always test-fire your bow to make sure the scope remains in its original position.

Are scope sights for every archer? Definitely not. But manufacturers have steadily improved designs in recent years, and the pros are beginning to outweigh the cons. At the very least, you owe it to yourself to scope out the latest models and see if you're missing out.

46   Modern Carbon Arrows: Why Use Anything Else?

BY BOB ROBB

If you haven't tried today's carbon shafts, you may be handicapping yourself when it comes to both accuracy and performance on game.

L et's cut to the chase. With aluminum arrows a proven, top-quality product, is there any practical reason at all why you should try a dozen carbon arrows this year? Are they the shafts of the future, or just a passing fancy?

A Little Background Music

The history of carbon arrows is a relatively brief one, and one that continues to evolve annually. Way back in the days of love beads and sit-ins—the early 1970s—carbon technology gained widespread use in the aerospace industry. Carbon fibers, which are strong, lightweight, durable and resilient to stress, proved to be an ideal material for flight. As the years flew by, carbon fibers were used to build everything from the Stealth Bomber to Indianapolis race cars, fishing rods and tennis rackets, bicycle frames and golf clubs. It was just a matter of time before someone experimented with carbon arrows.

That someone was Beman, founded by a pair of engineers in Lyon, France, in the early 1980s. Their first arrow, the DIVA, was introduced in 1986. The DIVA soon gained a solid following on the international target archery circuit. In 1988, Beman introduced the first carbon arrows for hunters. As we forge ahead into the new century, there are several manufacturers offering pure carbon shafts for bowhunters.

The Carbon Advantage

Carbon shaft sales are growing annually simply because they provide several performance advantages over aluminum shafts. One is raw arrow speed, achieved because carbon shafts of the same length and spine as a comparable aluminum shaft weigh less. "While the exact numbers vary, of course, we figure you get anywhere from 20–30 fps more from a carbon shaft than a comparable aluminum arrow," said Jeff McNail, Beman U.S.A. Assistant Brand Manager.

Another advantage is durability. Carbon shafts are just plain tough, able to withstand as much or more abuse than aluminum and aluminum/carbon composite arrows. With carbon, the shaft is either as straight as it came from the factory or it's broken—they can't be bent—and it takes quite a wallop to break them. (When aluminum is involved, as is the case with the carbon/aluminum Easton A/C/C, the shafts can bend, often imperceptibly, though they can be straightened.)

Third, while there has been no empirical testing to show that this is true, there is at least a perception among today's shooters that carbon shafts out-penetrate any other arrow on the market. "Penetration is something we don't talk about all that much," McNail said. "There can be drawbacks with carbon shafts, too, if you get an arrow that is too light to have enough kinetic energy to penetrate deeply. However, the combination of a very small diameter, condensed mass, less drag on the shaft because the broadhead is cutting a much larger hole than the shaft diameter and less surface area for friction seems to play a role in the deep penetrating ability of carbon arrows."

"We are going to do some testing in the near future to try and find out for sure whether or not carbons really do out-penetrate comparable aluminum arrows," said John Gooding, president of True-Flight Arrow Co., Inc. True-Flight is a leading maker of finished arrow shafts, using Easton aluminum and both Beman and Gold Tip carbon shafts to create thousands upon thousands of finished arrows annually. "But in reality, at the distances at which most game animals are taken—25 yards and under—there really isn't much difference. Then, penetration is really as much a function of bow tuning, broadhead blade sharpness and shot placement as anything else."

Another advantage of carbon arrows is that a single shaft spine covers a much wider range than comparable aluminum arrows. For example, most carbon arrow makers offer only three different spine sizes to cover the entire range of hunting bow draw length/draw weight combinations. For example, Beman's ICS Hunter shaft is available in just three spine sizes—500, 400 and 340. One of these three arrow sizes will tune in bows ranging from 33 to 100 lbs. of draw weight, and draw lengths between 23 and 33 inches, depending on the combination thereof. This makes it easy to select the right arrow shaft spine for your bow, without worrying about being "on the cusp" of the right size. It also makes it easier for a pro shop to stock the right size shafts to take care of virtually all its customers without having to carry dozens and dozens of different aluminum shaft spines in stock.

No Free Lunch

The first carbon shafts were so small in diameter that archers were required to use an "outsert" to affix screw-on broadheads, field points and nocks to them. Outserts are carbon components that glue on over the shafts themselves, which creates a slightly larger diameter part than the rest of the shaft. Early on, there was some trouble attaching outserts to carbon shafts in a perfectly aligned manner, which adversely affected accuracy. Today outserts are built to exact tolerances, and the bugaboos of attaching them to the shaft have been reduced.

Fletching has been a historical problem for carbon arrows. "In the early days, the available adhesives didn't work all that well when it came to securing fletching to a carbon shaft," said McNail. "We've tried many different things over the years, including sanding the bottoms of the vanes and the shaft to create a rough edge to trying all kinds of different glues and glue systems. Today, however, this is not a real problem, as glue makers have developed some excellent adhesives for carbon shafts. For example, the Arizona Fast-Set Gel and plastic vanes work extremely well on modern carbon shafts."

"Any of the super glue-type adhesives work really well on carbon arrows," Gooding said. "The secret is to first meticulously prep the shaft. You have to carefully clean both the inside and outside of the shaft to remove any microscopic carbon dust particles that can inhibit adhesion. We've found that using isopropyl alcohol does this very well."

Because of the extremely small diameter of a carbon arrow, achieving adequate fletch clearance with the arrow rest has been a problem. The problems of both fletch clearance and outserts has been solved with the recent introduction of a "fatter" carbon arrow that can accept the same internal component systems used in aluminum arrows. Two companies—Beman and Gold Tip—began using internal component systems in their pure carbon shafts in 1997. AFC/Game Tracker followed suit in 1998, with the Carbon Impact Fat Shaft and Carbon Tech CT Rhino first appearing in 1999. Each of these shafts is able to accept internal component systems because they are larger in diameter than the original carbon arrow. "The larger-diameter carbon shafts are the wave of the future," McNail said. "They offer all the performance benefits of the smaller-diameter shafts, but make achieving fletch clearance so much easier. That makes it easier to tune the bow properly with them."

Gooding said the key to assembling carbon shaft insert systems begins with proper shaft prepping. "Clean the shaft, inside and out, with isopropyl alcohol," he said. "Then, screw a broadhead you know is straight into the insert. Lightly coat the insert with a 24-hour epoxy, then push it into the shaft, checking it for straightness before the epoxy sets up. We do this on a machine, but you can do it by performing the old 'spin test' on the shaft. If the shaft shows some wobble, it's not straight; so work with it, push it in a bit more and so on to try and make it straight. If it never gets straight, it may be because the machined tolerances of the insert itself are off. In that case I'd recommend tossing the insert and starting over. If it is straight, however, remove the broadhead and set the shaft in a vertical position on the nock end while the epoxy sets up."

"One trick we've found with the inserts is that, once we get them in and glued in the right position, if you apply 150 degrees of heat to the insert portion of the shaft for 15 minutes, it will set the epoxy in place," Gooding said. "I'd then recommend letting it cure overnight."

Consistency Problems

It was difficult to find a dozen pultruded carbon arrows that weighed the same, or nearly so, in the early years. Differences in weight will, of course, adversely affect arrow groups. Today's carbon shafts are much better about this, however. "Much of that weight differential was due to the outserts," McNail said. "That's one of the big advantages to an internal component system. Together with being much easier to set up and install properly, it is a lighter system and much more consistent on the assembly. There isn't a 1 to ½ grain difference in weight per dozen inserts now."

Gooding sees the problem of consistent shaft-to-shaft weight as the biggest bugaboo in using carbon arrows today, although it is rapidly disappearing.

"Weight disparities are the number one problem I see with carbon shafts today," Gooding said. "There used to be bigger disparities, on average, than you'd find with comparable aluminum arrows. We weigh each shaft closely when making our Pro Series of shafts, which we guarantee to be as closely matched in weight and construction as any finished arrow available today. We've found that with some carbon shafts, you can find a weight disparity of as much as 28 grains between individual arrows in a given dozen shafts. However, with the better top-quality carbon shafts, like the Bemans, on average you can find a weight differential of maybe 6–7 grains." In contrast, Gooding said the weight differences in top-quality XX78 aluminum shafts might run 6–7 grains, "which is extremely good," he said.

"The average guy shooting at 20 yards won't notice a difference in arrow groups with a weight difference of 6–7 grains," Gooding said. "But he just might with 28 grains."

Early carbon shafts also did not necessarily come consistently straight enough from the factory to make it a nobrainer to put together a dozen arrows that grouped tightly together. As we've seen, carbon shafts cannot be straightened, so unless they are perfectly straight from the get-go, there's nothing you can do about it. Today, however, the problem of initial straightness is not a factor. For example, in their 2000 literature top-of-the-line Beman, Carbon Impact and Gold Tip shafts tout a shaft straightness of .001 inch, while Carbon Tech touts a straightness of .002 inch. That's an initial straightness that matches top-of-the-line Easton aluminum shafts.

"The ability of the top carbon shaft makers to spot-check straightness has really improved over the years," Gooding said. "While we still find some shafts that are not as straight as advertised, they're pretty close."

Poltrusion vs. Radial Construction

The original small-diameter carbon shaft is made by a process called poltrusion. In a nutshell, long carbon fibers are laid out lengthwise, then pulled through a vat of dye, then a vat of epoxy resins to hold the fibers together, McNail said. The result is a tube-like shaft with all straight fiber. The various different spine sizes of the finished shaft are determined by the size of the carbon fiber being used and the diameter of the finished shaft.

The newer, fatter shafts are made from a process commonly called radial construction, McNail said. "Here we a use multi-layer, or cross-laminate, process," he said. "In it we alternate a layer of straight carbon fibers, then wrap them in a circular pattern with another layer of carbon fiber, and so on. Bemen ICS and

Hunter shafts use a total of four layers." Some manufacturers, notably Gold Tip, use a five-layer construction. It is this radial construction that gives the carbon shaft the strength to accept the internal component system, McNail said.

Preferred Fletching, Broadheads

The standard hunting fletch for carbon shafts is a four-inch plastic vane, McNail said, "although some guys like three-inch vanes when shooting mechanical heads." Generally speaking, when using poltruded shafts you need either straight fletch or just a slight off-set, but when using a fatter shaft with internal component system you can get away with 1–2 degrees of off-set while still achieving fletch clearance with the arrow rest. This also can vary with the rest type. Some bowhunters prefer feathers over vanes, which work well with carbon arrows, too.

Smaller-diameter, lighter-weight broadheads are also required when shooting carbon arrows than when shooting aluminum shafts. "Generally speaking, broadhead weight should be no more than 125 grains with carbon arrows," McNail said. "Heads in the 85- to 100-grain size are the choice of most bowhunters."

What Do They Cost?

When they first appeared, carbon arrows cost a lot more than comparable aluminum shafts. However, as more manufacturers begin to produce and sell carbon arrows, and as the technology to manufacture them improves, the price is coming down. Today they are very competitive in price with aluminum shafts. The new generation of "fatter" carbon shafts with internal component systems and radial construction are a bit more expensive than poltruded shafts, which are a bit more expensive than Easton XX78-class aluminum shafts. In 2000, the most expensive hunting shafts of all, the Easton A/C/C aluminum/carbon composite shafts, cost about twice as much as XX78s.

Carbon arrows have a lot going for them and are worth looking into. I've shot them almost exclusively for several seasons and have been mightily impressed. I've shot completely through big, tough game like Alaskan grizzly bears and large-bodied elk with carbon shafts. Using True Flights Pro Series carbon shafts has me shooting the tightest groups at distances that I've ever achieved. Does that mean the aluminum arrow is ancient history? No way! It just means that there is a new player in town, one that offers a viable alternative to aluminum shafts. The wise bowhunter will weigh the pros and cons of each before deciding which to carry afield this season.

47   Head Games

BY MICHAEL PEARCE

Choosing between cutting tips, replaceable blades and expandable blades is something every bowhunter must carefully do. Pick the wrong broadhead for your bow and you could set yourself up for a hunting disappointment.

For a sport that seems so simple, bowhunting requires many considerations. Stand placement takes hours of scouting and work to get a setup where you can get hip pocket-close to a buck or bull without it ever knowing you're around. And then there's making the shot—getting the bow drawn, finding the right angle, aiming at the right spot with perfectly tuned equipment, holding precise shooting form while your knees are knocking and your heart's pounding at a punk-rock rate.

But when you think about it, the entire sport comes down to broadhead performance. At its peak, a good broadhead brings it all to an enjoyable conclusion. But if it performs poorly—not striking where it's aimed, or not doing its job on impact—it can turn a dream hunt into a nightmare. Obviously the more research you can put into selecting a broadhead, the better. Read on for a quick course in picking what's right for you.

Cutting Tips

There are basically three styles of broadheads on the market. Cutting-tip heads are the old originals that have been around since the first primitive man decided to put a piece of flaked flint on the front of a wooden arrow. Though they were eventually made of metal, not a lot has really changed in cutting-tip design. Of course, there's been no real reason to change much.

Cutting-tip heads, as their name implies, start cutting from the point of the head on down. They're also the most durable and dependable broadheads of all since they're generally made from one main piece of steel. Most such broadheads also offer lots of cutting edge as well. In other words, should you clip a shoulder or other bone that instantly dulls the first inch of an edge, there's still plenty of scalpel-sharp blade coming to continue good penetration and leave a good blood trail.

Most come in a standard flat, two-blade design, which along with the other features aids in overall penetration, making them ideal for small-framed archers shooting low-poundage bows. Big cutting-tip heads are also great for big, tough game like elk and moose, where an arrow needs to get 18 inches or more of penetration even after it cuts through the super-tough hide. I've talked with several long-time elk guides who say they prefer their clients use such heads for just that reason.

But cutting-tip heads also have faults. One of the perceived major drawbacks is difficulty in sharpening them. While the other two styles just need new blades added, cutting-tip heads need their edges manually sharpened. Actually, it's not that hard. Last fall I started using an Accusharp sharpener, and it's amazing how quickly it got my Magnus heads shaving sharp! Still, if you're lazy or don't think you have the skills to bring a blade to a keen edge, these broadheads aren't for you.

Another possible problem is that many cutting-tip heads have just two blades, which means they don't have the total cutting area of the other styles. Of course, there are some legendary cutting-tip heads—Bear Razorhead, Zwickey, Satellite Titan—that can have pre-sharpened blades added, giving the hunter the best of both worlds.

Getting good broadhead flight can be either painfully simple or downright impossible with cutting-tip heads. Generally, there's little to no problem with moderate-speed bows, though planing can certainly happen when people try to push the two-blade heads at high speeds.

Those who are after speed won't find much of a selection in lightweight cutting-tip heads. Overall, 125 grains seems to be about the minimum, though Bear has had a 110 version of their popular Razorhead available for some time. Magnus has a head that weighs the same, though the company says one even lighter should be out eventually.

As for selection, thankfully most of the cutting-tip heads are made well and perform the same. Such long-time favorites as the Bear Razorhead and Zwickey-style cutting tip heads are still popular for good reason. In more recent years the Magnus, Satellite Titan and Patriot heads have developed strong followings.

Replaceable Blades

Replaceable-blade broadheads have only been on the market for about a quarter-century, but their impact was almost immediate and they still are the most popular style in use—for a number of reasons.

For one thing, they're extremely convenient to use. If a head gets dull, the bowhunter only needs to loosen the ferule from the shaft, slide some new blades into place and they're ready to go. Such a setup makes it much easier to use three- or four-blade broadheads, which add more cutting area.

Also, most such heads are aerodynamically designed to fly well out of most bows. Granted, they don't fly like field points, but a well-tuned bow will usually group good broadheads well. At some high speeds, however, they may not have the same point of impact as field points. Replaceable heads also come in a huge assortment of cutting diameters and weights, from 75 to 150 grains.

But such positives certainly have negative trade-offs. Since they rely on a pointed or chiseled tip, replaceable-blade broadheads won't penetrate as well as most cutting-tip styles. It may not make much difference on thin-skinned white-tails, but it can on bigger game. I once saw a demonstration where a bowhunter stretched a tanned elk hide on a wooden frame, then dropped a well-sharpened Zwickey from three or four feet. It split the hide. He then dropped several replace-able-blade heads from the same distance. None penetrated at all.

Replaceable heads do usually have more blades, but they're certainly more easily broken than sturdy cutting-tip heads. While they may have a lot of cutting distance in all, the real cutting length per blade isn't a lot. Also not all replaceable heads—or their components—are created equal. Some brands seem to fly more consistently and hold up better than others. Still, bowhunters who stick with well-respected name brands like Thunderhead, Satellite Mags and others generally have no problems.

Expandable Heads

The new kid on the bowhunting block, heads utilizing hidden blades that open upon contact have certainly gotten their share of attention and action within the last decade. There's no question they have some advantages the other two styles don't.

Just slightly larger than field points, with no angling blades to catch the wind, expandable heads fly like a dream. In fact, most will impact a target the exact place as like-weight field points! That's a huge advantage for those shooting sensi-tive, super-fast set-ups and for those who don't have the time or the place to prop-erly tune and sight in other kinds of broadheads. Last fall hunting buddy Kendall Shaw took a friend's advice and simply screwed a NAP Spitfire onto a shaft and headed to the woods shot unseen. The first morning out a 145-class P & Y white-tail offered Kendall a shot, and he hit the exact hair he was aiming at. "Man, the confidence these kind of heads give you is incredible," he said. "You know where they're going to hit because they can't plane, and they're much more forgiving for bad shooting form than a regular broadhead."

Such broadheads can indeed be quite broad when opened; some early two-blade models had cutting diameters approaching two inches or more! Inch-and-a-half cutting diameters and slightly larger are common with three or four blades. Some of the holes I've seen in the sides of whitetails have been downright scary.

As they say, "now for the rest of the story."

There's no question expandable-blade heads have the worst penetration rates on the market. With points rather than razor-sharp tips, they poke their way in rather than cut, and it takes more of an arrow's energy to open the blades on the way in compared to a replaceable-blade head. Also, a lot of the expandable blades stick up when shot at fairly steep angles, which can significantly impede penetra-tion. Bowhunters who've had cutting-tip heads stick three inches in the ground after going through a whitetail have had expandable heads not even leave an exit wound.

Such severe angles on the long, thin blades can also lead to blades breaking. Four or five years ago a good friend, Marc Murrell, shot a turkey at about 15 yards with a new expandable head. The bird certainly died quickly, but Murrell found three of the four blades had snapped off inside the bird. Needless to say, those broadheads weren't on his shafts when whitetail season rolled around! But in fairness, I've also seen some reputable expandable heads center an elk rib and exit the other side without even a nick on the blades.

Another possible problem can arise if the broadhead nicks a weed or small limb on the way to the animal, opening the head prematurely and often sending it flying quite erratically. Granted, any arrow and any head can easily be deflected. But having hunted enough mule deer in CRP grass, I know there are times when you may need to nick the occasional thin blade of bluestem to get to the buck that's only a few inches behind it.

There's no doubt expandable heads are the most controversial piece of equipment in bowhunting, but their fans can be extremely avid. Some say the true flight increases accuracy enough that they can extend their shooting range an extra five to 10 yards over other broadheads. I've also heard that even with less penetration power there's usually always enough to make it into both lungs of a buck. Also, those who've shot such industry leaders as the Spitfire have had remarkably little problem with blade breakage.

Expandable heads certainly aren't for everybody, but no broadheads are, for that matter.

Picking What's Right for You

Broadhead needs are a bit different for everyone. While it's one thing to read about the great accuracy and huge cutting diameter of expandable heads, they may not be right for you. For instance, if you're hunting only whitetails from treestands, when shooting a 70-pound bow and midweight arrows you can use about any decent head you want. A cutting-tip head will no doubt bury deep into the ground behind any buck you shoot, and even expandable heads will probably leave an exit wound and a blood trail a blind man could follow.

But what about for the Western youngster who's barely pulling 45 pounds and has to shoot light arrows to get good flight from his bow? There's a decent chance the combination of light poundage and low-energy-delivering arrows won't be pushing an expandable head fast enough to push through a rib or the edge of the shoulder and into both lungs. This hunter is a prime candidate for a good two-blade cutting tip, so penetration will be maximized. Ditto for the person who's shooting just 60 pounds and wants to take on a big Arizona elk.

You need to be honest with yourself and try to pick the broadhead that best complements your positives and might cover-up your negatives. If you shoot with less than perfect form, that's a huge reason to go with an expandable. If you shoot fine, but can't put an edge on a broadhead, then the replaceable could be the ticket. Should your shots be long and your arrow energy fair at best, like on western mule deer, a sturdy cutting tip is worth serious consideration.

Actually, the only way to decide what head is best for you is to talk with lots of other bowhunters, look at the deer they bring in and shoot as many broadheads as you can into foam or sandy banks. Make sure you have a perfectly tuned bow and double check all your arrows for straightness or nicked vanes.

Don't practice by yourself, either; have a buddy looking over your shoulder, watching your arrows to make sure they're flying straight. Any wobble at all will greatly decrease penetration and accuracy. Never sacrifice anything for those two features. The sharpest cutting head in the world will bring you nothing but grief if it planes in the wind and causes a clean miss . . . or worse.

Of course, the only way to improve accuracy is to practice with the broad-heads. At least in the case of cutting-tip and replaceable-blade heads, forget the old adage "of just shoot field points of the same weight and you'll be fine." Sorry, it quite often doesn't work that way, at least not with many of my bow/arrow/ broadhead combinations.

If, for whatever reason, they fly fine and group tight somewhere other that where your field tips hit, just go ahead and move your sights. Practice, practice, practice with broadheads (I always keep a half-dozen older heads around for just that purpose) until you have total confidence in yourself and your shooting system. Gradually, move your practice distance back a bit each day until you get where you can consistently put four out of five arrows into a five- or six-inch target. When you've done that you'll know the exact edge of your shooting range. Then with complete confidence in your broadhead and rig, you'll be able to focus all of your attention on your knocking knees!

48   10X Better Accuracy

BY JEFF MURRAY

Every bowhunter can be up to 10 times more accurate! Follow these steps, and you'll be amazed at your improvement.

Stopping a bounding buck for a quality shot is every bowhunter's dream. So when the big eight-pointer froze dead in his tracks when I made a timely mouth-grunt, I thought I was dreaming. I promptly drew my bow and sent an arrow sailing for . . . the nearest tree branch. Needless to say, my arrow deflected low and the buck escaped unharmed. How come I hadn't seen that twig? Because I hadn't looked. I'd been immersed in aiming and "forgotten" to adjust my line of approach to accommodate the buck. Ironically, most bowhunters miss because they do the opposite: They fail to aim properly and blame phantom tree branches.

Although neither is acceptable, I believe every bowhunter can be a better shot than he or she realizes. In fact, I'll go on record as saying you can be up to 10 times more accurate. You may not score on 10 times as many bucks, but your arrow groups could be that much tighter. Here's a tried-and-true process that works for beginners, intermediates and advanced archers alike.

Eliminating Equipment Failure

The first place to look for improvement is equipment. It's easier to blame your bow or arrow or broadhead than the person in the mirror, and it's equally easy to identify and prevent equipment-related problems. If deer routinely "jump" your bowstring, for example, one of three factors is to blame. Either your setup is unacceptably noisy, your arrow speed could stand improvement or the animal was on red alert.

Just as quiet camo clothing is a must for bowhunting big game, so is a quiet bow. Yet each fall I see hunters committing the same basic mistakes. The most common is noise resulting from arrows gliding over a metallic arrow rest. The next most common is when an arrow slips off a rest and clanks against a riser or sight. To silence your rest's prongs, you can use everything from moleskin to hockey tape. A simple, long-lasting commercial product is Gibbs Archery Gear's Super Slicks. So is the Whisper Prong Silencer, from Coffey Marketing Corporation. Need I say that covering your riser and bowsight with fleece tape is not an option?

Regarding bow-generated noise, technological advancements in design and mass production continue to reduce recoil and vibration, which, in turn, cuts down on noise and shooter error (more later). But if you can't afford a new bow, some innovative aftermarket accessories can make a difference. Sims Vibration Laboratory has an impressive background in shock-absorption with aluminum bats and golf clubs. Now the company's gone archery. Check out its Limb Savers, rubber shock-absorbing stick-on devices for each limb. The new String Leech is excellent for dampening bowstring noise without hampering arrow speed, and the Enhancer 2000 makes any stabilizer even more effective in reducing shock.

If you can improve arrow speed without affecting accuracy, do it. Although speed is clearly secondary to shooting accuracy, achieving a certain velocity threshold does wonders in the whitetail world. Experience suggests that the 250 to 275 fps plateau is needed to prevent deer from consistently "jumping the string." I believe it's based on reaction time. As an example, a major-league batter facing a pitcher tossing an 85-mph fastball can usually make solid contact. But increase the pitch to 90 mph, and only upper-echelon hitters can react in time. Increase ball speed to the 95-mph mark, and almost all batters have a hard time adjusting. So it is with a typical deer in a typical situation, with a moderately fast arrow. There are exceptions, of course, such as hunting deer over bait (you might have to aim intentionally low).

Increasing arrow speed also increases one's margin of error for range estimation, particularly at common "deer distances" of 25 yards or so. It's a tremendous advantage to be able to hold one pin right on out to 30 yards because of flattened arrow trajectory! On the other hand, if your speed isn't quite up to snuff, you'll need 20- and 30-yard sight pins (not too long ago, we relied on 10-, 20- and 30-yard pins to get the job done). Moreover, you'll need to know which pin to use should a buck saunter within 30 yards. Which is to say, faster arrows can greatly simplify the short-range game of bowhunting.

Five ways to get faster: 1) Shoot lighter arrows (ounce for ounce, carbon shafts are lighter and have stiffer spines than aluminum); 2) muscle up to shoot more poundage (but don't overdo it); 3) reevaluate bowstring-alignment devices (peeps requiring rubber tubing cost about 12 to 14 fps); 4) lighten up nocksets, servings and string silencers (replace a pair of brass nocksets with a dacron string loop and use the smallest, lightest silencers possible, positioning them toward the end of the bowstring) and 5) add a pair of brass nocksets just above the bottom cam (cover them with shrink tubing).

Another equipment-related miscue is failing to tune broadheads. Unfortunately, the greater the arrow speed, the more critical this becomes. The exposed blades compete with fletching in steering the arrow, causing wind-planing. The key is proper alignment of the broadhead's ferrule and the arrow's insert. The tip should not wobble when spun on a hard surface. Shoot every single hunting head ahead of time (replacing or retouching blades).

An increasingly popular alternative is a quality expanding head, such as Rocky Mountain's new Warhead or Wasp's well-established Jackhammer. These designs sport a rugged chisel tip (for better penetration) and improved separation of the blades (to reduce deflections). Yet another option is switching from vanes to more-forgiving feathers. Feathers are a little less durable and slightly noisier in flight, but they definitely stabilize broadhead-tipped arrows quicker.

Not all arrows are created equal. Develop the habit of numbering every arrow so you can distinguish the "fliers." Though arrow-manufacturing tolerances improve steadily, it's impossible to clone arrow shafts. Some might be bent, the axis might be off on others, and still others just may not cycle the same due to differences in spine characteristics. Never assume anything about a brand new arrow. Test it.

And speaking of testing equipment, be sure to familiarize yourself with every accessory—including your range finder. Even electronic range finders are not foolproof. Some need to be calibrated, and some don't work well in low-light conditions. But all electronic range finders can be "fooled." Each year I hear stories of bowhunters "dialing in" a deer, only to miss low. Why low? Because in the excitement of a close encounter, the unfortunate bowhunter punches up an untimely false reading; range finders have the vexing habit of recording reeds, tall grass and branches that tend to get in the way at the worst possible moment (remember my miss earlier?). So practice with your range finder, and always double-check readings when time permits.

Finally, make sure your bow fits you like an old shoe. If it doesn't, the rest of this article won't fit, either. For starters, be sure your bow's draw length isn't too long. When I first shot a compound, my full-length arrows measured just more than 29 inches. Then I cut back to 28, and now my actual draw is between 26½ and 27 inches. Although I can shoot a longer draw length—and certainly do appreciate the extra speed from the elongated power stroke—I shoot noticeably better when I'm not "reaching."

It's easy to tell if your draw length is too long. One way is checking your "arrow line extension" while you're at full draw. Have a friend stand at your side and visualize an imaginary line running from the arrow shaft past your elbow. If the line runs through the middle of your elbow or below it, you're in good shape. But if your elbow is well below the arrow shaft, accuracy is going to suffer.

Another tip-off is your anchor point. "Floating" anchor points off the face represent the extreme. You shouldn't anchor much past your ear lobe. Also, if you find yourself leaning backward, away from the shot, you're drawing too much bow length. Again, accuracy suffers if you can't maintain an erect upper torso that's perpendicular to your arrow.

Shooting Flaws

The guy in the mirror is the next place to look to tighten arrow groups. Archery is amazingly similar to golf in three distinct ways: No two shots are exactly alike; both sports are games of inches; and form is critical. Never take form for granted. For years I thought I could shoot a bow well as long as it felt "natural." But thanks to the advent of the professional 3-D circuit, I discovered that geometry, not comfort, is the key. Good form and perfect practice is what allows the pros to reproduce impressive accuracy. Here's a closer look.

Start with the grip. Most experts recommend a low to medium grip (the pressure is in the middle of the palm, not in the fleshy web of the thumb and forefinger). "It's more solid, and you won't torque the handle as much" said Mathews pro-staffer Jesse Morehead. "Your bow will shake less, too, making right and left misses less common." Indeed, missing east and west, according to most archery coaches, is caused by torquing the riser (up to 75 percent of the time).

Next is the draw. If you can't point your pin at the target at the beginning of the draw cycle and keep it there till you come to full draw, you're pulling too much weight; you should be able to release when you want to, not when you have to. And when you consider that there are no warm-up shots in bowhunting, you'd better be able to draw your bow fluidly first thing in the morning. The proper way to draw a bow, incidentally, is pushing with the bow hand while simultaneously pulling with the release hand.

The hold is next. Hard-core archery research suggests that the compound bow is designed to be drawn and released in a time frame of five to 10 seconds; any shorter, and concentration suffers; any longer, and oxygen depletion and lactic-acid buildup in muscles begin to take their toll. So as you practice, try to stay within these limits. However, because deer aren't always cooperative, practice getting off a "quick" arrow as well as "waiting" on other shots. And by all means, practice from elevated positions, and practice with the exact same clothing you expect to hunt in (this goes double for facemasks).

Holding the bow isn't a meaningless task, either. Learn to use the large muscles (rhomboids) between your shoulder blades to help hold rock-solid. Your chosen anchor point is the backstop of your draw and should never be taken for granted. Pick an anchor point that can be attained blindfolded (a protruding cheek bone, jaw bone or tooth helps). You might be able to make some shots with any old anchor point, but consistent results come from a consistent anchor point.

Aiming technique is perhaps most important. In fact, books could be written on this controversial subject. Suffice to say, accurate archery demands aiming through the shot. That is, you must be immersed in maintaining the pin on the target well after the bow fires. You can't harbor any other thoughts at the conscious level at this time, or the aiming process will be interrupted. This means you must develop a subconscious release. "You'll know you're heading in the right direction if the bow 'just goes off' when you're aiming," Morehead said. "But if you're mind's eye sees your fingers on the bowstring or release, you're dead. You can't think 'release' and 'aiming' at the same time."

The next segment of the shot sequence is the release. Today, the vast majority of bowhunters rely on mechanical release aids to fire a bow. And why not—such releases are smoother and crisper and therefore more accurate over the long run. But they can also be persnickety to master and are another thing that can go wrong.

There are three "secrets" to conquering a release. One is making sure it fires with the proper tension so you don't have to worry about it going off unexpectedly or to exercise excessive force. In between is the fine line. Second, your release should fit your hand, not someone else's; for index-finger-operated releases, which are most popular among bowhunters, the triggering mechanism should fall between the first and second fold of the finger (never near the tip). And third, to avoid anticipating the release going off—which may evolve into a nerve-wracking case of target panic—rotate releases. Shoot a back-tension release for a couple of days, then return to a finger-activated model.

The completion of the release is the follow-through. Never quit shooting until the arrow strikes the target. It's the hardest easy task in all of archery—hard because you want to see where the arrow lands, easy because all it takes is another second of effort. Trust me when I say that a solid follow-through may be all that separates you from advancing to the next stage of archery prowess.

Because I'm never happy with my shooting, I'm always looking for ways to increase my accuracy. If I can dump arrows in a coffee can at 40 yards, I won't be satisfied till I can dump them in a coffee cup. Then a tea cup, then a thimble. . . . But that's what archery is all about: constant improvement.

Quick-Missers

Once you've sighted-in your bow, some arrows are going to stray from the bull's-eye. You're only human. Although a number of factors affect point-of-impact, the following generally apply to right-handed shooters (the reverse for lefties). If arrows tend to stray:

Left, your bow might be too long, causing: plucking the release, torquing the bow hand and string-clearance problems associated with bulky clothing.

Right, you're probably torquing the bow; your draw may also be too short.

High, you could be "heeling" the bow; that is, overemphasizing the bottom of the hand at the shot. Or you might be creeping (letting down on the draw slightly before releasing). Overestimating yardage is another cause of the high shot—an especially common mistake when shooting from an elevated tree stand.

Low, the bow could be too long (this symptom is most prevalent when the target is above or below the shooter); you might also fail to follow-through as you collapse at the shot prematurely.

The Startling String Loop

The day I installed a string loop on my Mathews Ultra-Max—an ultra-fast bow with a relatively short brace height—is the day I learned how to improve arrow flight without spending an extra hour on the practice range each day. The string loop is very light, so it won't reduce arrow velocity; is durable and extends serving life indefinitely; gives the arrow a smooth send-off, because it caresses the nock from the top and bottom, thereby reducing pinch; improves arrow stability by re-leasing it from directly behind the nock; and gives a crisper release with fixed re-lease aids that don't rotate.

See your local pro shop about replacing brass nocksets with a dacron string loop.

Buck Fever Simplified

Buck fever can strike anyone at any time. When it comes down to it, buck fever is essentially the fear of failing. The best antidote is a commitment to making the best shot possible (using the best form under the circumstances) and forgetting about "getting" the deer. Practice unfamiliar shots at different angles and distances, and you'll develop good muscle memory to draw upon at the moment of truth.

But that's not enough. You must train (or trick) your mind into thinking, Pick a spot. Many bowhunters miss high because they rush the shot. That shouldn't happen if you glare at "the spot on the spot" until you see or hear your arrow strike its intended target. Again, you need to be immersed in aiming as the arrow leaves the bowstring. Think, Good shot, and not, Good buck, and you'll make better shots and harvest more game.

49   Carbon or Aluminum?

BY THOMAS L. TORGET

Carbon shafts are the rage these days. But are they the best choice for whitetails?

When I started bowhunting in the early 1960s, arrow choice was easy because there was no choice. Everyone used cedar shafts because that's all there was. While pretty to look at, cedar arrows broke easily and spine inconsistency was a problem.

Fiberglass soon entered the market and these glass arrows were straight and durable. But they were much too heavy to suit most bowhunters. Then aluminum came along and solved the weight problem. These new metal shafts were extremely straight and very consistent in weight and spine. In fact, aluminum arrows were so superior to other materials that they quickly came to dominate the arrow industry. Aluminum remained essentially unchallenged until the mid-1990s.

That's when carbon arrived on the scene and growth in demand for these arrows has been phenomenal ever since. Carbon arrows have become so popular that they're now making serious inroads into aluminum's market share.

If you're thinking of making the switch, this story is for you. Let's look at the key differences between carbon and aluminum.

Durability

Advantage Carbon. With carbon, the arrow is either straight or it's broken. There's no middle ground. This resistance to breakage means most carbon arrows live longer than aluminum arrows.

Ease of Tuning

Advantage Carbon. When you release your bow string, the arrow flexes as it absorbs the forward-driving energy of the string. Aluminum continues flexing much longer than carbon. It's not uncommon for an aluminum shaft to be oscillating 10-15 yards downrange, while a carbon shaft usually stops flexing within five yards. This factor negates the need to produce carbon shafts with a multitude of different spine values. Most manufactures make only three spine sizes, which is enough to accommodate draw weights of 35-90 pounds. With aluminum arrows, each spine value performs well in a much narrower range of draw weights. Selecting the aluminum shaft size that's just right for your bow is therefore a more difficult task. It often requires substantial trial and error shooting because Easton's arrow selection charts usually list five choices of acceptable spine values for any given draw weight.

Weight Consistency

Advantage Aluminum. The mass weight of every aluminum shaft in a given size is nearly identical. That's not always true with carbon. Within a set of 12 carbon shafts, it's not uncommon for the weight of individual arrows to vary by as much as 10-15 grains.

Straightness

Advantage Aluminum. Most aluminum arrows have a straightness factor of plus or minus 2 to 3 one-thousandths of an inch. Carbon arrows have a greater range of straightness, from 1 to 6 one-thousandths of an inch. The straighter the shaft, the higher its price.

Penetration

Advantage Carbon. Carbon is a stronger material than aluminum and, therefore, carbon arrows can be made with thinner walls and smaller diameters. Carbon stops flexing soon after leaving the bow and carbon arrows fly faster because the shafts weigh less than aluminum. These factors all combine to give carbon the advantage in penetration. However, for most whitetail hunters shooting well-tuned bows in the 55-65 pound range, penetration is a minor issue at best.

Price

Advantage Aluminum. Most pro shops sell a dozen finished aluminum arrows for $40-$65, depending on the shaft model selected. Most finished carbon arrows sell for $50-$125 per dozen, with the straightest shafts fetching the highest prices.

Reliability

Advantage Aluminum. Easton has been producing high-quality aluminum arrows for decades. Today's leading carbon arrow makers, on the other hand, have been at their game only a few years. They're learning, experimenting and improving their products every year. But as mentioned above, every carbon arrow maker uses a manufacturing process that's at least somewhat different from that of his competitors. So no two brands of carbon arrows are quite the same. Some are constructed with three layers of fibers, while others use five layers. Some manufacturers use a weave pattern. Some grind or sand the surface of finished shafts. Some manufacturers produce carbon arrows that allow you to insert supplemental weights into the shaft to bolster arrow weight. All these variables suggest that it's wise to investigate several brands of carbon arrows before deciding which is best for you.

50   Are Mechanical Broadheads for You?

BY THOMAS L. TORGET

Expandables account for more than one-third of all broadheads sold. But they're not for everybody.

Today nothing is simple. Technology improvements come at warp speed. Before it's out of its box, a new computer is obsolete, overtaken by something faster, stronger, better. Some say it's the same with broadheads. Long-established models like Muzzy, Thunderhead, Satellite and Rocky Mountain—while still effective—are . . . well . . . kinda boring. Perhaps it's time to toss them aside and try something more high-tech, like a broadhead with blades that lie along the ferrule during flight and then explode open upon impact. Could this be a better mousetrap?

That's certainly the intent behind expandable heads. By reducing the effect of wind planing, a mechanical broadhead's flight characteristics resemble those of a field point. When the expandable reaches its target, the blades pop open.

But as Mr. Murphy has taught us, anything that can go wrong will go wrong, at least some of the time. Logic says that a mechanical device is inherently less reliable than the equivalent nonmechanical device. So any broadhead that operates with moving parts will fail more often than an equivalent head without moving parts. "Equivalent" is the key. The quality of materials and the manufacturing process used to produce a broadhead are as important as its design. That's why today's marketplace includes fixed-blade heads and mechanical heads that are both superb and mediocre.

Let's consider three key factors: flight characteristics, reliability and penetration.

Flight Characteristics

Advantage Expandable. Arrows launched from Fred Bear's 65-pound recurve likely traveled about 180 feet per second. That's 100 feet per second slower than many of today's fastest shooting compounds. While a lightning-quick bow offers many advantages, it can be tricky to tune, particularly with broadhead-tipped arrows. The difficulty in achieving tight groups with hunting arrows is what's driving sales of expandable heads. Because most modern compounds shoot well right out of the box, many archers who've entered this sport during the past five years have never mastered the nuances of fine-tuning their bow to achieve superb arrow flight. For these hunters, expandables offer great appeal. A hunter can use field points right up to opening day, then swap practice points for expandable broadheads and know his hunting arrows will be on target.

Even the most low-profile fixed-blade head is subject to wind-planing as it sails downrange. The larger the blade surface, the more wind-planing occurs. Most fixed-blade heads have sections of the blade removed, a design feature that mitigates this effect. A knowledgeable archer can tune the hottest-shooting bow to handle a fixed-blade head like the Muzzy or Thunderhead, in 75 to 130-grain size. With larger and heavier fixed-blade heads, especially when combined with a bow shooting at speeds higher than 250 feet per second, the challenge of achieving good arrow flight is magnified.

Reliability

Advantage Fixed. A fixed-blade head is always open and ready to carry out its mission. There is no spring, lever or other device that must perform as intended before the broadhead's blades begin cutting. Early versions of expandables featured designs more complex than today's products. The reliability of some of those heads was fair at best, a factor that gave expandables a black eye early on.

Today's mechanical heads are much improved. Designs are simpler and quality control has been tightened. But because there are mechanics involved in springing the cutting edges into position, the failure rate for expandables will always be greater than zero.

Penetration

Advantage Fixed. Kinetic energy (a function of the arrow's mass weight and the bow's draw weight) is the key to arrow penetration. Some of the kinetic energy imparted to the arrow by the bow is consumed by the process of springing open the blades of a mechanical head. And because most expandables are still opening as the broadhead pushes through the animal, movement of blades against bone and tissue as the blades open saps additional kinetic energy. The result can be an arrow that runs out of kinetic energy before creating an exit hole.

The absence of an exit hole, combined with a small entry hole, makes for a tough trailing task. On the other hand, when an expandable punches through the far side of a deer (as it will usually will), trailing can be a snap because most expandables create larger wounds than most fixed-blade heads.

It's Your Call

In just a few years, expandable heads have captured 35 percent to 40 percent of the broadhead market. That wouldn't happen if these products didn't meet a need in the marketplace. For any hunter who lacks the knowledge, time or inclination to fine-tune his equipment, a top-quality expandable broadhead offers many advantages. As for me, I'm sticking with my old reliable fixed-blade Muzzys and Thunderheads. I know they work every time without exception. That gives me peace of mind as I ponder what will happen when that world-class 16-pointer tiptoes through my shooting lane later this fall. (This is the year it's gonna happen! Honest!)

51   Glassing the Deep Woods

BY BILL MCRAE

The biggest bucks live in the thickest cover, but if you're not bowhunting with a good binocular,
you'll never see them.

Y ou won't need a binocular here," the would-be guide said, "because the cover
is so thick that you can't see more than 20 yards in any event."

Being stubborn, I took my battered 7x50 anyway, and later that day when
it allowed me to see through intervening branches and spot a well-camouflaged
whitetail buck at, yes, 20 yards, I was glad that I did.

Like most hunters, the guide thought that binoculars are for long-range
viewing only and, therefore, have no place in thick brush or deep-woods habitats.
Nothing could be more erroneous. Dense cover of any type—usually consisting of
a disordered mass of twigs, branches, leaves, evergreen needles and tree trunks,
punctuated by deep shadows and blinding bright spots—is a very confusing environment to the unaided human eye, which is why many species of game often
hide in such places. The good news is that binoculars, for reasons that I'll explain,
allow our eyes to selectively pierce the clutter of such places and see what's really
there.

Cover Penetration

The ability of binoculars to penetrate or "see through" thick cover is so astounding
that, although I've known about it for years, it still boggles my mind. My latest experience with this magical phenomenon happened one morning in April while I
was hunting spring turkeys at the famous YO Ranch near Kerrville, Texas. My entirely natural ground blind consisted of live junipers with branches cut from
nearby trees to fill the gaps and hide me from the sharp eyes of approaching
turkeys.

The turkeys weren't cooperating that day. So I entertained myself by learning
to use the remarkable mapping features of a new Lowrance GPS (Global Positioning System) that I was field testing and intermittently watching the various black
buck, sika, and axis and whitetail deer, which meandered past the blind. The amazing thing was that, while the animals couldn't see me (although they apparently
smelled me) I could catch only glimpses of them with my naked eye; by using my
8x42 binocular, I could look through the cover, in practically any direction, and
see whole animals clearly.

Since you're probably not in the woods right now, a good way to experiment with and experience this unusual phenomenon is by looking through a Venetian blind having one-inch slats tilted so that only very narrow slits (about ⅛-inch wide) are left open. While standing back several feet, first note that you can see almost nothing through the blind with your naked eyes. Then using a binocular, with at least 30mm objective lenses and focused for about 20 yards, look through the blind again. You'll be amazed to find that, while the out-of-focus slats appear very narrow and indistinct, nearly 100 percent of the sharply focused background will be clearly visible.

A similar and equally revealing experiment is to poke a pencil-sized hole in each of two pieces of dark-colored paper and to place them over the binocular's objective lenses. Now, with at least 90 percent of the lens areas covered, you'll find that the binocular's field of view is not decreased and that you can still see everything quite clearly. The only noticeable difference will be that objects appear somewhat darker.

How can such things be? Without getting into mind-numbing details about how optics work, I can say that it has to do with the large light-gathering and image-forming areas of the binocular's objective lenses versus the tiny light-gathering and image-forming areas of our eye lenses. In low light, our eye pupils have lens openings of about five millimeters. This means that very small obstructions, such as twigs or blades of grass as narrow as five millimeters, can at times obscure objects from our view.

In contrast, the 50mm objectives of a 7x50 binocular have light-gathering areas 100 times larger than our eyes, and therefore, it takes opaque objects at least 50mm wide to block their views. The clincher is that a binocular needs only a tiny hole in the intervening cover to gather enough light to form usable images.

Depth of Field and Stereopsis

Other factors that help us see better in thick cover with binoculars are their shallow depths of field and their increased stereopsis. Depth of field is the area, from near to far, in which objects appear acceptably sharp when a lens is focused for a particular distance. Human eyes, because of their low magnification (1X), have lots of depth of field, which is good for everyday living; otherwise, nature wouldn't have made them so. The problem, when trying to spot well-camouflaged game in thick cover, is that having lots of depth of field makes similar objects—such as a buck's antlers surrounded by brush—merge into homogeneous mosaics that strain our eyes and befuddle our brains, which is how camouflage works.

Binoculars, because of their higher magnifications, have very shallow depths of field, which make sharply focused objects (even of similar color, tone and texture) stand out in stark contrast against their surroundings. I first observed this while photographing wildlife with long telephoto lenses, but it works equally well when glassing with binoculars. The proper scanning technique is to slowly shift the focus from near to far, focal plane by focal plane, and back again.

Stereopsis is depth perception that results from our individual eyes viewing objects from slightly different positions. The farther the eyes are apart the greater the stereopsis, and vice versa. As with depth of field, this, too, helps our eyes separate well camouflaged animals from their surroundings. Any binocular will increase the eyes' natural stereopsis by magnifying the viewed image, but certain types are better than others. Inverted porro prism models (with their objective lenses closer together than the eyepiece) are the least effective. Roof prism models (with their objectives lenses and eyepieces in straight alignment) are better. And, full-sized porro prism models (with their objective lenses farther apart than the eyepieces) are best.

Opening the Shadows

Woodland species, such as deer, elk, moose and bear, love deep shade so much that, unless feeding, they spend practically all their time under its cool concealing mantle. Logically, one would think that they are avoiding human hunters, but there is more to it than that, because even in national parks where animals haven't been hunted for generations and, thus, have no fear of man, their habits remain the same.

Perhaps bright light hurts their eyes—it hurts most people's eyes and animals' eyes are much more light-sensitive than ours. Unlike people, animals don't have hat brims or hands with which to shade their eyes. Therefore, when they want to keep the sun out of their eyes so as to see better, they get in the shade. Also, they are very adept at shading their eyes with their ears or, in the case of bull moose, their antlers.

Furthermore, animals instinctively, or perhaps intelligently, know that shade makes them harder to see and, therefore, affords protection from predators, including man. It is analogous to being in a dimly lit room and watching people outside in the bright sunlight—you can see them, but they can't see you. As if that weren't enough, shady spots afford protection from the elements, such as wind, rain, snow, cold and heat.

To us as hunters trying to spot game, this means that (except during the brief periods of dawn and dusk when animals are moving about feeding), we must eschew the bright places and turn our eyes and, especially, our binoculars toward the shadows. A revealing experiment here, which also serves to check the apparent brightness of optical instruments, is to stand outside in the bright sunlight and to peer through an open doorway into a dimly lit room. If you are several yards from the doorway, you'll see little or nothing with your unaided eye, whereas, a binocular will open the shadows, allowing you to see the interior of the room quite well. This is precisely what happens when binoculars are used to search dark woodland environs for game.

For example, once while prowling a thick lodgepole-pine forest glassing for elk, I spotted a big six-point bull sleeping flat on his side with his head on the ground in a mosaic of mottled shade and sunlight. Having caught him napping, I moved closer and shot him with my weapon of choice, a 35mm camera. But, I've had similar experiences when hunting with guns and bows. Another time, I glassed a very dark shadow that, through my binocular, turned out to be a black bear.

Two factors contribute to a binocular's ability to open the darkest shadows: The first has to do with the way that our eye pupils automatically adjust to different light levels. In bright light, they constrict, admitting less image-forming light, thereby making surrounding objects appear darker. While, in dim light, they dilate (enlarge) to admit more image-forming light and make objects appear brighter.

Accordingly, when we are surrounded by bright light, our eye pupils constrict, darkening everything in sight and causing shaded areas to appear black and, therefore, visually impenetrable. But, when we look through a binocular, the eye cups and the blackened interiors of the barrels exclude the extraneous brightness, which allows our eye pupil to adjust for the lower light levels within the shadows, thus, enabling us to see detail. A related fact is that we can see better in heavy cover on cloudy days because there is less contrast.

The second factor that makes objects in shaded area easier to see when viewed through binoculars involves the intrinsic brightness of the particular instrument used. Some binoculars produce brighter images than others, and the brighter the image the better you can see into dark shadows.

Choosing the Right Binocular

Any binocular of any type will give the deep-woods hunter a distinct advantage, but, as we've seen, certain optical and mechanical attributes combine to make certain binoculars perform better than others. These factors include magnification, objective diameter, body style with regard to prism types and, above all, optical quality.

MAGNIFICATION: If you've been expecting me to recommend low-powered binoculars, such as 7X or 8X, for deep-woods use, I won't disappoint you. They are indeed best, first, because their inherently wider fields of view will allow you to glass more area, and, second, because at the relatively short viewing distances encountered, little magnification is needed. I will admit, however, that 10X binoculars do have a slight advantage when it comes to penetrating thick brush, distinguishing well-camouflaged animals, and peering into deep shadows. So, 10X binocular users needn't feel underprivileged.

LARGE OBJECTIVE LENSES: An immutable law of optics is that, all else being equal, larger objective lenses are optically superior. They produce brighter images by delivering more light to the user's eyes. They produce sharper images for reasons that are too complex to explain here. And, as explained earlier, in thick cover, it takes larger obstructions to block their view. Fifty millimeter objectives are best, but, since binoculars having them tend to be big and heavy, size- and weight-conscious users will be better served by smaller objectives of 35mm to 42mm.

BODY STYLE: Also as previously explained, full-sized porro prism binoculars, with their widely spread objective lenses, are superior to either roof prism or inverted porro prism models. Beside having greater stereopsis, their offset barrels act like small periscopes allowing the user to look around the edges of intervening objects, such as trees with diameters of up to about five inches. The result is that you can sometimes see game that might otherwise remain hidden to narrower-spaced objectives or to your unaided eyes. To put this in perspective, I must tell you that the 8x42 binocular that so successfully penetrated the cover surrounding my blind at the YO Ranch in Texas was a roof prism model.

OPTICAL QUALITY: This catchall term embraces all the factors that, when positive, combine to make people say "Wow!" when first looking through certain binoculars. So many factors exist—ranging from meticulous workmanship to the use of high-grade glass in the manufacture of optical components—that it would take a giant textbook to cover them all.

I hope that you are now convinced that you need a binocular in thick cover. But, simply carrying a binocular will not automatically change your hunting fortunes. You must use it, and use it often—even when the visibility is limited to just a few yards. Given our deeply ingrained beliefs that binoculars are for long-range use only, you'll find, as I have, that you must literally force yourself to do so. You'll also find, as I have, that doing so pays dividends.

Part Eight
Making the Shot,
Recovering the Game

If there's anything worse than making countless hunts and not seeing any game, it's having a shot and blowing it. And when that shot involves a true trophy of a lifetime, such as a big whitetail buck, the pain . . . Well, you just don't want to know!

52 Six Reasons We Miss Deer

BY THOMAS TORGET

Getting close to a deer is the easy part. Turning a shooting opportunity into a tagged whitetail is when things get interesting.

I'm convinced that Mr. Murphy coined his law ("Anything that can go wrong will go wrong") while trudging away from a treestand after yet another botched bowhunt. Murphy's law captures the essence of this sport's challenge. Bowhunt just one season and you quickly learn that getting close to a deer isn't nearly as difficult as finishing the job once you're there.

When you place your body within 20 yards of a deer's body, you give him a huge advantage he doesn't enjoy when he's 100 yards from you. At close range, the mere hint of odor, noise or movement will send that deer racing away. And when I say hint, that's precisely what I mean. Move your hand at the wrong time or let your treestand squeak ever-so-slightly and Mr. Deer will be near no more. If he's a young buck, the experience will make you scowl. But if he's the great-grandfather of a young buck, the experience will make you cranky for a very long time.

Of the multitude of reasons bowhunters bungle their moment of truth, these six miscues are the most common:

Miscue #1: Mediocre scent control. Friends, I hate to say it but it's true: You stink, I stink, we all stink. And many whitetails are alive today because of it. A single whiff of human odor will send even a half-witted yearling racing away in panic. Inadequate scent control is perhaps the surest way of all to foul up a high-potential stand site, not just for today's hunt, but for days or even weeks to come.

I'm continually amazed at the number of bowhunters who—due to laziness or ignorance—fail to take all steps necessary to minimize the amount of human odor they carry with them into the field. While it's never possible to totally eliminate human scent, it's quite possible to minimize it. Think of your body's odor as the music from a radio. While you may not be able to turn the sound off, you can certainly turn it down.

Comprehensive scent control is—I admit—a royal pain in the rear. It requires tedious effort, and then you have to do it all over again. But skip a single step and you compromise your chances for success. You never know when the season's best buck may tiptoe toward your stand from downwind. If you're stinky that day, you'll wish you stayed home to mow the yard.

Minimizing human odor begins by laundering all hunting clothes in unscented soap and storing them in scent-proof containers such as stout trash compactor bags. Many hunters wash their camo shirts and trousers with scentless soap, but then launder underwear and socks in regular detergent. While that makes for clean socks, it also makes for socks that emit perfumed odors that are sure to spook deer. Use unscented soap for everything you carry into the field, including underclothes, hats, belts, face nets, handkerchiefs and backpacks. Never wear the same clothes on two consecutive days, and shower and change outerwear and underwear between morning and evening hunts whenever possible. Scent-absorbing garments such as those offered by Scent-Lok provide valuable protection against spreading human odor in your hunting area. I've worn Scent-Lok suits for several seasons and have watched countless deer pass on my downwind side with no hint that I'm near. That didn't happen in the days before I wore Scent-Lok.

Treestand placement is a critical component of scent control. Always place stands downwind of where you expect deer to pass and look for opportunities to increase your stand's height. Hanging stands just a few feet higher than the normal 15 to 18 feet sharply reduces your risk of being scented. The higher your body, the farther its scent plume travels before gravity brings it to ground level. The calmer the wind speed, the more important this becomes.

Miscue #2: Noisy equipment. A deer's ears are his second-best defense system. At close range, these mega-sized sound receptors can detect the tiniest peep from a bow, treestand or other gear. And because such metallic sounds are unfamiliar to a deer, his reaction is invariably alarm, which is usually followed by panic and departure.

Most bowhunters are unaware of how much racket their equipment makes. Next time you're on the practice range, pay attention to the noise of your buddies' bows. You'll hear creaking cams, twanging strings and rattling accessories—sounds you and they aren't hearing because you've become so accustomed to them. But a deer is not accustomed to those sounds. So when he hears them at close range, he knows it's time to be elsewhere.

Whitetails pay scant attention to sounds they expect to hear, such as rumbling farm tractors and rustling squirrels. But any noise that's unfamiliar to them—no matter how low its volume—will alarm them. Squeaky arrow rests, "groaning" treestand seats and other unnatural sounds have saved the lives of many a deer. Some years ago, an unexpected squeak cost me an opportunity at a trophy class, nontypical Texas whitetail. I'd lured the deer to me with my grunt call and watched in gleeful anticipation as he stepped to within 10 yards of my stand, turned broadside and looked away. If ever there was a can't-miss opportunity, this was it. But just as I reached full draw, my finger tab moved a quarter-inch along the arrow nock and emitted a barely audible (to me) squeak. In an eyeblink, the buck became a blur of gray, disappearing into the brush, never again to be seen by me or any other hunter on that ranch. It was a painful lesson that taught me the importance of inspecting my gear for any and every possible source of noise. (I corrected this particular problem by wiping a light coat of Vaseline on my arrow shafts between the end of the fletching and the tip of the nock.)

To soundproof your bow, lubricate cams and wheels and install moleskin on your sight window and arrow rest. Tighten all screws and nuts on sights, quivers and other bow-mounted accessories. A loose nut will rattle loudly at the instant you release your bow string, causing a deer to instinctively duck beneath your arrow. Test treestands near ground level for squeaks and creaks and other noises. A combination of lubrication, Teflon washers and duct tape will silence most sounds.

Miscue #3: Incomplete concealment. Some hunters believe if they minimize human odor and quiet their gear, it's only a matter of time before they'll be posing for pictures at the deer camp game pole. Perhaps. But flashbulbs won't pop if a hunter doesn't first spend the time and energy to ensure complete concealment of his treestand, gear and body.

Set up each stand with the assumption that every passing whitetail will stare directly at it, then cross your fingers and hope you're wrong. Even if a deer looks up at your stand, he's not likely to "see" you if you and the stand are fully camouflaged. Achieving that level of concealment begins by positioning the stand in a location that has ample foliage behind and to each side of you. Try to place stands among a clump of trees rather than in a single tree that's isolated from others. If you have a multitude of branches to your rear and sides and you don't move, it's very tough for deer to find you.

In late season, when leaves have fallen, supplement background cover with camo netting. And move stands higher in late season because of the absence of foliage. Whether it's early or late season, always set up with the sun behind you or to your side. If an approaching deer has to squint into bright sunshine to find you, he probably won't.

Complete concealment includes all of your body, not just your torso. Camo gloves and face nets are absolutely mandatory for any bowhunter hoping to stage a surprise ambush. If your hands and face never moved, the disadvantage of not camouflaging them would be reduced. But it's your face and hands that move most when you're on stand. So conceal them. And make certain all the equipment you carry to your stand also is camouflaged and positioned out of sight of passing game.

Miscue #4: Range estimation goofs. An arrow's arc as it flies toward its target is more severe than many bowhunters realize. The tendency to underestimate this factor is especially common among treestand hunters because of the downward angle of their shots. Add to this our inherent inability to accurately judge distance and you have a recipe for missed shots at game.

A gun hunter can misjudge distance to a deer by 50 yards or more and still make a killing shot. But a bowhunter's guess must be almost 100 percent accurate to ensure a clean kill. Even when a deer is just 30 yards away, if the archer's brain tells him "26 yards" or "33 yards," the result will likely be a complete miss or—much worse—a bad hit.

There are two keys to minimizing range estimation goofs. The first is to constantly practice estimating distances. When shopping, pick out a car in the parking lot, estimate the yardage and pace it off. Guess distances to the mailbox, street signs, and other objects in your yard and neighborhood. Practice in low light, in open terrain and in thickly wooded areas. Then practice some more.

The second key to avoiding distance errors is to use a range finder. While more expensive, laser range finders are far superior to dial-operated models. Laser units work in the dark and give an instant reading that's plus or minus one yard of the actual distance. Personally, I wouldn't bowhunt without a laser range finder.

When setting up a treestand, use your range finder to gauge distances to game trails and other areas where deer might appear. If a buck shows up near that game trail, it's much easier to discern that he's about five yards beyond the trail than to accurately discern that he's 28 yards away.

Miscue #5: Failure to interpret body language. When the boss is in a foul mood, you know it at a glance. His furrowed brow, tightened jaw and glaring stare suggest that this may not be the perfect moment to ask for a raise. Like humans, animals convey much about their mood through body language. When a deer is calm, his movements are easy and steady. When alerted, however, his chin comes up, eyes dart and ears twist left and right. There is nothing "easy and steady" about his posture or movement.

Understanding the mood of a deer that's near your stand is important because it gives clues about what may happen next. Knowing what's coming guides you in deciding whether and when to take your shot.

Let's say an approaching buck is ambling slowly, nibbling on leaves here and there as he calmly moves along the trail toward your stand. This is a relaxed animal and unless you alert him to your presence, he'll remain that way, allowing you to patiently wait for the very best shooting opportunity.

If, however, that deer is trotting toward you with head held high, he's likely a disturbed whitetail. Or if he's walking briskly, his movements are jerky and he's constantly looking around, you're watching a very nervous deer. If he pauses in your shooting lane, you'd better be ready because it's now or never.

Likewise, if the deer approaches in a calm manner but becomes skittish after stepping into bow range, he's probably detected your presence. Get ready to shoot because Mr. Deer is fixin' to leave.

Studying hunting videos is a great way to hone your ability to read whitetail body language. Buy or rent a dozen videos and carefully study how deer react to unexpected noises, scents and sights.

Miscue #6: Failure to concentrate. Early one October morning several seasons ago, I had a slam-dunk shot at a six-point buck that was calmly feeding 18 yards in front of my stand. For some reason I became fixated on the perfect symmetry of his antlers. I recall pondering how nice his rack would look in photos because it was so perfectly balanced. These thoughts filled my mind as I came to full draw, released and watched my arrow sail over the buck's back. I stared in disbelief as he raced away, taking his symmetrical antlers with him.

Just as a place kicker sometimes misses a chip-shot field goal, bowhunters sometimes botch perfect shooting opportunities because they fail to concentrate. After a miscue, most field goal kickers and bowhunters could probably hit their targets 20 times in a row. But the only shot that really counts is the first one.

To put an arrow through a whitetail's chest, a bowhunter must be 100 percent focused on the job at hand. That means picking a dime-size spot on the deer's body and blocking from your vision everything other than that dime. It means concentrating on your posture, grip and arm position so that everything is identical to the shots you take on the practice range. And most important of all, total concentration means continuing to focus on that dime until after your arrow strikes its target.

Unconsciously jerking the bow aside at the moment of release in order to see your arrow hit its target is a common bugaboo. The problem here is lack of concentration. While there's no substitute for the experience of shooting at live game, concentrating intently during practice sessions is the key to training your mind to block out extraneous information. I do this by shooting only at deer targets, varying the distance on every shot and using a single arrow. The routine mimics the conditions I face in the field. The use of a single arrow forces me to concentrate on each shot because—just like when it really counts—one shot is all I get.

Tactics at a Glance:

- Bowhunting is an up close and personal sport magnifying even the smallest miscues.
- Comprehensive scent control is of utmost importance. Wash your body and all your clothing in odor eliminating detergent.
- Deer pay little attention to sounds they expect to hear like tractors, squirrels, etc. Foreign sounds are another matter.
- Range misestimation costs hunters more deer than any other factor. Practice constantly—even while walking down the street.

53   After the Shot

BY BILL BUCKLEY

Knowing what to do after hitting a big game animal is rarely cut and dried, but if you follow these common-sense tips, your recovery rate will soar.

If you bowhunt big game long enough, you'll soon realize that putting meat in the freezer actually involves two separate hunts: one that culminates in a shot, the other that leads you to the fallen animal. While being unsuccessful with the first certainly won't ruin your day, failure on the second hunt will. That's one of many reasons why it's so important to know how to trail the game you shoot.

The good news is, unlike Tonto you don't have to be so accomplished that you can tell how many horses passed through a canyon yesterday, and whether one of the riders was a one-eyed drifter with a bad left leg. In fact, in most cases all you have to do to recover a mortally wounded animal is exercise some common sense and lots of patience. But you'd better be paying attention once the arrow leaves your bow. That's when things start happening in a hurry, and the more information you can remember, the better off you'll be.

Let's say a buck stops 20 yards from your treestand and, at the shot, bolts into the brush. What should you do first to have the best odds of finding that animal? Certainly not let out a war whoop or the Rebel Yell (that comes later once you're standing over the carcass). Instead, all you should be concentrating on is the deer's path of departure. Watch carefully where he goes and disappears in the brush, then track his progress with your ears. Listen for that loud crash, followed by abrupt silence, that marks the final fall. If it doesn't come, then make note of the last place you heard the buck running and visualize the direction he took. Ground hunters have to rely much more on their ears than eyes, but regardless of your vantage, concentrating on the escape route and committing it to memory will make an easy trailing job easier, and a difficult one possible.

Now relax for a while—at least a few minutes for your adrenaline rush to subside and the strength to return to your legs. There's never any reason to rush down a tree, and you might as well not add to the casualty list by slipping off tree steps. But it is necessary to make as little noise as possible. Avoid any metallic clanking on your stand, talking, blowing your nose, whatever. As long as the animal doesn't know you're around, he's not likely to go far, even if your shot placement was less than ideal.

Use this time to relive the shot and picture how the deer reacted to being hit. There's a good chance you saw where you hit him, but even if you didn't you can tell a lot from his body language. If the buck bolted by running flat out, not by bounding away, and crashed blindly through the brush, you can almost be assured of a heart/lung hit. If, on the other hand, he hunched up and ran slowly away, you hit the paunch. A deer that bounds off as if you spooked him might be mortality wounded, but might only have a flesh wound. Or you could have grazed him or missed completely. An inspection of your arrow will paint a more complete picture.

Once you're on the ground, and still next to the tree, mark the direction you last heard or saw the deer by scraping your heel in the dirt or by laying an arrow on the ground. If you're ground hunting, use surveyor's tape to mark your location (preferably off the ground for increased visibility), then the direction of the animal's departure. Now quietly proceed to where the deer was standing when you shot.

An arrow that passes through the animal and sticks into the ground can give you immediate confirmation of the shot you think you made. A shaft covered with bright-red blood, often with small air bubbles, indicates a lung hit. Darker blood might mean a liver shot—lethal, although the deer could travel quite a ways before dropping. If the blood covering the arrow looks muddy and gritty, you've almost surely made a gut-shot, and the smell of the shaft will quickly confirm it. Another sign of a bad hit is an arrow lined with fat and hair and only a little bit of blood. This indicates a flesh wound. If the hairs are long and dark, chances are the arrow passed through the brisket. In any case of a flesh wound, your chances of recovering the deer are slim to none. More than likely the animal is in no danger of dying.

Even should the arrow stay in the deer when he takes off, chances are whatever is sticking out will break off where it meets the body soon after the animal enters thick brush. Find that part of the shaft and you'll get a good idea of what tracking job you're facing. If the broken shaft contains the broadhead, then you know you got complete penetration; what blood you find on the arrow will tell you where you hit. If the shaft has fletching, then deduct its length from how long the rest of your arrows are and you'll see how much penetration you got. Hitting a deer's shoulder might lead to poor penetration, but if enough of the shaft makes it through to enter the lungs, the deer should be dead. Broken arrow or complete pass-through—what clues they give you will tell you what to do next.

To Wait or Give Chase?

Most deer-hunting authorities recommend waiting at least a half-hour before moving from your stand, and if you suspect a bad hit, waiting much longer. The fact is, as long as you're quiet it's important to get to the site of the hit while every detail is fresh in your mind. That way you can map out the deer's travel route more exactly. Besides, chances are you know where the arrow struck, and if it was a good shot you've already heard the deer go down. Then sitting on your stand, killing time, won't make the deer any more dead. If your shot was bad, then it's all the more important to get your ducks in a row for the long trailing job ahead.

Let's say your arrow indicates a lung shot and you thought you heard the deer go down. Since you've probably spent the last five to 10 minutes calming down, sneaking down from your stand, and marking where he stood and where he went, there's no benefit to waiting around, especially if it's warm out or daylight is limited. Take a line from your marker and walk directly to where you think it fell, watching out for a blood trail, as well as a body, once you near your intended spot. If you reach the spot but can't find the deer, no worry. Go immediately back to the site of the hit (which you've already marked) and walk slowly along the deer's exit route, looking for signs of blood or cut hair.

If you know you made a bad hit, or debris on your arrow makes the shot suspect, then a different approach is necessary. Quietly follow the route the deer took and scan the ground for blood and hair. Don't be surprised if you have to go 20 to 30 yards or more before locating sign. But once you do, stop, mark the spot with surveyor's tape, then scan ahead for the bedded deer. A gut-shot animal won't go far before bedding. If you don't see or hear it, continue until you find the next blood sign, then mark it too. Should the quantity of blood be significantly more than the first sighting, there's a good chance the hit was more lethal than you suspected, so stay on the trail, marking sign, until you either find the buck or decide, with a dwindling blood trail, that it's better to quit and come back later. There's no sense having a deer lie dead, not field-dressed, any longer than necessary.

But if the blood sign remains scant, and you still think or know the shot was bad, then sneak silently back to your stand and wait, or go back to the truck and grab some water or coffee. You'll want to give the deer at least a couple hours before returning to pick up the trail.

Locating the first few signs of blood is worth the risk of bumping a badly hit deer because it's important to be able to get on its trail upon your return. With two blood spots you can draw a line and determine which direction it's heading. And fresh blood is easier to find than dried, which it's likely to be if you have to wait long to resume trailing. The weather might also turn for the worse in the interim; if it starts to rain or snow before your return, at least you'll waste no time picking up the trail.

In fact, weather should decide how long you let a wounded deer rest more than the sign on your arrow. If it's been raining or is about to rain or snow, the wet earth could dilute the blood trail and obliterate it. So you'll have no choice but to take up the trail almost immediately. A smart hunter will wait next to the first blood sign and gauge the weather's effect on it, then decide how long he can wait. A dry windy day can similarly hamper your efforts if you wait too long. Leaves with blood sign can overturn, and the drying blood will turn black and blend in with the forest floor. Dry snow, on the other hand, preserves a blood trail for a long time, not to mention the added benefit of being able to follow the deer's tracks when the blood trail thins out. Then waiting four or more hours can only work to your advantage.

But its effect on a blood trail is only one weather consideration. The other is how the weather will affect the meat if the animal dies long before you find it. It may be smart from a tracking standpoint to leave a questionably hit animal in the late afternoon until the next morning, but if the night is warm and the deer dies soon after you shot it, then you've just wasted a lot of good meat. Whenever I have to choose between risking tracking a deer too soon or waiting too long and ruining the meat, I'll opt for the former every time. I'm not about to waste that much meat.

Walking the Line

Sometimes a lung-hit deer will leave an obvious blood trail in his wake, but more often than not, even well-hit animals take a little more woodsmanship to find. And the hardest blood to find is usually the first drop. That's because it takes time for the internal bleeding to start leaking from the wound or through the animal's nose. Arrow placement also determines how quickly a blood trail will form. A deer hit in the heart or lower lungs will leave blood faster than one hit high in the lungs. A liver or paunch shot will take much longer to show blood, and then in less quantities. That's why you've got to be patient and not get discouraged if you don't find a blood trail right away. And why you have to be careful how you mark a trail and where you step in locating the next piece of the puzzle.

On almost any ground, where the deer bolts after being hit should show up in the form of splayed hoof marks and kicked up dirt and leaves. The drier the earth, the harder they are to see, but they are there if you look closely enough. If you can, follow these prints and they'll eventually lead to blood. If newly fallen leaves make that impossible, stand in the exact spot the deer was hit, then walk toward where you saw it disappear. Go slowly and bend down so you can study every detail on the ground. The first blood you find might only be a speck. Once you hit the first drop, mark it plainly so you'll be able to look back and refer to it.

Be sure to stand to one side of the deer's trail so you don't obliterate any sign. That can't be emphasized enough, and is why having any more than two people trail wounded game a big mistake. Oftentimes successfully following a blood trail depends on detecting minute flecks of blood that can so easily be stepped on and lost. Also, unless the blood trail is heavy and you know the deer dropped nearby, mark every drop you find, even if it's only five feet from the last one. That will save you from having to retrace your steps if you run out of fresh blood. Once you have two or three blood drops marked, you can draw a line on where the deer headed. At this point it never hurts to look ahead once in a while. You'll often spot the deer's white underbelly or antler in the distance, making further painstaking tracking unnecessary. Or, if it's still alive, you might be able to stalk in for a finishing shot instead of bumping it, or back off if it looks like it could travel far once jumped.

If you start running out of blood sign on the ground, pay attention to the sides of bushes and tall grass, where blood seeping out of the wound may rub against them. Also look carefully just past any obstacle the deer has to cross, like a deadfall or fence. A wounded animal having to jump over them often jars loose drops of blood. Although small drops of blood few and far between aren't positive signs of a mortally wounded animal, that doesn't mean he's not dead. Some wounds plug up fast, and a deer could be badly hemorrhaging internally yet show few outward signs. So don't give up. The one rule I've found to be invariably true is that if a wounded deer keeps following established game trails and you don't find it dead within 200 yards, chances are it's not hit well and will lead you on a wild goose chase.

Sometimes a blood trail will lead you to an intersection of deer trails or to an opening, but you can't tell which direction he went. If making narrow sweeps of the ground ahead fails to turn up obvious sign, return to the last blood drop and look at its shape. Blood dropped from a moving animal will usually splatter, if only a little bit, in the direction the animal is going. Then you can concentrate your efforts in whatever direction the blood points you and maybe pick up another drop 20 to 30 feet farther on.

When a blood trail peters out and you can't find another drop no matter how many times you look, take a line with the last drops you marked and walk ahead, eyeing the ground for blood or tracks, but mainly looking for the body. Then check out any thickets you see where it might have bedded, and any streams it might have crossed, where you can find a hoof print embedded in a muddy bank or water recently dripped on to rocks or leaves. And if all that comes to not, try walking in grids or widening circles to cover a big area. On a few occasions I've located fallen deer long after I lost the blood trail by doing this.

When all else fails, call up a few hunting buddies and return in force to the last sign you found. Then spread out and methodically cover as much ground as you can. If you still can't find the buck, he'll probably live to see another day. At least you'll know you did everything you could to find him.

Fact is, nothing makes a tracking job easier than a well-placed shot, and you should always try to do whatever it takes to ensure you hit a deer in the right spot. Ultimately, that's the best advice on blood trailing you'll ever receive.

Part Nine
Final Exam—A Bowhunter's Quiz

If this little quiz seems threatening, relax. It's a fun thing that veteran bowhunter Bob Robb has packed with information. No matter how many questions you answer correctly, you'll come out ahead.

54 What Should You Do?
A Friendly Quiz

BY BOB ROBB

O.K. Take out a piece of paper and a No. 2 pencil—it's time for a POP QUIZ on whitetails.

When you consider everything that can go wrong just getting into bow range (usually 30 yards or less) of a whitetail deer, and then all the things that can make you botch even a "gimme" shot, it's a wonder we harvest any deer at all. There are few things in life more difficult, but offhand I'm hard-pressed to think of many. A tax audit, perhaps. Alligator wrestling. Or maybe catching rattlesnakes bare-handed, and putting them into a gunny sack. But not much else.

One way to up your odds on bagging a whitetail this fall is to increase your overall knowledge of deer habitat and behavior, bow shooting, and hunting in general. Take our Bowhunter's Deer Quiz and see how you rate, keeping in mind that there might be—and often is—more than one right answer. You'll find the correct answers to the questions at the end of the quiz on page 318.

1 Scouting is a very important part of any deer hunter's strategy. In anticipation of opening morning, the best time to scout for deer is:
   a) two months before the season opener;
   b) two weeks before the season opens;
   c) one week before the season opens;
   d) not at all, to prevent polluting the area with human scent and activity.

2 Scouting has shown a high deer activity level in a specific location. However, in four mornings and evenings of hard hunting you haven't seen a single deer feeding. What do you do?
   a) hunt an hour longer in the mornings and an hour earlier in the evenings;
   b) hunt the middle of the day only;
   c) hunt all day long, dawn to dusk;
   d) give up and move into another area.

3 You have found a deer "funnel," a narrow gap through a hilltop saddle, that is 100 yards wide with lots of sign. However, you can't seem to anticipate just where the deer will move through and get close enough for a shot. You should:

a) set up several different stands, watch the wind, and plan the hunt accordingly;

b) set up several stands, observe which one the deer pass closest to most often, and sit there;

c) pile up brush, dead limbs, and other natural barriers to form a small fence that will force the deer to funnel past your stand site;

d) use a lure-type deer scent to bring the animals closer to your stand site.

4 The rut is on, and you've found a red-hot scrape in a good deer area. The best place to set up your treestand is:

a) on a trail leading directly to the scrape, about 30 yards from the scrape itself;

b) directly over the scrape;

c) 30 to 50 yards below the scrape;

d) crosswind from what looks like the most heavily-used trail leading to the scrape.

5 A buck is within 30 yards of your stand, feeding slowly. He stops behind a screen of brush, with only his neck protruding. You come to full draw, but the deer doesn't move for nearly a minute. You should now:

a) take the shot;

b) wait for the buck to drop his head, or turn away, let your arrow down, and wait for a better chance;

c) blow a grunt call, hoping to make him move forward;

d) stay at full draw no matter what, and wait.

6 Practice makes perfect in bow shooting. However, improper practice habits can result in bad shooting once the season opens. To increase your field shooting skills, in practice you should:

a) practice from an elevated stand the same height at which you'll be hunting;

b) wear your hunting clothing while practicing;

c) use broadheads, not field points, when doing the final sight-in on your bow;

d) all of the above.

7 You're in the market for a new bow this year. In deciding what to buy, you should:

a) listen to your best hunting buddy, and buy the bow he suggests;

b) read magazine articles and advertisements, and choose a bow based on what they say;

c) visit your local archery pro shop, look over and shoot lots of different bows, and choose the one that "feels" best to you;

d) go for the "he-man" approach, and buy the heaviest poundage bow you can draw—barely.

8 It's two weeks before the season opens, and you haven't taken your bow out of the closet since last fall. To get ready for this year, you should:

a) wait until opening day to mess with it, so you won't change a bow that was shooting good last year;

b) check all screws for tightness, metal parts for rust and wear, string for fraying, and broadheads for sharpness;

c) give the bow a tune-up that includes checking and lubricating parts;

d) shoot at targets with broadhead-tipped arrows after the "tune-up," to ensure perfect arrow flight, and re-sight it in with your hunting broadheads.

9 You're in luck! A friend has given up bowhunting, and offered you his arrows. You should:

a) thank the stars you don't have to buy another dozen expensive shafts this fall;

b) make sure they are the same spine stiffness and length of your current arrows;

c) if they're a different length or spine from what you shoot now, shoot them anyway—arrows are expensive;

d) practice with them with broadheads in place to make sure they fly straight and true for you.

10 The weather has turned unseasonably hot, too hot for most bowhunters, who stay home. But you're dedicated, and want to up your odds. To that end, you should:

a) stay home and avoid the mosquito bites and ticks, as there won't be any deer moving anyway;

b) hunt all day near a water source that scouting has shown to be actively used, especially midday;

c) be sure you're on stand well before daylight and until it's too dark to see, returning to camp for a midday nap;

d) in the evening, set your stand on a travel route between a bedding area and a water source, not a food source.

11 Whitetails have tremendous noses. One of our most difficult tasks as bowhunters is to keep them from smelling us. To that end, we should:

a) always hunt into the wind;

b) use masking scents with regularity;

c) wear freshly-laundered clothing at all times, washed in a non-scented soap and stored away from human odors;

d) lay down several scent trails to and from the stand to confuse a deer's sense of smell.

12 Any day you can get out and hunt is the best day to be hunting, of course. However, if you had a choice, the best day to be out there hunting hard all day is:

a) a beautiful, sunny, "bluebird" day;

b) one with light rain or drizzle, coupled with high overcast skies;

c) during or just after a light snow;

d) the day before a strong storm front passes through.

13 You generally hunt an area of public land that receives fairly heavy hunter pressure. You scouted hard, and found some deer. Your best chance of success in this area is:
   a)   opening day, particularly opening morning;
   b)   the first week of the season;
   c)   the first two weeks of the season;
   d)   the first month of the season.

14 You are buying some new hunting arrows, and can't decide between bright-colored and dull fletching and nocks. Your best choice would be:
   a)   dull-colored shafts, fletching, and nocks, to avoid spooking sharp-eyed deer;
   b)   dull shafts and fletching, but a brightly-colored nock;
   c)   bright fletching and nocks, to make it easier to find your arrows after you've shot them;
   d)   all-white fletching and nocks, to help you actually watch the arrow in flight to the deer.

15 A deer's body language will often help us tell if a shot was a hit or miss. If the deer has been hit, it will probably:
   a)   run off with its tail down between its legs;
   b)   run off with its flag up and head down;
   c)   jump straight up at the sound of the bow, then stand completely still;
   d)   slowly begin walking off, head and ears erect and alert.

16 You've shot a deer, and are sure you hit it solidly. You should now:
   a)   come right down out of the tree and begin looking for blood;
   b)   remain in your tree for several minutes as you recompose your nerves, allowing the deer to run off and bleed to death;
   c)   mark the spot where the deer was standing when you took the shot by either taking careful landmarks, or shooting another arrow into the ground at that same spot;
   d)   jump down out of your tree, dance around excitedly, then begin tracking the deer.

17 You've marked the spot of the deer carefully after the shot, but after several minutes of searching can find no blood for 50 yards. It's now safe to assume that:
   a)   you missed cleanly;
   b)   you only grazed the deer, and need track it no further;
   c)   you hit the deer hard, and need to track it more diligently by following hoof prints, broken twigs, and other sign indicating a running animal;
   d)   mark the spot, and go get help.

18 To bowhunt a specific area productively, you need:
   a)   one treestand, placed in the area where deer seem to be most active;
   b)   two treestands that cover both sides of the most productive-looking area on the land;

  c) a portable treestand that allows flexibility in moving where the deer move;

  d) several treestands placed in both the most likely looking deer-use areas as well as some fringe areas.

19 Selecting the proper broadhead for bowhunting is very important. The most effective broadheads for bowhunting whitetails are:

  a) two-blade, 125-grain, cutting-tip broadheads;

  b) three-blade, 125-grain, chisel-point broadheads;

  c) four-blade, 145-grain, chisel-point broadheads;

  d) any well-constructed broadheads with razor-sharp blades that fly straight and true with your hunting setup, and that comply with state regulations and laws.

20 Whitetails are social creatures, and can often be called in. The most likely way to get a deer to come to you by calling is:

  a) aggressively using rattling antlers in a loud, combative manner;

  b) just tickling the rattling antlers together in a soft, sparring sound;

  c) softly using the grunt tube, generally calling infrequently;

  d) grunting loudly and often.

21 You've hunted hard, but haven't had a shot at a buck. Your area allows the harvest of does, and a fat doe has just stopped broadside 15 yards in front of your stand. What do you do?

  a) just watch her. Shooting does is too embarrassing, and your buddies would rib you unmercifully;

  b) take the shot. Harvesting does is an important part of deer management, and her meat will be delicious;

  c) leave her alone, using her as a possible live decoy for any bucks in the area;

  d) shoo her away, so she won't discourage any bucks who might be in the area.

22 You want to stay in your stand all day, but find it difficult to concentrate or remain comfortable for that length of time. To combat these problems, you could:

  a) bring a paperback book with you to read;

  b) pack along a little food and drink to ward off hunger;

  c) carry a small plastic bottle in case you have to answer "nature's call;"

  d) use a safety belt to prevent falling out of the tree in case you do fall asleep.

23 You like to "age" your venison to get it nice and tender for the table. To do that properly, you should:

  a) field dress and skin the deer, then leave the carcass hanging outside in a cheesecloth bag for a week if it's winter and freezing outside;

  b) field dress and skin the deer, and let it hang in a meat locker with a controlled temperature between 36 degrees and 38 degrees F;

    c)   field dress and skin the deer, and let it hang in a meat locker at a controlled temperature between 40 degrees and 42 degrees F;

    d)   field dress the deer but leave the skin on, then let it hang in the barn in the chilly autumn air.

24   Arguments abound over a whitetail's "live weight." To calculate the live weight of a deer, you can:

    a)   field dress the deer, leaving the head and skin on, weigh this carcass, and multiply that weight by 1.25;

    b)   field dress the deer, remove the head and skin, weigh the carcass, and multiply that weight by 2.00;

    c)   use a tape measure to measure the deer's chest girth just back of the front legs, then use a conversion table available from many sources as your live weight;

    d)   bone out the deer, weigh the boned out meat, and multiply that weight by 5.00.

25   Antler growth in whitetail bucks is an annual process. To find bucks with maximum antler growth, you must hunt areas that have quality feed, good genetics, and deer at least:

    a)   1½ years of age;

    b)   2½ years of age;

    c)   3½ years of age;

    d)   4½ years of age.

Answers

How do you rate in our quiz? If you got 22 to 25 (88 percent to 100 percent) you're a real pro. 19 to 21 correct (76 percent to 84 percent), and you're very good. If you scored between 15 and 18 correct answers (60 percent to 72 percent), you're doing OK. If you got 12 to 14 right (48 percent to 56 percent), you're fair. Under 12 right, and you need to study up before opening day!

1   c) One week before opening day. While all scouting can be beneficial, if you scout too early the deer may change their pattern before the opener. No scouting at all leaves you blind going in, and blind luck isn't good enough.

2   c) Hunt all day long. If you don't see deer you know are there, they have either gone nocturnal or are using the area during midday hours. Since you can't hunt at night, the alternative is hunting all day. Then if no action is forthcoming, it's time to move to a new area.

3   c) By carefully creating a natural funnel within a funnel, you can often influence deer to move the easy, unobstructed way—right to your stand. Setting different stands is, in this case, a shotgun approach since you can only sit in one stand at a time. And while scents may work, they may not. A brush funnel often will.

4   c) 30 to 50 yards below the scrape. Below, in this case, means downwind, the direction a buck will normally approach a scrape from. A buck often checks

the wind to see if a doe is waiting near the scrape before moving in; therefore, hunters on the upwind side will possibly be smelled.

5   b) Wait for a better shot. Neck shots are iffy at best. Blowing a call may work, but may also alert the deer to your position while he's still screened. Call if the deer begins to move away from your shooting lanes.

6   d) All of the above. You should practice from a treestand that closely resembles your own, wear your hunting clothing, and shoot broadheads as often as possible to simulate actual hunting conditions.

7   c) Visit a pro shop and shoot lots of different bow makes until you find one that just "feels" right to you. Magazine ads and articles, as well as advice from a buddy, are good places to start, but should not be the final determiner.

8   b,c,d) The only thing you should not do is not touch your bow before opening day.

9   b,d) If the shafts are the same spine stiffness and length as your current shafts, shoot them with broadheads to make sure they fly straight and true.

10 b,d) In hot weather, deer often water several times a day, including midday, so it pays to be on stand all day long. They will also often move to water before they feed in the afternoon, not waiting until afterwards to shake their thirst. Returning to camp for a nap isn't the best idea now.

11 a) Always hunt into the wind. Both b and c are good ideas, of course, but not foolproof, and should not be depended on to totally mask human scent.

12 d) Just before a heavy storm front passes through, deer often feed more heavily than normal to stock up in case bad weather lasts a long time. Watching the barometer fall will help alert you to this phenomenon.

13 a) Opening morning, before other careless hunters have disturbed the deer's usual pattern, is the best time for your scouting to pay off with success in this case. After heavy pressure, the deer may change their patterns, forcing you to start all over again.

14 Because there is no evidence to make us believe that deer are spooked by colored fletching and nocks, any answer will work here. I prefer bright fletching because it does help me locate my shafts easier after a shot, but it's a personal thing. And while all-white will help you see the arrow in flight against the dark body of a deer, it may also cause you to not follow through with the shot as you lift your head and eyes and try to see the arrow, and therefore miss.

15 There is no every-time answer to this question, but the most common reaction is a) drops his tail between his legs as he runs off. I have had deer do b, c, and d at least one time each, however, so be sure you always check for other physical signs of a hit.

16 b,c) Once you've shot a deer, you must immediately mark the spot with visual markers; shooting an arrow into the ground is a good way of doing this. However, before you do anything get control of your nerves so you don't

lose the spot or cover up any potential tracking sign with excited carelessness.

17   c) Deer can travel a long way without leaving any blood at all, or a very scant trail. Assume nothing until you've tracked the animal at least 250 yards without seeing blood before giving up. If that's tough for you to do, then mark the spot well and go get the help of one who has those skills.

18   d) The more treestands available, the better you can cover an area. Portable stands (answer c) are good, too, but several permanent stands placed well before the season are the preferred alternative.

19   d) Deer are not that difficult to cleanly kill with a bow and arrow, provided they are hit in the thoracic (chest) cavity. To that end, any well-constructed broadhead that flies straight and true with your bow-and-arrow setup should do the job. Just make sure it conforms to state laws governing the minimum number of blades and cutting diameter.

20   c) While all the mentioned methods will work at times, the most effective day-in and day-out calling technique is softly blowing the grunt call. Rattling is most effective during the rutting cycle, and when buck to doe numbers approach a 1:1 ratio.

21   b) There's nothing wrong in taking a doe with either a gun or a bow, and any bow-shot deer is a trophy. In fact, in many areas the older herd does are much tougher to lure into bow range than young bucks. If you just have to have a buck, then "c" is a plausible answer, but "d" is not.

22   a,c) All of the answers are good ideas. I often read a paperback book while on stand, especially at midday. Food, water and a "nature's call" bottle are always with me, and anyone who doesn't use a safety belt while up a treestand is crazy.

23   b) The only temperature at which venison ages is between 36 and 38 degrees F. Above that, it begins to spoil, and near freezing it doesn't degenerate at all. If you don't have the proper aging temperature or a controlled hanging room, it's best to cut and wrap the deer, then get it into the freezer as soon as possible.

24   a,c) There is a conversion table available that correlates the girth of the chest size to live weight very accurately. If you have already field dressed the deer and can weigh the carcass, multiplying that weight by 1.25 will yield a very close live deer weight for you.

25   d) Whitetails do not reach their full size physically until 4½ years of age. Up until that time, all their energy goes toward growth and sustenance. After reaching maximum physical size, the calories that previously went to body growth now go to antler development. Deer will continue to grow larger antlers each year up until they are at least 8½ years old, after which the antlers may begin to decline, depending on many factors.